The Cambridge Companion to Rossini

The Cambridge Companion to Rossini is a collection of specially commissioned essays on one of the most influential opera composers in the repertoire. The volume is divided into four parts, each exploring an important element of Rossini's life, his world and his works: biography and reception; words and music; representative operas; and performance. Within these sections accessible chapters, written by a team of specialists, examine Rossini's life and career; the reception of his music in the nineteenth century and today; the librettos and their authors; the dramaturgy of the operas; and Rossini's non-operatic works. Additional chapters centre on key individual operas chosen for their historical importance or position in the present repertoire, and include *Tancredi*, *Il barbiere di Siviglia*, *Semiramide* and *Guillaume Tell*. The last section, Performance, focuses on the history of Rossini's operas from the viewpoint of singing and staging, as well as the influence of editorial work on contemporary performance practice.

Cambridge Companions to Music

Topics

The Cambridge Companion to Blues and Gospel Music
Edited by Allan Moore

The Cambridge Companion to Conducting
Edited by José Antonio Bowen

The Cambridge Companion to Grand Opera
Edited by David Charlton

The Cambridge Companion to Jazz
Edited by Mervyn Cooke and David Horn

The Cambridge Companion to the Musical
Edited by William Everett and Paul Laird

The Cambridge Companion to the Orchestra
Edited by Colin Lawson

The Cambridge Companion to Pop and Rock
Edited by Simon Frith, Will Straw and John Street

The Cambridge Companion to the String Quartet
Edited by Robin Stowell

Composers

The Cambridge Companion to Bach
Edited by John Butt

The Cambridge Companion to Bartók
Edited by Amanda Bayley

The Cambridge Companion to Beethoven
Edited by Glenn Stanley

The Cambridge Companion to Benjamin Britten
Edited by Mervyn Cooke

The Cambridge Companion to Berg
Edited by Anthony Pople

The Cambridge Companion to Berlioz
Edited by Peter Bloom

The Cambridge Companion to Brahms
Edited by Michael Musgrave

The Cambridge Companion to Bruckner
Edited by John Williamson

The Cambridge Companion to John Cage
Edited by David Nicholls

The Cambridge Companion to Chopin
Edited by Jim Samson

The Cambridge Companion to Debussy
Edited by Simon Trezise

The Cambridge Companion to

Rossini

. . . .

EDITED BY
Emanuele Senici
University of Oxford

CAMBRIDGE
UNIVERSITY PRESS

PUBLISHED BY THE PRESS SYNDICATE OF THE UNIVERSITY OF CAMBRIDGE
The Pitt Building, Trumpington Street, Cambridge, United Kingdom

CAMBRIDGE UNIVERSITY PRESS
The Edinburgh Building, Cambridge, CB2 2RU, UK
40 West 20th Street, New York, NY 10011–4211, USA
477 Williamstown Road, Port Melbourne, VIC 3207, Australia
Ruiz de Alarcón 13, 28014 Madrid, Spain
Dock House, The Waterfront, Cape Town 8001, South Africa

http://www.cambridge.org

First published 2004

Printed in the United Kingdom at the University Press, Cambridge

Typeface Minion 10.75/14 pt.   *System* LATEX 2ε   [TB]

A catalogue record for this book is available from the British Library

Library of Congress Cataloguing in Publication data
The Cambridge companion to Rossini / edited by Emanuele Senici.
        p.   cm. – (Cambridge companions to music)
Includes bibliographical references and index.
Contents: Biography and reception – Words and music – Representative operas – Performance.
ISBN 0 521 80736 0 (hardback) – ISBN 0 521 00195 1 (paperback)
1. Rossini, Gioacchino, 1792–1868 – Criticism and interpretation.   I. Senici, Emanuele.   II. Series.
ML410.R8C17   2003
782.1′092 – dc21
[B]   2003048560

ISBN 0 521 80736 0 hardback
ISBN 0 521 00195 1 paperback

Contents

Illustrations

Between pp. 215 and 216

14.1 Giuseppe Borsato, *Prison*, stage design for the first performance (Venice, La Fenice, 1813) of *Tancredi* (Bibliothèque de l'Opéra, Paris)

14.2 Giacomo Pregliasco, *Elisabetta d'Inghilterra*, costume sketch for the first performance (Naples, San Carlo, 1815) of *Elisabetta regina d'Inghilterra* (Biblioteca Civica, Turin)

14.3 Alessandro Sanquirico, *Nino's Tomb*, stage design for *Semiramide* (Milan, La Scala, 1824 or 1825) in *Nuova raccolta di scene teatrali inventate da Alessandro Sanquirico e pubblicate da Giovanni Ricordi* (Milan, 1827–32)

14.4 Sanquirico, *Hall in Argirio's Palace*, stage design for *Tancredi* (Milan, Carcano, 1829) reproduced in *Nuova raccolta di scene teatrali inventate da Alessandro Sanquirico e pubblicate da Giovanni Ricordi* (Milan, 1827–32)

14.5 Sanquirico, *Maometto's Tent*, stage design for *L'assedio di Corinto* (Milan, La Scala, 1829) in *Nuova raccolta di scene teatrali inventate da Alessandro Sanquirico e pubblicate da Giovanni Ricordi* (Milan, 1827–32)

14.6 Pierre-Luc-Charles Cicéri, *Mahomet's Tent*, stage design for the first performance (Paris, Opéra, 1826) of *Le Siège de Corinthe* (Bibliothèque de l'Opéra, Paris)

14.7 Giuseppe Bertoja, *The Lake of the Four Cantons*, stage design for *Guglielmo Tell* at the Teatro Regio, Turin in 1840 (Civico Museo Correr, Venice)

14.8 Giuseppe Bertoja, *Piazzetta S. Marco*, stage design for *Otello* at La Fenice, Venice in 1846 (Civico Museo Correr, Venice)

14.9 Anonymous, *Scene from 'Matilde di Shabran' as performed at the Italian Opera in London* reproduced in *Panorama universale*, 16 June 1855, p. 80 (Biblioteca Civica, Turin)

14.10 Thomas Grieve, *The Acropolis of Corinth*, stage design for *The Siege of Corinth* at Drury Lane, London in 1836 (University of London Library, Grieve Collection, London)

Contributors

Marco Beghelli is Professor of Music History at the Conservatorio 'Rossini', Pesaro. He has collaborated with the Deutsche Rossini Gesellschaft and the Fondazione Rossini, editing *L'equivoco stravagante* (with Stefano Piana) and the cantata *Omaggio umiliato a Sua Maestà*. He is also co-editor of *Tutti i libretti di Rossini* (Milan, 1991).

Charles S. Brauner is Professor of Music History and Chair of the Department of Theory, History and Composition of Roosevelt University. He is co-editor of Rossini's *Armida* (Pesaro, 1997) and author/editor of *Armida*, volume VII of the series *I libretti di Rossini* (Pesaro, 2000), and has published articles on nineteenth-century opera and Lieder and on Monteverdi.

Patricia B. Brauner is Coordinator of the Center for Italian Opera Studies at the University of Chicago and a member of the Editorial Committee of the Fondazione Rossini. Among her articles on Rossini is 'La primaria importanza delle fonti secondarie' in *Gioachino Rossini, 1792–1992. Il testo e la scena* (Pesaro, 1994). She is editor of the critical edition of the cantatas *La riconoscenza / Il vero omaggio*, and co-editor of *Ermione* and *Armida*.

Damien Colas is *chercheur* at the Centre National de la Recherche Scientifique, attached to the Institut de Recherches sur le Patrimoine Musical en France, Paris. His research interests focus on exchanges between France and Italy in the realm of opera, specifically the evolution of melodic writing and of the opera orchestra in the nineteenth century, and the transformation of the aesthetics of Classicism from the seventeenth to the nineteenth century.

Paolo Fabbri is Professor of Music History at the University of Ferrara, director of the Fondazione Donizetti, Bergamo, and president of the *edizione nazionale* of Donizetti's operas. He has been a member of the editorial committee of the Rossini critical edition and deputy director of the Fondazione Rossini, and has published several books and articles on Italian madrigal and opera. He is the author of *Rossini nelle raccolte Piancastelli di Forlì* (Lucca, 2001) and editor of *Gioachino Rossini, 1792–1992. Il testo e la scena* (Pesaro, 1994), Rossini's *Sinfonie giovanili* (Pesaro, 1998) and the volume on *L'italiana in Algeri* in the series *I libretti di Rossini* (Pesaro, 1997, with Maria Chiara Bertieri).

Philip Gossett is the Robert W. Reneker Distinguished Service Professor at the University of Chicago and the general editor of both the *Edizione critica delle opere di Gioachino Rossini* and *The Works of Giuseppe Verdi*. His reconstruction (with Ilaria Narici) of *Gustavo III*, the original version of Verdi's *Un ballo in maschera*, was performed for the first time in Gothenburg, Sweden, in September 2002.

Leonella Grasso Caprioli is Research Fellow in the Department of Music and Art History, University of Padua. Her research interests are in musical lexicography and the history of Italian singing. The historical dictionary *CANTO. Lessico italiano del* *canto*, edited by her under the general editorship of Sergio Durante, is forthcoming on cd-rom from Olms Verlag.

Heather Hadlock is Assistant Professor of Music at Stanford University. She is the author of *Mad Loves: Women and Music in Offenbach's 'Les Contes d'Hoffmann'* (Princeton, 2000) and is currently at work on a book on female cross-dressing in nineteenth-century opera. She is reviews editor of the *Cambridge Opera Journal*.

Janet Johnson is Associate Professor of Music at the University of Southern California. Her three-volume reconstruction of Rossini's *Il viaggio a Reims* appeared in 2000 as part of the *Edizione critica delle opere di Gioachino Rossini*. Her work on Rossini, Donizetti and the Parisian Théâtre Italien has appeared in numerous European books and journals, and she is a contributor to both *The Cambridge Companion to Berlioz* ('The Musical Environment in France') and the revised *New Grove Dictionary of Music and Musicians* ('Stendhal').

Cormac Newark is currently Leverhulme Trust researcher at the University of Ferrara. He has published in the *Cambridge Opera Journal*, the *Journal of the Royal Musical Association* and the *Guardian*, and has contributed to various collections of essays, including *Reading Critics Reading* (Oxford, 2001) and the *Cambridge Companion to Verdi* (2003).

Richard Osborne is the author of the 'Master Musicians' *Rossini* (London, 1985; rev. edn 1993) and the Rossini entries in *The New Grove Dictionary of Opera* (London, 1992). His most recent publications are *Herbert von Karajan: A Life in Music* (London, 1998; Boston, 2000) and '*Till I End My Song'. English Music and Musicians 1440–1940: A Perspective from Eton* (London, 2002).

Emanuele Senici is University Lecturer in Music at the University of Oxford and Fellow of St Hugh's College. He is the author of '*La clemenza di Tito' di Mozart. I primi trent'anni, 1791–1821* (Turnhout, 1997) and works on Italian opera of the long nineteenth century. He is also co-editor of the *Cambridge Opera Journal*.

Mercedes Viale Ferrero, a graduate of the University of Turin, is an expert on scenography and author of several books, among them *La scenografia del '700 e i fratelli Galliari* (Turin, 1963), *Filippo Juvarra scenografo e architetto teatrale* (Turin, 1970), *La scenografia della Scala nell'età neoclassica* (Milan, 1983) and, with James Hepokoski, '*Otello' di Giuseppe Verdi* (Milan, 1990). She has contributed to several exhibitions, such as *L'aspetto visivo dello spettacolo verdiano* (Parma, 1994) and *Giuseppe Verdi: l'uomo, l'opera, il mito* (Milan, 2000–1). She edits the series 'Musica e spettacolo' (Milan, Ricordi) with Francesco Degrada.

Benjamin Walton is Lecturer in Music at the University of Bristol. He works on French and Italian opera and musical Romanticism. Recent publications include articles on 'The Operatic Coronation of Charles X' in *19th-Century Music* and Rossini's *Guillaume Tell* in the *Cambridge Opera Journal*. He is currently working on a book about music and modernity in Restoration France.

Preface

The aim of *The Cambridge Companion to Rossini* is to present a series of essays providing a rounded and informed view of Rossini's works. The book is divided into four sections. The first, 'Biography and reception', opens with a chapter by Richard Osborne in which the main events of Rossini's life are not only situated historically, but also explored psychologically in terms of the composer's character and outlook; his activities other than musical composition receive special attention, as does the contentious issue of his early 'retirement' from the operatic agon and its possible connection to his physical and mental health. In 'Rossini and France' Benjamin Walton probes the relationship between Rossini and his 'other' country, where he spent a significant part of his life and on whose music and culture he had an enormous influence. Charles S. Brauner charts the reappearance of Rossini's operas on the stage in the last fifty years and their increased presence in histories of music and opera, advancing some hypotheses on the reasons of this ongoing Renaissance.

The second part, 'Words and music', approaches Rossini's *oeuvre* from a number of historical and analytical standpoints. Paolo Fabbri presents Rossini's librettists, charts their relationship with the composer, and introduces the sources, language and structure of the librettos, which differ significantly between Italian and French works. Presenting a wealth of newly discovered materials, Philip Gossett illustrates Rossini's working methods, paying particular attention to compositional revisions and placing his practice of self-borrowing in the context of operatic conventions. Marco Beghelli's chapter on the dramaturgy of the operas answers the crucial question 'how is a Rossini opera made?', considering not only the formal construction of single numbers and the logic of their succession, but also their dramaturgical implications and functions. In the next chapter Damien Colas analyses Rossini's melodies as rhetorical utterances, demonstrating the integral rôle of ornamentation in their construction and signification, and suggesting how a singer who wants to ornament a melodic line according to contemporary practice should proceed. Richard Osborne's intriguing proposal that 'there was always something of the court composer about Rossini' introduces a survey of the composer's non-operatic works, from the early *sonate a quattro* to the *Petite messe solennelle*, including the occasional cantatas of the Italian years and the piano music and songs from his 'retirement'.

Part III comprises three chapters that introduce in detail four operas, chosen for their historical importance and/or privileged position in the repertoire. Heather Hadlock discusses the *opere serie Tancredi* and *Semiramide*, Rossini's earliest theatrical success and his most influential mature Italian work; Janet Johnson deals with his most famous comic opera, *Il barbiere di Siviglia*; and Cormac Newark presents *Guillaume Tell*, his last opera and most important French work. Each chapter discusses the historical and biographical background of the operas and pays particular attention to their literary sources. A recurring theme is the dialectical relationship between the conventions of a given operatic genre and Rossini's innovations, which in turn modify generic expectations.

Finally, Part IV, 'Performance', focuses on the history of Rossini's operas from the point of view of singing and staging, and on the enterprise of critically editing these works – undoubtedly a major influence on contemporary performance practice. In 'Singing Rossini' Leonella Grasso Caprioli presents the composer's ideas on and attitudes towards the theory and practice of singing as an entry into his operatic aesthetics; she emphasises the crucial rôle that some singers had in shaping both the music and the dramatic profile of the operas they premièred, and also in promoting a Rossinian singing ideal through their pedagogical activities. Mercedes Viale Ferrero gives a brief history of 'staging Rossini', explaining practices in Italy and France in the early nineteenth century and introducing the most important designers who first staged Rossini's operas. Finally, Patricia B. Brauner charts the process of editing an opera for the complete critical edition (in press with the Fondazione Rossini), from tracing and selecting the sources to preparing the score for the final printing; moreover, she discusses in fascinating detail a few specific editorial cases.

The community of Rossini scholars is an eminently international one, and this characteristic is reflected in the list of contributors to the present volume, which includes American, British, French and Italian authors: some are familiar and experienced Rossinians; others are well-established authorities in related topics who newly bring their unique insights to bear upon Rossinian matters; others are younger, up-and-coming scholars. I am grateful to them all, especially those who have had to wait longest to see their chapters in print. I am also grateful to the Faculty of Music, University of Oxford, and to St Hugh's College for grants towards meeting the cost of translation, and to the team of translators, who are all scholars in their own right: Laura Basini, Cormac Newark (who, beside writing the chapter on *Tell*, also helped with last-minute editing) and Rosa Solinas. I would also like to thank Marco Beghelli, Mauro Bucarelli, Stefano Castelvecchi, Paolo Fabbri, Philip Gossett, Roger Parker and especially Mercedes Viale Ferrero for their suggestions and practical help in planning the volume and bringing it to completion. A special *grazie* to Vincenzo Borghetti, who, among other things, put my mind at rest that there is no comma in the title of *Elisabetta regina d'Inghilterra*. Finally, many thanks to Victoria Cooper of Cambridge University Press for her support.

Emanuele Senici

Note on the text

In present-day Italian the correct spelling of Rossini's forename is 'Gioacchino'; Rossini himself spelt it with either one 'c' or two in the first decades of his life, eventually settling on 'Gioachino' in the 1830s. Rossini experts consider 'Gioachino' the more accurate form, which is therefore used throughout this volume. Bibliographical citations maintain the spelling as it appears there.

Abbreviations

BCRS   *Bollettino del centro rossiniano di studi* (Pesaro: Fondazione Rossini, 1955–)

GREC   *Edizione critica delle opere di Gioachino Rossini* (Pesaro: Fondazione Rossini, 1979–) (see chapter 15 for details)

GRLD   *Gioachino Rossini. Lettere e documenti*, 3 vols. to date (Pesaro: Fondazione Rossini, 1992–)

1 Introduction: Rossini's operatic operas

EMANUELE SENICI

'Since the death of Napoleon, another man has appeared who is talked about every day in Moscow as in Naples, in London as in Vienna, in Paris as in Calcutta. The fame of this man knows no bounds save those of civilisation itself; and he is not yet thirty-two!'[1] The opening words of Rossini's first biography – by none other than Stendhal, and published in Paris in 1824 – help introduce what at first might seem an extravagant claim: Rossini was Europe's most famous composer in the first half of the nineteenth century; his music reached the largest number of listeners, whether in opera houses, or concert halls, or played in countless arrangements printed for all sorts of performing forces, or simply whistled in the streets. In other words, nineteenth-century musical culture cannot be understood without taking Rossini into prominent account; any history that relegates Rossini to a secondary rôle must to some extent ignore the tastes of those who inhabited the period. And yet such histories have been the norm rather than the exception in the past century, especially in the English-speaking world.

The reasons behind this historiographical neglect are numerous and diverse, but chief among them is probably the progressive disappearance of Rossini's works from the repertory of opera houses during the second half of the nineteenth century, a trend not reversed until the later decades of the twentieth. Only a handful of his comic operas were performed, especially *Il barbiere di Siviglia*, which remains the most popular and frequently revived. In the past half century, however, Rossini's fortunes have undergone a substantial and perhaps surprising reversal, with his works, including the *opere serie*, regaining a footing in the operatic canon. Music historiography has followed suit, with an increasing wealth of books and essays devoted to Rossini's *oeuvre*. The inclusion of the present volume in a book series in English devoted to the most important composers of the past, unlikely even thirty years ago, may be taken as a sign that modern Rossini scholarship has come of age. These considerations raise a number of important questions: why were Rossini's operas so famous in the first half of the nineteenth century? Why did they mostly disappear between 1850 and 1950? And why have they now returned to the stage?

Understanding the reasons behind Rossini's meteoric rise and unprecedented success is made particularly difficult by our rather sketchy knowledge of opera in Italy at the turn of the nineteenth century. To judge from what we know, Rossini's strength seems to have been his prodigious capacity for rationalising and codifying a number of disparate dramatic and musical solutions already explored by his predecessors, and then employing them with single-minded attention to coherence, balance and clarity. In the words of Philip Gossett, 'Rossini's formal procedures were compelling because they fused in a simple yet satisfactory manner the urge for lyrical expression and the needs of the drama'.[2] Similarly, he devised a melodic style that offered the singers scope for both syllabic *cantilena* and melismatic coloratura, each kept within the boundaries of clearly defined formal moulds. Over the past few decades Rossini scholars have extensively and persuasively explored how his operas are made, from overture to *finale ultimo*, from the distribution of numbers within a work to minute details of thematic construction. In fact, the dramaturgy of Rossini's operas has been the main concern of recent scholarship (together with source studies and editing), and the very considerable fruits of this research are evident throughout the present volume.

What has been addressed less strenuously are the motives behind such a dramaturgy, and this makes it all the harder to answer the question of why Rossini was so successful. If we believe that dramaturgy must ultimately be the manifestation of an ideology, of a particular worldview, then the central issue becomes the ideological outlook that lies behind Rossini's operas. The theme has not often been addressed by modern scholars, but recurs in nineteenth-century writings, albeit not always explicitly. Stendhal, for example, tried to explain the relative lack of success of Mozart's operas in Italy in terms that illuminate by reflection the peculiar attractions of Rossini:

> Love is not the same in Bologna as it is in Königsberg; love in Italy is far more dynamic, more impatient, more violent, less dependent upon imagination. It is not a gradual tide which sweeps slowly, but for ever, into the farthest recesses of the soul; it takes the whole being by storm, and its invasion is the work of an instant; it is a frenzy. Now, frenzy knows nothing of melancholy, since frenzy is a wild explosion of all kinds of energy, while melancholy springs from an absence of energy. No novel, as far as I know, has ever described love in the Italian manner; and Italy, as a consequence, is a land without novels. Instead, Italy has her Cimarosa.[3]

Whereas the 'Northern' Mozart puts on the stage characters who evolve and develop but, more importantly, who constantly reflect upon their development – as novelistic characters do – the 'Southern' Cimarosa (read Rossini) presents us with characters whose subjectivity is conceived in terms not of modern sentiment, but rather of a pre-modern ideal of the self as resistant to change, as a 'mere' vessel for emotions. Expression in opera is, then, the expression not of a subject, but rather of a passion, of an emotion that takes over the self and makes it utter this emotion in song. According to

Stendhal, this conception of human character stands behind Rossini's musical dramaturgy, and the success of Rossini's operas is due to their masterly translation into music of this very conception. Saying that Rossini's music is 'the music of the soul' means saying that it is not 'the music of a character', or 'the music of the composer's interiority', and therefore can speak directly to each member of the audience who wants to listen and knows how to do so.

Other prominent contemporary commentators agreed with Stendhal, offering their interpretation of what had doubtless become a critical commonplace. Reviewing the first London performance of *Il barbiere di Siviglia* in 1818, Leigh Hunt reminded his readers that 'they [Italian opera composers] take up one passion after another, and give you the genuine elementary feeling of it', but he added that this was not Rossini's most prominent quality:

> We have a strong recollection of the most striking passages. Some of them fairly beat it into us. They were the more hurried parts in general, the entrance of the *Count* in the disguise of a singing master, the groans of old *Bartolo*, and the scene where *Figaro* and his master have so much difficulty in getting rid of a set of fellows who have a prodigious pertinacity. We never met with a composer who gave us such an harmonious sense of discord, who set to music with such vivacity what is vulgarly called a *row*. The rest of the opera is of a piece with this kind of talent, not good in the graver, more sentimental, and graceful parts; but exceedingly promising in the ardent, vehement, and more obviously comic.[4]

Another Englishman, Thomas Love Peacock, writing in 1834, established a link between Hunt's interpretation of Rossini and 'reality':

> There has been an increase of excitement in the world of reality, and that of imagination has kept it company . . . The public taste has changed, and the supply of the market has followed the demand. There can be no question that Rossini's music is more spirit-stirring than Paësiello's, and more essentially theatrical: more suited to the theatre by its infinite variety of contrast and combination, and more dependent on the theatre for the development of its perfect effect.[5]

Rossini's operas, then, do not simply present a succession of sudden, passionate utterances in music; they are not just old-fashioned products of a Southern imagination for a Southern public. Their modernity lies in their privileging of vehement emotions, in staging the excitement of the contemporary world. But the operas are also modern because they are 'essentially theatrical', because they exploit to the full the possibilities of the theatrical medium.

Scholars have recently advanced interesting hypotheses about this heightened theatricality, concentrating on Rossini's comic operas and interpreting them in what might be called 'metatheatrical' terms. Paolo Gallarati contrasts what he calls the 'everyday' realism of Mozart's comic works with the grotesque, deformed version of reality presented in Rossini's *opere buffe*. It is as if Rossini's characters have always worn masks, self-consciously staging their actions in a theatrical (as opposed to real) fashion, constantly aware that they are operatic characters, rather than real human beings. These characters have no past and no future, no memory of who they have been and no anticipation of who they may become; they live exclusively in the theatrical present – in Freudian terms, they have no unconscious.[6] The only reality known to Rossini's comic operas is operatic; in other words, the subject of Rossini's comic operas is comic opera itself.

Gianni Ruffin suggests that this heightened self-referentiality is achieved through a conflict between the diachronic dimension of text and the syncronic dimension of music, which negates development as a compositional and aesthetic principle, operating instead through repetition. This music is openly anti-realistic because openly anti-mimetic: its repetitive mechanisms highlight the gap between the stage and the real world, forcefully negating any realistic dimension to the musical action unfolding on the stage.[7] Alessandro Baricco emphasises how this anti-mimetic quality rests on what he calls Rossini's 'sabotage of the signifying function of words', which are treated instead mostly as phonetic support for the music – hence the crucial importance of coloratura in Rossini's vocal aesthetics.[8] Carl Dahlhaus also notices how 'Rossini not infrequently gives precedence to rhythm over themes, to instrumentation and coloratura over melodic contour, to intensified repetition over motivic manipulation.'[9]

Dahlhaus's observations extend to Rossini's serious operas, which in his analysis share most – if not all – of their musical language with the comic ones. This switching of genres can be interpreted in both historical and psychological terms: 'The extremes meet: the farcical takes on catastrophic proportions in the frenzy of the music; the tragic, in its moments of greatest despair, exposes the marionette strings from which the characters are dangling. For a skeptic like Rossini, whose cheerfulness is simply the obverse of a melancholy that affected not just himself but his entire age, these extremes prove to be complementary.'[10] This interpretation squarely locates Rossini in the historical and ideological context of post-Napoleonic Restoration, an epoch characterised, according to Dahlhaus, by a resigned detachment, 'a detachment of cheerful skepticism or melancholic self-absorption'.[11] Heinrich Heine forcefully expounded this position in his *On the French Stage* of 1837: since Rossini's operas are mostly concerned with the isolated passions of individuals, and since these self-contained passions are best expressed in melody, Rossini is the absolute master of melodic expression. The ideology behind this approach to opera is, according to Heine, that of the Restoration, when, after the great struggles and subsequent bitter disappointments of the Napoleonic years, individuals retreated from the public arena into the private sphere, forgetting for a while collective interests and 'the destiny of the people'.[12]

Heine contrasts Rossini with Meyerbeer, whose *grands opéras* best epitomise, according to him, the new era in French history ushered in by the 1830 July Revolution. However, if 1830 marks the end of the Bourbon Restoration in France, in Italy the régimes that had gained power in 1815 lasted well into the second half of the century; having survived more or less intact the revolutions of 1848–9 – as was the case in many other European countries – they were finally ousted by the proclamation of the Kingdom of Italy in 1861. The first half of the century encompasses therefore both the heyday of Rossini's success and fame, and the Restoration régimes in Italy and other parts of Europe. I am not suggesting that there is a simple cause-and-effect link between these two phenomena; simply that, when discussing Rossini's gradual disappearance from the operatic stage in the central decades of the century, the political and ideological contexts should not be forgotten. As we have seen, commentators of the time had them in vivid focus.

As did Rossini. His few declarations of poetics, all made after he had retired from the operatic agon, sometimes refer to 'modern' music and its performance in political terms, linking contemporary opera and its vocal execution to revolution, 'steam, theft and barricades'.[13] More generally, Rossini's pronouncements measure the distance between his aesthetics and a new conception of opera that emerged after his retirement. As Paolo Fabbri has argued, the central issue is that of imitation. According to Rossini, 'music is not an imitative art, but is at root entirely abstract; its purpose is to arouse and express'.[14] The musical parameter on which this abstractedly expressive function mainly falls is melody, especially the kind of 'beautiful', 'Italian' melody designated *cantilena* at the time. Rossinian *cantilena* expresses general and idealised emotions, never descending to the aesthetic lowliness of giving prominence to single words, since this would ruin its beautiful, 'musical' flow. This, the older Rossini felt, was the ruinous direction taken by modern opera, a direction which he was proud never to have considered himself.[15] Recalling terms mentioned above, we could say that, for Rossini, operatic music ceased to be the music of the soul and became the music of a character, in the process losing its ideal abstraction. This was a fundamental aesthetic shift, linked on the one hand to a political, social and ideological evolution and, on the other, to profound changes in the performance of opera, especially its vocal style. Hence the older Rossini's frequent and loud complaints about the decline of singing standards and the prevalence of 'shouting' among singers who had lost the true art of executing 'beautifully' his dear, old, beautiful *cantilena*.[16]

Perhaps we should be surprised that, in the face of such fundamental changes, a few operas by Rossini managed to maintain a foothold in the repertory of opera houses after the mid nineteenth century. But it is important to remember that the very concept of an operatic repertory appeared first in connection with repeated revivals of Rossini's operas in the same theatre. This fundamental shift is closely connected to the mounting importance of the composer vis-à-vis the librettist. It was with Rossini that, for the first time, the composer was indisputedly considered the author of an opera, with the librettist simply a supplier of words – it is precisely in the early nineteenth century that the word 'librettist', originally derogatory, began to substitute for the eighteenth-century 'poet'.[17] In the eighteenth century the author of an opera was the author of its words, which could be set to music by different composers and be heard in the same theatre repeatedly, always in new settings. Operatic scores had travelled increasingly as the eighteenth century progressed, but were very seldom performed in the same city in more than one season. Some operas by Mozart, especially *Le nozze di Figaro*, *La clemenza di Tito* and above all *Don Giovanni*, became repertory pieces in the German-speaking lands and in London in the early nineteenth century.[18] But it was Rossini's works which were first revived over and over again throughout Europe in the first half of the century, so that for the first time in the history of opera a spectator in Milan, Paris, London and Vienna, but also in many provincial cities, could attend performances of the same opera at more or less regular intervals during the course of his or her life.

The astonishing success of several of Rossini's operas and their rapid conquest of operatic stages in Europe and beyond turned them into 'classics', a word that can be meaningfully applied to Rossini's works for the first time in the history of opera (with the partial exception of Mozart, as mentioned above). The composer himself was taken by surprise by this canonisation; in a recently discovered letter about *Otello* he frankly confessed that he could hardly believe he was the author of such a 'classic'.[19] I would suggest that it was precisely their swiftly acquired status as classics that secured the survival of a handful of Rossini's works in the nineteenth-century operatic repertory.

If we look at the chronology of La Scala, Milan, for example, we can see that *Otello* was frequently performed there until 1870; *Mosè* (an Italian version of *Moïse et Pharaon* rather than the original *Mosè in Egitto*) survived until 1869, but *Semiramide* was performed as late as 1881, and *Guillaume Tell* (as *Guglielmo Tell*) even later, 1899. Among the comic operas only *Il barbiere* remained in the repertory after the 1860s, but it did so in an astonishingly healthy manner: the longest audiences at La Scala went without a *Barbiere* was only fifteen years, between 1890 and 1905; since its house première in

1820 the opera was performed in eighteen years of the nineteenth century; and of course there were other theatres in Milan where *Il barbiere* was performed, at some point even more frequently than at La Scala, especially in the late nineteenth and the early twentieth centuries, when comic opera was produced more frequently at secondary theatres. *Il barbiere* is, quite simply, the first opera to have been constantly revived all around the operatic world ever since its première.

Il barbiere is, though, the only Rossini opera to have done so. All his others, with the partial exception of *Tell*, at some point lost their status as classics, or, rather, retained that status only in a few music history books. The presence of Rossini's operas in the repertory reached its lowest point from c. 1890 to c. 1920. Then the curve started a slow but steady rise, however, eventually leading in the last few decades to a phenomenon called the 'Rossini Renaissance', explored in detail by Charles S. Brauner in chapter 4. Why have Rossini's operas returned to the stage in the last half century? Brauner points out that several other composers have enjoyed 'renaissances' in the last few decades. The ever-increasing historicism of the culture of opera in the twentieth century is surely a crucial factor. This is not the place to investigate the reasons of this trend – although the fundamental rôle of recordings in shaping it should be mentioned more often than it is. It is clear, in any case, that revivals of old works have taken the place of premières of new ones (and their failure to enter the repertory in most cases). In this sense the Rossini Renaissance has much in common with the so-called early music movement, with the difference that, in the case of Rossini, and of opera in general, the emphasis is on 're-discovered' works rather than on familiar works performed in new styles – the exception being Handel's operas, re-discovered works performed in new styles. On the other hand, the rôle of historically aware performance practice, especially vocal, in making the rediscovery of Rossini's operas possible should not be underestimated. Finally, as Brauner reminds us, musicology has been an important player in the Rossini Renaissance, especially the enterprise of the critical edition and the activities of the Fondazione Rossini and of the Rossini Opera Festival in Pesaro, an institution explicitly devised as a meeting ground between performance and musicology.

There are other reasons, however, aesthetic and ideological, behind Rossini's return to the operatic stages. Perhaps it is precisely the qualities that Stendhal and his contemporaries saw as quintessential to Rossini's operatic aesthetic that have a particular appeal for present-day audiences and critics. According to Herbert Lindenberger, the Rossini of our time is a 'performing figure' who speaks out 'in diverse voices no one of which has any special authority nor reveals the essentials of its creator nor of the voice it purports to represent'.[20] To recall terms introduced above, the very fact that Rossini's music is 'the music of the soul' and not 'the music of a character' or 'the music of the composer's interiority', perceived as a problem from within a Romantic and post-Romantic aesthetic paradigm, finds in the climate of the present a potentially sympathetic terrain. If, as Lindenberger suggests, 'excess and repetition display themselves as Rossini's guiding principles',[21] it is not difficult to see how a culture which takes excess and repetition as some of its most salient characteristics may hear Rossini with some degree of sympathy, perhaps even of recognition. If the very concept of reality is under scrutiny – as it undoubtedly is at present – the fact that the only reality known to Rossini's operas is operatic may chime with our scepticism towards any form of representation that claims a more or less direct link with reality.

The present volume cannot entirely escape this 'presentist' perspective, nor does it attempt to do so, since in part it owes its existence to this very perspective. Its purpose is rather to give a historically grounded view of Rossini and his works from an early-twenty-first-century point of view, conscious that its object of enquiry is as much part of the present as it is of the past. If it succeeds in mediating between the two, it will have fulfilled its purpose.

PART ONE

Biography and reception

2 Rossini's life

RICHARD OSBORNE

Rossini is one of the most enigmatic of the great composers. The reasons for the popularity of his best-known compositions have never been difficult to fathom. His music is sensuous and incomparably vital: 'Full of the finest animal spirits', wrote Leigh Hunt in his *Autobiography* in 1850, 'yet capable of the noblest gravity'.[1] It is also somewhat detached, causing his admirers to think him a fine ironist, his detractors to dub him cynical. Rossini himself was happy to cultivate the mask of casual unconcern. But the image which devolved from this – the gifted but feckless amateur who at an early age abandoned his career for a life of luxury and the otiose pleasures of the table – bears little relation to the facts of his life as we have them.

The formative years, 1792–1810

Rossini was born in the small Adriatic town of Pesaro during a time of severe political upheaval. Both his parents were musicians. His father, Giuseppe Rossini (1764–1839), a robust character, energetic, querulous and a touch naïve, was Pesaro's town trumpeter and a horn player of sufficient distinction to be admitted to Bologna's Accademia Filarmonica. An outspoken Republican, he was briefly imprisoned by the Austrians in 1799, a circumstance which forced his young wife into making more of her untrained talent as an operatic soprano than might otherwise have been the case.

Anna Rossini (1771–1827) was the daughter of a Pesaro baker, Domenico Guidarini, with whom Giuseppe lodged. After falling pregnant in the summer of 1791, she married Giuseppe in the town cathedral on 26 September and gave birth to their only child, Gioachino Antonio, on 29 February 1792. Rossini was five when his mother first took to the professional stage. For the next eleven years she appeared regularly in local opera houses, eventually acquiring a repertory of some fifteen rôles, all of them comic. 'Poor mother!' Rossini later told Ferdinand Hiller, 'she was not without talent, even though she couldn't read music.'[2]

In 1802 the family moved to Lugo, near Ravenna. Yet despite their partly itinerant life, the Rossinis saw to it that their precociously talented child received a basic grounding in reading, writing, mathematics and Latin. Musically he was well catered for. Under the guidance of Canon Giuseppe

Malerbi he studied the rudiments of composition and had the run of the Malerbi family's extensive music library. It was here that he first delighted in the works of Haydn and Mozart ('the admiration of my youth, the desperation of my mature years, and the consolation of my old age'), whose music remained something of a closed book to conservative, chauvinistic taste in early nineteenth-century Italy. By the age of twelve Rossini was already ahead of the game, as proven by the six *Sonate a quattro*, composed in 1804 for performance in the villa at Conventello of the wealthy young amateur musician (and Republican sympathiser) Agostino Triossi (1781–1822). The attestation Rossini later added to the autograph manuscript is typically self-deprecatory:

> First violin, second violin, violoncello, and contrabass for six *horrendous* sonatas composed by me at the country house (near Ravenna) of my friend and patron, Agostino Triossi, at the most youthful age, having not even had a lesson in thorough-bass. They were all composed and copied in three days and performed in a doggish way by Triossi, contrabass; Morini (his cousin), first violin; the latter's brother, violoncello; and the second violin by myself, who was, to tell the truth, the least doggish.[3]

Opera was meat and drink to him from an early age. On 21 April 1804 a formal application was submitted in his name for the use of Imola's Teatro Comunale. This evening with the Rossinis, mother and son, featured among other things a 'Cavatina sung by Citizen Gioachino Rossini, who will act fully-costumed in a *buffo* part'.[4] In the autumn of 1805 he appeared on stage at the Teatro del Corso, Bologna (where the family had moved the previous year), in the cameo rôle of the boy Adolfo in Ferdinando Paer's *Camilla*. During Rossini's time in Bologna two singers visited the city who made a profound impression on him. One was the Spanish soprano Isabella Colbran (1785–1845), for whom he would write some of his most dramatically powerful roles, and whom he would later marry. The other was the great castrato Giovan Battista Velluti (1781–1861). Although the castrato tradition was all but extinct in contemporary operatic life, Rossini claimed to have been deeply influenced by what he called the purity and the miraculous flexibility of those voices and 'their profoundly penetrating accent'.[5]

In 1806, at the precociously early age of fourteen, he had entered Bologna's Liceo Musicale, initially to study singing, though he was quickly admitted to the composition class of the director of the Liceo, Padre Stanislao Mattei (1750–1825). He produced some accomplished work during his time at the Liceo, both privately (the so-called 'Ravenna' Mass, another Triossi commission) and for examination within the Liceo itself (his fine early cantata *Il pianto d'Armonia sulla morte d'Orfeo*); but when, in 1810, a further two years of study were proposed (plainsong and canon the prescribed topics), his instinct to continue his education in the real world finally asserted itself.

Venice and Milan, 1810–1815

Rossini's decision to cast his bread on the waters was not inherently risky, given the nature of his talent and the huge demand for new works which existed in Italy's opera houses at the time. But where to start? It was the singer Rosa Morandi and her husband Giuseppe who, on the advice of theatre impresario Francesco Cavalli, pointed the eighteen-year-old Gioachino in the direction of Venice's Teatro San Moisè. It was there, on 3 November 1810, that he made his professional début as an opera composer with the one-act *farsa La cambiale di matrimonio*. What is remarkable about the piece, apart from the sheer vitality of the writing, is how an unusually successful structural plan appears to have formed itself in Rossini's mind at the very outset. Conditions in theatres such as Venice's San Moisè were ideal for an apprentice composer. Working to a strictly limited budget, a small company of singers (without chorus) would stage a one-act opera with minimal scenery and limited rehearsal. Between January 1812 and January 1813 Rossini wrote four such *farse* for the San Moisè, beginning with the hugely successful *L'inganno felice* and ending with *Il Signor Bruschino*, whose mixture of sharp wit and sentimentality makes it perhaps the most successful of Rossini's works in this genre.

Initially Rossini had less success away from the San Moisè. The ambitious two-act *dramma giocoso L'equivoco stravagante* (Bologna, October 1811) was costly to stage and ran into trouble with the local censor. This first encounter with a more complex plot and large-scale formal structures did, however, give him the necessary confidence to mastermind his first genuinely successful two-act opera, *La pietra del paragone* (Milan, September 1812). Stendhal thought the opera's Act 1 Finale the funniest of all Rossini's comic finales. His penchant for nonsensical banter ('Ombretta sdegnosa' with its 'Missipipì, pipì, pipì' refrain) and quotable jokes (the 'Sigillara' sequence in Act 1) made him the toast of Milan and guaranteed fifty-three performances of the opera in its first season. *La pietra* also cemented some important partnerships with singers, notably the contralto Maria Marcolini, for whom Rossini was to create a number of bespoke rôles, and the bass Filippo Galli. After his Milanese success, Rossini was able to designate himself a *maestro di cartello*, a composer whose name alone guarantees a public. He was also exempted from military service, no mean concession in 1812.

Tancredi (Venice, 1813) was a further landmark in his career, his first truly (and immensely) successful *opera seria*. In this two-act heroic idyll he wrote some of his most flawlessly beautiful early music, whilst at the same time significantly advancing his mastery of individual forms and their co-ordinated use in ensembles. The opera also included a smash-hit which quickly travelled beyond Italy, the protagonist's cabaletta 'Di tanti palpiti'. Two months after the première of *Tancredi* Rossini was engaged at short notice by Venice's Teatro San Benedetto to re-work a contemporary story about an Italian girl in Algiers. Nothing demonstrates more clearly his emancipation from eighteenth-century Italian operatic practice, his innovative genius and the purely musical basis of much of his humour than this opportunistic reworking of Angelo Anelli's libretto for *L'italiana in Algeri*, which Luigi Mosca had first set to music in Milan in 1808.

Naples, 1815–1822

The year 1814 brought Rossini no runaway successes, but his new-found status was sufficient to land him a contract which would change the direction of his own career and the future course of Italian opera. It came from the Teatro San Carlo in Naples, one of Europe's most lavishly financed houses, built in 1737 by the Bourbon King Charles III as part of a programme of beautification of the city. The man who secured Rossini for Naples was the multi-millionaire builder, gaming magnate and impresario Domenico Barbaja (1778–1841). Barbaja was reputed to have made his money out of a coffee and whipped cream concoction which he invented whilst working as a waiter in Milan. In reality, building contracts, wheeler-dealing in military supplies during the Napoleonic wars and a gambling concession at La Scala, Milan, were the basis of his fortune. When the Teatro San Carlo burned down on the night of 13 February 1816 Barbaja himself advanced the entire cost of the rebuilding in return for an exceptionally generous concession on the opera house's future gambling revenues. His letters are full of cajolery, abuse, hectoring and self-pity. Yet he was the greatest musical entrepreneur of his day, with a nose for quality and a passion to promote it. Since his arrival in Naples in 1809 he had lured to the city a superb roster of singers, including Isabella Colbran (his mistress and later Rossini's wife), three distinguished tenors – Giovanni David, Manuel García and Andrea Nozzari – and the bass Michele Benedetti.

Rossini's contract with the Neapolitan theatres was an appropriately lucrative one and allowed him leave to work away from Naples. That said, its terms were complex, its schedules strenuous. These involved the composition of a series of grand new *opere serie*, the musical preparation of other composers' works (in 1820 Rossini oversaw the Italian première of the revision of Spontini's *tragédie lyrique Fernand Cortez*), and a good deal of day-to-day administration. Rossini bridled at the work-load (he once expressed surprise that Barbaja had not insisted on him doing the washing-up as well), but the obsessive side of his nature ensured ready compliance with Barbaja's desire to have each new production meticulously staged, played and sung.

Rossini's reception in Naples in the late summer of 1815 was not especially warm. The *Giornale delle Due Sicilie* (25 September) was typically condescending: 'And finally a certain Signor Rossini, a choirmaster, who has come, we've been told, to present an *Elisabetta regina d'Inghilterra* of his at this S. Carlo theatre, which still resounds with the melodious accents of the *Medea* and the *Cora* of the distinguished Signor Mayr.' When *Elisabetta* triumphed and *L'italiana in Algeri* had the audience at the home of Neapolitan comedy, the Teatro dei Fiorentini, in paroxysms of delight, the *Giornale* (31 October) was vaguely abashed: 'Signor Rossini – some will have found it strange that, the last time, we ignored his merits – today triumphs in the principal theatres of this ancient cradle of science and musical genius.'

The hostility of the press notwithstanding, Rossini was quickly absorbed into Neapolitan society. Outside the court, one of its hubs was the Palazzo Berio, home of the well-to-do literary dilettante Francesco Berio di Salsa (1765–1820), Rossini's librettist for *Otello* and *Ricciardo e Zoraide*. The Irish-born novelist Lady Morgan would recall in her *Italy* (1821):

> The *conversazione* of the Palazzo Berio is a congregation of elegant and
> refined spirits, where everybody converses and converses well; and best
> (if not most) the master of the house . . . Rossini presided at the
> piano-forte, accompanying alternatively, himself, Rosetti in his *improvisi*
> [*sic*], and the Colbrun [*sic*], the *prima donna* of San Carlo, in some of her
> favourite airs from his own *Mosè*. Rossini at the piano-forte is almost as
> fine an actor as he is a composer.[6]

Excluding the semi-pastiche *Eduardo e Cristina* (Venice, 1819), Rossini wrote eighteen operas in the six-and-a-half years between his arrival in Naples in 1815 and his departure in March 1822, nine of them for the San Carlo company. Sources ranged from the Bible, Tasso and Shakespeare to Racine and Sir Walter Scott, many of them ground-breaking initiatives, with Rossini himself taking a close interest in the drafting of the librettos. Away from Naples, he would consolidate his reputation as a composer of *opera buffa*. *Il barbiere di Siviglia* (Rome, 1816) is a brilliant re-appropriation of Beaumarchais's play that iconoclastically outmanoeuvres Paisiello's earlier setting at almost every point, whilst *La Cenerentola* (Rome, 1817) mixes *buffo* antics with a degree of pathos unheard thus far in Rossini's comic operas, and perhaps influenced by the sentimental *semiseria* tradition.

Rossini's huge capacity for work and obsessive attention to detail are well illustrated by his involvement in 1817–18 with the gala opening of Pesaro's new opera house. On 27 January 1818 he wrote to the project's organisers, Giulio Perticari and Antaldo Antaldi, confirming that he was trying to engage the services of Colbran and Nozzari, possibly with *Armida*, his newest Neapolitan opera, in mind. The negotiations dragged on for two months, during which time it became clear that Pesaro could neither afford such celebrities nor give clear indications as to when they would be required. Eventually *La gazza ladra* (Milan, May 1817) was chosen, though this proved almost as difficult to cast and even more expensive to stage, not least because of Rossini's insistence on employing La Scala's distinguished stage-designer, Paolo Landriani (1757–1839), and his star pupil, Alessandro Sanquirico (1777–1849).

When a plea to his old friend Rosa Morandi to sing Ninetta came to nothing, Rossini engaged the eighteen-year-old Giuseppina Ronzi De Begnis and, at a reduced fee, her husband Giuseppe De Begnis as the Mayor. The savings made on the De Begnises enabled him to engage his protégé, the tenor Alberico Curioni, as Giannetto and Raniero Remorini as Ferrando. As the star of the show, Remorini was both expensive and difficult. 'He has put me through three days of hell', Rossini informed Perticari on 20 May, referring to Remorini's insistence on having an additional solo. 'Oh, what trouble!' This was nothing, however, to the trouble Rossini himself was taking over the production. Every inch the obsessive perfectionist, he insists on nominating and acquiring the finest local instrumentalists; the layout of the orchestra, the spaces between players, and the lighting of the music-stands are all specified; the co-ordination of designers and stage machin-ists is set in train; a reminder is issued about the whereabouts of the fake magpie.[7]

The gala opening on 10 June was a triumph, though shortly afterwards Rossini was struck down with 'a severe inflammation of the throat', perhaps an early warning of more serious stress-related illnesses to come. His death was noised abroad as far afield as Naples and Paris, but he survived. The following May he returned to Pesaro only to be hounded out of town by thugs in the pay of Bartolomeo Bergami, the lover of Caroline of Brunswick (the estranged wife of the English Prince Regent), whom Rossini had appar-ently snubbed the previous year. Rossini was twenty-seven, and though he survived into his seventy-sixth year, he never set foot in Pesaro again.

Though he returned to Naples in the autumn of 1818, talk in operatic circles was all of him leaving Italy, possibly for Paris, where *L'italiana in Algeri* had recently taken the Théâtre Italien by storm. In practice, the French musical establishment was in no mood to negotiate with him, nor was he perceived by musicians who knew him to be ready to go abroad. On

25 August 1818 the violinist Jean-Jacques Grasset wrote from Bologna to a friend in Paris: 'He is in good hands here for the two things he loves, the table and women.'[8] In the summer of 1820 there was a rising against the Bourbon régime in Naples. Although it was rapidly quashed by the Austrians, it unnerved Rossini. The following year Barbaja signed a contract to take the Naples company to Vienna. Rossini, it was proposed, would also visit Paris and London before returning to Naples. He never did return. The press now worshipped him, but Neapolitan audiences were tiring of his high-minded *opere serie* as much as he was tiring of Neapolitan audiences (the failure of *Ermione* in 1819 had been a particular cause of distress).

Europe and Paris, 1822–1829

Rossini's last Naples opera was *Zelmira*. Setting out for Vienna on 6 March 1822, three weeks after the *prima*, he and Colbran broke their journey at Bologna where they were married in the small church of San Giovanni Battista in Castenaso. Rossini's parents were both present. Many years later he told the painter De Sanctis that it was his mother who had urged him to marry, possibly on grounds of propriety. Money may also have been a consideration: Colbran had recently inherited lands in Sicily as well as the villa at Castenaso. The near-hysteria with which the Viennese greeted Rossini confirmed that there were worlds beyond Italy waiting to be conquered. During his stay in Vienna he had a brief meeting with Beethoven. If, as Rossini reported, Beethoven really did say 'Above all, make more *Barbers*!', it was a fine compliment: proof that Beethoven had read this musically radical work with a good deal more insight than many of his contemporaries.

Returning to Castenaso in the late summer of 1822, Rossini closeted himself with his old friend, the librettist Gaetano Rossi, to work on *Semiramide* (Venice, February 1823), the swan-song of his Italian career. In November 1823 he and Colbran travelled to Paris, where they were fêted on a grand scale and where negotiations finally began about the possibility of Rossini accepting some kind of permanent position in the city's musical life.

The following month the Rossinis moved to London. After a stormy channel crossing, from which it took Rossini a week to recover, the couple settled in rooms at 90 Regent Street. On 29 December Rossini was received by George IV at the court in Brighton. His performance of Figaro's 'Largo al factotum' was well received, but his falsetto rendition of Desdemona's Willow Song scandalised staid opinion. The *Quarterly Musical Magazine* found him genial but bland: 'He certainly looks more like a sturdy beef-eating Englishman than a sensitive, fiery-spirited native of the soft climate of Italy. His countenance when at rest is intelligent yet serious, but bears no marks of the animation which pervades and indeed forms the principal feature of his compositions.'[9]

Rossini's immediate responsibility was the musical direction of a season largely given over to his own operas in the partly refurbished King's Theatre. Neither *Il barbiere di Siviglia* nor *Zelmira* were much liked (an expensive mistake for the impresario Benelli, given the £1,500 fee Mme Colbran-Rossini had demanded), but *Otello* and *Semiramide* with Pasta and García won a large measure of approval from the public, though not from Rossini, who is reported to have remarked that Pasta sang 'false'.[10] The composer amassed a small fortune during his time in London, largely through numerous private appearances for which he made extortionate charges (100 guineas a 'lesson' at a time when the more usual rate was one guinea). These money-making sorties, which included two star-studded concerts at Almack's Rooms, were ill-received in the press. Nor was his newly written *Il pianto delle muse in morte di Lord Byron* spared, despite exertions which left the soloist, Rossini himself, red-faced and perspiring in the summer heat. The Byron elegy and a *Duetto* for cello and double bass, written for the banker David Salomons and the double bass virtuoso Domenico Dragonetti, were the only works Rossini completed in London. A proposed opera, *Ugo, re d'Italia* (a reworking of music from *Ermione*), was never finished.

A draft contract with the French government was signed in London in February 1824. It proposed that, within the year, Rossini would provide for the Paris stage a new *grand opéra* and a shorter *opéra comique*. In the event it would be four years before he produced either. There were sound reasons for this delay. His command of French prosody and the French declamatory style had to be worked on; moreover, singers needed re-schooling as part of a process of re-aligning French and Italian traditions and methods. Rossini was also called upon to assist in the running of the Théâtre Italien, which his music had already taken over: in the season before he arrived in Paris, 119 of the theatre's 154 performances featured works by him.

After the move to Paris in the autumn of 1824, Rossini's first unavoidable duty came with the coronation of Charles X in June 1825. The celebrations spawned a score of official entertainments of which Rossini's *Il viaggio a Reims* was one. It delighted everyone except the king himself. After four performances Rossini withdrew the score, not because of royal disfavour but because he had more permanent plans for the music, much of which would re-appear in intriguing new configurations in *Le Comte Ory* three years later.

Rossini's first French-language operas for the Paris stage were revisions of earlier works: *Le Siège de Corinthe* (from *Maometto II*) and *Moïse et Pharaon* (from *Mosè in Egitto*). The composer was prudently testing French musical waters, making numberless changes to the scores, both large- and small-scale. Theatrically, however, the revisions were far from prudent. In revising *Maometto II*, originally a story about Venetians and Turks, Rossini and his librettists turned the drama into a tragedy of the Greek people at a time when the French government was in strategic alliance with the Turkish cause but public opinion was sympathetic to the Greek one. The staging itself was also revolutionary, not least the final scene depicting the sacked and burning Corinth: 'The entire stage is on fire!', notes the production book; 'the curtain falls on this horrifying tableau'.[11] Rossini's promised *grand opéra*, *Guillaume Tell*, which eventually had its première in August 1829 – after an eleventh-hour battle of wills with the government over Rossini's demand for a life annuity – offered a very different view of the world, embodying ideals which were rather closer to Rossini's heart: familial harmony and the politics of a people who seek independence with peace.

Bologna and Paris, 1829–1836

In September 1829 Rossini returned to Bologna. It was a sad homecoming. His mother had died two years previously after a short illness and, though his father soldiered on, Isabella was becoming progressively more impossible, bored and addicted to gambling. The following spring Rossini was in correspondence with the French government about the possibility of an opera based on Goethe's *Faust*. Then, in the summer of 1830, the government fell. Charles X fled into exile to be replaced by Louis-Philippe, the 'citizen king'. Committed to policies based on 'fairness' and 'accountability', the new government slashed investment in the Civil List, cancelling Rossini's life annuity and invalidating his contract with the Opéra. Rossini rushed back to Paris to attend to the matter, but it was only after five years of lobbying and litigation that the annuity was restored when an appeal by the Ministry of Finance against an independent tribunal's ruling in Rossini's favour was thrown out by the courts (the fact that Charles X's own signature was on the contract of April 1829 had proved decisive).

Well-off now, but wearied by litigation and in increasingly poor health (he had contracted gonorrhoea in 1832), the 43-year-old Rossini was in no fit state to return to the operatic fray. There had been talk of his retiring from operatic composition as early as 1816, after the fiasco of the first night of *Il barbiere di Siviglia*. Clearly such talk was premature, but his father's remark in a letter written in 1827 – 'he has toiled long and wearily enough' – is very much to the point. Certainly thirty-nine operas in nineteen years, few of them outright failures, many of them masterpieces or works of significant imagination or innovation, is a formidable record. Tiredness, family concerns, and political, artistic and social change all played their part in what Rossini biographer Francis Toye misleadingly termed 'the great renunciation'.

Rossini was thirty-seven at the time of the completion of *Guillaume Tell*, an age when even the most naturally gifted composers can lose the facility they once possessed. Creative failures, suicides, unanticipated deaths and lapses into silence far more complete than Rossini's have been legion at this stage in the lives of many great artists. Rossini had made his mark and established his line. Returning to the Théâtre Italien in 1830, he was able to watch with interest the work of Meyerbeer, Donizetti and Bellini. His grief at Bellini's death at the early age of thirty-three in 1835 was marked; difficult though Bellini had been, he was one of the first of Rossini's several surrogate sons, the exemplary bearer of the torch Rossini himself had lit.

In February 1831 Rossini, now based mostly in Paris, travelled with his friend, the Parisian banker Alexandre-Marie Aguado, to Madrid, where he was persuaded to create a new work for Aguado's friend, the priest and state counsellor Don Francisco Fernández Varela. A *Stabat mater* was suggested. Rossini accepted the commission and half completed it before farming out the remainder of the work to his colleague Giovanni Tadolini. The Rossini/Tadolini setting was first performed in Madrid on Good Friday 1833. Rossini did not travel to hear it. Furthermore, he stipulated that, after its first performance, the work should remain in manuscript, unpublished and unperformed, a stipulation which would return to haunt him.

In the midst of the *Stabat mater* project Rossini wrote a cantata for voice and piano, *Giovanna d'Arco*, 'expressly for Mademoiselle Olimpia Pélissier'. Born in 1797, Olympe was the illegitimate daughter of a woman who later married Joseph Pélissier, whose name she adopted. The erstwhile mistress of the painter Horace Vernet, Olympe was described by Balzac as 'the most beautiful courtesan in Paris'. The character of Fedora in his novel *La Peau de chagrin* (1831) was partly inspired by her. Fedora is described there as being physically opulent, sexually chilly (the one aspect of the character probably not inspired by Olympe), snobbish and insecure, yet possessed of a strange inner warmth, a private serenity.

Although it would be a mistake to think of Balzac, Rossini and Olympe as a *ménage à trois*, they certainly saw a good deal of one another in the early 1830s. Balzac was a Rossini addict who physically rather resembled his hero and was, like him, subject to a form of manic depression. To judge by the pages devoted to the Rossini cult in *La Peau de chagrin*, Balzac understood the ambiguous nature of the phenomenon as well as anyone. Seen from one perspective, Rossini is an urbane figure from a bygone age, a musician descended from the school of Cimarosa and Paisiello, an emblem of that sweetness and classical decorum which the besotted wretches of Parisian society yearn for in their morning-after moods. Seen from the other perspective, his music is disruptive and noisy, representative of a world where dissipation, high living and heightened sensation are the order of the day. Both were true, but it was the former vision to which Rossini himself clung: in his *Les Soirées musicales* (1835) populist material is treated with courtly sophistication.

Bologna and Florence, 1836–1855

His annuity secured, in the autumn of 1836 Rossini moved back to Bologna, Olympe following him there a few months later. By now he was suffering a hell of his own devising: the effects of gonorrhoea and its attendant afflictions. Although he is said to have 'at the age of forty-four tempered his passion for women and stopped the abuse of liquors and heating foods',[12] it was too late. Nowadays his condition could be cured with a mixture of antibiotics or chemotherapy; in the 1830s there was no known cure. He also suffered from chronic dysuria and various bladder infections. A predisposition to manic depression was almost certainly exacerbated by the pain and humiliation these illnesses brought in their wake.

By now Olympe had ceased to be Rossini's lover and become his nurse. In 1837–8, after Rossini had formally separated from Colbran, he and Olympe wintered in Milan, where he met and befriended Franz Liszt. But events continued to wreak their havoc. A fire at the Théâtre Italien in Paris in January 1838 claimed the life of Rossini's friend Carlo Severini. In October his father celebrated his eightieth birthday, but he was in poor health and died the following April. News also reached Rossini of the death of Varela and the appearance in a Parisian auction room of the manuscript of the Rossini/Tadolini *Stabat mater*. He immediately set about establishing his legal rights to the piece. More importantly, he determined to complete it. The new, all-Rossini *Stabat mater* made its sensational public début in Paris in January 1842. Two months later it was performed in Bologna: too nervous to conduct, Rossini asked Donizetti to take charge of the performance. Rossini was in poor physical and mental shape and might well have died, had it not been for a decision in the spring of 1843 to return to Paris to consult France's leading urologist, Jean Civiale. The treatment lasted three months, during which time Rossini was confined in a semi-darkened bedroom, much obsessed, it is said, with thoughts of death.

In October 1845 news reached him that Colbran was gravely ill. He visited her shortly before her death on 7 October 1845. The following August he and Olympe were married. The year 1846 also saw the election of Pope Pius IX, a liberalising pontiff who, it was hoped, would help reconcile Catholicism and Italian nationalism. Rossini honoured the Pope's election with a grand cantata (his last such work) for performance in Rome on New Year's Day 1847. What neither Pius IX nor Rossini had bargained for was the disruptive power of the revolutions which were about to engulf Europe. With Italian nationalists confronting Austrian troops on the streets of Bologna in April 1848, Rossini beat a hasty retreat to Florence, where he remained until 1855, returning to Bologna only to settle his affairs and sell the villa at Castenaso. His uneasy but none the less co-operative relationship with the Austrians was noised abroad by radicals as the collaborative act of a decadent bourgeois. Rossini retaliated by dubbing Bologna 'that sewer'.

To pass the time he buried himself in the minutiae of domestic and legal affairs. Visitors, whom he often burdened with gruesome and embarrassing details of his physical condition, found him morbid and excitable. He claimed to have contemplated suicide but confessed that he was too much of a coward to take the decisive step. Gossips reported him incurably insane. He was not, but his mood-swings were extreme. Amid the gloom there are letters from this period in his best *buffo* style. The new complete edition of the works of J. S. Bach gave him real pleasure, and he continued to pass amusing and acerbic judgements on fellow composers. Hearing music in his own home often left him in a distracted and tearful state, but his executive skills remained undimmed. Emilia Branca Romani recalls him weaving a brilliantly improvised accompaniment round Matilde Juva's rendering of 'Bel raggio lusinghier' from *Semiramide* and describes his improvisation on Desdemona's Act 3 romance in *Otello* – a 'fantasia alla Thalberg' as Rossini called it – as 'magnificent, astonishing, dumbfounding'.[13]

Paris, 1855–1868

In 1855 Olympe insisted that they return to Paris, to French doctors and French society. The removal had no immediate effect, but slowly the clouds began to lift. On 15 April 1857 Rossini presented to Olympe a set of songs entitled *Musique anodine*. The dedication reads: 'I offer these modest songs to my dear wife Olympe as a simple testimonial of gratitude for the affectionate, intelligent care of which she was prodigal during my overlong and terrible illness (Shame of the [medical] faculty).'[14]

The Rossinis took an apartment in the rue de la Chaussée d'Antin and land was acquired in Passy for the building of a sumptuous new villa. On 18 December 1858 the first of the famous *samedi soirs* was held. The food bordered on the execrable (Olympe making good use of the endless 'samples' sent to the gourmet maestro) and Rossini himself often stayed apart in a nearby room chatting with cronies. But the music, much of it newly written by him for the occasion, was exquisite. Rossini dubbed these pieces 'Sins of

Old Age'. Over the next ten years musical Europe beat a path to Rossini's door. Few invitations were more coveted.

Rossini led a carefully regulated life in Paris. After rising at eight and breakfasting, he would attend to his mail and, if circumstances were propitious, take a brief walk or drive or visit one of a select band of well-to-do friends. He rarely ate lunch, dined at six and, after a short nap, might receive friends before retiring on the stroke of ten, 'the canonical hour'. He assumed no public duties (his presidency of a government commission on musical pitch was purely honorary) and attended no public performances of his, or anyone else's, music.

He was fascinated by young musical talent, however. In 1860 the Marchisio sisters – Barbara (1833–1919) and Carlotta (1835–72) – starred in a new production of *Semiramide* at the Paris Opéra. Although Rossini was firmly of the opinion that the art of singing had fallen into decay by the time of *Guillaume Tell,* he seems to have found in the voices of the Marchisios echoes of past beauties. On the evening of Good Friday 1861 a musical soirée was given over to his *Stabat mater,* performed by a chamber ensemble which included the Marchisio sisters and, in lieu of the orchestra, a double string quartet.

This was the prelude to an altogether more important initiative, the creation of his last major work, the *Petite messe solennelle,* written for the dedication in March 1864 of the private chapel of the Countess Pillet-Will. In an epigraph to the *Messe* Rossini tells his Maker:

> Dear God, here it is finished, this poor little Mass. Is this sacred music which I have written or music of the devil? (Est-ce bien de la musique Sacrée que je viens de faire ou bien de la Sacrée Musique?) I was born for *opera buffa,* as you well know. A little science, a little heart, that's all. Be blessed, then, and admit me to Paradise. G Rossini. Passy 1863.[15]

The Mass's title is not a joke (*solennelle* indicates a sung mass, a *missa solemnis* as opposed to a *missa lecta*), although it does hint at its scale: just twelve voices, including the four soloists, two pianos and harmonium. The work has moments of radiance and uninhibited joy, but also a stranger, darker side, which tests conventional faith to its limits. In something like the irksome little E minor figure which dominates the Agnus Dei there is a sense of death as extinction, empty of all meaning.

Towards the end of 1866 Rossini suffered a mild stroke from which he made an unexpectedly full recovery. He was pathologically obese, however, with hardening of the arteries in his legs making walking increasingly difficult. The following February he celebrated his seventy-fifth birthday. In 1868, while the Paris Opéra celebrated the '500th performance' of *Guillaume Tell,* he became embroiled in controversy about the funding of Italy's music schools. In August he received a letter from a young composer, Costantino Dall'Argine, who proposed to dedicate his own setting of *Il barbiere di Siviglia* to him. Rossini wrote a wise, witty and gracious reply acceding to the young man's request. Later that same month he penned a long and wide-ranging letter on musical aesthetics to the critic Filippo Filippi, in which for the last time Rossini affirmed the classical virtues of the early *Ottocento* style and railed against 'imitative' (as opposed to 'expressive') music and the decline of vocal art.[16]

The final *samedi soir* was held on 26 September 1868. For some time Rossini's doctor had been aware of what he took to be a rectal fistula. It was in fact a malignant tumour. Rossini was referred to Professor Auguste Nelaton, a pioneer of abdominal surgery at Paris's Hôpital St Louis, who scheduled an operation for 3 November. Since chronic bronchitis and cardiac weakness made Rossini an anaesthetic risk, Nelaton removed as much of the malignancy as he could in a five-minute operation, which he was forced to supplement with further surgery two days later. Nelaton was confident of success, but the use of unsterile equipment proved fatal, causing a rapidly spreading infection of the skin. Delirious with fever and pain, Rossini lapsed into a coma and died shortly before midnight on Friday 13 November.

The funeral, which took place at the church of the Trinity in Paris at noon on 21 November, was attended by over 4,000 people, after which Rossini's body was laid to rest in Paris's grandest cemetery, Père-Lachaise. He died a wealthy man. His estate passed to Olympe and, after her death in 1878, to the municipality of Pesaro for the founding of a new Liceo Musicale, which opened on 5 November 1882. In 1887 his remains were removed to the church of Santa Croce in Florence, a temple to the glories of the young Italian nation modelled on Westminster Abbey. Olympe had been apprised some years earlier that this would be the case. When she proffered the hope that she might be moved there too, Italian opinion (including Verdi's) was scandalised, a situation this most resolute yet modest of musical wives accepted with characteristic grace and forbearance: 'After the removal of my husband's mortal remains to Florence', she wrote in her will, 'I shall remain there [Père-Lachaise] alone. I make this sacrifice in all humility; I have been glorified enough by the name I bear. My faith and my religious feeling give me the hope of a reunion which escapes earth.'[17] It was not until 1902 that a proper memorial was erected at Rossini's tomb in Santa Croce, the words 'Pesaro–Firenze–Parigi', which are engraved on it, an obvious (and surely intentional) slight to Bologna and Naples.

3 Rossini and France

BENJAMIN WALTON

The nationality of Rossini

For those who wander Père-Lachaise cemetery in Paris in search of celebrity graves, the tomb of Rossini is mercifully easy to find. By contrast with the narrow, winding paths to Chopin's memorial, or the detour through undergrowth necessary to pay homage to Bellini, Rossini's dwelling, in death as in life, sits squarely on a main boulevard. His name carved in capitals on the lintel, the grave follows the Second Empire entrance porch design, rejecting the faded, overgrown decrepitude of the simple stele for the solidity of a miniaturised Haussmannian apartment block. Rossini, however, is no longer there. The grave is an empty memorial, robbed of the invisible remains that give such visits their existential satisfaction.

Any literal suggestion of robbery is, of course, unfounded. On a cold, rainy day in the late spring of 1887 the Italian ambassador to France, the head of the Paris Conservatoire, and other notables from the two countries gathered for an official ceremony. Rossini's body was disinterred, his coffin opened to confirm his identity, and music and speeches provided to mark the transfer of the composer from French to Italian authorities.[1] He was then taken by train to Florence, where a series of more elaborate celebrations took place to welcome his corpse to its final location in the church of Santa Croce. Yet the speech given in Père-Lachaise by the Prefect of the Seine, Eugène Poubelle, while not explicitly mentioning theft, conveyed a marked lack of conviction about the return of Rossini to the country of his birth. Having pointed out that Rossini's grave had been constantly visited since his death, Poubelle went on to list various ways in which the composer belonged in and to France. These included the suggestion that the protagonists of the composer's works were all in some way French. Figaro was a true Parisian, and as for Guillaume Tell, 'the passion of the French for national independence almost makes us think that we once fought alongside him in delivering Switzerland from the clutches of the German empire'.[2]

Most strikingly, Poubelle asserted that apart from a break of a few years in Italy, Rossini had lived in Paris from 1823 until his death. In truth this break lasted almost two decades, from 1836 to 1855, a quarter of the composer's life. Poubelle's disdain for such chronological detail, however, only served to reinforce his central purpose of naturalising Rossini. As such, his speech over the composer's beautifully preserved cadaver stands as the culmination (or the last gasp) in a long process to claim Rossini for France, where, in the wishful words of one of his obituarists, 'he would have liked to have been born'.[3]

On the eve of Rossini's exhumation, one newspaper prefigured Poubelle in asking simply: 'Was Rossini French or Italian?'[4] In late 1823, at the time of Rossini's first trip to Paris en route to London, such a question would have seemed ludicrous. He was not merely known to be Italian, but was crucially defined by his foreign status in the eyes of both admirers and detractors. Over the intervening decades Rossini's contact with France went through several distinct stages, and the question of his national identity would be answered differently at different times, in accordance with his country of residence but also, less tangibly, with his changing place in French consciousness.

The first stage of Rossini's French career was also the most active, lasting from the early 1820s until the completion of *Guillaume Tell* in 1829: the time both of his greatest renown in France and of the greatest controversies surrounding his music. Indisputably Italian on his arrival, by the end of the decade he had been accorded the status of an honorary Frenchman on account of his works for the Paris Opéra. A year after the première of *Tell*, Rossini took rooms at the top of the Théâtre Italien, and discreetly oversaw much of the theatre's direction, largely out of the public eye. His relative invisibility combined with his long compositional silence pushed him back towards Italy in the public mind, foreshadowing his actual return to Bologna in 1836. Between 1836 and 1855 Rossini stayed in Italy, and French performances of his operas flagged. As the excitement over his isolated visit to Paris in 1843 demonstrated, however, he was not forgotten. In the absence of concrete detail, he and his music were instead fictionalised, making appearances in short stories, travelogues, anecdotal essays and even full-scale fabricated biographies.

Rossini returned to France in 1855 as a grand old man, after decades of illness, depression and inactivity. In comparison with the preceding years, this last period is relatively well documented. Yet for all the extant eye-witness accounts of Rossini's unalterable routines – of daily strolls, weekly salons, winters in central Paris and summers spent in the village-suburb of Passy – these years remain elusive, the accumulated detail obscuring as much as it reveals.

Biographers ever since have sought the 'real' Rossini, the man concealed behind countless and often baseless anecdotes. But to understand his place in nineteenth-century French cultural life it is as revealing to pay attention to the various Rossinis of the national imagination that came in time to shape any new reality. Beginning in the Restoration, the degree of his celebrity, the continued debates over the significance of his music and his avoidance of public utterance all served to make the composer uniquely susceptible to mythologising (and demonising) in the celebrity-hungry culture of post-Napoleonic Paris.

It is in this context that the famous opening image of Stendhal's magnificent *Vie de Rossini* resonates most strongly: 'Since the death of Napoleon, another man has appeared who is talked about every day in Moscow as in Naples, in London as in Vienna, in Paris as in Calcutta.'[5] Deprived of a charismatic leader after Waterloo, subjected first to the dessicated remnants of an ex-monarchy and, after 1830, to a bourgeois king, the French needed new heroes. If the figure of Rossini now seems unlikely next to more familiar Bonaparte substitutes such as Byron or Liszt, this is to overlook the power of Rossini's music in its time to symbolise political liberty, sexual potency, amorality, the thrill of battle and other heady themes of the Romantic era in France. Later, Rossini's voluntary abdication after *Guillaume Tell* somewhat altered the stories that surrounded him; the eventual length of his retirement, in flat contradiction of all the imperatives of Romantic creative genius, would allow these stories to be retold many, many times.

1815–1829

As early as September 1818, Giacomo Meyerbeer wrote to his brother from Milan with the news that Rossini was in negotiations with the Paris Opéra. Rossini's conditions were steep, Meyerbeer said, but if accepted, 'he moves to Paris, and we shall witness strange things'.[6] Three years later Rossini received further offers and by January 1822 newspapers in Italy and France announced a forthcoming visit by the composer to Vienna, Paris and London. Finally, after a separate stay in Vienna, he set out for London via Paris in October 1823.

The timing was auspicious. At the time of Meyerbeer's letter, Parisians had been exposed to very little of Rossini's music. Extracts from *Tancredi*, *La pietra del paragone*, *Demetrio e Polibio* and *L'italiana in Algeri* had appeared as early as 1813 in the *Journal d'Euterpe*, a periodical for new vocal pieces.[7] But only *L'italiana* had been publicly performed in Paris (1 February 1817), and it had failed completely. By the time negotiations were renewed in 1821, despite persistent rumours that the director of the Théâtre Italien, Ferdinando Paer, resented Rossini's success, the theatre had staged four works in two years, would produce four more (including a revival of *L'italiana*) in 1821, and a further four in 1822.[8] Paris, or at least the enthusiasts at the Théâtre Italien, had succumbed to Rossini's charms, and a visit from the composer himself would clearly be well received.

As excitement about Rossini's music spread, protests began to surface from those less susceptible to the new style, and irritated by the composer's mounting popularity. The newspaper reviews from these early years – declaring *Il barbiere* colourless or *L'inganno felice* weighed down by its harmonic complexities – seem comical now. But for all their surprising conclusions, they mark the beginning of a decade of argument over the meanings and importance of Rossini, during which his music became a symbol for a wide range of contemporary concerns. As a result such reviews can rarely be taken at face value, since all writings about Rossini in the gossipy, slanderous and often short-lived 'theatrical' journals of the period exist within networks of vested interests, political affiliations and volatile feuding that are largely lost to view today.[9] Nevertheless, the intertwined issues which surrounded Rossini's music still remain visible, and can be teased into four separate strands: personal, musical, political and national.

The most readily apparent is the first. The personality problem lay not with Rossini himself, but with his fans, the notorious group of regulars at the Théâtre Italien whose collective title of 'dilettanti' took on the mantle of an insult, a shorthand for the blind excesses of Rossinian admiration. Such enthusiasts, who listened exclusively to Italian music at their predominantly aristocratic theatre, are frequently portrayed as insufferably snobbish, but there was equal snobbery in their dismissal. Scorn was heaped on these 'demi-savants', who lacked proper musical understanding of complex material yet were too sophisticated to grasp the simple 'truth' of the genuinely beautiful melodies of earlier French music.[10]

In opposition to such truth, anti-dilettantes labelled Rossini's melodies tasteless, over-embellished and above all false. The most vehement exponent of this line of attack was Henri-Montan Berton, an ageing French composer who had been something of a musical revolutionary in his youth. In the summer of 1822 Berton produced a detailed critique entitled 'On Mechanical Music and Philosophical Music', republished as a pamphlet in 1826.[11] In Berton's terms, mechanical music, epitomised by Rossini, lacked soul, dramatic truth and an appreciation of proper rules of declamation, offering in their place only 'rhythmic incoherence, pretentious harmonic ideas, mannered melodic turns and above all an impossible profusion of semiquavers'.[12] For Berton this constituted an attack on musical purity equivalent to the Barbarian invasions during the late Roman empire, with Rossini's Gothic music trampling over the Greek temples of Gluck and Mozart (and of Berton himself).

Berton's writings frequently exhibit the same paranoia that would reappear in fulminations against the dangers of jazz in the 1920s or rock-'n'-roll in the 1960s: a fear of impurity, of foreign infiltration and above all of the physical force of Rossini's music, of its intense, indeed excessive stimulation.

As one journal described: 'See the pretty girls at the Italian opera; how their complexions colour, how their eyes shine, what a delicious expression animates their faces during a performance of *La gazza ladra* or *Il barbiere*! I would like to ask the regulars at the Opéra whether they often get to see anything like it.'[13] Indeed, bits of Berton's own list of Rossini's faults – 'ambitious modulations, extraordinary transitions, multiple parts' – sound like a recommendation for a thrillingly new kind of musical experience.

The provision of this pleasure could moreover be figured as a political act, artistic liberty being linked to political liberty in a way that would become ever more familiar leading up to the Revolution of 1830. Such an idea is clearest in the articles which had goaded Berton to his choleric response, by a man Berton sarcastically addressed as 'le grand juge'.[14] Their author, Henri Beyle (better known as Stendhal), back in Paris after seven years in Italy, heard the sounds of great Napoleonic battles in Rossini's percussive accompaniments. And in the stultifying atmosphere of Restoration Paris these sounds offered him the idealised aesthetic modernity that he would later describe as Romanticism: 'The art of presenting people with . . . works which, in the present state of their needs and beliefs, will give them the greatest possible pleasure'.[15]

Nationalistic rhetoric gathered around Rossini's first visit to Paris in 1823, arguably the high point of his entire French career. By this time twelve of his operas had been premièred at the Théâtre Italien, and any failures such as *Torvaldo e Dorliska* (two performances) and Stendhal's favourite *La pietra del paragone* (three) were quickly forgotten next to the huge success of *Tancredi* (thirty-two performances by the time of Rossini's arrival), *Otello* (thirty-six) and *La gazza ladra* (forty-four). Their fortune was helped by a formidable troupe of soloists, including the soprano Joséphine Fodor-Mainvielle, the tenor Manuel García, the bass Felice Pellegrini and (from 1821) the *prima donna assoluta* Giuditta Pasta. Pasta's performance of *Tancredi*, in particular, was central to Stendhal's conception of the piece, and still proverbial many years later in Balzac's *Illusions perdues* (set in the Restoration). Most successful of all, however, was *Il barbiere di Siviglia*, first produced only at the insistence of García, which by the end of 1822 had appeared without a significant break for three years in a row.[16]

Rossini's arrival in Paris on 9 November 1823 set in motion four weeks of public and private festivities which included trips to the Opéra and the Théâtre Italien, serenades in the streets, visits to prominent Parisian musical figures and soirées with nobility both blue-blooded and theatrical. Each appearance of the composer was covered in detail by pro-Rossinian journals, and no rumour was left unreported, from accounts of the great man's table manners to his skill at speaking French.[17] Critics of the brouhaha sought to deflate the celebrations, and affected bewilderment that the simple arrival of an Italian composer in the French capital should be regarded as especially newsworthy.[18] Meanwhile, parodies published at the expense of these same critics depicted them as blind nationalists, and invented an ancient country in Asia Minor called *Idiopatrie* (Stupidland) from which they apparently originated; a place that denied the existence of its neighbours altogether, and punished its citizens with three days of verbal abuse for naming anything beyond its borders. When some of Idiopatrie's populace finally emigrated, they nevertheless retained their original character, and over the centuries dogmatically resisted the introduction of gunpowder, eye glasses, windmills, printing, Copernicus, vaccination, steam engines and lightning conductors; 'today they want to forbid the music of Rossini'.[19]

There was concern, however, over the effects of rampant 'rossinisme' even among some of the composer's supporters.[20] During Rossini's Parisian visit a single act vaudeville by Edouard Mazères and the young Eugène Scribe appeared, entitled *Rossini à Paris, ou le grand dîner*. Hailed by anti-Rossinian papers as a decisive blow against the composer and his devotees, the play is a relatively mild satire in which a group of dilettanti excitedly awaiting the composer's arrival at one of the gates into Paris mistake a young French composer, Giraud, for the great Italian. In the confusion, Rossini enters the city without anyone noticing. The play's gags must have seemed deliciously predictable. When Giraud plays bits of famous French operas for the dilettanti they respond with delight, believing the music to be by Rossini, too clueless to notice the obvious differences. Ultimately, however, the most significant moment of the play lies not in the antics of the dilettanti, but in the fact that Giraud himself has an opera that he is unable to get performed, because all theatres want is Rossini or mimicry of Rossini. The future for French opera looks bleak.[21]

This was a serious matter in a city with tight government control over operatic production, and all the more so since indigenous opera had been in poor shape before Rossini arrived. Even supporters of French music observed that the great genre of the *tragédie lyrique* was dying, singers at the Opéra had begun to copy Italian methods of ornamentation, everyone was bored to death with the same ancient repertory, and the only new works submitted were comedies.[22] As if to prove the point, when Rossini visited the Opéra on the day after his arrival, he witnessed a production of Rousseau's *Le Devin du village*, written in 1753 as a challenge to the mid-eighteenth century domination of *tragédie lyrique*, paired with *Lasthénie*, a one-act comedy by Rossini's Italianate friend Ferdinand Hérold.

Rossini did what he could to defuse the national rivalry. He paid visits to distinguished members of the Paris Conservatoire, and at the lavish dinner held in his honour he responded to a welcoming toast with one of his own to the composers of the French school and to the prosperity of the

Conservatoire. But in the end, all his critics' fears came true, if not in quite the way they imagined. In the years following his return to Paris from London in August 1824, Rossini would indeed take over French opera and transform its style, and he would continue not just to dominate the Théâtre Italien but also (temporarily) to run it.[23] Worse still for his opponents, other theatres would also turn to his music for commercial success, most notably the Odéon.[24] Added to the performances by street musicians, the sales of sheet music and vocal scores, the arrangements of 'Di tanti palpiti' or 'Una voce poco fa' as fantasies or variation sets for piano, the reality must frequently have seemed as Joseph d'Ortigue described in 1829: 'From dances at the city gates to churches where an organ accompanies the singing, everything bears witness to the fact that art has taken shelter in the genius of a single man.'[25] And although for the rest of the decade the criticisms continued – pamphlets were published, articles written, dilettanti mocked – from an artistic and administrative point of view Rossini successfully shaped Parisian musical life into his own image.

The possibility of Rossini producing a work in French, whether new or in translation, to revive the fortunes of the Opéra had been discussed as early as 1821. Three years later, in February 1824, Rossini's first contract with the French government specified two new works, one for the Opéra and one for the Théâtre Italien. Rossini ultimately took a further five years to produce his single completely original French opera, *Guillaume Tell* (3 August 1829). But the works that led up to it were equally significant in adapting his own musical style to the grander, less ornamented tradition of Gluck and Spontini while responding to some of the dominant themes of the later 1820s. His first work for the Opéra, *Le Siège de Corinthe* (9 October 1826), changed the opposition between Venetians and Turks of its model, *Maometto II* (1820), into a conflict between Greeks and Turks, in line with the immense French interest in the Greek cause during their war of independence against the Ottoman empire.[26] The tragic ending, too, corresponds directly with pessimism over the Greeks' fate at the time of the work's conception and première. In Rossini's telling, the Greeks commit mass suicide and the heroine, Pamyra, deprived of the final aria granted to her predecessor Anna in *Maometto*, is overwhelmed by the unleashed orchestral forces.[27] As if in direct response to his critics, Rossini provided the aural representation of an instrumental army wreaking havoc on the action on stage; if they had thought he was noisy before, this time he would make sure that they left the hall deafened.[28]

After the première of *Le Siège de Corinthe* Rossini relinquished his official duties at the Théâtre Italien and took instead the honorific titles of Composer to the King and Inspector General of Singing. His time at the Italian theatre had produced only one new work, the *pièce de circonstance*

Il viaggio a Reims (19 June 1825), written to celebrate the coronation of Charles X. He withdrew the piece after four performances, and later reused the music for his French comic opera *Le Comte Ory* (premièred at the Opéra; 20 August 1828).[29] In addition he oversaw new productions of *Semiramide* (8 December 1825) and *Zelmira* (14 March 1826), his most recent works before his arrival in Paris, and mounted the Parisian première of Meyerbeer's *Il crociato in Egitto* (1825). In part through sustained journalistic attacks, however, his tenure was widely (if unjustly) seen as a failure, and nothing more than a reinforcement of his Parisian monopoly through lack of new competition.

Freed from the time-consuming administration of the Théâtre Italien, Rossini set to work on his final two French grand operas, *Moïse et Pharaon* (an arrangement of *Mosè*; 26 March 1827) and *Guillaume Tell*. Like *Le Siège de Corinthe*, both depict the struggles of oppressed peoples, if with happier outcomes than in the earlier work. The temptation to connect such a shared theme with the Revolution of 1830 is strong. To give in, however, involves the replacement of the more intricate contexts that surround each individual work with a potentially deadening generalised hindsight. Later in the century *Guillaume Tell* would come to be uncomplicatedly interpreted as politically revolutionary. In 1829 the only indisputable revolution offered by the work was a musical one. Having provided his long-awaited model for a new French grand opera, Rossini's major task over the following years would be to resolve the question of his annual state pension, payable independently of obligations. The age of Rossinian grand opera had reached its end.

1830–1855

After the triumphant première of *Guillaume Tell* Rossini received a serenade under the windows of his apartment, just as he had on his arrival in 1823, and just as he would again for the 500th performance of *Il barbiere* shortly before his death in 1868. In 1823 the honour of the serenade had been extended to a famous foreign visitor; in 1868 it was meant as an act of thanksgiving for Rossini's music and as an opportunity to marvel that there could really be a direct connection between this ancient Parisian and such familiarly classic music. What then did the serenade for *Guillaume Tell* signify? In part, no doubt, a sigh of relief that Rossini had finally produced the brand new French opera he had promised for so long; also perhaps astonishment that the work was so magnificent, so epic in scope. But the serenade further bore witness to Rossini's acceptance as an honorary Frenchman, as incontestably significant to the history of the nation's operatic tradition as those other foreign Frenchmen, Lully and Gluck. Accordingly, in 1835, Rossini appeared in the centre of an English lithograph showing a pantheon of eight 'celebrated French composers', next to three other Italians (Cherubini, Spontini and Paer), a German (Meyerbeer) and three composers born in France (Berton, Boieldieu and Auber).[30]

In the 1830s, however, Rossini showed few signs of believing himself French. His last contract in 1829 carried an explanation of his need to go to Italy both for family reasons and for his health.[31] When he returned to Italy again in 1836, having finally resolved the matter of his pension, he wrote to Carlo Severini, one of the directors of the Théâtre Italien, that 'I assure you that up to now I feel the greatest indifference over having abandoned the capital of the world.'[32] Moreover, for French writers Rossini seemed to become more Italian the longer he failed to produce any more operas. Recent research has begun to show that Rossini's second period in Paris, between 1830 and 1836, was a great deal more active than it may have appeared to his contemporaries. Behind the scenes at the Théâtre Italien Rossini was busy hiring and training singers, advising composers (including Bellini, Donizetti and Mercadante), and acting as a full financial partner in the running of the theatre.[33] But to the casual observer Rossini's apparent dormancy while waiting around for his pension could best be rationalised as a return to his Italian roots, to the land of *dolce far niente*.

The best-known account of Rossini's music from the period relies heavily on the idealised otherness of a soporific Italy. Written after a trip to Italy in 1838, Balzac's novella *Massimilla Doni* is set in a decaying Venice and includes a famously long analysis of Rossini's *Mosè* by the eponymous heroine. Many of the themes of the tale, which takes place in 1821, seem designed as much in tribute to Stendhal as Rossini, not least Massimilla's extended political interpretation of the opera's plot. Yet whereas Stendhal rarely resorted to poetic imagery in his efforts to capture the indescribable effects of Rossini's music, Balzac's tale is written in a Hoffmannesque tone of German Romantic awe that Stendhal frequently mocked. As a result, Rossini's music risks seeming ridiculous in Balzac's hands, described in ecstatic terms originally conceived for the cerebral, instrumental alternative to the sensory delights of Italian opera. Balzac's tale stands as an intriguing attempt to celebrate a Romantic Rossini who by the 1830s no longer existed in the public mind. Twenty years later one Rossini biographer still recalled the ridicule that Balzac had suffered for daring to claim so much for *Mosè*.[34]

Other writers tended to avoid discussion of Rossini's music in favour of accounts of conversations with Rossini, a kind of literary sub-genre through the 1830s and 1840s. Even when these trips actually took place, the written reports sound contrived, either dominated by deep philosophical reflections or skewed to reveal a particular angle on Rossini's life. A biography published in 1836, for instance, concluded with a walk taken with Rossini along the Parisian boulevards, discussing the aesthetics of musical expression.[35] The result is very convincing, more so than Alexandre Dumas's account of discussing the art of writing a libretto with Rossini over dinner, or Jules Janin's tale of visiting him in Bologna after a strange experience in the local graveyard.[36]

The most believable works often proved the most fallacious. In 1845 a work by Edouard Oettinger appeared in Leipzig, in which the author claimed to have known Rossini in Paris in 1830 and to have listened to stories of the composer's youthful exploits while seated by the fire in the living room of his apartment. Three volumes of these tales followed, ending with an account of a visit to Rossini in Bologna and a conversation with him about Meyerbeer and Verdi. When Rossini himself encountered the book in French translation in Brussels thirteen years later, he insisted that he had never met Oettinger, in 1830 or later. His displeasure at the work's contents led to a series of damning articles that spread through the Parisian press.[37] Fétis declared the book beyond contempt, the Escudier brothers described it as 'a bad book, and a bad deed'.[38] One review, however, by Pier-Angelo Fiorentino in *Le Moniteur universel*, was particularly significant, as it progressed from the claim that the book was written in 'Belgian patois', each page containing an outrage against truth, to the statement that 'the time has passed when it might be permissible to deny the genius of Rossini or to attack his works'.[39]

Oettinger's book is an entertaining read, well written and well translated into entirely correct French. And the author's unfortunate claims to have spent time with Rossini co-exist with his admission in his preface that the work is a mixture of fact and fantasy. More accurately, it is Rossini's life replayed as *opera buffa*, complete with sub-plots, intrigues, disguises and recognisable comic stereotypes. Domenico Barbaja, entrepreneur of the San Carlo theatre in Naples, is the buffo, Nozzari, Rossini's protégé, is the young romantic lead, Rossini and Colbran the canny protagonists, the Figaro and Rosina of the piece, and so on. Why did Rossini object to it so strongly? The answer appeared in an article in the *Revue et gazette musicale*: he did not want the work to be seen in thirty or forty years as unimpeachable truth.[40] After years of studied indifference, Rossini had taken control of his image for posterity, and wanted it shaped to his own specifications.

1855–1868

An earlier article by Fiorentino had stated that Rossini never minded stories about him that were written in good faith, and in which the anecdotes were worthy of him. The criterion was not then whether the anecdote was true, but whether a dignified, noble Rossini could potentially have said it.[41] Attacking the life of Rossini (partially based on Oettinger) published by Henri Blaze de Bury in the *Revue des deux mondes*, Fiorentino accused the author, among other things, of an anachronistic view of Italy: 'In this age of rapid communication and electric telegraphs, it is time to put an end to this grotesque and wild Italy which has kept in business . . . the vaudeville and the novel; and it is time to put an end to the Italy of M. Scribe, full of monks and brigands, of daggers and mandolins.'[42]

At a stroke, the imagery of Italy was swept aside, and with it Rossini's identity as an Italian, which, as Fiorentino suggested, had always been based on a stereotype. In its place, a Rossini of the telegraphic age. Such a leap into modernity, however, still only skirted reality. Fiorentino's earlier demolition of Oettinger had prefaced a description of Rossini's present existence notable for its idealised imagery and hagiographical overtones. Rossini had just left his beautiful Paris apartment, Fiorentino told his readers, for the pure air of the loveliest villa in Passy. Meanwhile his health, fully returned, 'will only get stronger given the great joy of his friends and admirers, which is to say all intelligent beings who have had the happiness to hear one of his masterpieces . . . He arrived among us from Italy sick, depressed, languishing; he is not only cured, but rejuvenated.'[43]

There is an element of truth in all of this; Rossini's health did improve enormously once he was in Paris, his sense of humour returned, as did, famously, his urge to compose. Nevertheless it is as if a pact had been tacitly agreed. If France unconditionally accepted the genius of Rossini, Rossini would accept the honorary citizenship of France, and allow her to claim the credit as Rossini's new native land. Such an agreement could only involve rewriting the past, perhaps beginning to play down Rossini's Italian years as Eugène Poubelle would do at the exhumation ceremony, or perhaps smoothing over the old controversies, replacing them with the definitive elevation of Rossini into a timeless pantheon of great composers. Both Rossini's dwelling places, in Paris and Passy, included such a pantheon; in Paris there were busts, and in Passy specially commissioned paintings of great composers, including Beethoven, Grétry, Boieldieu and, yes, Rossini. Rossini had already found his place in history, and intended to enjoy the status accorded him as a living relic.

The most striking thing about this final period, aside from the musical compositions that suddenly flowed easily again, is its limited orbit. Fiorentino warned biographers away from the desire to delve into Rossini's private life, yet the last years of the composer's life were entirely created within the private sphere. We know from eye witnesses every detail about the layout of the interior of his Paris and Passy residences; not only the number of rooms, but the furnishings, where Rossini hung his wigs, what he would wear, his tendency to sit in the room next door playing cards during the famous Saturday evening salons, attended by all the luminaries and great performers of the Second Empire.[44]

We also know that he would eat dinner out only twice a year, once on his first night in Passy for the summer, once on his return to Paris. Yet, it is as hard to connect Rossini's interior world with the rapidly changing city outside as it is to connect the great man with his earlier selves. All around Rossini's apartment, on the corner of the Boulevard des Italiens and the Rue de la Chaussée d'Antin, Paris was changing and modernising, entering the world of the electric telegraph. Within sight of his drawing room windows, the hôtel de Montmorency was demolished the year before Rossini's death to make way for the new Théâtre du Vaudeville. A five minute walk away, the Avenue de l'Opéra was being carved through diagonally from the Palais Royal to Garnier's new opera house (begun in 1861 but not completed until 1875). And turning to the right outside Rossini's front door, down the Chaussée d'Antin, the church of La Trinité could be seen under construction, finished just in time for Rossini's funeral in November 1868.

The architect of Paris's transformation, Baron Haussmann, attended the Saturday evenings; at one meeting, Marie Taglioni was apparently moved to the back so that he could have a good seat.[45] But we no longer can know whether he talked about the noise of building work going on outside Rossini's window. Although the salon was prestigious, its very exclusivity shut it away from public view, with nothing more than visitors' lists and reports of the composer's legendarily caustic wit seeping out to the world beyond. Inside, Rossini was called upon simply to receive homage, in a style that his obituarist in *The Times* compared with the ageing Goethe, while Saint-Saëns described the Parisian enthusiasm for Rossini as nothing short of religious in nature.[46] Given his status as a worshipped ancestor, prematurely immortal, his death appears consequently to have occasioned little widespread grief. The *Journal de Paris* even dared to suggest that Rossini had died years before, at the time that he had stopped writing.[47] And at Rossini's funeral, several newspapers reported that the event was more like a festive concert, or an opera, the crowds there to hear great singers perform, and to pay tribute to a man who had lived beyond his time.

4 The Rossini Renaissance

CHARLES S. BRAUNER

We may define the Rossini Renaissance as the reappearance of his forgotten operas after decades of neglect. The word 'forgotten' is an important qualifier because one opera, *Il barbiere di Siviglia*, was never forgotten, and in fact remained a constant presence in opera houses from its première in 1816. Even if we discount the anomalous popularity of *Il barbiere*, it would be inaccurate to say that Rossini ever completely disappeared from the repertory: performances cropped up every few years at one house or another.[1] Still, there is no escaping the dwindling of his presence: both the number of Rossini's operas performed and the number of productions and performances of them declined.

It was not his other comic operas but the French serious ones – particularly *Moïse/Mosè* (as opposed to the Neapolitan *Mosè in Egitto*, 1818, of which it was a substantial revision) and *Guillaume/Guglielmo Tell* – that were most persistent in the six decades or so following the composer's death. A revival of the *opere buffe* began between the world wars – mostly *L'italiana in Algeri* and *La Cenerentola* but occasionally others – alongside the continued occasional presence of *Mosè* and *Tell*. In a Rossinian season in Paris in 1929 *Guillaume Tell*, *L'italiana*, *La Cenerentola* and *Il barbiere* were all presented.[2] Largely missing were the *opere serie* and *semiserie*; aside from *Semiramide* at the 1940 Maggio Musicale, Florence,[3] and *La gazza ladra* in an adaptation by Riccardo Zandonai in Pesaro, 1942, their revival took place after World War II, and this will be the focus of the remainder of this essay.[4]

The fate of Rossini's *opere serie* and *semiserie* – the last to survive were *Otello* (disappeared in the 1870s) and *Semiramide* (1890s) – differed from those of his younger contemporaries Bellini and Donizetti. For both composers there was a decline in performances in the second half of the nineteenth century and the first half of the twentieth, but Donizetti's most successful survivor was an *opera seria*, *Lucia di Lammermoor*.[5] Three of Bellini's ten operas, *La sonnambula* (an *opera semiseria*), *Norma* and *I Puritani*, maintained places in the repertory. Thus there was already a presence of bel canto *opera seria* in the repertory upon which to build the revivals of Rossini's. Up until the early 1960s these were very sporadic. Exceptional was the 1952 Maggio Musicale, which presented *Armida* and *Tancredi* as well as the comic rarities *Il conte Ory*, *La scala di seta* and *La pietra del paragone*, plus *Mosè* and *Guglielmo Tell*. These aside, there were stagings of *L'assedio di Corinto*[6]

(Florence 1949, repeated in Rome 1951 and Naples 1952), *L'inganno felice* (Rome 1952 and Bologna 1954), *La donna del lago* (Florence 1958), *La gazza ladra* (Wexford 1959), *Otello* (London 1961), *Semiramide* (Milan 1962), and concert performances of *Elisabetta regina d'Inghilterra* (Milan 1953) and *Otello* (New York 1954 and 1957, Rome 1960). Starting in 1964 the number of productions (both staged and concert) of Rossini *serio* increased slowly, as did, in the late 1970s, the list of operas revived, so that all his *opere serie* and *semiserie* have finally reappeared (the last *seria, Eduardo e Cristina*, in 1997; the last *semiseria, Adina*, in 1999). The following statistics will show the trend:[7]

Productions of Rossini's *opere serie*

Years	Average number of productions (staged and concert) per year	Average number of staged productions per year
1949–63	0.8	0.5
1964–79	3.7	2.9
1980–90	10.0	7.1

The increase starting in 1980 coincides with the inauguration of the Rossini Opera Festival in Pesaro. The first season consisted of the *semiserie La gazza ladra* and *L'inganno felice*. The next three summers saw *La donna del lago*, *Tancredi* and *Mosè in Egitto* – a commitment to Rossini *serio* that has continued to this day. Commercial recordings of many of the *opere serie* have been issued, at first only *Semiramide* (1966), then a steadily increasing number beginning in the mid-1970s.

Up until 1970 the most frequently performed of these operas was *Otello*; especially noteworthy was the production of the Rome Opera of 1964, with Virginia Zeani, which then travelled to Pesaro, Berlin and New York. But *Otello* was soon surpassed in popularity by *Semiramide*, whose 1962 revival at La Scala saw the first appearance in Rossini of Joan Sutherland. In the mid-1970s *Tancredi* also became quite popular, so that by 1989 *Semiramide* had had forty-eight productions and *Tancredi* thirty-three; *La gazza ladra* led the *opere semiserie* with twenty-one.

Critical response

As they had during his years of popularity, critics' opinions of Rossini differed during the years of decline.[8] One school of criticism viewed him as the epitome of Italian melody whose quality had become lost at the hands of modern composers, a creator of 'beauties that are absolute and not dependent on the diversities of time and place'.[9] The more progressive critics, especially those who supported the 'music of the future' (that is, Wagner), objected especially to the formal conventions and elaborate vocal style as undermining drama and expressivity. (An intermediate critical view saw Rossini's late works – *Mosè* and *Tell*, in which the use of conventional forms and ornamentation was reduced – as themselves harbingers of the music of the future.) And yet even as pro-Wagner a critic as George Bernard Shaw, after denouncing Rossini as 'one of the greatest masters of claptrap that ever lived. His moral deficiencies as an artist were quite extraordinary,'[10] wrote of his surprise at finding Rossini's music genuinely moving.

> Yet the Swan came off more triumphantly than one could have imagined possible at this time of day. *Dal tuo stellato soglio* was as sublime as ever . . . The repeats in the overtures were, strange to say, not in the least tedious: we were perfectly well content to hear the whole bag of tricks turned out a second time. Nobody was disgusted, *à la Berlioz*, by the 'brutal crescendo and big drum'. On the contrary, we were exhilarated and amused; and I, for one, was astonished to find it all still so fresh, so imposing, so clever, and even, in the few serious passages, so really fine.[11]

The complaints that Rossini's music was formulaic, overly ornate and therefore inexpressive go back to his own day and remain constants of Rossini criticism.[12] Around the time of the revival of Rossini's *opere buffe* in the 1920s, these aspects of his style became objects of praise by neo-classicists and Futurists who, in reaction against both Romanticism and Impressionism, saw Rossini as the cure for what ailed music: 'After the magnificent heroics of Wagner, the austere and pathetic dissertations of the Franckists, the iridescent shimmerings of the impressionist school, we should doubtless have more ease and simplicity. In this regard, the example of Rossini would be salutary. Our young musicians would find in him precisely what they themselves lack: youthfulness [la jeunesse].'[13] The composer and critic Alfredo Casella, a self-proclaimed Futurist, declared Rossini 'the man who was the last to know how to laugh. Rossini has been reproached with shallowness . . . He was quite probably a smaller genius than the great Germans. But then a "small" genius is so often more amusing than a great one.'[14] Casella noted support for Rossini by Honegger, Milhaud and Poulenc.[15] However, these writers thought of Rossini as a composer of comedies, and it is doubtful whether hearing Rossini as a proto-Futurist ironist could ever have led to an appreciation of his serious works.

From this same period, but quite different in tone, came the magisterial study of the composer by Giuseppe Radiciotti.[16] Radiciotti, for whom Rossini was 'the greatest Italian composer of the nineteenth century, one of the most remarkable geniuses by whom humanity is honored', announced as his goal the production of 'a biography that is neither an apology nor a diatribe', based on 'documents, positive facts, [and] irrefutable testimony', together with 'a serene and unprejudiced analysis of his works' (p. ix). At 1,429 pages it was certainly the longest study of an Italian composer to that time. To be sure, not every 'positive fact' has proved true, and the author offers many judgements that are debatable, but the work is still useful to scholars, particularly for the wealth of primary-source material (letters, contemporary reviews and comments) that it reproduces.

At a time when Rossini's *opere serie* were completely absent from the opera house and from critical discourse, Radiciotti examined them all and found much to praise: in *Tancredi*, *Armida*, *Mosè in Egitto*, the third act of *Otello*, the first act of *La donna del lago* – all of which he thought, on the whole, moving and dramatically convincing. Nevertheless, he too was bothered by the same things that bothered earlier critics: the extensive use of coloratura and the conventionality of form.[17] The French operas, particularly *Guillaume Tell*, are for him the culmination of Rossini's art, at least in part because they contain more of the simplicity that Radiciotti admires and less of the conventionality that he dislikes.

In the English-speaking world, the beginnings of a Renaissance may be observed in the 1934 biography of the composer by Francis Toye.[18] He begins candidly:

> To the best of my belief there is no demand whatever for a life of Rossini in English. Supply, however, sometimes creates demand . . . Moreover, there are undoubted signs of a renewed interest in his music other than the immortal *Barber of Seville*. The most important overtures . . . are beginning to creep back once again into the programmes of our more enterprising concerts. Some of the songs . . . have made many new friends in recent years. (p. vii)

Toye goes on to chastise current English musicology ('too often inspired by a *furor Teutonicus* surpassing that of the Teutons themselves' (p. ix)) for ignoring the importance of Rossini for the history of music. Toye acknowledges his great debt to Radiciotti, and his judgement of the operas, like Radiciotti's, is not very different from the critics of the 1860s. He shows enthusiasm for the *opere buffe*; towards the *opere serie* he is more equivocal. He too is unable to accept the formal conventions of Rossinian *opera seria*, to hear Rossini's musical language (including the tradition of *fioritura*) as sufficiently expressive. He generally prefers the French operas, especially *Moïse*.

Toye's sense that the 'furor teutonicus' had passed and that the Anglo-Saxon world might be ready for a Rossini revival was borne out by a comment by Shaw on the publication of his collected criticism in 1935. He no longer found all musical truth to reside in Wagner: 'When the wireless strikes up the

Tannhäuser overture I hasten to switch it off, though I can always listen with pleasure to Rossini's overture to William Tell.'[19] However, after the war critics both scholarly and journalistic continued to reject or ignore Rossini *serio*. In Donald Jay Grout's *A Short History of Opera* (New York, 1947), two pages are devoted to Rossini in 536 pages of text (as opposed to five for Weber; perhaps the 'furor teutonicus' had not quite passed after all). Like Toye, Grout seems to prefer the comic operas, but he offers no strong judgement of the *opere serie*. In the second edition (1965), the section on Rossini is expanded to three pages, and Grout praises the third act of *Otello* as 'some of the most beautiful music he ever wrote' (p. 353). This is a step forward compared to the British *Pelican History of Music* (1968), which in praising his comic operas grants only that Rossini outshone his contemporaries in 'light, catchy melodies' and, like Casella, forgives him for 'declining the effort which could have revealed greater depths of expression';[20] Rossini's two pages are found in the section on French opera (Bellini and Donizetti are in the section on Wagner).

Many newspaper critics, reviewing post-war revivals of the *opere serie*, heard in them at best occasions for beautiful singing, at worst dramatic incongruousness and absurdity. Franco Abbiati, long-time critic of the leading Italian daily *Il corriere della sera*, denounced both *Armida* (at the 1952 Maggio Musicale) and *Semiramide* (La Scala, 1962) as overly ornate, prolix and old-fashioned (*Semiramide* 'expressed sentiments that we no longer understand' and 'transmits the echo of musical and theatrical practices and customs that had faded in the same period in which Rossini was alive', 18 December 1962). In the *New York Times*, we read, from 1954, that ' "Otello", like *William Tell*, is an ungainly great brute of a score, magnificent passages alternating with tedious ones' (J[ohn] B[riggs], 11 November 1954); to 1968, that 'Rossini's "Otello" . . . is not a particularly interesting work. It is one of Rossini's formula operas, organized like so many early 18th-century [*sic*] Italian operas' (Harold C. Schonberg, 16 June 1968); and then to 1990, that 'the evening offered the opportunity not so much for music drama as for a feast of voices, as any work in the bel canto tradition should' (Donal Henehan, 3 December 1990).

There were dissenters, to be sure, who took serious Rossini seriously. In the sympathetic category we should especially mention Andrew Porter, whose lengthy reviews in *The New Yorker* magazine from 1975 to 1986 are some of the most thoughtful pieces written about this music.[21] Some post-war critics found themselves unexpectedly moved by Rossini's serious operas, as Shaw had been in the late nineteenth century, e.g. Howard Taubman (chief critic of the *New York Times*, as Schonberg and Henehan were to become): 'At its best, [Rossini's] operatic setting of *Otello* is a work of stunning power and searching pathos . . . [O]ne wondered how the world could afford to neglect an opera of this stature' (11 December 1957);[22] or Stanley Sadie: 'There are . . . fine things [in *Elisabetta*]. A superb first Finale, for one . . . – a scene of splendid tension and excitement, musically sustained . . . a trio . . . with three-part writing of uncommon beauty and subtlety . . . a prison scene for Leicester, where Florestan-like he sees his beloved in a vision – comparable, this, with *Fidelio* (almost) or Handel's *Rodelinda*' (*The Times*, 28 February 1968). These opinions, although a minority view, suggest that neither neo-classical praise nor Romantic rejection, two sides of the same coin, told the whole story, and at least for some listeners there was more to Rossini's music than pretty tunes and sparkling wit.

Singers

Nor did providing occasions for vocal display explain the Rossini Renaissance, since, as several critics noted, the early revivals were frequently populated by singers inadequate to the demands of the music, and the vocal writing was often simplified to accommodate the limitations of the performers. However, there were singers who could have sung Rossini *serio* had they so chosen, singers adept at bel canto and coloratura who sang *opera seria* rôles by Bellini and Donizetti and sometimes Rossini's *opere buffe*. Lily Pons, for example, made her Met début as Lucia in 1931 and sang ninety-three performances of the rôle in her twenty-nine seasons there. She also sang Rosina in *Il barbiere*, Amina in *La sonnambula* and two additional Donizetti rôles (Marie in *La Fille du régiment* and the title rôle in *Linda di Chamounix*). Norma attracted a different sort of singer – Rosa Ponselle, Gina Cigna, Zinka Milanov – who sang such heavier rôles as Aida, Leonora (both *Forza* and *Trovatore*) and Santuzza, and in fact Cigna sang Anaide in *Mosè*.

I therefore disagree with the more or less general consensus among modern critics that bel canto was dead before it was revived by Maria Callas.[23] And while Callas through her dramatic force gave a new respectability to bel canto *opera seria* and expanded the repertory slightly (she also sang Bellini's *Il pirata* and Donizetti's *Anna Bolena*), her direct contribution to the Renaissance of Rossini *serio* was small. She sang only one Rossini *opera seria*, *Armida*, part of the 1952 Maggio Musicale devoted to Rossini, and despite the spectacular showpiece it makes for a soprano (and, several commentators notwithstanding, the relatively minor demands on the numerous tenors called for), Callas never attempted this opera again, nor did anyone else until 1970, nor did Callas ever record it (pirated recordings exist).

In addition to Callas, some very fine singers participated in the early years of the Rossini Renaissance before going on to quite different repertories – Renata Tebaldi, for example, a native of Pesaro (*L'assedio*, 1949–52; *Tell*, 1952); Teresa Stich-Randall (*Tancredi*, 1952); Eileen Farrell (*Otello*, 1957); Janet Baker (*La gazza ladra*, 1959). Towards the end of her career, Jennie Tourel sang in two serious operas, *Otello* (1954) and *Mosè* (1958). However, the only singer from before 1960 who could remotely be considered a true Rossinian was the mezzo-soprano Giulietta Simionato, who sang Tancredi opposite Stich-Randall's Amenaide and later Arsace opposite Joan Sutherland's Semiramide.

Sutherland's appearance as Lucia at Covent Garden in 1959 had been sensational. Then, when she made her New York début, in a concert performance of Bellini's *Beatrice di Tenda* in 1961, joining her as a last-minute replacement for Simionato was the relatively unknown Marilyn Horne, also making her New York début. Thus was inaugurated a partnership that was to be extremely important for Rossini. Sutherland and Horne sang together again in *Norma* (Vancouver, 1963) and then finally *Semiramide*. Sutherland had sung her first *Semiramide* (the first post-war *Semiramide*), with Simionato, at La Scala in December 1962. In January 1964 she was joined by Horne in this same opera, touring from Los Angeles to New York to Boston. They also performed it together in London (Drury Lane, 1969) and Chicago (1971), and both sang the opera with others, Horne as late as 1990 at the Metropolitan. At least as important as the performances was the recording of the complete opera in 1966, which allowed for its far wider dissemination than individual performances and also made the music permanently available.

Semiramide was uniquely suited to this pair of singers. Its use of mezzo-soprano for the 'male' lead gave Horne an appropriate rôle, but the opera shares this feature with a number of Rossini's *opere serie*. *Semiramide* combines the mezzo-soprano hero with a queen rather than a young girl as soprano (the statuesque Sutherland excelled as the queenly Norma and Anna Bolena, although of course she also sang the more girlish Lucia and Amina). Moreover, the writing is especially brilliant, and the musical forms are closer to those of Bellini and Donizetti than is true of Rossini's earlier *opere serie*. Finally, the tenor rôle is relatively unimportant and is easily reduced without affecting the story.

This appropriateness perhaps explains why, despite her considerable success in this rôle, Sutherland never sang another Rossini opera. Horne, on the other hand, has sung many Rossini rôles, both comic – Rosina, Cenerentola, Isabella in *L'italiana* – and serious. Between 1964 and 1989, Horne sang seven *serio* rôles – Arsace (*Semiramide*), Neocle (*L'assedio di Corinto*), Tancredi, Malcom (*La donna del lago*), Falliero (*Bianca e Falliero*), Andromaca (*Ermione*), Calbo[24] (*Maometto II*) – opposite eleven sopranos: Sutherland, Beverly Sills, Joan Carden, Margherita Rinaldi, Katia Ricciarelli, Montserrat

Caballé, Frederica von Stade, Lella Cuberli, June Anderson, Paula Scalera, Christine Weidinger – a list that includes some of the greatest voices of the late twentieth century. As Horne explained it, 'mezzos are *always* looking for interesting rôles, because there are so few in the standard repertory . . . [I]t's heaven to sing beautiful music of the kind Rossini wrote for his favorite artists.'[25] She has also sung and recorded many Rossini songs. No singer comes near her in importance for the Rossini Renaissance.

As late as the mid-1970s critics still noted a shortage of adequate singers, but there was no longer talk of simplified vocal lines (however much there may have been simplification in actuality, as we may hear from Salvatore Fisichella as Rodrigo on the 1979 recording of *Otello*). Thereafter critics may be critical of individual singers, but they assume that it is reasonable to expect good singing. In fact, many sopranos and mezzo-sopranos capable of meeting Rossini's vocal demands have emerged over the last several decades. The number of good Rossini tenors has remained smaller, however. While a light lyric tenor can perform much Bellini and Donizetti adequately, Rossini expected his tenors to have the same vocal flexibility as his sopranos. Moreover, Rossini wrote many of his *opere serie* for two principal tenors, and this has perhaps kept these operas from assuming a larger place in the repertory.

Musicology

After Radiciotti, little of significance occurred in Rossini studies until the 1960s. Friedrich Lippmann's 1962 dissertation on Bellini for Kiel University[26] brought a new level of scholarship to the study of bel canto opera, including a fifty-page chapter on Rossini, although his conclusion that 'the dominant colour in the manifoldly iridescent spectrum of Rossini's style is playfulness . . . Rossini's most fundamental achievement was the preservation of lightness' (p. 206) seems not very different from the *Pelican History*. More important, and in contrast to Bellini and Donizetti, the revival of Rossini has been aided by the musicological enterprise of the critical edition. The idea of critical editions of this repertory was in the air by the mid-1960s when Philip Gossett began work on his dissertation, 'The Operas of Rossini: Problems of Textual Criticism in Nineteenth-Century Opera' (Princeton, 1970), and had spread to Italian thinking, to judge from Fedele D'Amico's acerbic comment that those who dream of critical editions should instead defend the traditional editions against new editions that are much worse (Claudio Abbado's rewriting of Bellini's *I Capuleti e i Montecchi* was his example).[27] In response was the conductor Alberto Zedda's edition of *Il barbiere di Siviglia* (conducted by an evidently repentant Abbado at La

Scala in 1968, published in 1969); based on Rossini's autograph, it stripped away the layers of orchestration added in the late nineteenth century.

In 1971 Gossett made contacts among interested Italian scholars and musicians, especially Bruno Cagli, who had recently become artistic director of the Fondazione Rossini, and Zedda. The Fondazione, founded by Rossini's legacy for the purpose of supporting a conservatory in Pesaro, had begun two publishing ventures: editions of music in the *Quaderni rossiniani* (nineteen volumes from 1954 to 1976, mostly of chamber works, cantatas and songs) and Rossini scholarship in the *Bollettino del centro rossiniano di studi*. Begun in 1955, the *Bollettino* at first published very short articles (one to three pages) mostly tied to the activities of the conservatory; beginning in 1971 under Cagli's direction, it became an international scholarly journal.

Spurred by the much-criticised edition of *L'assedio di Corinto* used in the 1969 production at La Scala,[28] the Fondazione in 1973 undertook the publication of a critical edition of the composer's complete works (discussed in chapter 15 of this volume), with Gossett, Cagli and Zedda serving as the editorial board. The first volume, *La gazza ladra*, appeared in 1979, edited by Zedda. The Fondazione is also publishing Rossini's letters and two additional series, one on librettos, which includes facsimiles of the first edition of the libretto and other relevant historical documents, and the other on iconography, that is, historical sets and costumes. It has also sponsored conferences and published their proceedings as well as other collections of scholarly essays.

The enterprise of the critical edition in turn inspired the creation of the Rossini Opera Festival, which describes itself as having been started 'with the intention of backing up and developing, by means of theatrical performances, the scientific work of the Rossini Foundation (in particular ... the publication of Rossini's complete works in critical editions)'[29] and which performed the Fondazione's *Gazza ladra* in 1980, its inaugural season. This has led to a collaboration between musicology and opera house that is very unusual, perhaps unique. The Festival has first rights to perform the edition, which serves the two organisations' mutual interests: the Festival has the prestige of offering the premières of the critical editions, while the Fondazione sees its scholarly work realised in the theatre. In practice, not all of the Festival's productions have been based on critical editions, and sometimes preliminary versions of the critical edition have been first performed at other venues. Nevertheless, the Fondazione has adhered to the principle of hearing its editions performed before they are published.

The other area of musicology directly affecting the Rossini Renaissance, and the one most visible (or audible) to the audience, is performance practice. In Rossini, this has meant primarily the art of vocal ornamentation. Rather than the simplifications critics used to report, singers have increasingly adopted the historically based practice of embellishing Rossini's vocal lines, thereby helping fulfil the operas' potential as vehicles for spectacular singing. However, one aspect of bel canto vocalism has rarely been adopted. We know that bel canto tenors used falsetto in the upper registers, a technique that even Rossini specialists today do not adopt for fear the sound would be too foreign to the ears of modern audiences. Curiously, Rossini (and Italian opera in general) has not been much affected by the movement to use period instruments. The Rossini Opera Festival, for one, has resolutely refused to experiment with them. This may be due in part to its reliance on outside orchestras brought in for the festival, but it would surely be possible to engage an original-instruments band if the Festival so chose. So far at least, the Festival's musical leadership has resisted the idea, and even Roger Norrington, whose reputation was made in the original-instruments movement, conducted a conventional orchestra in Pesaro.

Why the Rossini Renaissance?

The post-war Rossini Renaissance was slow at first, led, it would seem, not by demands from singers or audiences, but by a few dedicated conductors (Vittorio Gui for *opera buffa*, then Tullio Serafin and Gabriele Santini in Italy and the now-obscure Arnold Gamson and his American Opera Society in New York), impresarios (like Francesco Siciliani, responsible for the Maggio Musicale of 1952), and the response of some listeners, reflected by some critics of the 1950s and 1960s, that these operas were in fact works of great beauty that still had the power to move. The growing number of singers adept at the style and the musicological commitment to the repertory has surely contributed to Rossini's increasing presence in the opera house since 1980. An additional factor has been the initiative of Pesaro, a small city (90,000) whose chief attraction was its beach. The commitment of that community, in the forms of the Fondazione Rossini and the Rossini Opera Festival, has made it and its favourite son a focus of international attention.

But then the revival of forgotten operas by many composers has been an important aspect of post-war musical life: Monteverdi, Handel, Donizetti, Massenet, Janáček have all had renaissances. We might well ask why, when such bel canto *opere serie* as *Norma* and *Lucia di Lammermoor* had remained in the repertory, Rossini's struggled to regain their place. The possible factors are many, stemming from Rossini's position at the crossroads between the eighteenth-century tradition of *opera seria* and the emerging Romanticism of the nineteenth, as seen, for example, in the transition from the castrato to the tenor in the heroic male rôles or from the happy ending to the tragic. The scarcity of Rossinian tenors and the assigning of heroic male rôles to female mezzo-sopranos have surely hindered these works' acceptance. Then there is the problematic nature of Rossini's librettos, whose implied musical forms are similar to those of Bellini, Donizetti and early Verdi but whose plots favour complication and the fraught situation rather than logically directed action. That *Tancredi* and *Otello* had both happy endings and tragic endings suggests a lack of the dramatic inevitability that modern audiences expect. Other structural problems abound; for example, Act 1 of *La donna del lago* introduces three characters in three substantial arias, the succession interrupted only by a short *duettino*, which render the action inert.

The characteristics of Rossini's style that many critics have found disturbing have also been a contributing factor to the slowness with which his *opere serie* have regained acceptance. However, some recent critics have detected in opera audiences a growing anti-Romanticism[30] and anti-realism[31] that reminds us of Alfredo Casella and the Futurists of the 1920s. A paradoxical aspect of the Rossinian cult at Pesaro is that it is a descendant of the cult of Wagner at Bayreuth, and more broadly of the veneration of the heroic individual – quintessentially Romantic phenomena – but that it focuses on an altogether less pretentious artist than Wagner, one whose self description was 'little science, a little heart', whom commentators often oppose to Romanticism. To compound the irony, a small Rossini festival has recently begun in Bayreuth itself. Perhaps Rossini is the right heroic figure for an age that distrusts heroic figures.

However, the critics notwithstanding, signs that the general public is tiring of late-Romantic melodrama are scarce. Performances of Rossini's serious operas are still relatively infrequent, especially at the major opera houses, whose repertories have broadened in many directions but whose heart is still Verdi and Puccini. In 1971 the critic Glenna Syse (*Chicago Sun-Times*, 25 September 1971) predicted that *Semiramide* would return to Chicago, but thirty years later it had not yet reappeared. Anne Midgette, in the *New York Times* of 1 July 2001, calls *La donna del lago*, *La gazza ladra* and *Otello* 'little-played works' and wonders 'whether the bel canto revival . . . remains a force in today's repertory'. On the other hand, in 2001 the Rossini Opera Festival did more performances of its operas than in previous years. There are those, few in number compared with the opera-going public as a whole, who return to Pesaro in August, year after year, those who attend a second Rossini festival in Bad Wildbad and now the one in Bayreuth, who seek out Rossini *serio* in other venues – who hear in Rossini not post-modern irony but the qualities that have surprised receptive critics from Shaw to Sadie, 'beauties that are absolute and not dependent on the diversities of time and place'.

PART TWO

Words and music

5 Librettos and librettists

PAOLO FABBRI

Still more apprehensive of the disagreeable impression which might be gleaned from the *libretto*, Signora B***, in Venice, used to refuse to allow anybody at all to bring it into her box, even at the *première*. She used to get someone to prepare her a summary of the plot, some forty lines in all; and then, during the performance, she would be informed, in four or five words, of the theme of each aria, duet or ensemble, which had previously been numbered 1, 2, 3, 4 . . . etc., as each item was introduced in the performance; for instance, simply: *Taddeo is jealous; Lindoro is passionately in love; Isabella is flirting with the Bey*, etc. – this condensed summary being followed by the first line of the aria or duet which happened to be in question. I observed that everyone approved of this procedure, and thought it most suitable. In such a fashion should *libretti* be printed for the *amateurs*.

Such were the observations and proposals put forth by Stendhal in the chapter on *L'italiana in Algeri* in his *Life of Rossini* (1824).[1] Happily, fewer and fewer people today consider the libretto to be little more than a pretext for an opera, a thin canvas threaded with commonplaces unworthy of serious consideration, or even an obstacle to enjoying the music undefiled. But it is still worth reiterating the case that the libretto of an opera simply cannot be ignored, and that it is the premise of all musical efforts. To appreciate fully the composer's work, it is absolutely necessary to give due consideration to the literary object on which it is based: its authors, events, stylistic levels, structures and conventions, the models from which it derives and its relationship to the contemporary theatre and other literary genres.

When Rossini began to compose opera shortly before 1810, the fashionable genres in Italy were *opera seria*, *opera semiseria* and *opera buffa* in two (occasionally three) acts, and the one-act *farsa*. Certain broad, endemic rules presided unchallenged over the genres. Everything was sung (unlike, for example, in French *opéra comique* or German *Singspiel*).[2] Set 'numbers' alternated with recitative passages. The latter were organised in *versi sciolti*, a free mix of *settenari* and *endecasillabi* without a predictable rhyme scheme; the former were in *versi lirici*, in any metre, arranged in one or more blocks of the same metre and rhymed.[3] According to a convention established at the end of the eighteenth century, the curtain usually rose on an ensemble with chorus (the *introduzione*), and the act ended with a piece for a number of characters, often also with chorus (the Finale). For the rest of the opera, the numbers were arranged with a considerable degree of flexibility, taking into account various factors, most prominently matters of balance and hierarchy in the company of singers (the so-called 'convenienze').

Rossini's librettists

The 'Elenco de' Poeti Drammatici e loro dimora' ('List of dramatic poets and their dwellings') in the 1808–9 almanac *Indice dei teatrali spettacoli* offers a useful survey of librettists on the theatrical scene at the time of Rossini's début:[4]

> Anelli Angelo from Desenzano, Public Professor at the Brera Academy (lives in Milan); Boggio Angelo from Turin (Turin); Buonavoglia Leonardo from Leghorn (Amsterdam); Camagna Giulio from Genoa (Venice); Caramondani alias de' Filistri Antonio from Venice (Berlin); Foppa Giuseppe from Venice (Venice); Gasbarri D. Gaetano from Naples (Florence); Gonella Dr Francesco from Florence (Florence); Palomba Giuseppe from Naples (Naples); Prividali Luigi from Gorizia (Venice); Prunetti Michel Angelo from Rome, Member of the Accademia dei Quirini (Rome); Romanelli Luigi from Rome (Milan); Rossetti Dr Domenico from Bologna (Bologna); Rossi Gaetano from Verona (Venice); Sgatizzi Steffano from Leghorn (Leghorn); Smith Vincenzo from Leghorn (Naples); Sograffi Antonio Simeone from Padua (Padua); Tarducci Filippo from Rome (Rome); Tottola Andrea from Naples (Naples).

In the course of his career, Rossini had dealings with a dozen of these poets, and with others who are not listed here because they were not yet working, because their work as librettists was sporadic, or because their librettos were not in Italian.

The broad range of Rossini's operas offers a representative illustration of the figure of the theatrical poet throughout the period.[5] First we meet librettists by profession working stably in a specific city, such as Gaetano Rossi and Giuseppe Foppa in Venice, Luigi Romanelli and Felice Romani in Milan, Andrea Leone Tottola, Giuseppe Palomba and Giovanni Schmidt in Naples, Cesare Sterbini and Iacopo Ferretti in Rome, Luigi Balocchi, Eugène Scribe and Etienne de Jouy in Paris. Some of these, however, only worked for the theatre part-time, their permanent and primary jobs being elsewhere. Foppa, for example, was Clerk at the Venice Tribunal, Ferretti a state employee of the tobacco works in Rome. There were also dilettantes active in the theatre world such as the actress Vincenzina Viganò Mombelli (*Demetrio e Polibio*), the journalist and theatre agent Luigi Prividali (*L'occasione fa il ladro*) and the scenographer Gherardo Bevilacqua Aldobrandini (*Adina*). As well as these, aristocratic amateurs passionate about the theatre were also employed: the Ferrarese Count Francesco Aventi (*Ciro in Babilonia*), the 'Neapolitans' Francesco Berio, Marquis of Salsa (*Otello* and *Ricciardo e Zoraide*), and Cesare Della Valle, Duke of Ventignano (*Maometto II*). The level of expertise of these librettists fluctuated widely, ranging from débutant to established poet, craftsman to intellectual, untrained amateur to ambitious man of letters.

In the beginning the young Rossini obviously had to consider himself lucky to acquire any libretto free of charge. The libretto for his first *opera seria* (*Demetrio e Polibio*, c. 1809–11) was sent to him piecemeal, in instalments, by the singer Domenico Mombelli, as his wife Vincenzina wrote it. But as early as *Ciro in Babilonia* (1812) we see a less servile attitude: Rossini insisted that the initial libretto, supplied by an unknown poet unfamiliar with structures for musical setting, was replaced by another by the more proficient Count Aventi.[6]

By the Spring of 1815 Rossini was in a position to turn down a libretto by the famous professor Anelli, and to treat him as an equal. 'I must compose a *new* opera' he wrote to Anelli, 'and you offer me an old libretto? Where is your genius, your beautiful fantasy? But by God, perhaps you don't believe that I am capable of setting your verses to declamatory, expressive, touching (*parlante*) music?' (GRLD, vol. I, no. 41). In this instance – Rossini was under contract for the Carnival season of 1816 at the Teatro Valle in Rome – it was up to the composer to find and pay for his libretto. Usually, however, this task fell upon the theatre management, as in the case of the 1815 and 1816 Rome contracts with Duke Francesco Sforza Cesarini for *Il barbiere di Siviglia* and Pietro Cartoni for *La Cenerentola* (GRLD, vol. I, nos. 58 and 68).

In the case of *La gazza ladra* Rossini was presented with a libretto acquired in truly unusual circumstances. In April 1816 the impresario of La Scala, Angelo Petracchi, had announced a public competition to establish 'a collection [of operas] for the company, from which all the new operas that the aforesaid company will commission in the course of its contract until Carnival 1820 must, without fail, be chosen' (*Corriere delle dame*, 6 April 1816). Petracchi himself would judge the entries, along with his associate Francesco Benedetto Ricci and one of the most respected literary authorities in Italy, the poet Vincenzo Monti. The system of public competitions judged by competent juries was an inheritance from the years of the French Revolution, born of the desire to replace privilege with merit, caprice with competence, and arbitrariness with objectivity. The Restoration barely re-established, Petracchi adopted these principles in a more innocuous context.[7] As an immediate result, Felice Romani's *La testa di bronzo* was set to music by Carlo Soliva and staged at the beginning of September 1816. The following year it was the turn of Giovanni Gherardini's *L'avviso ai giudici*, assigned to Rossini with a new title. The composer wrote to his mother in March 1817: 'I'm writing an opera entitled *La gazza ladra*. The libretto was versified by a beginner, and consequently it's driving me crazy; the subject, however, is very beautiful indeed' (GRLD, vol. I, no. 99).

In general, however, Rossini's librettos were obtained in less unusual circumstances, often brand new, but sometimes modernised versions of pre-existing models. These models might be rather dated, like the works by Caterino Mazzolà (*Il turco in Italia*, 1788) and Gaetano Sertor (*Zenobia in Palmira*, 1789) which Rossini re-worked as *Il turco in Italia* and *Aureliano in Palmira* respectively.[8] They could even be second-hand librettos hardly altered (Anelli's *L'italiana in Algeri* had already been set by Luigi Mosca for La Scala in 1808).[9] The contractual terms of the two works for Rome mentioned above (*Barbiere* and *Cenerentola*) seem to suggest a situation in which the composer was obliged to subject his own will to that of the impresario. The well-known anecdote on the genesis of *La Cenerentola* related by Iacopo Ferretti in his autobiography, however, mitigates such a negative image, demonstrating how in reality the composer was involved in such decisions.[10]

One variable not to be neglected when choosing a subject was the composition of the company of singers. Even if the variety and balance of the different vocal ranges was standard, it was still necessary to mould the roles as much as possible to the personal aptitudes of the singers. The poet and composer also had to agree on the nature and scansion of the 'numbers' within the opera, within the framework of the conventions. Those agreed upon for *Il barbiere di Siviglia* are outlined in a declaration signed by the librettist Cesare Sterbini in January 1816 (GRLD, vol. I, no. 63):

> *Introduzione.* First Act.
> Scene I: Tenor's Serenade and Cavatina with choruses and *introduzione*.
> Scene II: Figaro's Cavatina. Tenor's Cavatina. Another for the Prima Donna. Duet for the Prima Donna and Figaro: Figaro explains the Count's love to the Prima Donna. Grand Duet between Figaro and the Count. Vitarelli's aria. Aria for the Tutor with *pertichino*. Finale with a lot of action and motion [di gran scena e giocato assai].
>
> Act Two.
> Tenor disguised as Music Teacher gives a lesson to the Prima Donna and then there is the aria for the Prima Donna – this scene also full of action. Aria for the Seconda Donna. Quartet. Subject for the Quartet: Figaro prepared to shave the Tutor, while the Count flirts with the Donna. The Tutor believes he is ill and is made to leave. Terzetto for Figaro, Donna and Tenor. Tenor's Grand Aria. Finaletto.

In the Autumn of 1822, with *Semiramide* in sight, Rossini summoned Gaetano Rossi to his villa in Castenaso. On 10 October Rossi informed his friend Meyerbeer: 'We're drafting the outline: he approved all the situations that I had already settled on. He began to compose yesterday' (GRLD, vol. II, no. 344). And at the end of the month he announced: 'I did the *introduzione* à la Meyerbeer: even Colbran will appear in the *introduzione*. A grand spectacle, a massive scene' (GRLD, vol. II, no. 347, 28 October 1822). He probably had in mind the opening scenes of *Romilda e Costanza* (Padua, 1817) and *Emma di Resburgo* (Venice, 1819), for which he had supplied Meyerbeer with the librettos.

Rossini's own letters, unfortunately, rarely contain such revealing comments. But some indication of creative intentions can be deduced by comparing a finished work with its literary sources, or at least the works from which it derives. For example, compare the libretto of Mosca's 1808 *L'italiana in Algeri* with Rossini's version, with its additions, omissions and alternative pieces. The largest discrepancies obviously concern the set numbers, most significantly the two solos for Mustafà. First, the entrance aria 'Ho inteso che in Italia' from the *introduzione* (no. 1) was replaced by 'Delle donne l'arroganza', a most effective self-introduction, whose impact relies on the character's attitude on stage, rather than on a verbose disquisition on the relative merits of Italy and Algeria. Second, the aria 'Star soggetti a un sesso imbelle' (no. 7) made way for 'Già d'insolito ardore nel petto' (even though it is less effective at this point to have the tyrant already seized by nascent passions of love rather than still bragging and arrogant). The recitative and duet between Isabella and Lindoro in Act 2 (no. 11) was replaced by a further aria for the tenor, a less theatrically convincing situation provided to satisfy the singer, who had lost an aria in Act 1, rather than to develop the action. The second part of the sextet (no. 13, a quintet in Rossini, Zulma having been left out) was modified and trimmed. The unidentified poet who adapted the libretto for Rossini saw fit to cut the whole of Taddeo's entrance aria (no. 4, a harsh loss for the character), and Lindoro's second cavatina (no. 8, compensated for by the new aria in Act 2). Rossini then gave the heroine Isabella a much greater stage presence, having fifteen more verses added to her entrance aria ('Già so per pratica'), which he then set as a cabaletta with an unusual musical reprise on new text. In addition, Isabella was given an aria at the mirror during her toilette in Act 2 ('Per lui che adoro'), a situation originally set in simple recitative. Finally – and most prominently – Rossini's version added the onomatopoeic episode in the first Finale, the absurd 'Nella testa ho un campanello', which exaggerates the sound effects for which Neapolitan opera had been renowned since the middle of the eighteenth century, and which would be aptly defined by Stendhal in chapter 3 of his *Life of Rossini* as 'organised and complete folly'.

Farse

Rossini made his début, like most others, with the less exacting genre of the *farsa* – the setting in music of a 'short comedy (*commediola*), in one or two acts, which corresponded to the "petite pièce" or short comedy of the French, which could belong as much to the noble as to the middle or the lower comic genre' (Francesco Albergati Capacelli, 1796).[11] The *farsa* was a one-act piece: two works were usually performed each evening as a pair with a *ballo* between them. Five were written for Rossini between 1810 and 1813 by Rossi, Prividali and most importantly Foppa. They are representative of the main contemporary trends: exaggerated and absurd comic effect (*La cambiale di matrimonio*); semiserious and sentimental stories with happy endings (*L'inganno felice*); plots with many twists and turns (*La scala di seta*); the comedy of errors (*L'occasione fa il ladro*, *Il signor Bruschino*). For the first of these, Rossi had as a model the five-act comedy by Camillo Federici (1749–1802) *La cambiale di matrimonio* (Venice, 1790), already re-worked by Giuseppe Checcherini as the two-act *burletta per musica Il matrimonio per lettera di cambio* (Rome, Valle, 1807, set to music by Carlo Coccia). The literary source for *L'inganno felice* – if indeed existing – is as yet unidentified. The remaining works all had French ancestors: respectively, Planard's and Gaveaux's *opéra-comique en un acte L'Echelle de soie* (1808), the *opéra-comique en un acte et en prose mêlée de couplets* attributed to Scribe *Le Pretendu par hazard, ou L'Occasion fait le larron* (1810), and Chazet's and Ourry's *comédie en cinq actes en prose Le Fils par hasard, ou Ruse et folie* (1809).

Because of its modernity and its 'low' position in the hierarchy of genres (it did not boast noble ancestors in the classical theatrical tradition), novel elements could be incorporated into the *farsa* more easily than the older and more established repertories. *La cambiale di matrimonio*, for example, revolves around the classic plot of a young couple in love thwarted by a scornful father. The plot is updated, however, by a setting in the new and novel world of business, commercial and financial affairs. The father, Tobia Mill, is a London businessman; the husband he proposes, one of his associates from the New World, is the Canadian Slook. Rossi not only appropriates contemporary trading jargon, but also applies it wholesale to the subjects of love and marriage – to bizarre effect. The marriage union is equated with a 'compagnia' (company), the wife with a 'ditta' (firm), and Slook's physical appearance to contractual 'condizioni' (conditions; scene 2). Fanny is called 'fondo' (property/estate; 7), 'manifattura' (manufactured goods; 9), 'capitale' (capital; 10). Her love for Edward, however, makes her 'ipotecata' (mortgaged; 10–11, 13) and even – with a rather heavy double entendre – 'sforzata' (forced/broken open; 13, final scene). Besides all this, there are witty pretexts for moral polemics on marriages made for interest, paternal tyranny and the affectations of the European man on the up, all mixed with a parody of the *bon sauvage*. The Canadian sparkles with 'ingenuità' (naïveté): 'È un vero e raro tratto / della semplicità del secol d'oro' ('It is a rare and genuine example of the simplicity of the golden age'), pronounces Mill in scene 2, later bursting out with 'Viva pure la bella / semplicità d'America!' ('Long live the beautiful simplicity of America!', scene 6). Slook, on the other hand, finds it rather difficult to get used to European good manners, and immediately before the end will savour the pleasure of heartily denouncing the emptiness of all those formalities: to his formerly hostile and now downright arrogant rival ('Voi non siete già in mezzo a' Americani', 'You are not now among Americans'), he retorts easily, 'Lo so. Un americano / non avria minacciato in propria casa / a un ospite la vita' ('I know. An American would not threaten the life of a guest in his own house', scene 13).

The succession of set pieces in Rossini's *farse* clearly betrays their nature as compressed *opera buffa*. After the introductory Sinfonia (a separate piece: only in *L'occasione fa il ladro* is it specifically tied to the *introduzione*), a series of eight or nine pieces unfolds, starting with an *introduzione* and duets or arias introducing the characters.[12] Up to this point the procedure is similar to that of *opera buffa*; here, however, the farce skips quickly to the concertato (in *opera buffa* usually left until the middle of Act 2). A 'minor' aria for a secondary rôle then precedes the protagonist's much more taxing and complex one. This functions as the climax and prepares the denouement of the whole plot in the Finale.

Opere buffe

Rossini's *opere buffe* display both varieties on which the late eighteenth century had focused: excessive and gratuitous buffoonery, with its cross-dressing, pranks, fanciful intrigues, disguises and caricatures; and comedy, with more realistic events and plot, and characters who are less schematic, and not just mechanisms in a perpetually moving action.[13] Neither of these two streams is ever found in its pure state, of course, but they are nonetheless useful coordinates for a general orientation.

L'equivoco stravagante and *La pietra del paragone*, for example, start out in the vein of a comedy of manners, only to change tack quickly to a mode of excess and buffoonery. The prize for 'topsy turvy', however, goes to *L'italiana in Algeri*; a recycled libretto, admittedly, but nonetheless the most beautiful and amusing that Rossini ever set. Anelli's subject presents themes not uncommon to musical theatre – neither the examples of female shrewdness nor the Turkish setting could really be called a novelty (though the analogy with the 1782 *Die Entführung aus dem Serail* by Stephanie and Mozart should not be counted, since it is highly unlikely that Anelli was familiar with it). But again we see the modernisation of these themes. Consider the implied confrontation between Italy and Algeria – between the 'modern' West and peoples not 'redeemed' by the French revolution – as regards relations between the sexes: Mustafà's explicit confrontation with two different conjugal examples (on the one hand Elvira, docile and submissive even though spurned by him, and on the other the indomitable Isabella, who ridicules him); the husband–wife model he provides for Lindoro and Elvira; his own unexpected metamorphosis from 'leone in asino' ('a lion into an ass'), from 'flagel delle donne' ('the scourge of women') to foolish dolt; the title of 'Pappataci' conceded in Italy 'a color che mai non sanno / disgustarsi del bel sesso' ('to those who never tire of the fair sex'), condemned to have to close their eyes to the initiative of too emancipated women; and finally the polemic against arranged marriages. All these elements of the plot clearly harbour polemical intentions, present even in what seem to be the most innocuous passages. The scene of Taddeo's appointment to Gran Kaimakan has a clear literary model: the 'Turkish ceremony' in Act 4, scene 5 of Molière's *Le Bourgeois Gentilhomme* (1670) in which the foppish protagonist Monsieur Jourdain is ennobled for a joke to the rank of Mamamouchi at the will of the Grand Turk's false son.[14] The parallel investiture of Mustafà to the Order of the Pappataci, on the other hand, is a parody of initiations into the secret clubs in great vogue at the time (Anelli himself belonged to the Masons).

Even in the context of an ambiguous, double-edged satire, the 'virile' characterisation of Isabella (Act 2, scene 9: 'alle vicende della volubil sorte / una donna t'insegni ad esser forte'; 'when confronted with the vicissitudes of fickle fate, a woman will teach you to be strong'), reminiscent of classical heroines, also constitutes an element of modernity.[15] A greater rôle for women in society, and claims of sexual equality, were ideals agitated (and to a certain degree actually active) in Italy in the context of the new political and social conditions introduced by the arrival of the Napoleonic army. In homage to the spirit of the times, Isabella, besides being cunning (a typical spirited woman in the comic tradition), is determined and courageous to the point of leading men in arms. Once her doubt about her beloved's faithfulness has dissipated, she does not hesitate, scorning Taddeo's cowardliness and heartening the feminine, 'gentil' Lindoro who pales in the face of danger. It is Isabella who decides the decisive turn of events in the crucial musical number, her aria 'Pensa alla patria': it is to her that the troops of 'Italian slaves' longing for liberation from their chains turn, putting their faith in her, and acclaiming her leader of the troops on their territory.

This scene is an example of faultless dramatic construction, with an irresistible climax. In her *scena*, Isabella first frees herself of the faint-hearted Taddeo, then gives Lindoro courage, evoking 'Patria, dovere, onor' ('Homeland, duty, honour') and urging him 'a mostrarsi Italiano' ('to show himself worthy of being Italian'). She then immediately reasserts her argument with an emphatic change of poetic and musical régime, from recitative to aria, in the section which begins 'Pensa alla Patria, e intrepido / il tuo dovere adempi: / vedi per tutta Italia / rinascere gli esempi / d'ardire, e di valor' ('Think of your homeland, and fearlessly fulfil your duty: see examples of bravery and valour re-born throughout Italy'). After this, she puts aside private affairs to address the troops, who respond with reciprocal enthusiasm, repeating the initial self-confident assertion: 'Quanto vaglian gl'Italiani / al cimento si vedrà' ('It will be seen how much Italians are worth when they are put to the test'). The ideal of a solicitous and impartial mother country to be loved, and if necessary defended, was a value continually proclaimed and propagated in the Jacobin republics born in Italy in 1796 after the French invasion. The states derived from these (the Cisalpine, then Italian Republic, 1800–2, then 1802–5, and the Reign of Italy, 1805–14) acted on this legacy by promulgating laws which imposed obligatory military service for men between the ages of twenty and twenty-five (1801). The call to arms resonating on the most important stage of the capital of the Reign of Italy (1808, La Scala, Milan; and again 1813, for Rossini) alluded powerfully to themes of acute topicality.

By contrast, librettos tending to comedy like *Il barbiere di Siviglia* or *La Cenerentola* abound with situations and characters which exchange seriousness for the opposite extreme, buffoonery. Moreover, comparing *Il barbiere* with Paisiello's then-venerated precedent (1782, derived from Beaumarchais's 1775 *comédie*) illustrates the dramaturgical shifts of the intervening thirty years.[16] The same kind of comparison can fruitfully be made between *La Cenerentola* and its French and Italian predecessors, Etienne's and Isouard's *opéra-féerie Cendrillon* (Paris, 1810) and Fiorini's and Pavesi's *Agatina, o La virtù premiata* (Milan, 1814). Ferretti's *dramma giocoso* also contains a pathetic and sentimental vein that brings it close to the semiserious genre. The adjustment of the original model (*Cendrillon*, *conte* in prose by Perrault, 1697) to the paradigms of comic opera, with the expunction of its fantastic and magic elements (the stepmother turned into a father and traditional comic bass; the fairy godmother made masculine in the form of the more prosaic tutor Alidoro, another bass; and a valet, who does not exist in the fairy tale but usually figures in the comic genre), highlights the absence of the fantastic from the Italian operatic stage.

Il turco in Italia, finally, is a unique case. Drawn from Mazzolà's homonymous libretto for Seydelmann (1788), Romani's 1814 version is enriched with a meta-theatrical plot of a poet at work on a comic opera inspired by the main action. This play of frames refers not only to Goldoni's *La bella verità*, set to music by Piccinni in 1762, but to a long tradition of opera within opera.[17]

Opere serie

During his years at Naples (1815–22) Rossini worked primarily for the most important royal theatre in the city, the San Carlo, in collaboration with its house poets. As we have seen, these poets were both professionals such as Schmidt and Tottola, and noble amateurs like Berio and Della Valle. The theatre staged only *opere serie*: the comic masterpieces of this period, *Il barbiere di Siviglia* and *La Cenerentola*, were born elsewhere. Up until *La Cenerentola* the composer had on the whole shown equal interest in serious and comic works; after it, his excursions into the latter field were sporadic. If we were to believe the confession made directly to the 'Bon Dieu' in the preface to his *Petite messe solennelle* (1863: 'I was born for comic opera'), we should think that since 1817 Rossini had been working almost constantly against his true inclinations. But the composer was being economical with the truth, as usual, when playing down his work in the serious genre. In fact that work had, on the contrary, intensified, and encompassed a broad range of experiments which, though concentrated mainly in the Naples operas, were grounded in the preceding years, and continued to be developed in *Semiramide* for Venice (1823). Rossini's compositional trajectory unfolded without ruptures or regressions, guided by a highly individual personality, well-thought-out ideas and a strong sense of direction.

Chance drew this strand of Rossini's career into a perfect circle. His first and last successes, *Tancredi* (1813) and *Semiramide* (ten years later), had a common venue, librettist and literary source: La Fenice in Venice, Gaetano Rossi, and the Voltaire of *Tancrède*, 1759 and *Sémiramis*, 1748. Tragic tension permeates more than one of the titles between these extremes. The main influence is not, however, the ancients, but rather the French authors of the *grand siècle* such as Racine (*Andromaque*, 1667, is the source of *Ermione*) and their eighteenth-century heirs Voltaire, Antoine-Vincent Arnault (whose 1789 *Blanche et Montcassin ou Les Vénitiens* is the basis for *Bianca e Falliero*), Dormont de Belloy (whose 1762 *Zelmire* generated *Zelmira*), and Italians such as Della Valle (*Anna Erizo*, which became *Maometto II*). Although it might seem unlikely at first, Shakespeare appears too. However, Berio's *Otello*, set by Rossini in 1816, relied largely on the versions produced by Jean-François Ducis (Paris, 1792) and Giovanni Carlo Cosenza (Naples,

1813), in which the 'irregularities' of the original had been 'regularised' in tragic and classical terms.

As well as these embodiments of tragic pathos, Rossini's serious works include other equally 'high' subjects: the Scottish Middle Ages of Walter Scott (*La donna del lago*), viewed as the modern heir of the boreal Ossian and his 'barbaric' energy; and the biblical Middle East (*Ciro in Babilonia, Mosè in Egitto*), which, particularly in the Lenten season, had for some decades colonised the Italian stage, inducing a religious *gravitas* and meditative attitudes previously quite foreign to that hedonistic world. All three of these trends testify to an ever-increasing interest in the late-eighteenth-century category of the sublime, an inheritance to which various European Romanticisms were heavily indebted. A gravitational pull towards full-blown tragedy permeated Italian opera in the late eighteenth and early nineteenth centuries, with more or less radical results, but surely significant repercussions on compositional style. It pulled towards a musical language that was at times learned, at times grandiose and elevated, but also towards expanded musical forms, as proven by many numbers from Rossini's Naples operas, and especially in the sumptuous *Semiramide*, the culmination of Rossini's Italian career not just in a chronological sense.

At times, though, we are catapulted from grandeur to the opposite extreme, to headlong action at lightning speed, accompanied by an intensely laconic style à la Alfieri. Consider for example the Act 2 Finale of *Semiramide*:

OROE	Ninia, ferisci!	Ninia, strike!
ASSUR	Ninia!	Ninia!
NINIA	Assur!	Assur!
SEMIRAMIDE	Il figlio!	My son!
ASSUR	Arsace!	Arsace!
	Ov'è?	Where is he?
NINIA	Pera . . .	He must die . . .
SEMIRAMIDE	Si salvi . . .	Save him . . .
NINIA	Padre mio,	My father
	ecco la tua vendetta . . .	Here is your revenge . . .

Another instance of such terseness is the almost unheard-of breathlessness with which *Otello* ends, as the protagonist stabs himself and expires over just seven bars in the orchestra and with a single cry from the onlookers. The curtain falls without a chorus, a *rondò*, or even a cavatina (as in the tragic Finale of *Tancredi* re-worked for Ferrara, Lent 1813), in the same short time taken by the 'Fiat Lux' in Genesis, or 'Qu'il mourût!' of Racine's *Horace*, two famous archetypes of the laconic style always evoked in the literature on the sublime.

Opere semiserie

As well as the two main genres, Rossini also composed *opere semiserie*, which had been defined as a relatively autonomous genre in the last few decades of the preceding century. The semiserious genre had also started to contaminate works which previously would have been either serious or comic: *Eduardo e Cristina*, for example, is a primarily serious opera with comic elements, whereas *L'inganno felice* and *Matilde di Shabran* are primarily comic operas with serious elements. Works such as *Torvaldo e Dorliska* and *La gazza ladra* embody in full the variety of semiserious opera which had come into being in the preceding revolutionary decades, and which twentieth-century musicology would term 'rescue opera'; at the same time, however, they also document an adjustment to the changed political and cultural climate of the Restoration. Compare the political motivations for the persecution of Armand and Constance in Cherubini's *Les Deux Journées* or Leonore and Florestan in Beethoven's *Fidelio*: the two protagonists of *Torvaldo e Dorliska* are victims only of a foolish amorous jealousy, while the maid of *La gazza ladra* indeed risks immediate execution, but because accused of the mere theft of a piece of silverware.

Gherardini, although a novice, wrote a theatrically effective as well as extremely interesting text.[18] *La gazza ladra* was based on the *mélodrame historique* by Caigniez and D'Aubigny *La Pie voleuse, ou La Servante de Palaiseau* (Paris, 1815), and was at first more polemically titled *Avviso ai giudici*, admonishing against judiciary error. As an *opera semiseria* it has unusually broad dimensions, a musical and rustic equivalent of mid-eighteenth-century bourgeois drama, of Diderot's *tragédie domestique et bourgeoise* and Lessing's *bürgerliches Trauerspiel*, which had been discussed and popularised in Italy at the end of the century by Idelfonso Valdastri in his *Dissertazione sulle tragedie cittadinesche* (1794). In the nineteenth century the mixture of drama and comedy proved of no small interest to the new Romantic poets bent on overcoming the boundaries between the traditional literary genres. In its events and tone, *La gazza ladra* seems to anticipate Alessandro Manzoni's *I promessi sposi* (*The Betrothed*, 1827, after a first draft completed in 1823 entitled *Fermo and Lucia*), the most important Italian novel of the nineteenth century. Its protagonists also belong to the 'gente meccaniche, e di piccol affare' ('mechanical folk, and of but small account') which concerned Manzoni, and the story revolves around an ingénue pursued by the evil mayor of the town, saved at the end by providential intervention, just as in the novel. Secondary character actors appear with equal prominence in the background, broadening further the stylistic spectrum (which with Ninetta, Fernando, Giannetto and the Mayor was already shifting from the graceful to the dramatic, from the comic to the sublime, from the colloquial to the pathetic) in the direction of *sermo humilis*, the lowest stylistic level (Lucia and Fabrizio), or the picturesque (the Jewish pedlar Isacco, Pippo with his dithyrambic drinking song in Act 1, scene 5 'Tocchiamo, beviamo'). *La gazza ladra* was premièred in the Romantic Lombardy of 1817, Gherardini having shortly before published a translation of Schlegel's *Corso di letteratura drammatica*. In this context the Manzonian premonitions may appear less unfounded.

French operas

The first talk of taking Rossini to Paris dates back to 1818; it was only substantiated, however, in 1823–4. Once in the French capital (from the end of 1824), the composer came into direct contact with dramaturgies, styles, systems, organisational procedures and methods of work often notably different from those he had previously known and practised. These differences also involved librettos and librettists: their conceptions and structures, cultural assumptions and *modus operandi*.

A sort of embassy of Italian opera in France existed, however, in the Théâtre Italien, which in general conformed to Italian theatrical practices. The theatre had a house poet on its permanent staff; at the time Rossini moved to Paris this position had been filled for more than fifteen years by the Piedmont librettist Luigi Balocchi (1766–1832). The theatre staged both imported and new works, but always in Italian; Balocchi's job therefore consisted of making small adjustments to librettos by other people or writing new ones and rehearsing them.

The most important theatre in the capital, however, was the Opéra (officially the Académie Royal de Musique), where French was the mandatory language. Here there functioned a commission, the 'Jury littéraire et musical', made up of about fifteen members: literary men, composers and representatives of the administration (in November 1826 Rossini himself became a member, in accordance with his appointment the previous month as 'Inspecteur général du Chant', as well as 'Compositeur du Roi'). The Jury's function was to sift through the proposed librettos, approving them, rejecting them or suggesting modifications. Shortly after settling in Paris, Rossini was offered *Le Vieux de la montagne*, a libretto by Victor-Joseph-Etienne de Jouy approved on 3 November 1824 (GRLD, vol. II, no. 466). The procedure demanded that the poet read his text and then leave the room. At that point, the president would pose the following queries to the members, to be voted on individually: 'Is this work suited to the lyric stage?', and 'Is the work approved as it stands?' In this case, Jouy's declamatory performance had charmed the majority of the committee into responding positively to both questions.

In view of his move to Paris, when Rossini was still in England in 1824 he had signed the contract offered to him by the Opéra administration on 27 February. It required that he compose a French opera and an Italian opera, the latter either semiserious or comic. The choice of the libretto for the French work had to be agreed between Rossini, the administration of the Opéra and the Jury, the administration offering to present the composer with a number of possible texts (GRLD, vol. II, no. 436). The unexpected coronation of a new sovereign (Charles X) in 1825, however, resulted in Rossini's first work for the French stage being another Italian opera, albeit the highly exceptional and idiosyncratic *dramma giocoso Il viaggio a Reims*. Intended for the Théâtre Italien, the libretto was the work of Balocchi. The large number of characters (necessitated by the desire to employ the whole company of singers simultaneously) and their rôle in shaping the overall structure of the libretto, not to mention the nature of some of its numbers, gave it an eccentricity of conception which reaches its apex in the Finale – a completely atypical structure governed strictly by the exceptional solemnity of the occasion.

Despite plans to compose *Le Vieux de la montagne* for the Opéra, and *La figlia dell'aria* for the Théâtre Italien, Rossini's next Paris operas were re-workings, or simple translations, of previous Italian operas. *Ivanhoé* falls into the latter category, a pastiche which drew from a good ten Rossini operas, staged by Antonio Pacini with the collaboration of the composer himself at the Odéon on 15 September 1826. In this case Emile Deschamps and Gabriel-Gustave de Wailly had crafted a made-to-measure libretto, superimposing French verses onto the pre-existing Italian ones.

Similar work was needed to transform the *dramma Maometto II* (Naples, 1820) into the *tragédie lyrique Le Siège de Corinthe* (Opéra, 9 October 1826), and the *azione tragico-sacra Mosè in Egitto* (Naples, 1818–19) into the *opéra Moïse et Pharaon* (Opéra, 26 March 1827). When still in Naples in the spring of 1821, Rossini had written to Giovan Battista Viotti of the Théâtre Italien: 'According to a common friend [Ferdinand Hérold, on a mission to Italy on the theatre's behalf], the oratorio *Mosè*, which I composed three years ago, seems to be the score most suited for French translation' (GRLD, vol. I, no. 255). Castil-Blaze explained the reason for this at the beginning of 1822, as he finished translating *Mosè in Egitto*, which he had been sent the previous summer. The score possessed 'grandiose and colossal forms that are appropriate for our principal opera house. Its style is severe, but vehement and impassioned; the effects, produced mainly by the crowd, put the Opéra's excellent chorus to good use. A flower of innovation also reigns in this marvellous work, a force of colour, an originality in the structure and pace of musical pieces' (GRLD, vol. I, no. 303).

As early as the summer of 1826 Ferdinando Paer wrote from Paris to the theatre agent Benelli in Bologna that 'Rossini is trying out his *Maometto* reworked into French for the grand Opéra, helped by Balocchi, and by a certain Mr [Alexandre] Soumet, tragic poet' (GRLD, vol. II, no. 624). Paer wrote again to Benelli at the beginning of 1827: 'Rossini is fully intent on smearing new French words onto his old *Mosè*' (GRLD, vol. III, no. 721). In addition to Balocchi's usual help, this time Rossini was further supported by Jouy. During the same period, Etienne Pellot wrote to Giuditta Pasta: 'We are caught up in arranging *Mosè* for the Opéra. The Maestro and Monsieur de Jouy have finished the necessary groundwork. The poem is entirely changed. The scenic effects will be spectacular' (GRLD, vol. III, no. 711). Quite apart from the authors' different dispositions towards Rossini, their two viewpoints reflect the amphibious nature of these operations. On the one hand entire numbers, or significant portions of them, were transferred intact, with French verses substituted for the Italian ones. (Soumet on the whole respected Della Valle's poetic metres in his work; Jouy, on the other hand, went so far as to recast the verse in metres better suited to the contour and rhythmic scansion of the sung phrases. Both, obviously, abided by the metrical laws of French poetry, which were different from those of Italian verse.[19]) But significant parts of these librettos were completely original. For these, the two poets had to furnish new verses and Rossini new music.

Le Comte Ory was not a brand new opera either, given that Rossini had 'quarried many pieces from his *Viaggio a Reims*', as Luigi Goffredo Zuccoli wrote to Bartolomeo Capranica (GRLD, vol. III, no. 845). Even though *Il viaggio a Reims* was a recent opera, it was little known, due to the minimal number of its performances. The transfer did not cause many problems of dramaturgy or structure. *Il viaggio a Reims* strung together a series of loosely connected scenic and musical situations, without being too concerned with normal sequential coherence. Once what was unusable in a more common context had been eliminated (for example, the whole banquet passage and the homages to the various nations), it was not difficult to re-assemble its situations according to more conventional dramatic logic (and to much greater theatrical effect).

The plot of *Le Comte Ory* derives from a medieval ballad published in the late eighteenth century by Pierre-Antoine de la Place (*Pièces intéressantes et peu connues pour servir à l'histoire et à la littérature*, Brussels–Paris, 1785) in the context of a literary historiography which emphasised primary sources, and an incipient passion for the middle ages and for apparently 'popular' art. In just a dozen stanzas, the *ballade* recounted one of the erotic exploits of the terrible Comte Ory, predator of wild beasts and women, hero of revelry, brawls and festivities. Eugène Scribe (1791–1861) had early in his career drawn from it a light-hearted vaudeville in one act titled *Le Comte Ory. Anecdote du XIᵉ siècle*, written in collaboration with Charles-Gaspard Delestre-Poirson. This had been staged at the Théâtre du Vaudeville on 16 December 1816, and must have generated significant interest, since Louis-François Raban then recast it as a huge novel in three volumes (*Le Comte Ory*, Paris, 1824). Thanks, perhaps, to this renewed attention to the subject, the plot was reworked for Rossini by Scribe, who versified it afresh and provided a brand new first act in order to provide a full evening of entertainment and a libretto fit for the greatest Parisian stage.

In this form, *Le Comte Ory* made its début at the Opéra on 28 August 1828. Its anti-clerical elements had been attenuated: the monastery was transformed into a castle, the abbess into a countess and the nuns into grass widows; Ory's followers in Act 2 became generic women pilgrims instead of, again, nuns. But the tone of the opera still remained irreverent. The theatre which only a few decades earlier had staged ancient and venerated classics such as Gluck's *Orphée* and *Alceste* (1800 and 1803), Rousseau's *Le Devin du village* (1810) and the masterpieces of Mozart, and more recently great historical frescos such as Spontini's *Fernand Cortez* (1817), Rossini's *Siège* and *Moïse* (1826 and 1827) and Auber's *La Muette de Portici* (29 February 1828), opened its doors to erotically titillating plots. The vogue for all things medieval had been influential for some time: champions of Romanticism exalted it as an era of triumphant Christianity opposed to pagan classicism and its modern secular – when not irreligious or even atheist – promoters. Just a few years earlier (22 September 1825) *Il crociato in Egitto* by Rossi and Meyerbeer had made its début in Paris, having first been staged in Venice in March 1824. In this context, the adventures of a pleasure-loving and sceptical shirker such as Comte Ory, who lay traps for wives and sisters of cavalier colleagues while they were busy at the Crusades, could not but seem like a quick-witted spoof of the medievalising fashion – and even as being acrimoniously sarcastic toward religion. Journals hostile to Rossini like *Le Constitutionnel* and *Le Corsaire* did not pass up this opportunity to attack, and stigmatised the 'boulevardier' tone as inappropriate at the Opéra.

The *opéra Guillaume Tell* (premièred on 3 August 1829), destined to become Rossini's artistic testament, was of a very different rank. Written by Jouy some years previously, it was judged in need of some revision; this was entrusted to the younger Hippolyte-Louis-Florent Bis, who had recently achieved theatrical acclaim. The well-educated and literary tenor Adolphe Nourrit, the future protagonist of the opera, also made a significant contribution – for his good offices Rossini began good-naturedly to call him his 'poëte adjoint' (GRLD, vol. III, no. 974).

The great epic canvas conceived by Jouy, enhanced by the individual and personal event of Arnold's heroic 'conversion', followed a fashion for spectacle and a penchant for politics well established at the Opéra, but also built on the cornerstones of Rossini's two preceding works. Both *Le Siège de Corinthe* and *Moïse et Pharaon* as well as *Guillaume Tell* (and *La Muette de Portici*) set on stage the historic events of a people's struggle for liberty (Greek, Hebrew, Neapolitan, Swiss), and collective rebellion guided by great individual personalities (Moses, Masaniello, Tell). The contemporary events of the Greco-Turkish war, which French public opinion followed passionately – siding with the insurrection against the Ottoman oppressors – furnished obvious parallels.[20] But these were also themes crucial to contemporary historiography, which reinterpreted with relative detachment the great revolutions and subsequent Napoleonic epic that had recently raged through France and Europe. The writings of François Guizot (1787–1874), Augustin Thierry (1795–1856) and, a little later, Jules Michelet (1798–1874) had as protagonists concepts such as the People, Liberty, insurrection and national identity. The great choral scenes of Rossini's French operas and their intensely characteristic (as opposed to merely pictorial) *couleur locale* translated these abstract concepts onto the musical stage, adumbrating a kind of militancy that imminent political events themselves, beginning with the July Revolution of 1830, would take to a degree of explicitness far beyond the intentions of the composer.

(*translated by Laura Basini*)

6 Compositional methods

PHILIP GOSSETT

The peculiar shape of Rossini's theatrical career encouraged the circulation of a host of anecdotes about his compositional methods. Their function was to provide a rationale for both the miracle of creativity that permitted the composer to write some forty operas in twenty years, many of them enduring achievements, and the psychological mystery that surrounded his withdrawal from the operatic stage after *Guillaume Tell* in 1829. These anecdotes tended to trivialise Rossini's works and to cast doubt on his seriousness as an artist. Some of them emphasise Rossini's habit of employing the same music in more than one opera, without making any effort to describe his practice more precisely. Others claim to enter into the workings of his creative spirit. A fabricated 'letter' tells us that the overtures to *Le Comte Ory* and *Guillaume Tell* were prepared while Rossini was fishing with his banker friend, Alexandre Aguado, 'as he spoke to me about the Spanish economy'.[1] Another favourite site for creative work was said to be a crowded room, amidst the hilarity of friends laughing, drinking and singing.[2] According to another anecdotal tack, implicitly emphasising his sloth, Rossini was said to have composed in bed. When a sheet of music paper fell to the ground, the story continues, the indolent Rossini did not deign to go after it, but instead took another piece of paper and started again. I have always wondered why this anecdote is thought to emphasise Rossini's laziness, as opposed to his extraordinary creativity.[3]

Just as these anecdotes suggest that Rossini was less than serious about how his music was composed, so too was he said to have been indifferent to the fate of the autograph manuscripts of his works. Responsibility for this reputation rested in part with the composer himself. In Paris during his later years (1855–68), when asked about the whereabouts of his manuscripts, he would respond that he never asked to have them back once a work was finished.[4] But this was a simple lie, one of Rossini's many efforts to conceal the truth about his artistic life from a curious world. When during the 1860s he believed the autograph of *Otello* to have disappeared from his home in Paris, the furious composer added a codicil to his will, insisting that the thief be found and punished (in fact, the manuscript had merely been misplaced).[5] Once his fame permitted him to have control over the fate of his operas, Rossini conserved as many of his manuscripts as possible, both those of his operas and those of the pieces composed in his last years, the *Péchés de vieillesse.* After his death the autograph manuscripts in the composer's possession passed temporarily to his second wife, Olympe Pélissier. At her death, apart from those manuscripts that Olympe gave away as gifts to her doctors, lawyers and bankers, the entire collection was inherited by the city of Pesaro, where it continues to be housed under the auspices of the Fondazione Rossini.

The fate of these manuscripts, and the care with which they have been preserved, is crucial to our understanding of Rossini's compositional methods, for it is through them that we can develop some understanding of how the composer worked. Far from being indifferent to his manuscripts, Rossini was extraordinarily attentive to every aspect of their elaboration. That does not mean that he left them in a state ready for publication. Composers of Italian opera in the nineteenth century could not have imagined that the full scores of their operas would ever be published. Indeed, during the 1810s Rossini did not even expect that his operas would be printed in reductions for piano and voice: vocal scores became widespread in Italy only during the 1820s, following a practice already well established in northern Europe. With the generation of Bellini and Donizetti, the immediate publication of the vocal score of an opera became the norm. It was not until the very last years of the nineteenth century, however, with Verdi's *Otello* and *Falstaff,* that printed orchestral scores of Italian operas began to circulate regularly to theatres: before then, operas were usually made available in manuscript copies.

Rossini knew very well that the autograph manuscripts of his operas would therefore be the point of departure for the process by which his music would circulate. From them manuscript copies would be made in the *copisterie* found throughout the peninsula, wherever there was an active theatrical life, and from those first copies other copies would follow. The theatre that originally commissioned a work would try to control its diffusion wherever possible, but it was a losing battle. Within the fragmented world of separate states that constituted Italian political reality during the 1810s and 1820s, once a theatre obtained a copy of a score – whether legally or illegally – it could not be prevented from preparing derivative materials and organising a performance. Legislation concerning authors' rights had no practical influence.

The extent to which performances reflected the notated intentions of the composer, therefore, depended on this system of production, and the quality of the product depended on the quality of the starting point: the composer's autograph manuscript. Rossini was fully aware, of course, that a theatre would make changes to satisfy contingent needs: the vocal limits of a particular singer, the demands of a prima donna to have an aria where the composer and librettist had planned something else, the need to make cuts for a foreign public unaccustomed to the length of a typical Italian opera of the period. Rossini himself, directing revivals of his works, participated fully in similar revisions. Whether within a congenial or uncongenial social and artistic context, however, the quality of the composer's autograph would remain decisive in determining the extent to which his musical and dramaturgical desires could eventually be realised in the theatre.

During the earlier part of his career (up until about 1820), Rossini often completed several operas each year. To do so, he was compelled to prepare his scores within a relatively brief time frame, although rarely as brief as the few weeks employed for the principal comedies written for Roman theatres, *Il barbiere di Siviglia* (1816) and *La Cenerentola* (1817).[6] It was, in fact, during the years before 1818 that the bulk of Rossini's self-borrowing took place, as we shall see. There is growing documentary evidence, however, that for many of his more mature works Rossini's creative process required many months. Already in mid-June 1816, for example, he wrote to his mother that he was composing *La gazzetta*, a comic opera based on a Goldoni comedy, whose première at the Teatro dei Fiorentini in Naples did not take place until 26 September.[7] Already at the end of August 1819 Rossini and his librettist Felice Romani were preparing *Bianca e Falliero*, which opened the Carnival season at the Teatro alla Scala of Milan on 26 December.[8] Beginning in 1820 Rossini composed no more than a single opera each year, a creative rhythm he maintained until his retirement from the theatre at the end of the decade. Bellini, who boasted about the deliberateness of his compositional method, was simply imitating the practice of his older colleague.

Preliminary sketches

Not until 1820, after Rossini had already composed some thirty operas, do we have evidence that he prepared preliminary sketches. Unlike the mature Verdi, who preserved his elaborate sketches from the time of *Luisa Miller* (1849) until the end of his career,[9] Rossini does not seem regularly to have kept such documents. We can neither be certain that they are representative of what once may have existed, nor assume that similar sources were not prepared for earlier works. Yet the pattern of survival (sketches have been identified for *Maometto II* of 1820, *Semiramide* of 1823, *Le Siège de Corinthe* of 1826, *Moïse* of 1827, and *Le Comte Ory* of 1828) is suggestive, as is the fact that surviving sketches are often related to complex ensembles (the *terzettone* from *Maometto II*, the Act 1 Finale from *Semiramide*, the trio from *Le Comte Ory*).

The earliest known Rossini sketch, part of the Lord St Davids collection at the Fondazione Rossini, is related to *Maometto II*.[10] It pertains to the great

Example 6.1 *Maometto II*, *terzettone* Anna–Calbo–Erisso, 'Ohimè! qual fulmine', sketch for the cadence of Anna's prayer, 'Giusto ciel, in tal periglio'

terzettone for Anna, Calbo and Erisso from the middle of Act 1, one of the most complex ensembles Rossini ever wrote, incorporating many different musical sections, dramatic actions and even changes of set. The sketches, which occupy both sides of a single leaf, refer to neither the beginning nor the end of the ensemble, which might suggest that other pages of sketches for the *terzettone* once existed. Yet this single leaf provides a wide range of examples of how Rossini's sketches allowed him to develop his art in works from the 1820s.

There is no trace of the *scena* or canonic trio ('Ohimè! qual fulmine'), or of the Turkish assault (which motivates the change of set), or of the women's chorus and the beginning of Anna's prayer ('Giusto ciel, in tal periglio'). The first music sketched is the highly chromatic cadential phrase for this prayer (ex. 6.1). For Rossini a sketch leaf of this kind may not have been employed *before* he began preparing his autograph manuscript (as in the case of Verdi), but rather during the process of drafting the skeleton score (see the next section for further details). The sketch seems to have functioned as a separate physical location, where the composer could work through a difficult passage. Yet even here Rossini's instinct was strong: this sketch from Anna's prayer is essentially identical to the final version.

The page continues with a complete sketch for the following recitative ('Ahi, Padre!'), where the three characters reassemble after the beginning of the assault. In most cases Rossini captured the spirit of the passage's ultimate form, even if details remain to be defined. A recurring orchestral figure sketched as the arpeggiation in crotchets of a major chord, for example, will ultimately be fleshed out into a pattern of semiquavers (ex. 6.2). About halfway through the recitative, however, the sketch begins to differ markedly from the final version, so much so that Rossini drafted the passage a second time. Example 6.3 gives Erisso's description of the military situation as notated in the original sketch, together with the second sketch (essentially identical to the final version).

Example 6.2 *Maometto II*, *terzettone* Anna–Calbo–Erisso, 'Ohimè! qual fulmine', sketch for an orchestral figure from the recitative

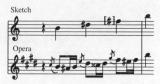

Example 6.3 *Maometto II*, *terzettone* Anna–Calbo–Erisso, 'Ohimè! qual fulmine', two sketches for Erisso's recitative

The two sketches diverge in tonal direction, melodic detail and declamation. The first is tonally more predictable, with two full cadences: from E major to V of VI at '[Sulle mura è il ne]-mico', which resolves to C♯ major at '[Mao]-metto', and finally modulates to F♯ major. Not only does the melody meander and repeat itself (notice the identical 'il corso arresta' and 'e attender vuole'), but the full close at 'Maometto' contradicts the sense of the text, while the emphatic '*di* sua vittoria', reached by the largest upward leap in the melody, a sixth, has no textual motivation. The revised version is a more sensitive treatment of the words: the initial phrase is highlighted effectively, the absence of a full close in the middle allows the passage to sweep on towards the cadence, where Rossini gives enormous prominence – through the upward leap of a seventh, rhythmic displacements and a more

Example 6.4 *Maometto II, terzettone* Anna–Calbo–Erisso, 'Ohimè! qual fulmine', sketch for the reprise of the principal melody in the cantabile, 'Mira, signor, quel pianto'

florid style – to Erisso's final words ('e attender vuole il giorno'). It is a lovely example of the composer's self-criticism at work.

After a brief sketch for the opening of the B major Allegro giusto, 'Figlia . . . mi lascia', Rossini devotes most of the verso of the leaf to the G major cantabile, Andantino, 'Mira, signor, quel pianto'. In its final form, this cantabile consists of the following: a thirteen-bar melodic period sung by Calbo (the mezzo-soprano); a contrasting section begun by Anna (the soprano), joined in counterpoint after four bars by both Calbo and Erisso (the tenor); a reprise of the melodic period, with Anna singing the entire melody and contrapuntal accompaniments for the other singers; a cadential section for all three singers (five bars, repeated, plus two bars, with a varied repeat).

Rossini's sketch begins at the eighth bar of the thirteen-bar melodic period (as if he had written the initial seven bars directly into his autograph manuscript before deciding to work with a sketch), and continues through to the end of the cantabile. It holds many surprises, all of which help us to understand the composer's art. Here are two examples. What should be the 'reprise' of the opening thirteen-bar melodic period is instead an eight-bar melody (sketched without text), entirely different from what will become the final version (ex. 6.4). It is a lovely, lyrical melody in its own right, yet Rossini ultimately rejected it. The melody he chose instead is equally lovely, but its construction from smaller melodic fragments, with accented chromatic appoggiaturas from below, allowed the composer to introduce a series of intense contrapuntal imitations in the reprise, imitations that would have been impossible with the lyrical melody he had originally sketched (ex. 6.5). A comparison of the sketch and the final version, in short, demonstrates that the composer was not simply looking for an appropriate melodic idea, but was concerned with intensifying the emotional effect of the reprise by integrating all three characters into a more complex musical texture.

Even the five-bar repeated phrase within the cadential section of this cantabile is the product of multiple drafts. Originally Rossini sketched the phrase in four bars; then he made a separate sketch, extending the phrase

Example 6.5 *Maometto II, terzettone* Anna–Calbo–Erisso, 'Ohimè! qual fulmine', reprise of the principal melody in 'Mira, signor, quel pianto'

to six bars; only in his autograph manuscript did he settle on the five-bar phrase of the definitive version (ex. 6.6). Although the first and last bars are the same in all three versions, at issue here is the approach within the phrase to f″ (with which the tonic triad momentarily becomes V of IV) and its duration. Related issues are the introduction of sufficient diversity among the sextuplets in the cadence and the handling of the upper register. In the original four-bar sketch the ascent to f″ is singled out as important (only at this point is the sextuplet rhythm momentarily modified), and its arrival on the third beat is rhythmically effective, but the pitch is rapidly passed over and the following melodic figures are faceless. In the six-bar sketch Rossini gives much more prominence to the f″, holding it for more than a full bar, but its appearance on the downbeat is more predictable and the patterns leading up to it are overly extended. There is more variety in the patterns following the held f″, but the upper note of the phrase (repeated three times) is only g″. In the final version the composer markedly improves all these elements. The f″ falls on the third beat, as in the original four-bar sketch, but is prolonged over the barline, giving momentum to the ensuing patterns, which share the variety of those in the six-bar sketch. The nicest touch, though, is the ascent to a″ in the penultimate bar, which provides a powerful pivot to prepare the cadential figure in the final bar.

While these examples have all been taken from a single ensemble in *Maometto II*, they provide a fair measure of the nature of Rossini's sketching. For *Semiramide* a much wider range of sketches has survived, which cover almost the entire Act 1 Finale, as well as significant sections of the *gran scena* for Arsace and a few key moments of the *gran scena* for Assur.[11] The sketches, which often involve multiple renderings of the same passage, use a fascinating notation for several florid passages or cadenzas: Rossini would write the first notes, then render the remainder with wavy lines that define the shape of the music, without making the pitches precise. An important group of sketches for *Le Comte Ory* (much of which is derived from *Il viaggio a Reims*) includes all sections of the trio for the Comtesse, Isolier and Ory, the

Example 6.6 *Maometto II*, *terzettone* Anna–Calbo–Erisso, 'Ohimè! qual fulmine', two sketches and the final version of the cadential phrase in the cantabile, 'Mira, signor, quel pianto'

a) Four-bar sketch

b) Six-bar sketch

c) Five-bar final version

opera's masterpiece and its principal original composition. Also sketched is the orchestral introduction, which precedes the *introduction* (largely taken from *Il viaggio a Reims*).[12]

That these sketches exist at all is evidence that, by the 1820s, Rossini felt the need to develop some of his musical ideas on paper. Study of the sketches provides striking instances of the composer's musical judgement at work. Ultimately they can help us develop analytical insights into compositions for which no sketches survive, insights that reflect the issues that demonstrably mattered to him.

Skeleton scores

To judge by the nature of the surviving material and by the appearance of the autograph manuscripts, it seems likely that before 1820 Rossini did not normally make sketches and certainly not the kind of extensive sketches we find in the case of *Semiramide*. Instead, he inserted his ideas for a musical number directly in the manuscript that would become the autograph score of that number. We can see with clarity how he proceeded thanks to the survival of two unusual autograph manuscripts: the choruses and incidental music for *Edipo Coloneo* of Sophocles, in the translation by Gianbattista Giusti, and the beginning of the *introduzione* for an opera in which the characters Teodora and Ricciardino appear. In both cases Rossini began to write the music, but failed to complete it. In the case of *Teodora e Ricciardino* he pursued the composition for a while, then abandoned it.[13] In the case of *Edipo Coloneo* he actually 'composed' the entire score, but did not complete the orchestration. Later another composer, one whom Rossini knew well (since he also composed music for both *Adina* and *La donna del lago*), filled in the remainder of the score.[14] Still, observing with attention what Rossini himself wrote down, we can obtain a relatively clear idea as to how he prepared numbers for which no sketches survive. More important, we can use the information obtained from these unusual sources to help us examine the compositions he brought to completion. Such a study fully confirms the testimony of the incomplete manuscripts.

Normally Rossini wrote his music on single bifolios of oblong music paper. In this he was quite different from Verdi, for example, who normally used large fascicles of vertical music paper, composed of five or more nested bifolios. A composer who sketches his music in full, before writing out his autograph manuscript, can permit himself to use larger fascicles, since he has a precise idea about the length of each musical number. It is easy to understand why a composer who does not normally make continuous sketches of his music (or does not work out all details of the structure in such sketches), and is therefore less sure of the exact dimensions of each piece, might prefer the greater flexibility of working with single bifolios, rather than larger fascicles. As for the two types of format, the horizontal format used by Rossini allowed him to write more bars on each page, but reduced the number of staves at his disposal (normally between ten and sixteen for his Italian operas, somewhat more in his French ones, depending on the type of composition: recitative, aria, ensemble). For more complex numbers, therefore, Rossini was often forced to employ a supplementary 'spartitino', grouping instruments for which there were insufficient staves in the principal score. Verdi, who normally used a larger orchestra than that of Rossini, soon found an oblong format inconvenient, and already near the beginning of his career he adopted a vertical format with sixteen to thirty staves per page.

When beginning to write out a musical number in full score, Rossini would first assign each stave to one of the instruments or vocal parts.

Although not all instruments appear in every opera, or even in all numbers of a single opera, the basic order of staves remains unvaried, for the most part, throughout the operas of his maturity. The upper three staves are assigned to the upper strings (first and second violins and violas), followed by the winds (flutes and/or piccolos, oboes and clarinets). These are followed by parts for the brass and bassoons (horns, trumpets, bassoons, trombones and serpentone) and those for harp and percussion (timpani, triangle, bass drum and cymbals). The solo vocal parts follow, in descending order of tessitura, followed by the chorus. Finally, he signals a stave for the cellos, but fills it in only when they have an independent part; normally they are notated together with the double basses on the lowest stave of the score.

After having thus specified the vertical structure of his score, Rossini would then lay out the skeleton score of the piece. This usually consisted of the principal vocal line, text and music, most of the double bass (and cello) part and important instrumental ideas: accompanimental figurations, unusual harmonic progressions, crucial instrumental solos. Composers of nineteenth-century Italian opera considered this phase of their preparation critical. Once the skeleton of an opera was prepared, they considered the creative work finished. Completion of the orchestration could be undertaken at a later moment. In fact, when Gianbattista Giusti, who commissioned from Rossini the stage music and choruses for *Edipo Coloneo*, objected that Rossini had left the full score incomplete, the composer did not understand his lament: he was prepared to complete the orchestration once a performance was planned.

The skeleton scores of Rossini's operas are largely free from errors or even uncertainties. The clarity of the composer's thought, even in complex ensembles, is extraordinary. The internal voices in a sextet such as 'Quest'è un nodo avviluppato' from *La Cenerentola* are written with precision and conviction, even though they are entered in ink. When Rossini did make a correction, however, its significance is often immediately evident: eliminating a superfluous phrase, changing a detail within a lyrical period, improving a melodic line. Significant musical changes are almost always undertaken in the skeleton score phase, before the music is fully orchestrated. A large-scale change of particular importance, for example, is found in the autograph of *Semiramide*, where the cantabile of Semiramide's cavatina, 'Bel raggio lusinghier', was originally much longer, ending in conclusive cadences, without a cabaletta. Only later did Rossini modify the form in order to add a cabaletta, 'Dolce pensiero'.

If it is true, then, that Rossini did little or no independent sketching before 1820, how was it possible for him to write his first thirty operas, including all the major comedies, directly on pages that would become his complete

Example 6.7 *La Cenerentola*, duet Cenerentola–Ramiro, 'Un soave non so che', Allegro, orchestral theme

autograph manuscripts? The answer must be sought not simply in his genius, however unusual, but in the stylistic world to which his operas belong. Italian operas of the first decades of the nineteenth century were much dependent on a series of compositional models for individual numbers, many codified by Rossini himself, models that continued to play a significant rôle throughout the first half of the nineteenth century.[15] Thus, the points of significant invention for the skeleton score of many musical numbers were limited in number and the structural elaboration of these ideas tended to obey categorical imperatives. In an aria or cavatina, for example, Rossini had to invent principal melodies for the cantabile and for the cabaletta, although the internal structure of these melodies often involved further repetition, reducing the actual invention required.[16] To these melodic ideas, he would need to add an instrumental theme over which the voice could freely declaim in transitional passages, an orchestral theme to serve as the basis for a crescendo, and some cadential material. Having invented this musical material, whether entirely in his head or at the keyboard or even with the possible aid of written notation, Rossini could depend on structural models to guide his hand in laying out the skeleton score.

These formal procedures, of course, were available to every composer working in the first decades of the nineteenth century, many of them thoroughgoing professionals. Yet only Rossini succeeded in endowing them with the melodic charm, harmonic intensity and rhythmic energy that made them seem compelling to generations of composers and listeners. Most important, he joined to these structural conventions a keen sense of the theatre, which allowed him to mould his musical inspiration to the particularities of a dramatic situation. His instinct is usually so sure that there is little tangible evidence of how he arrived at his goals, but one lovely example in *La Cenerentola* is worth citing.[17]

In the duet for Cenerentola and Don Ramiro, a middle section (Allegro) opens with a symmetrical, eight-bar melody in the first violins, beginning in the tonic D major and closing in the dominant (ex. 6.7). Over it Don

Ramiro freely declaims his text (here slightly adjusted in accordance with the original printed libretto): 'Del Baron le figlie io cerco. / Dove son? Qui non le vedo'. Cenerentola responds over a simple set of orchestral chords, returning the music to the tonic: 'Son di là nell'altre stanze. / Or verranno. (Addio speranze.)' At this point Rossini must have continued in his skeleton score by beginning to write the orchestral melody again in the first violins. He got as far as the sixth bar of the phrase (with the two d'''s written an octave lower, as d''), then stopped cold. At that point he reduced the theme to its first three bars, then resolved it on the next downbeat with a quaver d''.

Although the conventional continuation Rossini originally entered into his skeleton score was perfectly functional, he had a precise dramaturgical reason for this change. The dialogue now moves from two verses per character to one, and then to a half:

RAMIRO	Ma di grazia, voi chi siete?	
CENERENTOLA	Io chi sono? Eh! non lo so.	
RAMIRO	Nol sapete?	
CENERENTOLA		Quasi no.

The composer could easily have entered this text under the complete theme, but by truncating the theme and by repeating the last verse ('Nol sapete? Quasi no'), he gave the final interchange more prominence and dramatic effect, setting the stage for Cenerentola's confused patter about her family ('Quel ch'è padre, non è padre') that soon wins Ramiro's heart.

After having completed his work with the skeleton score, the composer would return to the same manuscript in order to complete the orchestration. We know almost nothing about the time Rossini needed for these phases of the compositional process. For Verdi, on the other hand, we know that the composer gave his skeleton score directly to the copyists, who derived from it parts for the singers. Once these parts were in the hands of the singers, making rehearsals possible, Verdi orchestrated the score. It is likely that Rossini worked in a similar fashion. His orchestration is almost always a model of clarity. There are few rethinkings in his manuscript with regard, for example, to figurations in the accompaniment, in contrast with the Bellini manuscripts which frequently reveal significant indecision on the part of the Sicilian composer. In his orchestration Rossini can even seem parsimonious, using only instruments he truly needs, nothing else. But this apparent simplicity is deceiving, for instrumentalists are continually asked to play like soloists: not only are the scores difficult to execute, but they demand great skill if their orchestral qualities are not to be trivialised.

In some ways, however, Rossini's autograph manuscripts do reveal the speed with which they were often prepared. He made no effort to furnish dynamic levels for every instrument in the orchestra, or to provide complete articulation signs (slur, staccato, accent) throughout a composition. He employed these signs as models, generally specifying them at the first appearance of a particular musical figuration and leaving to his musicians the task of extending that model as the composition proceeds. In an operatic world where performers played stylistically homogeneous scores, all composed within a brief chronological period, such shorthand was deemed more than sufficient. In fact, there are cases in which interpreting Rossini's articulation, whether because it is insufficient or seems contradictory, may have posed problems even for his contemporaries. Experience with the critical edition, however, has demonstrated that Rossini's notation usually provides all the elements required for a reasonable interpretation. That it is necessary for a critical edition today to 'complete' his notation, extending the signs he furnished and removing uncertainties and contradictions, reflects more the nature of today's operatic world (where theatres pass, without batting an eye, from *Il barbiere di Siviglia* to *Lulu* to *La Bohème* to *Death in Venice*) than fundamental deficiencies in Rossini's notation.

Self-borrowing and the use of collaborators

That Rossini borrowed from himself is well known. As with Handel, this petty larceny has been used as a weapon to excoriate a composer whose seriousness and artistic integrity it presumes to negate. This was particularly true in a world where the autonomy and uniqueness of each work of art was becoming part of the philosophical underpinnings of German music. The roots of such criticism of Rossini, which became prevalent in German musical circles during the 1820s, stretch back into Italy of the mid 1810s. After the Milanese première of *Il turco in Italia* on 14 August 1814, for example, reviewers for the *Corriere milanese* and the *Corriere delle dame* both accused Rossini of having repeated himself: 'C'est du vin de son cru' says one; the young composer, says the other, has 'gathered together the various beauties and metrical jewels that are found spread through *L'italiana in Algeri*, in the *Pietra del paragone* and in other operas'.[18] This for a notably original *dramma buffo*, in which only a handful of short orchestral motifs are actually derived from earlier works. Critics, however, in the absence of any printed scores, were often unable to differentiate between stylistic consistency and actual self-borrowing.

Rossini grew to maturity in an artistic milieu in which very few operas survived for more than a few seasons and in which operas in Italy circulated only through manuscript copies and in performance. Since one-act operas had an extremely limited circulation, for example, four of the five *farse* he wrote between 1810 and 1813 for the Teatro San Moisè of Venice, a theatre that specialised in such pieces, were essentially never revived elsewhere. It should come as no surprise, then, that the composer treated these works as repositories for musical ideas on which he felt free to draw for later use. The wonder is that, despite it, Rossini's *farse* are so different from one another in musical language, ranging from the hilarious *Il signor Bruschino*, rooted in the shenanigans of improvisational comedy, to the graceful *La scala di seta*, whose nocturnal Finale owes much to Mozart's *Le nozze di Figaro*.

When Ricordi announced plans to publish vocal scores of all of Rossini's operas during the 1850s and early 1860s, the composer was not altogether pleased with the project. As he wrote to Tito Ricordi on 14 December 1864: 'The edition you have undertaken will give rise, justifiably, to much criticism, since the same pieces of music will be found in various operas: the time and money accorded me to compose were so *homeopathic* that I barely had time to read the so-called poetry to set to music.'[19] From 1812 to 1819 Rossini wrote twenty-seven operas,[20] an extraordinary compositional pace. Yet, with few exceptions, Rossini's borrowing was selective. He usually turned to works that had not circulated widely or that he did not expect to survive. Once an opera was popular, he left it alone. Nor did he usually engage in self-borrowing for the major works of his maturity, neither the principal comedies nor the great Neapolitan operas and *Semiramide*. The few exceptions reflect unusual situations. He lost interest in the Sinfonia as a genre by the mid-1810s, and for several years either recycled old ones or avoided a Sinfonia altogether. Since he never expected that *Il viaggio a Reims*, written as a celebratory work for the coronation of a king, would be revived, he found a new home for some 50 per cent of the score in *Le Comte Ory*. He would sometimes address a new audience by drawing on music he valued from operas that were less effective in their entirety. So, when Rossini composed his first work for Naples in 1815, *Elisabetta regina d'Inghilterra*, he drew heavily on themes from *Sigismondo* and *Torvaldo e Dorliska*, both unknown there. For his second Neapolitan opera, *La gazzetta* (1816), he turned to *Il turco in Italia*, but it was *La gazzetta* that the composer did not expect to circulate, since its principal character sang in Neapolitan dialect.

La gazzetta is based on a famous comedy by Carlo Goldoni, *Il matrimonio per concorso*. It consists of a Sinfonia and sixteen musical numbers, joined together by secco recitative. All the recitative and two musical numbers were prepared by a collaborator (for Rossini's use of collaborators, see below). Four numbers (and much of the Act 1 Finale) are entirely new. Five are taken in their entirety from earlier operas (four from *Il turco in Italia*, one from *La pietra del paragone*). Major sections of three others (including the *introduzione* and the Act 1 Finale) are derived from earlier operas (*Sigismondo* and *Torvaldo e Dorliska*), while a few melodies in the two remaining pieces, and the Sinfonia, are borrowed. What does this extensive self-borrowing tell us about Rossini's compositional methods?

In some cases, the structural conventions of Rossini's style encouraged self-borrowing. The theme in the dominant from the Sinfonia for *La gazzetta*, for example, is borrowed from the same structural point in the Sinfonia to *Torvaldo e Dorliska*, while in the quartet from *La gazzetta* the thematic material for a crescendo comes from a trio in *Il turco in Italia*: plugging these borrowed ideas into the new context caused Rossini no more difficulty than inventing an original melody. When adopting entire musical numbers, however, he needed to work closely with his librettist, Antonio Palomba, both to introduce the borrowed compositions elegantly into the new opera and to recast their poetry appropriately. In Act 1 of *La gazzetta* the job was simple: Goldoni's plot could easily accommodate a cavatina for the heroine, Lisetta, and a confrontation between Lisetta and her father, Don Pomponio. For the three borrowed numbers in Act 2, however, Palomba had to stray far from Goldoni: he needed to justify a comic trio for Don Pomponio, Filippo and Alberto, borrowed from *La pietra del paragone*, and to introduce a masked ball, so that Rossini could use a chorus and quintet from *Il turco in Italia*. The latter is not a particularly successful innovation, since it redundantly introduces a second set of disguises into the opera.

In *La gazzetta* Rossini notated every one of these borrowed pieces anew. Some changes are obligatory: new words and a reduction of instrumentation (*La gazzetta* uses only a single bassoon, for example, whereas most of the source operas used two). But throughout the composer recast his orchestration in large and small ways, modified vocal lines and rewrote cadenzas. There is nothing mechanical about his work, in short: he was both borrowing and recomposing. It hardly seems as if he saved very much time by engaging in this kind of self-borrowing, yet the practice may have eased somewhat the pressure of writing one new work after another, as many as five operas in a single year.

Occasionally Rossini met his frenetic compositional schedule during his Italian career by engaging a collaborator to assist him. When we possess the autograph manuscript of an entire opera (as we do for most of Rossini's works) the presence of a collaborator is self-evident. It is not only that some music within Rossini's complete manuscript is written in a different hand, but rather that the music is represented by a composing score, not by the fair copy of a previously composed piece. While sometimes we cannot identify the collaborators, in other cases they were important young composers with whom Rossini had cordial relations throughout his life: Michele Carafa for *Mosè in Egitto*, Giovanni Pacini for *Matilde di Shabran*. Even in his use of music by collaborators, however, the composer's practice was more interesting than facetious anecdotes would suggest.

Rossini generally assigned collaborators two tasks: to compose secco recitative and to write an occasional short piece of lesser importance, including so-called *arie di sorbetto* ('sherbet arias') sung by secondary characters. This is the case in *L'italiana in Algeri*, all of whose recitative and two short arias in the second act (for Lindoro and Haly) are by an unknown collaborator, and in *La Cenerentola*, with recitative and three numbers (the arias for Alidoro and Clorinda and a brief chorus opening the second act) by a Roman musician, Luca Agolini. In both cases, though, Rossini was under immense time pressure: he agreed to prepare *L'italiana in Algeri* after another composer had failed to live up to his contract; the time between the decision to compose *La Cenerentola* (which replaced a libretto considered inappropriate for the Papal censorship in Rome) and its première was little more than one month. Even when Rossini called on a collaborator to do more significant work, there were good reasons. Gaspare Spontini pulled out of a commitment to the Teatro San Carlo of Naples at the last moment, and Rossini agreed to produce *La donna del lago* in the Autumn of 1819 in a very brief period. That a trusted collaborator composed a major aria for Duglas (Rossini's spelling) and much of the opera's accompanied recitative is less surprising than the quality and extent of the music Rossini himself composed under the circumstances, none of which is borrowed from earlier works.

More important, Rossini often participated in revivals of operas for which he had originally employed a collaborator, and on those occasions he would replace all or most of the complete musical numbers by another hand with new music of his own composition: that is the case with *L'italiana in Algeri*, *Il turco in Italia*, *La Cenerentola*, *Mosè in Egitto* and *Matilde di Shabran*. Some of these new numbers are particularly beautiful: the Lindoro aria from the second act of *L'italiana in Algeri* ('Concedi, amor pietoso') and the Alidoro aria for *La Cenerentola* ('Là del ciel') are lovely examples. The conclusions to be drawn could not be clearer. While Rossini was working in a system in which he was driven to make accommodations to the realities of theatrical life, he went out of his way to reassert his artistic integrity when he had the opportunity to do so.

The late music

Towards the end of his life, after the long suspension in his compositional activities following *Guillaume Tell*, Rossini produced an important group of pieces, which he called his *Péchés de vieillesse*.[21] The manuscripts of these late compositions, for the most part either for voice and piano or for piano solo, suggest quite different compositional methods from those of his operas.

Although Rossini always affirmed that he composed these late pieces for his personal pleasure, even if he shared them with friends who frequented his Parisian salon, he nonetheless wrote them with exceptional precision.

This preoccupation with detail may be related to the harmonic and melodic language he developed in the *Péchés de vieillesse*, which delight in unusual modal mixtures, harmonic detours and wayward voice-leading. Often the intention is parodistic, but Rossini's humour is intensely musical. Immediately after having finished a piece, he would have a copy prepared by an associate, and these copies were employed for performances at his *samedi soirs*. But the copyist occasionally 'corrected' what seemed to him errors. Rossini carefully reviewed the copyist's work and usually reinstated his original versions. There might be errors, he told a friend, but at least they were his own errors.[22] In fact, Rossini often went far beyond simple corrections of the copyist's errors: he made various emendations, adding signs of dynamics, pedalling, fingering, always in search of notational precision unthinkable during his operatic career. His efforts are amply visible in the 'Choeur de chasseurs démocrates', first composed in 1862 and later collected in the *Album français*. The piece went through a complex series of at least eight compositional stages, revolving around two strikingly different versions, each of which was elaborated in many copies and autographs. Everywhere the chorus was subjected to a continuing series of corrections involving every element of the music: articulation, voice-leading, melodic details, dynamic levels, harmony.[23] This intensive search for improvement in the context of pieces Rossini had no intention of publishing is quite extraordinary. Similar efforts are apparent in Rossini's compositional work on the masterpiece of his old age, the *Petite messe solennelle*, whose original scoring for two pianos and harmonium we now know to exist in two distinct versions.[24]

To the end, Rossini remained a composer intensely engaged in his art. At the same time he presented himself to the public behind a mask of irony, seeking to protect himself from hostility and incomprehension. His musical manuscripts, whether from his theatrical career or from his final years, reveal the seriousness of his engagement. Not through unfounded and facetious anecdotes will we understand the composer's attitude towards his own music, but rather through the clarity and precision of his musical notation. His compositional methods offer precious testimony to Rossini's humanity and artistry.

7 The dramaturgy of the operas

MARCO BEGHELLI

The idea of a 'Rossinian dramaturgy', which is occasionally given an airing, may be a misleading abstraction: much as *Tancredi* or *La Cenerentola* may seem epiphanies of a personal poetic, to what extent were they the largely predictable results of contemporary artistic convention? The 'author's intentions', however powerful, always have to reckon with a sort of 'opera's intentions', a fixed framework within which the composer has limited space for manoeuvre: to compose within a genre means, after all, submitting at least partially to its language and structure, if one does not want to see the work excluded from the genre itself. While this is the case for every artistic genre, it is all the more so for Italian opera, which until the early nineteenth century flourished on this fertile dialectic between originality and convention.

What is more, opera could be called a trinitarian text: a syncretic product resulting from the confluence of three distinct texts, verbal, musical and visual, technically known as the libretto, the score and the *mise en scène* or staging. Each has a different author: poet (librettist), composer and staging director respectively. (The identity of this last gradually changed over time, and is fragmented today into the different professions of director, scenographer, costume designer, choreographer and lighting designer. For convenience we will consider these as one 'author', similar to librettists or composers who worked as a pair.) Each of the three texts has a different weight: on the creative level, the verbal text precedes and conditions the others; on the level of transmission and reception, the score becomes the primary aesthetic object, the only one capable of sustaining theatrical interest in the work; and finally, on the executive level, the staging inevitably boasts a prominence which at times overwhelms (or impoverishes) the musico-dramatic text upon which it is superimposed.

Rather than Rossinian dramaturgy, then, we might speak of a dramaturgy of Rossini's operas, in which artistic responsibility is divided among a group of authors just as in other contemporary operas. The more individual and original aspects of each opera, meanwhile, elude any attempt at classification precisely on account of their idiosyncrasy. They include the stylistic traits which differentiate *opera seria* from *opera buffa*, the early works from the mature ones, Italian from French: every genre, every style, even every score, it could be argued, presents its very own dramaturgy. What we seek to delineate here, therefore, is a 'lowest common denominator' of Rossini's operas – which is inevitably common to all early nineteenth-century Italian opera.[1]

While the three constituent texts of an opera are autonomous, each is, however, insufficient in itself. Furthermore, the visual text is much less codified than the other two; we have little evidence of its original appearance (that is, what the audience saw at the première of *Semiramide* or *Guillaume Tell*): a few images in prints and sketches in addition to brief stage directions annotated in the libretto and score, realisable in an infinite number of different ways. In Rossini's time as well as today the visual text was as changeable from one production to another as it was vital for its impact on the audience, and in this sense comparable to the creative input of singers through their stage presence and vocal gifts. These contributions were indeed crucial in the economy of the opera, often bearing the real responsibility for its success or failure, and often overly influential in modifying or distorting the dramatic design of the original text. However, the ephemeral nature of both the visual dimension and such personal inflexions, lying beyond the fixity of a written text, precludes discussion of them here, even though their influence on the act of composition is clear: the composer worked with the scenic and vocal capacities of a theatre company already in mind. We will concentrate, then, on the verbal and musical texts of opera as fixed on paper.

A morganatic marriage between words and music

The libretto is a fully fledged poetic work, even though it has traditionally been neglected by literary historians, who tend not to consider it literature because it is not aesthetically autonomous. Although structured in acts and scenes and furnished with stage directions like any verse tragedy for the spoken theatre, without song an opera libretto would be completely inadequate for recitation on account of specific characteristics which mark it out as expressly predisposed for setting to specific musical forms. For example, we see a clear opposition between two distinct metrical systems specifically designed for corresponding compositional systems: sections in *versi sciolti* alternate with sections in *versi lirici*.[2] In the Metastasian system, current for a good part of the eighteenth century, *versi sciolti* had been used for dialogue between the characters, to inform the spectator of the minute details of the plot and advance the action, while *versi lirici* had dealt more specifically with moments of reflection, 'lyrical' outbursts in which a sentiment or thought was extended in a brief composition of one or two stanzas. In the nineteenth century, on the other hand, a decisive homogenisation occurred: rhymed strophes of *versi lirici* were used to set passages of action just as often as soliloquies.

The juxtaposition of these two metrical systems was however functional in the construction of the musical score, which adopted an equally polarised compositional style. *Versi sciolti* are sung to rapid, stereotyped melodic formulas (more or less unchanged from the Baroque era), sustained by simple harmonies in either the basso continuo (secco recitative) or the strings (accompanied recitative). The name 'recitative' refers to the character of simple recitation, with a declamatory rhythm that closely follows that of an actor in the spoken theatre. The attention of the spectator is directed wholly to the 'referential' meaning of the word, the music remaining in a supporting rôle deprived of aesthetic prominence. *Versi lirici*, on the other hand, are intended for real musical composition (arias, duets, choruses, etc.), where the spectator's attention is firmly directed towards the 'poetic' dimension of sound, particularly the voice. The verbal text often seems nothing more than a pretext for triggering communicative processes more complex than the simple narration of an event in music: displays of vocal virtuosity, but also of expressivity, dramatic force, compositional skill and everything else that makes an opera score like any other musical score. It is, in fact, these truly 'musical' moments – the so-called 'closed pieces' – that demonstrate the stylistic differences between composers, historical periods and genres.

In musical performance *versi sciolti*, subordinated to recitative formulas, stretch out into prose, while *versi lirici* risk being blurred by the stretching and compression, expansion and acceleration, omission and repetition to which the musical declamation often subjects the text after a first linear exposition. The same verse, for example, can be sung with a scansion relatively similar to spoken recitation – save for some stretching which exaggerates its regularity (ex. 7.1a) – or it can be drowned in a sea of notes, the word becoming a mere support for the singing, pure phoneme (ex. 7.1b). As much as the intonation of recitative verses allows semantic perception to be safeguarded, in closed pieces this tends progressively to diminish the more the voice shifts away from dry declamation towards sheer vocalisation. This is exacerbated by the singing technique adopted in the opera house, which hampers clean, consonant articulation, particularly in female voices and in the highest registers.

The limited comprehensibility of the verbal text is in fact a distinctive trait of opera that sets it apart from other theatrical genres. The classic anxiety of the first-time spectator to understand every word said by every character is unjustified – understanding the text is a feat impossible even for mother-tongue spectators. Especially in the sections of *versi lirici*, librettos are by constitution redundant texts, awash with words necessary only to sustain melody. As Stendhal wrote, 'whoever worries about the *words* in *opera seria*? They are always the same, *felicità, felice ognora, crude stelle*, etc.

Example 7.1a *La Cenerentola*, Andante maestoso, 'Parlar, pensar vorrei', in Act 1 Finale

(Par - lar, pen-sar vor-re — i, par-lar, pen - sar non — so).

Example 7.1b *La Cenerentola*, Andante maestoso, 'Parlar, pensar vorrei', in Act 1 Finale

(Par - lar, _____ pen - sar _____ vor - re — - - - i, par

- lar, _____ pen - sar _____ non _____ so, no, no, no, no, no, no, no, no).

etc., and I doubt if a single person in all Venice ever read the text of a *libretto serio*; not even the impresario himself who had commissioned and paid for it!'[3]

Situations and musical numbers

The merit of a libretto does not lie in its intrinsic poetic value, then; even Verdi, praising the libretto for *Rigoletto*, said that it was 'one of the most lovely librettos ever, except for the verses'.[4] Rather, the quality of a libretto depends firstly on its *appropriateness for musical setting*, determined by particular rhythms and structures in the text being suited to the given musical style (the predisposition of *versi sciolti* for recitative, *tronco* words at the end of each stanza, and the natural floweriness of the poetic style are relevant here). Secondly, and above all, the libretto must be *suitable for drama in music*, furnishing the composer with a series of scenic situations to spark the musical imagination. Stendhal, again, snapshots Rossini for us during a bout of fury with an unskilled librettist: 'You have provided me with verses but not with situations!'[5]

The nature of Rossinian opera, indeed Italian opera up to and including Verdi, rests substantially on the dramaturgical concept of *situazioni* (situations). This ambiguous term, used with different nuances by Italian opera librettists in their letters and by contemporary critics in their writings, should not be confused with the plot. The latter is the succession of various events that constitute the story to be told; *situazioni*, on the other hand, are the most powerful moments of that narrative, which punctuate the opera like the individual images in a picture book. They are the moments – for the most part stereotyped and common to the genre as a whole – on which the composer focuses his greatest attention: the serenade, the prayer, the solitary outburst, the palace feast, the drinking song, the hymn, the oath, the duel, the abduction, the recognition, the unexpected meeting, the public curse, the suicide, the hero's dying breath and so on.

Every situation, prepared through the recitative dialogue, gives rise to a single musical fresco, a 'closed piece' which can take the form of an aria, a duet, a trio, a chorus or a Finale. It is the situation which creates the music, sets the piece alight with a spark of drama; and the various pieces which constitute an opera are nothing but a succession of more or less conventional *dramatic situations*, transformed in turn into no less pre-constituted *musical situations*. Such musical passages, to which each section of recitative leads, were called 'numbers' by composers because they are numbered progressively from the first (usually called *introduzione*) to the last (in general a concluding grand aria, or a short Finale – *Finaletto* – for several characters). The sum of these various 'numbers' (fifteen, on average, in a two-act Rossinian opera; half as many in a one-act *farsa*), along with the intervening recitatives and an opening overture (Sinfonia), constitutes the musical score: a fragmentary and unhomogeneous product, in which the musical grey of the recitatives functions as an effective contrast to the intermittent colour of the musical numbers – a vital alternation which prevents monotony.

An opera of this type is thus rather like an exhibition of pictures in sound, which, although subject to a dramatic text and connected by a developing narrative, is dominant in aesthetic terms over the other artistic parameters. (One goes to the opera to enjoy musical, not verbal, narration; to be beguiled by a sonorous plot, not a dramatic one; to such a degree, indeed, that the lack of originality of the story was never considered problematic, most librettos deriving from stage dramas or novels.) But this musical predominance does not at all mean the reduction of opera to a concert of arias or duets: lack of originality in the plot does not mean lack of dramatic interest, which was instead always feared by librettists and composers alike. The narrative dimension of the music alone is not enough in itself, as recent staged exhumations of Rossini's *cantate sceniche* (cantatas for the stage) without any real stage action have demonstrated. 'The different *pezzi cantabili*, from which a libretto is woven', Carlo Ritorni wrote in 1841, 'should proceed from *situazioni*, each intended for musical setting.'[6] Without a strong dramatic situation to sustain a musical number, the score sounds like a series of effects without cause; this impression is given even in the best operas when an aria begins without a real dramatic reason, having been included solely to comply with theatrical conventions demanding a certain number of particular pieces in particular places in the score.

The *programma musicale*

The librettist's first task, therefore, was to parcel out the narrative into individual, well-defined dramatic moments, which were to become equally distinct musical forms. This was a process of continuous mediation between what compositional convention and customary expectation required and what the chosen subject suggested, the dramaturgical unit always remaining the musical number.

To see for ourselves how the structure of a Rossini opera was developed from an initial sketch or programme of musical situations ('programma' or 'ossatura'), we can read an account of the genesis of *La Cenerentola* left to us by librettist Jacopo Ferretti:

> There were only two days left before Christmas in the year 1816, when . . . I was begged to find and write a new subject at great speed . . . We holed ourselves up in the house . . . I proposed twenty or thirty subjects; but this one was considered too serious . . . this one too complicated, this one prohibitively costly for the impresario . . . and finally this one not suited to the singers for whom it was destined. Tired of suggesting, and half dead on my feet from fatigue, I mumbled through half a yawn: 'Cendrillon'; and Rossini . . . sitting up . . . 'Would you have the heart to write *Cendrillon* for me?', he asked me, and I replied to him: 'And you to set it to music?', and he: 'When will we have the programme?', and I: 'Despite my exhaustion, tomorrow morning' . . . and I ran home. There . . . I paced the length and breadth of my great bedroom with my arms folded, and when God willed it, and I saw the scene before my eyes, I wrote the programme for *La Cenerentola* and the following day I sent it to Rossini. He was happy with it.[7]

Unfortunately, no such outline for *La Cenerentola* seems to be extant; but it is easy to get an idea of its form by looking at the analogous 'programme' another librettist had formulated for *Il barbiere di Siviglia* a few months earlier (see chapter 5). Those who know the opera will see in this preliminary outline a good approximation of the layout of the final score. Note, though, that the sequence of events is viewed almost exclusively in terms of the music, and voices in particular ('Tenor's Cavatina', 'another for the Prima Donna'). There are very few indications about the development of the narrative; it is not a succession of events so much as a plan of musical numbers destined to incarnate single events, single situations.

'We have drafted the outline [ossatura]', wrote the librettist Gaetano Rossi to his friend Giacomo Meyerbeer, recounting his first meeting with Rossini about *Semiramide*. 'He approved all the situations that I had already settled on' (GRLD, vol. II, no. 344). Evidently the poet had satisfyingly distributed the dramatic material among the obligatory musical numbers. These usually included an *introduzione*, which is an almost ritual opening, formally complex and incorporating many voices. It often throws the audience into the thick of the action in a deliberately bewildering fashion, until events finally begin to be clarified in the first recitative (a similar opening gambit is used in many Steven Spielberg films). Then there was a series of dramatically static cavatinas, that is, arias which present the main characters (one was sometimes placed in the *introduzione*); they were so obligatory that not giving one to a protagonist only served to make her more conspicuous by her absence (see *Otello, Armida, Ricciardo e Zoraide, Ermione, Zelmira*). Duets for the principals in various combinations were interwoven throughout, and there were also numbers for groups of voices (trios, quartets, quintets, sextets, with or without chorus, according to dramatic necessity), of which one, the largest and most complex, functions at the end of Act 1 as the central Finale. There were usually a *rondò* for the protagonists, that is, grand arias with chorus placed in Act 2, one of which might function as the closing number (*Elisabetta regina d'Inghilterra, La Cenerentola, La donna del lago, Bianca e Falliero, Matilde di Shabran*). Otherwise, the closing number was a *Finaletto* in vaudeville style, where the characters sing in turn a short parting stanza, with the chorus providing interjections (*Tancredi, Aureliano in Palmira, Il barbiere di Siviglia, La gazza ladra, Ricciardo e Zoraide*); or a moral intoned collectively at the footlights, on the eighteenth-century model (*L'equivoco stravagante, L'italiana in Algeri, Il turco in Italia*, and the one-act *farse*); or some other less codified structure (*Mosè in Egitto, Maometto II, Semiramide*) composed according to the requirements of the action.

The rest of the opera the composer was free to shape as he wished, particularly the remainder of the second (or third) act, which might include supplementary arias. These were usually also called cavatinas, in the eighteenth-century manner, if in one movement (Amenaide's 'No, che il morir non è' in *Tancredi*, Uberto's 'Oh fiamma soave' in *La donna del lago*), or *romances* in French opera if they were strophic in form (Mathilde's 'Sombre forêt, désert triste et sauvage' in *Guillaume Tell*). There may also be *canzoni*, stage songs understood to be heard as songs by the characters onstage, and which would also be sung in the spoken theatre (Desdemona's Willow Song, Cenerentola's 'Una volta c'era un Re'); choruses that stood alone or, more often, were annexed to solo numbers (chorus and cavatina; chorus and *rondò*); generic *scene*, that is, recitatives with notable orchestral support which introduced solo numbers (*scena* and duet; chorus, *scena* and *rondò*); and instrumental pieces, from the overture to the dances and accompanimental pieces for marches, battles or other pantomimes. An early-nineteenth-century Italian opera is the sum of all this (see the list of numbers in the index of any score).

Once the outline was fixed, the librettist versified each item in accordance with the formal conventions for that particular musical number.[8]

This draft of the libretto inevitably proceeded in blocks: in the case of *La Cenerentola*, 'On Christmas Day [1816], Rossini had the *introduzione*; on Santo Stefano [26 December] the cavatina for Don Magnifico; on San Giovanni [27 December] the duet for the Prima Donna and Tenor', and so on, until the libretto had been completed.[9]

The value of conventions

La Cenerentola went on stage on 26 January 1817, exactly one month from the first contractual agreements. In those thirty days, a librettist reinvented a dramatic subject starting from an earlier libretto by somebody else (fairly distant from Charles Perrault's fairytale model), organised it into a musical outline suited to an opera score of the period, conceived dialogues and translated them into poetry. In the meantime the composer set the verses to music, while one of his collaborators was busy writing the recitatives and three less important numbers in order to speed up the work (as in Renaissance painting studios). A censor read the libretto and suggested modifications considered necessary to public decorum, while a typographer waited for the definitive version to set for printing. In the theatre, scenographers and costume designers were begging the librettist to tell them as quickly as possible how many and which characters would be employed onstage, in what dress and which settings, so that they could provide what was necessary, while a copyist extracted the parts from the score. These the singers and chorus members had to commit to memory, and the orchestral parts had to be duplicated the necessary number of times for the orchestra. The one who suffered most was the impresario, always at risk of a heart attack, terrified that the slightest accident would delay the opening night: given that in 1817 Carnival would end on 18 February – the unchangeable date for the Lenten closure of the theatres – very few days would be left to recover his costs from ticket sales (always assuming that a fiasco would not oblige him to retract the score on the opening night!).

In this finely balanced production line, the acceptance of convention by all parties was indispensable, speeding up work by eliminating the need for explanations and negotiations. Everything, in a sense, was defined *a priori*, beginning with the engagement of a company of singers formed according to a cast of stereotypical rôles, which then corresponded to the number and types in the libretto. A contralto *prima donna*, a soprano *seconda donna*, a *primo tenore*, a *buffo cantante*, a *buffo caricato* and a less important bass could competently perform not only *Il barbiere di Siviglia* but *La Cenerentola* or *L'italiana in Algeri* – or any other new comic opera, Rossini's or not. Shorthand phrases such as 'cavatina with choruses', 'aria for the tutor' or 'aria for the *seconda donna*' in the outline for *Il barbiere* imply a much more exact agreement between poet and composer than those simple words at first seem to indicate: behind the titles lie an extremely precise vocabulary, forms and styles familiar to everyone in the theatre from the impresario to the librettist, the composer to the singer, the audience to the reviewer. For the tutor's aria, for example (traditionally a comic aria), Rossini would certainly have expected the librettist to provide an endless series of stanzas, which most often derived their comic character from a barrage of words and images.[10] For the *prima donna*'s or tenor's aria, on the other hand – rôles that were vocally and dramatically more serious even in comic opera – the formal structure was the same multi-sectional one as in *opera seria* (see below). For a secondary rôle, the model remained the da capo aria of eighteenth-century lineage, in comic opera just as in the serious and semiserious genres. A quick glance at a libretto of the period therefore provides many signs as to the nature of the score, and the musical personalities of its characters. The structure of a libretto was prescriptive, even though the composer was free to interpret its suggestions in his own way.

The typical structure of a musical number

The most frequent formal model in a Rossini libretto is a structure as present in the repertory as it is elusive on account of its polymorphism. Before analysing this structure, typical of a good 70 per cent of Rossini numbers (duet or finale, in *seria* or *buffa*, Italian or French opera), we should recall part of our earlier discussion. The Metastasian dichotomy between action recitatives and reflective arias had been superseded by the beginning of the nineteenth century, with the steady introduction of action into the body of the closed number. The musical number continued to function as the 'emotional outcome', amplified and sublimated in music, of action conveyed in the preceding recitative; but more often it took that action further – in fact, almost everything significant in Rossinian drama occurs in a closed number. The moment of stasis, of reflection, does not disappear entirely: it remains the key moment, but it has to share with other elements of the drama, which encroach on it from either side. The closed number thus became less and less closed in itself, now articulated in *musical subsections*, each one of which corresponds again to *dramatic subsections*. Nobody at the time named this formal structure; nobody labelled its constituent parts; but its presence and persistence in contemporary writings, not to mention its distinctness in aural terms, is indisputable.

It is worth re-emphasising that the closed number is both dramatic and musical in nature; in this sense its lineage may be traced back to

late-eighteenth-century grand arias. As in many arias for Mozart's heroines, an Adagio was followed by an Allegro, melodic *cantabilità* by rigorous
virtuosity, self-reflection by renewed strength to react to events. These two
dramatic-musical sections, called 'cantabile' and 'stretta', provided the basis
for the early-nineteenth-century number.[11] Dozens of Rossini's arias are
limited to this simple two-part scheme, especially when the character finds
herself alone on stage without interlocutors to act as *pertichino* (literally,
'extra horse with the job of hauling', and metaphorically 'a sidekick who
provides interjections'). Consider, for example, the *scena* and cavatina for
Malcom (Rossini's spelling) in *La donna del lago*. After a long recitative
with orchestra (*scena*, 'Mura felici, ove il mio ben si aggira'), in which
the hero delights in thoughts of love, his affection for the woman is idealised in a bipartite aria (cavatina, with its cantabile 'Elena! oh tu, ch'io
chiamo!' and *stretta*, 'Oh quante lacrime – finor versai'). In the nineteenth
century, as in the eighteenth, a cantabile still relied on a variety of formal
structures (ABA, for example); the *stretta*, however, assumed a well-defined
shape: a melodic period, complete in itself, is repeated with the same text.
This is the 'cabaletta', a term of uncertain origin which probably implies
an 'intriguing little motive, captivating for its marked melodic character'.
Some 'bridge' bars, melodically 'grey', separate the two statements, the latter leading finally to a powerful coda. It does not need an expert in musical
analysis to identify this segmentation: the structure is clear to any theatre-
goer, now as then, and it is the essential foundation for the pre-ordained
rhetorical sweep from dry introductory recitative, through rocking cantabile
to the fireworks of the concluding *stretta* (which many call cabaletta, by
synecdoche).

In complex pieces, however, the two principal areas, cantabile and *stretta*,
share the musical number with more dynamic supplementary sections
which inject action into the piece, as mentioned above, and which can reach
massive proportions. (The single unifying element, among so much multi-
plicity, is the key of the piece, almost always re-established at the end of the
number, whatever deviations may have occurred unexpectedly during its
course.) Contemporary terminology helps us still less with these sections:
today the terms 'tempo d'attacco' or 'primo tempo' are common for the
opening section, which precedes the cantabile, and 'tempo di mezzo' is used
for the section between the cantabile and the *stretta*.

All this can be illustrated by a passage from *La Cenerentola*, a musical
number in clear four-part form, which the librettist would simply have indicated in the musical outline as 'grand'aria del tenore' – as did his colleague
for *Il barbiere* – or more technically, 'rondò' (in Rossini's autograph it bears
the generic title 'aria Ramiro'). The dramatic situation is quickly described:
Prince Ramiro has allowed the mysterious beauty he met at the palace to

escape, leaving behind a single clue to her identity (here a bracelet rather than a shoe). The long preparatory *scena*, first in secco recitative and then accompanied recitative, has advanced the action as far as the Prince's resolution to find his beloved at any cost, with the sole help of the clue; the shift from prosaic secco recitative (used throughout the preceding verses) to the noble accompanied recitative underlines the significance of the following aria in dramatic as well as musical terms:

RAMIRO
[. . .] di tante sciocche
si vuoti il mio palazzo.
(*chiamando i suoi seguaci, che entrano*)
        Olà, miei fidi,
sia pronto il nostro cocchio, e fra
   momenti . . .
Così potessi aver l'ali dei venti.

RECITATIVE
(0) preparatory *scena*

Sì, ritrovarla io giuro.
Amore, amor mi muove:
se fosse in grembo a Giove,
io la ritroverò.

ARIA
(1) *tempo d'attacco*
dramatically kinetic, in real time; communication between characters is active

(*contempla lo smaniglio*)
(Pegno adorato e caro
che mi lusinghi almeno,
ah come al labbro e al seno,
come ti stringerò!)
CHORUS
Oh! qual tumulto ha in seno;
comprenderlo non so.

(2) *cantabile*
dramatically static, in expanded time; introspection; communication among characters is for the most part suspended

RAMIRO AND CHORUS
Noi voleremo, – domanderemo,
ricercheremo, – ritroveremo.

(3) *tempo di mezzo*
dramatically kinetic, in real time; communication among characters resumes

RAMIRO AND CHORUS
Dolce speranza, – freddo timore
dentro al mio/suo core – stanno a pugnar.
Amore, amore – m'hai/l'hai da guidar.
(*parte con i seguaci*)

(4) *stretta* (cabaletta I, bridge, cabaletta II, coda) dramatically static, outside time: the action is already completed; strictly musical logic

It is worth taking time to discuss each segment in more detail.

No. 1: *tempo d'attacco*

'Yes, I swear I will find her again. Love, love moves me. Even if she were in the arms of Jove, I would find her again.'

Calling the moment dramatically *kinetic* calls attention to the sense of action within the aria:[12] the prince's emphatic oath before his court dignitaries unfolds before the audience as an event in real time. The florid technique that Rossini adopts here has no less an expressive value than the trumpets which sound ritually in the orchestra: virtuosity is by convention the language of nobility, of heroes. The style of this oath strengthens its rhetorical import, with the grandiloquence one might expect from a prince.

No. 2: *cantabile*

'(*contemplating the bracelet*) Beloved and adored token, that gives me at least hope, oh, how I will press you to my lips and heart!'

Here we arrive at the heart of the aria. The musical colours soften; the modern director lowers the lights – an effect already achieved in musical terms in the orchestra – and spotlights the character; he comes to the footlights, removing himself from the reality surrounding him. This is the moment of introspection; communication between characters is suspended, as the parentheses around the verses demonstrate, and the prince's thoughts go unheard by those on stage ('Oh, what tumult is in his breast! I cannot understand it'). We are in the realm of the unrealistic, in keeping with the operatic nature of such moments. In spoken theatre, or cinema, this brief act of passionate contemplation would be expressed in a simple languid sigh, a silent look; in opera, the introspective moment develops into a full musical passage which lyricises the fleeting moment. If a clock were onstage, its hands would have to slow down until they had almost stopped, illustrating the concept of the relativisation of time.[13]

No. 3: *tempo di mezzo*

'We'll fly, we'll question, we'll seek, we'll find.'

The lights come back on, real time resumes, as does communication between the prince and his dignitaries. If we were in spoken theatre or a film, the scene would end at this point, with the characters hurrying towards their new venture. But opera is a spectacle infamous for incongruous cries of 'I'm coming to save you' while the character remains onstage for repeat after repeat. This seems a little less absurd, though, if we consider it in the context of the operatic principle whereby the 'referential' function of the drama must always allow for the 'poetic' function of the music, vocal performance in particular. Therefore:

No. 4: *stretta*

'Sweet hope, cold fear within my/his heart are battling. Love, love, you must guide me/him. (*He leaves with his courtiers*).'

All that needed to be said has already been said; therefore the character promptly withdraws and yields to the singer – the prince to the tenor – for an impressive conclusion, outside dramatic time and intended to coax applause from the audience. The structure of this section is designed specifically for the gratification of the performer and his fans: in the customary repetition of the cabaletta (a practice that is slowly being revived today) the composer gave the performer free rein to intervene at will in the vocal line, in an outburst of musical invention and vocal display complete with a final high note on the dominant chord (not the tonic, as is so often heard today).

Such a dramatic-musical structure suits not only arias, but all the principal 'situations' of the plot, whether solos, duets or ensembles. An example of its typical application to a duet might be the following: (0) two lovers meet after a long separation, during which he has mistakenly understood her to be unfaithful; (1) the two confront one another, flinging accusations: 'Faithless one, don't come near me' – 'Don't treat me so unjustly', etc.; (2) an interior monologue for both, each on their own: 'What have I done to deserve such pain?'; (3) they advance reciprocal explanations: 'We have been misled, we should make peace'; (4) common joy: 'United forever!' Such a structure is even more suitable for a central Finale, the moment at the end of the first act where the plot is brought to a point of crisis: (0) the characters convene in the same place, often inadvertently; (1) they meet each other, and agitation mounts progressively until the explosion of a dramatic and musical bombshell (a curse, a fatal revelation, the unexpected appearance of another character who upsets everyone's plans, etc.); (2) grand ensemble of shock: everyone is astonished at the event, and expresses their dismay in a large ensemble, a broad tapestry of sound; (3) return to reality: dialogue until the definitive crisis; (4) great uproar, musical babel, with words that add nothing to the action, since everything has already been said.

Playing with forms

The single sections of this form – called *la solita forma* ('standard' or 'usual form') according to a neologism of dubious pedigree but effective impact[14] – are really self-contained modules (which is one crucial premise for the phenomenon of Rossinian self-borrowing).[15] They can also occur in a varied form, perhaps missing a section or engulfed by one much larger than the others, without losing their identity. The essence of a cantabile lies not in its placement in second position, but in its dramatic-musical nature. It is therefore still perceived as such both in a cavatina or a *rondò* without the first section (actually the majority of cases), or in an expanded sub-species of *rondò* which in Rossini goes by the name of *gran scena*, and provides two distinct cantabiles, the first a lyric episode in the introductory recitative (the cavatina of eighteenth-century heritage mentioned above), the other an integral part of the *rondò* proper (*Ciro in Babilonia, Tancredi, Aureliano in Palmira, Ermione, Bianca e Falliero*). The same can be said for certain central finales (in *Tancredi*, for example, or in *Otello*), where a double *coup de scène* provokes two distinct *larghi concertati* (the name given to section 2 of ensemble pieces, where 'largo' refers to the generic slow tempo and 'concertato' to the compositional technique, often a canonic opening in which each voice retains autonomy, 'concertising' with the other voices).

In other cases, numbers intersect, creating irregular forms. Usually, however, the classic subsections can still be discerned. In the sextet from *Il viaggio a Reims*, for example, a *canzone* of three whole strophes, accompanied by solo harp, is inserted wedge-like into the *tempo di mezzo*: a completely self-sufficient musical number is developed within another. Or there are numbers that never run their full course because another character arrives and cuts in, singing a new *solita forma* in all its glory (rather than the remainder of the number thus far sung). This is the case in Act 2 of *Elisabetta regina d'Inghilterra*, where the two women are interrupted by their common lover during the *tempo di mezzo* of their duet. This immediately mutates into a *tempo d'attacco*, which in turn starts off a full-scale four-part trio. (Interestingly, we can see from the libretto that the poet had foreseen quite another structure, with a single three-voiced concertato; the composer remodelled it to his own ends.)

A musical number therefore runs a well-defined course, both dramatically and musically, which is planned by agreement between a librettist and a composer who work within the same theatrical conventions, yet are always ready to subvert them quietly. The audience is nonetheless capable of perceiving the number (notwithstanding possible ambiguities) for what it is: a pre-ordained micro-drama presented in a rhetorically effective form. When such a four-part structure is applied to an encounter between two or more characters, the narrative trajectory is rendered even more vivid; even a solo aria, the most dramatically static piece, is however experienced as a musico-dramatic event complete in itself, with a beginning that seems to come from nowhere and a momentum towards a liberating end. As 'opera is a complete musical gallery' of contrasting affects, so the single number has to be 'a complete painting'.[16]

Action made music

An opera score of Rossini's time can therefore be read not only as a musical realisation of a succession of dramatic events, but also a 'dramatic' succession of musical events – in other words, the narration of a drama laced with musical, rather than verbal or visual, *coups de scène*. This was how Stendhal's Venetian gentlewoman with an aversion to librettos perceived the genre (see the beginning of chapter 5), and so might the cosmopolitan modern spectator, who through his or her own linguistic limitations grasps only the clues gleaned hurriedly from the programme book prior to the performance. Interest is maintained entirely by this musical drama, and the plot takes second place.

From this it follows that what really reaches the spectator's consciousness is not what is said, but what is sung: Rossini's Otello can express his love for Desdemona a million times, but if he never has a love duet with her the nature of his love will never be conveyed to the audience (a daring dramatic choice which, as is well known, Boito and Verdi subverted in their adaptation of the subject). By contrast, the protagonist of *La donna del lago*, wooed by three different suitors, continues to profess her faithfulness to her inexperienced teenage lover Malcom throughout the opera; but only when faced with the mature virility of the King does she sing, in turmoil, a musically overwhelming stretta *a due* ('Cielo! In qual estasi / rapir mi sento'). However much the words – incomprehensible, of course, to the listener – strain to affirm the contrary, any listener will perceive the heroine's unexpected desire, experienced for the first and only time in her life, and never to be revived for her young lover. The duet with the latter soon to follow is in fact a *duettino*, that is, a duet that stops after section 2 of the multi-partite structure: Rossini forbids her the thrills of excitement with Malcom in a *stretta*, allowing only a tender cantabile caress.

Vocal rôles

The all-musical dramaturgy of such a theatrical product ends up, then, transmuting into a narration of song-events: the characters of the plot are voices, which contrast and couple on behalf of the characters they represent. Everything is a function of voice, and on voice everything turns: the classic narrative triangle (him, her, the third party) could become a quadrilateral if, one season, there were an extra singer on a company's roster. Characters such as Rodrigo in *La donna del lago*, Calbo in *Maometto II* or Idreno in *Semiramide* (to mention three fully mature operas) could in other creative

circumstances just as well have been left out, or at least limited to secondary rôles. And perhaps it was no accident that, as if to justify their presence, Rossini gave them his most vocally arduous and thankless rôles of all.

That said, though, identifying a typical Rossinian triangle is far from straightforward, in so far as the years 1810–30 saw a decisive change in vocal practice – one which involved Rossini himself. The *prima donna*'s pre-eminence established and undisputed (be she a soprano or contralto, depending on availability), in comic opera the corresponding love rôle was usually in the tenor range, and 'mezzo carattere' (that is, neither completely serious nor completely comic). The antagonist was a 'buffo', a male character of low vocal register, and a comic part: a father, tutor, husband or someone else who could be characterised as an old grumbler. This vocal triangle is exemplified clearly by Isabella, Lindoro and Taddeo in *L'italiana in Algeri*, Rosina, Almaviva and Bartolo in *Il barbiere di Siviglia*, and Angelina, Ramiro and Magnifico in *La Cenerentola*. The contrast between the couple and the antagonist is clear in vocal terms: 'donna' and 'mezzo carattere' employ a 'noble', virtuosic style, while the buffo champions a 'prosaic', syllabic style (quite unrelated to social rank). Alongside this so-called 'buffo caricato', there is often a 'buffo nobile' or 'buffo cantante' (again, 'noble' in singing style, certainly not social rank) cast in the rôle of protagonist: Mustafà, Figaro and Dandini are typical examples, being the real driving forces of their respective operas even though they are outside the basic love triangles. Around this triangle a number of secondary characters, 'comprimari', also appear; however excellent these may be, they nonetheless remain secondary accessories – *seconda donna*, *secondo tenore*, *basso*, etc.

In *opera seria*, however, the rôle of male lover could be given to one of two voice types. According to the eighteenth-century tradition, he would be a 'soprano' or 'uomo' or 'musico', three equivalent but ambiguous terms used to indicate the rôle of a young male hero sung by a voice in the female range (castrato or woman; soprano, mezzo or contralto depending on the singer). On the example of *opera buffa*, however, the lover tended over the years to be given increasingly to the less idealised and more realistic timbre of a tenor. The antagonist (in general, a father, king or rival) would as a tenor make a triangle with the *prima donna* and the *musico* (*Tancredi*, *Aureliano in Palmira*, *Adelaide di Borgogna*, *Bianca e Falliero* etc.), while in the more modern vocal arrangement he occupied a lower male register, from the archetypical example of *Guillaume Tell* to more or less the whole production of Donizetti, Bellini and Verdi. The apparently anomalous vocal triangle of operas such as *Otello*, *Ricciardo e Zoraide*, *Ermione*, *Zelmira* and others from Rossini's period at the Teatro San Carlo in Naples (seven of his most productive years) is explained by the fact that, alongside the prima donna Isabella Colbran, a pair of first-class tenors (Andrea Nozzari and Giovanni David, however different vocally they may have been) was engaged – more impresarial contingency than real artistic choice.[17] 'Today, looking back upon the occasion with a cool and detached mind, I would say that it was a mistake to have written the parts of Norfolk and Leicester for *two tenors*. However, I can answer for Rossini's rejoinder to *that* criticism: "I happened to *have* two tenors at my disposal, whereas I had no *basso* to play Norfolk." The truth is that, before Rossini's time, it was a tradition that major parts in *opera seria* should never be given to the bass.'[18]

Voice duels

That it is the voice that 'makes the drama', more than the character who acts it out, is clearly demonstrated by the continual adjustment of formal structures on the basis of this assumption. A duet, for example, is not only the meeting of two heroes, but above all a duel between two heroic voices pitted against each other. When an Otello and a Rodrigo challenged each other to combat in the second act of the opera, the duel was fought, to put it bluntly, by Nozzari and David in front of the Neapolitan audience. With voices for swords, thrusts and parries take the form of rivalling high notes; at stake are fame and career, in a confrontation where the two singers are restricted to proving themselves with the same notes, one after the other. In a solo aria the individual singer gambles independently with the different vocal styles skilfully encapsulated in the multipartite form; in an ensemble each section is the property of every character, and each singer must have the chance to put their skills to the test in a display of rhetorical power meant to convince the other characters with their words and gestures, but really intended to win the audience over with their vocal reasoning.

The duet in the first act of *Bianca e Falliero* illustrates the typical division of the form between two characters, starting with the poetic text. 'The form of the duet is produced by one character answering the other in the same number of words', Ritorni tells us.[19] The *tempo d'attacco* opens with two parallel stanzas that express opposing concepts:

BIANCA	FALLIERO
Sappi che un rio dovere	Se tu mi sei fedele,
al nostro amor si oppone . . .	se il cor non hai cambiato,
Sappi che il padre impone ch'io	il genitore e il fato
più non pensi a te.	sfido a rapirti a me.
Know that sad duty	If you are faithful to me,
Sets itself against our love . . .	If your heart has not changed,
Know that my father insists	I dare your father and fate
I think no longer of you.	To take you from me.

These stanzas are rather like open letters sent to the opposite party in the presence of the audience, two equally appealing speeches composed, as is usual, of a first, melodically open part (the first couplet) and a second, closing one.[20] Grand vocal gestures, roulades and magniloquent cadences follow each other without rest, displaying mastery of the entire vocal range, underlining the elocutive force of the statement. Only when the first character triumphantly concludes her offensive does the letter of reply by the second character begin, with different words but the same music, in order to demonstrate his ability to match his opponent's rhetorical force (the tonality might change to suit the second character; here, Falliero, a contralto, sings Bianca's proposal in the dominant). Then the exchanges become swifter, the voices gradually get closer, until they unite in the cantabile, where they slide over one another in thirds and sixths:

FALLIERO	BIANCA
Ciel! Qual destin terribile	Ciel! Com'è mai possibile,
tronca ogni mia speranza!	serbar la mia costanza!

BIANCA and FALLIERO
A questo colpo orribile
manca la mia virtù.

[FAL: Heavens! What terrible fate puts an end to all my hopes! BIA: Heavens! How is it possible to keep my constancy! BIA and FAL: My virtue falters at this horrible blow.]

Whatever the words, it is this vocal embrace between the two characters, who become one in the so-called 'comune', the sensual cadenza *a due* without orchestral accompaniment, that is the crowning moment of such passages. Climax achieved, the *tempo di mezzo* shifts the voices apart once again, and they chase each other in a fast *parlante* (the technique where the rhythmic-melodic interest is borne entirely by the orchestra, the voices uttering fragmentary phrases over it). Only the *stretta* remains to complete the vocal drama of the duet, divided between the two voices in a number of ways. The calabetta theme may be sung by each voice in succession (similarly to the *tempo d'attacco*, especially if set to different words), delaying a vocal coupling until the repeat. Or – as here ('Ah! Dopo cotanto / penar per trovarsi') – it may be sung triumphantly together from the very first statement, and then repeated together with suitable ornamental variants.

The poetic of the double

This game of mirrors, the continual repetition of formal elements, permeates even the most minute details, going far beyond the contingency of two characters singing opposite one another. The use of repetition, of the 'double', in extreme cases takes us back into the realm of comedy (see the investiture of the 'Pappataci' in *L'italiana in Algeri*, and two similar gags in *L'equivoco stravagante*); but it is just as true that such musical parallelisms are fundamental to the artifice of early-nineteenth-century Italian opera and Rossini in particular. Everything, or almost everything, gets repeated, from macro-structures to micro-phrase-constituents. Behind such a behaviour lie deep-rooted anthropological models (parallelism of greetings, courtship, etc.), which have migrated to certain artistic forms.

In opera the benefits of repetition are felt on various levels. It provides for compositional economy, since the 'as above' and ritornellos indicated in manuscripts cover entire minutes of music without requiring further creative energy than writing the repeat sign. Comprehension of the verbal text is facilitated, since if the first statement is missed there is still a chance to understand the second. It is also more likely that significant melodic lines will be remembered, since already at the end of the first performance each important musical phrase has been heard at least twice. All this contributes to a satisfying listening experience.

This satisfaction is the real dramaturgical soul of an opera. Everything is meant to enhance the experience of listening, the *incontro* (the critics' technical term, literally 'meeting') with the audience constantly in mind. The audience is the motivating force of Italian opera, which is geared towards it and depends on it; and 'the gratitude of the audience towards whoever gives it great pleasure' wrote Balzac in *Massimilla Doni*, 'has something frenzied about it',[21] as Rossini proved in his day and does again in ours. He succeeded; other contemporary composers did not. Why does his *L'italiana in Algeri* delight us so much, while that composed by Luigi Mosca a few months earlier on the same libretto wrings from us a few smiles at most? 'Voilà, de l'électricité musicale!' they cried in Paris about Rossini's music. The real essence of his operatic dramaturgy – beyond the common traits of an entire production system examined here – could probably be traced by looking at these differences of 'incontro', through thorough examination of the strictly musical, audio-perceptual, elements. But investigations into this complex area are largely still to be undertaken.

(*translated by Laura Basini*)

8 Melody and ornamentation

DAMIEN COLAS

More than any other qualities of Rossini's operas, it was orchestration and melodic idiom that determined their success at the time of the first performances, and for us today they remain among the most significant aspects of the composer's art. While his orchestration displays distinctly novel tendencies, Rossini's melodic language is based on consolidation: an extreme refinement of two typically Italian traditions, the school of the castratos and the *concertante* aesthetic applied to the voice, coinciding historically with the disappearance of the first and the dwindling of the second. Rossini integrated into his writing for voices a system of expression perfectly suited to the training of the singers of his time. This continuity between Rossini's vocal grammar and that of his interpreters was crucial to the success of this art, and yet also precipitated its obsolescence when the performers, as time went on, lost the technical capacity to execute the proper diminutions and to ornament their own parts. But by that time Rossini's melodic language, directly as much as through singers, had already impregnated the music of numerous composers contemporary with, or immediately after, its progenitor. Even the most original among them – Donizetti, Bellini, Pacini, Mercadante, the young Verdi – had recourse to his style. It follows, then, that detailed knowledge of this style is a valuable tool in the study of all Italian opera in the first half of the nineteenth century.

Rossini's melodic aesthetic

By contrast with many composers, there is no significant divergence between Rossini's declared aesthetic ideals, in this case as they concern melody, and what is observable in his scores. This is evidence of an unusually close alliance of clearly defined artistic position and perfectly mastered technique. For Rossini, Italian music is not an imitative art, but rather one that is ideal and expressive. This art is incapable of representing human emotions and passions, as painting or sculpture do, but it has the power to awaken them in the soul of the listener. Its aim is to give pleasure and its means of doing so are based on rhythmic clarity and melodic simplicity. Like the Italian men of letters of his time, Rossini places melody at the centre of Italian musical art – postulates, indeed, that it is fundamental to Italian cultural identity. The limpid flow and firm metrical grounding of Italian melody are in opposition as much with the *mélopée* (dramatic monody) of the French *tragédie en musique* inherited from the eighteenth century as with the harmonic sophistication and finely honed inner parts of German Romanticism.[1]

Proceeding from these two basic criteria relating to melody and rhythm, it may be revealing to situate Rossini in a more general philosophical and aesthetic context, even if his standpoint remains above all that of a practical composer and not a theoretician. By rejecting the Aristotelian principle of imitation, Rossini was at the same time rejecting what was then its most current application to dramatic music, i.e. the tenet that music should submit to the text of the libretto. This position put the composer at odds with the doctrine of Classicism, aligning him instead with an older, Platonic, idea of the superiority of the art of the original creator over that of the imitator, who produces only a second-rate image of reality. By affirming, on the contrary, the primary (and primordial) rôle of melody and rhythm, Rossini was acknowledging music's autonomy, its special power, which he attributed in the first place to its formal properties. The exaltation of symmetry and reiteration, on which Rossinian melodic language rests, bespeaks an idea of beauty conceived from the harmony of proportions and the necessary relationship of the parts to the whole. We might say, then, that Rossini believed in the immanence of Italian musical art: the work owes the effect that it produces in the listener – in particular, the aesthetic effect sought by the composer – only to its internal formal qualities.[2] In Rossini's music, therefore, expression does not flow from the text. Yet, to the extent that it appeals to the aesthetic pleasure to be gained from the perception of form, neither is it apprehended instinctively; in this sense, it is fundamentally different from Romantic *Ausdruck*, which is opposed to rational perception. In sum, the *concertante* aesthetic of eighteenth-century Italian instrumental music – and not the theories of men of letters – is where the ideas behind Rossini's operas are rooted, and where their fundamental principles – autonomy of musical language, immanence of the musical work, the cult of form, rational expression and the pursuit of aesthetic pleasure – come together in a coherent way.

The position championed by Rossini, and by numerous Italian composers of his time, affirms the aesthetic validity of certain compositional practices usually condemned by critics, or at least looked upon with suspicion. One such practice was the recourse to *contrafacta*, i.e. melodies reused with new words, quite logically admissible in an aesthetic which treats melodic invention as autonomous with respect to text. Another, centrally important to the present chapter, was the systematic use of ornamentation, more or less generally disparaged in modern western culture. This disparagement is the end result of a departure from the ancient opposition of structural and ornamental laid down in the precepts of rhetoric, where ornamentation completes the *narratio*, or body of the discourse. The fall into disrepute of rhetoric came with French Classicism's quest for simplicity and the sublime; it is in this context that an opposition of essential and accessory was substituted for the ancient one of structural and ornamental. And yet this post-Classical conception of ornamentation is irrelevant to most of Rossini's melodic writing, from a number of different perspectives. For one, Rossini's melodies were not intended as the naïve or sincere form of expression sought by some of his successors, who opted for what became known as 'philosophical' music. Considering a melody very much as an artistic object in its own right, and not an imitation, Rossini had no reason to deprive himself of art's resources. For another, the opposition of structural and ornamental verges on the meaningless when it is remembered that ornamentation of melodic lines in fact works most of all towards the affirmation, even the exaltation, of their structure. Lastly, recourse to ornamented language and its formal conventions conforms to the very same idea of artistic codification lauded by Aristotle *à propos* of tragedy and respected by Italian *dramma per musica* right up until it was brought into question by French-inspired currents of reform in the middle decades of the eighteenth century – a reform on which Rossini, for the reasons set out above, decisively turned his back.

Constructing a melodic line

The cantabile of Idreno's aria in Act 2 of *Semiramide* sets the lines of the first quatrain in a way often found in Rossini (ex. 8.1). The first eight bars of the vocal line consist of three melodic segments: the first two (1 and 2) correspond to the first two lines (a and b) and the third groups together the second two lines (c and d). Each melodic phrase is made up of three parts: α = the anacrusis, which comes before the first beat; β = the kernel of the melody, constituted of whole bars (1 bar for each of the first two phrases, 2 bars for the third phrase); γ = the melodic desinence, corresponding to the syllables at the ends of lines, placed after the last stress. The space allotted to each of the building-blocks α, β and γ in a given phrase reflects the prosody of the line. For *tronchi* verses the desinence is absent (e.g. the termination of the third phrase on 'cor', bar 8). For lines in which the first prosodic stress falls on the first syllable (e.g. 'Pénsa alla patria, e intrepido'), it is the anacrusis that is missing (see ex. 8.5 below). When present, the anacrusis can be entirely without accent, comprising only the syllables before the first prosodic stress (as in Idreno's aria), or incorporate

Example 8.1 *Semiramide*, aria Idreno, 'La speranza più soave'

Example 8.2 *La donna del lago*, cavatina Malcom, 'Mura felici'

one or even several prosodic stresses, for example 'Oh quánte lágrime' (ex. 8.2). Phrases with a simple anacrusis and an ending but no kernel are numerous, particularly in settings of short lines (ex. 8.2). But, as will be shown below, the kernel is normally present in the melodic development that comes after the exposition of the initial phrases, where it is often associated with textual repetition within the line.

This way of structuring melody in phrases comprising anacrusis, kernel and desinence is not found either in recitatives – which are in no way anchored to the first beat of the bar – or in *parlante* passages in the dialogue sections of ensembles, but is typical of the *pezzo chiuso*, allowing for optimal setting of the prosodic rhythm of the line to the regular metrical scansion of the orchestral accompaniment. The present chapter will explore Rossinian melody with reference to this norm. Only cadenzas, which lie outside this regular scansion, do not conform to this morphology, and they will be described separately.

Melodic desinences have a special rôle to play in that they are the melodic equivalents of the rhyme, and hence signs of closure with decisive

Example 8.3 *L'italiana in Algeri*, cavatina Isabella, 'Cruda sorte'

importance in linking together the melodic phrases. Their periodic return, often emphasised by ornamentation (see below), plays a crucial rôle in the coherence of the 'melodic strophe', just as relationships of symmetry and reiteration do in tying the phrases together. Generally, the length of phrases and the ways of linking them are highly varied. In example 8.1 the first three phrases are separated simply by a pause for breath, but this pause may be much longer, and the melodic desinence in the vocal part (γ) may be answered by a counter-desinence in the orchestra (δ) (ex. 8.3).

Conversely, phrases can touch each other to the point of fusing together. This is the case in the third phrase of example 8.1, which has a two-bar kernel and is really a complex fusion of two simpler phrase-lines: 'e l'istante s'appressava' (c) plus 'più felice pel mio cor' (d), where the contiguity of the original melodic phrases verges on continuity as the internal desinence 's'appres*sava*' (γ) loses its feeling of closure. Such a fusion of the third and fourth lines into a single melodic phrase is often found in Rossini and corresponds, at the level of melodic construction, to the poetic procedure of enjambment.[3]

Line		Poetic desinence	Melodic desinence
a	La speranza più soave	*piano*	ornamentation
b	già quest'alma lusingava,	*piano*	ornamentation
c	e l'istante s'appressava	*piano*	enjambment
d	più felice pel mio cor.	*tronco*	–

Constructing an aria

Conforming to an Italian blueprint passed down from the eighteenth century, Rossini's arias are built upon a succession of differing melodic textures. These textures define closed sections, each associated with a particular orchestral accompaniment and constructed according to a general principle of progressive melodic development (see below).

Example 8.4 *Il barbiere di Siviglia*, aria Bartolo, 'A un dottor della mia sorte'

Si - gno - ri - na, un' al - trà   vol - ta   quan - do   Bar - to - lo an - drà   fuo - ri,   si - gno - ri - na, un' al - tra

vol - ta   quan - do Bar - to - lo an - drà   fuo - ri,   la   con - se - gna ai ser - vi - to - ri   a   suo mo - do far sa - prà

Recitatives and dialogue sections

Recitatives, in the serious as much as in the comic genre, are all written in common time (4/4): no metrical scansion is perceptible because the orchestra only provides, by turns, punctuation and harmonic support. The verses are not subject to any melodic periodisation: although most phrases have the final poetic stress falling on the first beat of a bar, a few have it in the middle of a bar. The effect of this aperiodicity of phrases and their extremely limited intervallic and rhythmic differentiation (in the biological sense of developing from rudimentary to particular), as well as their placement in the middle register of the voice, is to preserve as much as possible the intelligibility of the text and to keep the melodic texture of the recitatives as analogous as possible to the prose-like character of the *versi sciolti*, whose function is limited to narration and dialogue. In the serious register (*opera seria*, but also in the pathetic arias of *opera buffa*) recitatives may end with one or more cadenzas.

The *parlante* texture of the dialogue sections in ensembles differs from that of recitatives only in the stabilisation of prosodic stress on the first beat of the bar in order to establish the pulse as metrical. Melodic differentiation remains very limited, the syllabic recitation (*nota e parola*) still necessary for optimal intelligibility of the text.[4] An original characteristic of Rossini's language in the *buffa* register is in certain arias to transform, by extreme acceleration of the delivery, this rudimentary vocal texture into a virtuosic vocal style (ex. 8.4).

Open melodic texture

Characterised by a declamatory style well suited to rich and florid ornamentation, open melodic texture is encountered at the beginnings of arias and duets (ex. 8.5).[5] The orchestra assumes a punctuating rôle, making frequent use of the tutti; the vocal phrases are short, separated by multiple pauses, but widely differentiated, with a large range and complex rhythms. They succeed one another without any link immediately apparent to the listener, so as to give the impression of a through-composed structure – whence the term 'open' texture. Each phrase is, as it were, bipolar: the beginning syllabic, the end ornate. This type of writing, still very close

Example 8.5 *L'italiana in Algeri, rondò* Isabella, 'Pensa alla patria'

to the poetic verse-structure, obeys the laws of prosody and not those of 'pure' melody: an open melodic texture is simply the result of improvisation on the existing prosodic stresses, whose sequence generates the melodic phrases one by one. Consequently, this open texture lacks thematic character, which explains the use of generic devices, found in aria after aria (e.g. the descending arpeggio in 'imperative' arias).[6] In a morphological sense, then, open texture occupies an intermediate position between recitative and 'closed' texture, sharing with the former its properties of athematicism, apparent asymmetry and punctuating orchestra, and with the latter those of strong metrical sense, background symmetry and melodic differentiation.

Open texture is not used at the beginning of every aria. It is analogous in function to the rhetorical device of *allocutio*, when, by a familiar theatrical convention, a character addresses himself to the audience in the theatre as well as to an interlocutor on stage. Arias that begin with a section in open texture subscribe, therefore, to a dramatic aesthetic in which utterance is inductive and dialogic – thus justifying the use of rhetorical techniques of communication and persuasion – and no longer the monologic 'confession' of the typical solo aria, which is of a more poetic order of expression. It is by following this borrowed logic, dominant in the duet during Rossini's time, that an aria may begin in a peremptory tone, as in Isabella's *rondò* (ex. 8.5), and not in the sweet, lyrical one enshrined by tradition.

Closed melodic texture

Closed melodic texture appears whenever the orchestral accompaniment settles into formulaic regularity. The discourse of the vocal part becomes fluid: the interstices are reduced in length, the phrases by contrast elongated and brought closer together (ex. 8.6). Unlike in the prosy, through-composed sequence of phrases associated with open texture, here segmentation and periodicity prevail, fully justifying the parallel with versification – and helping explain Manuel García's term for this kind of writing, 'melodic verse'.[7] This term is in opposition to the word-fixated

Example 8.6 *L'italiana in Algeri*, *rondò* Isabella, 'Pensa alla patria'

Example 8.7 *Tancredi*, cavatina Tancredi, 'Tu che accendi'

mélopée of French *tragédie en musique* condemned by the defenders of Italian opera: unlike *mélopée*, 'melodic verse' is based on symmetry and reiteration between the melodic phrases, and this purely musical logic for constructing large-scale structures supersedes poetic organisation. The coherence of the phrases, together with the unified orchestral accompaniment, define melodic strophes that may be brought to a close by a cadenza.

If open melodic texture corresponds to the *allocutio* of a rhetorical discourse, closed texture is the *narratio*: a single expressive mood is sustained for an entire poetic strophe, with no attempt to render the content of the text word by word. This 'melodic unity', which Rousseau saw as emblematic of Italian music, is disturbed only by temporary modulations that, as a result, are brought into sharp relief, all the more tangible because of the clearly affirmed tonal context (ex. 8.7).[8]

A Rossinian characteristic is the absence of any archetype of phrase-distribution within closed-texture sections, such as exists for example in Bellini; on the contrary, Rossini's arias are distinguished by their diversity.[9] A rigorous typology of the different construction schemas would be rather complex and, what is more, perhaps of limited use, since it is not certain how far the more common schemas may be considered points of departure for the evaluation of those less common.

As Idreno's aria shows (ex. 8.1), melodic phrases are assembled to form strophes on the basis of two types of relationship, complementarity and similarity. The first type is represented by the opposition of antecedent and consequent, or by the insertion of contrasting (e.g. modulating) episodes; the second by the varied reprise of elements already heard, whether immediate, when the original is still present in the short-term memory of the listener, or deferred, when an entire section (e.g. a cabaletta) is reprised

Example 8.8 *Semiramide*, aria Idreno, 'La speranza più soave'

Example 8.9 *L'italiana in Algeri*, rondò Isabella, 'Pensa alla patria'

after an intervening episode. Of the two principles of construction, that of similarity and derivation is the more important: it gives rise to a gradual metamorphosis of the melodic line (a → a' → a''), in the course of which the individual phrase has meaning above all by virtue of its place in the dynamic process of transformation rather than its own morphological properties (ex. 8.8).

A Rossinian melodic phrase, then, often lacks the character of a theme. Because its plasticity and its aptness for transformation deprive it of the pregnancy and morphological rigidity proper to thematic material, even when presented for the first time it does not have that quality of instant recognisability typical of themes as such. This quality of Rossini's melodic language is perfectly suited to a musical dramaturgy blissfully ignorant of reminiscence themes and leitmotifs. Rather, in cabalettas and more rarely in cantabiles, two different types of closed-texture phrase may be distinguished: the first possesses a specific contour, is clearly separated and corresponds to the announcement of a 'subject' (ex. 8.9a);[10] the second is based on generic formulas, tends towards fusion with contiguous phrases, and corresponds to what Galeazzi called the 'passo caratteristico' (ex. 8.9b).

The principle of progressive melodic development

Apart from beginnings *ex abrupto*, which make use of highly developed melodic figures from the very first bars, each section of an aria by Rossini is built upon the progressive development of melodic phrases. As the section goes on, that is, intervallic and rhythmic differentiation increases, along with ornamentation, and the phrases become longer and fuse together. From time to time within a given section, however, a kind of enclave, a passage in a different texture, may be superimposed upon the teleological principle from which the overall dynamic proceeds. It is therefore not unusual to find closed-texture sections in the middle of a recitative, especially in the serious genre, or passages of recitative within an aria.

Rossini's ornamentation

With very few exceptions (*Armida*, Armida's 'D'amore al dolce impero' in the Act 2 Finale; *La donna del lago*, 'Fra il padre e fra l'amante', the cabaletta of Elena's *rondò* 'Tanti affetti in tal momento'), Rossini's arias are not in variation form. In nineteenth-century arias in variation form (frequently found in *solfeggi* of the time), ornamentation of melodic segments is continuous and regular, while in Rossini not all the melodic segments are equally susceptible to ornamentation: some are, some very much so, and others are not, depending on their precise position within the aria. This greater or lesser aptness for ornamentation underlines the formal properties of an aria, therefore, especially its points of articulation. It is in the context of the properties of these different segments that Rossini's ornamentation will be discussed here.

Desinences

The elongation of the final syllable of a verse or stanza and a fondness for drawing out closure of the melodic phrase together make up a marked characteristic of the Italian art of melody. When tempo and metre permit, desinences may be varied, but there is of course little room for manoeuvre because they are relatively limited in duration. Rossini's desinences compensate for this limitation with their astonishing plasticity, which results from two morphological properties: mutation and derivation. Mutation is the reprise of a desinence on a different scale degree by means of minimal modifications to its configuration; for example, the desinence on 'sguardo' from the trio 'Quel sembiante, quello sguardo' in *L'inganno felice* moves from the dominant to the tonic (ex. 8.10).

Derivation consists in a limited number of procedures that can be applied to any ornamented desinence. Expanding an ornamental figure towards the

Example 8.10 *L'inganno felice*, trio Isabella–Bertrando–Tarabotto, 'Quel sembiante, quello sguardo'

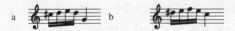

Example 8.11 (a) *Tancredi*, aria Isaura, 'Tu che i miseri conforti'; (b) *Otello*, aria Rodrigo, 'Ah, come mai non senti'; (c) *Semiramide*, duet Semiramide–Arsace, 'Serbami ognor sì fido'; (d) *Otello*, *canzone* Desdemona, 'Assisa appiè d'un salice'; (e) *Tancredi*, cavatina Amenaide, 'Come dolce all'alma mia'; (f) *La gazza ladra*, Act 2 Finale, 'Ecco cessato il vento'; (g) *L'italiana in Algeri*, Andantino, 'Oh! che muso', in Act 1 Finale; (h) *Semiramide*, duet Semiramide–Arsace, 'Ebben . . . a te: ferisci'; (i) *L'italiana in Algeri*, Moderato maestoso, 'Non sei tu che il grado eletto', in Act 2 Finale

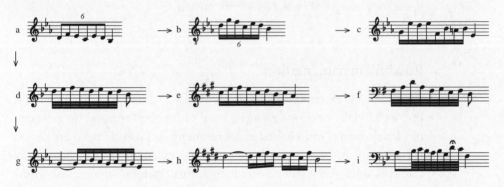

Example 8.12 *Tancredi*, cavatina Tancredi, 'Tu che accendi'

top of the range, always a good way of enriching a vocal line, is one such procedure, allowing, by means of appoggiaturas or arpeggiated leaps, a large number of derivations to be drawn from a single figure (ex. 8.11).[11]

Cadenzas

Not to be confused with desinences, cadenzas in Rossinian opera are ornamental passages indicated by a fermata and performed outside the metre.[12] The function of the vast majority of cadenzas is to provide an emphatic close to the melodic strophe in the same way as desinences underline the closure of the phrase. In a separate, smaller category are those cadenzas consisting of moderately elaborate figures placed exclusively on the dominant that are sometimes used to introduce strophes (ex. 8.12). Rossini hardly ever uses cadenzas for the purposes of suspense in the middle of melodic strophes; the proliferation of this kind of device is typical, rather, of singers and composers of the following generation, notably Bellini.

Example 8.13 (a) *Le Comte Ory*, *cavatine* Comtesse, 'En proie à la tristesse'; (b) *Semiramide*, duet Semiramide–Arsace, 'Ebben . . . a te: ferisci'; (c) *L'inganno felice*, aria Isabella, 'Al più dolce e caro oggetto'

The general shape of the cadenza is developed out of ornamentation of a part of the cadential sequence IV–V–I, within which metrical scansion is suspended.[13] The following features differentiate cadenzas from mere ornamented melodic kernels: (1) *passaggi* expanded to an undetermined number of notes – the free melodic elaboration of a given harmony, released from contrapuntal constraints; (2) the emergence of one or more apexes in the line, and the differentiation of the melodic contour by means of successive *passaggi* in opposite directions, which may be brought to a close by a brief syllabic phrase to allow the words to be taken up again at the harmonic resolution V(7)–I; (3) *passaggi* in segments made up of the regular repetition of a basic melodic cell in a scalic or arpeggiated pattern (see below, substitution); (4) large-scale asymmetry, in contrast with ordinary cadential passages that are ornamented but lack a fermata; (5) the separation of the cadenza from its context, so that it seems an autonomous unit which has no obvious connection with the compositional procedures of the preceding musical strophe and which, therefore, could easily be transplanted into another piece or itself substituted by a similar figure.

Any or all of the chords making up the harmonic steps of the cadenza may be thus elaborated, which means that the overall length is widely variable, and that it is possible, depending on the chordal point of departure, to distinguish the following types of cadenzas: (a) V(7)–I; (b) V(6/4)–V(7)–I; (c) IV (or II)–V(6/4)–V(7)–I (ex. 8.13). In the cases of b and c, only exceptionally is every chord of the cadence ornamented in turn. To put it simply, cadenzas are constructed on a series of ascending and descending *passaggi*, deployed at will save for the condition that there can be no change of chord

Example 8.14 *La Cenerentola*, Maestoso, 'Sprezzo quei don', in Act 1 Finale

between an ascending section and a descending section. The point of artic-ulation between two such sections, the apex, may be marked by a held note, but there may equally be no slowing-down at all, just a broad melodic arch (ex. 8.14).

Interpolation

Because Rossini's ornamentation is not tied down to illustrating the sense of individual words, local ornamentation – i.e. acciaccaturas, appoggia-turas and trills designed to highlight single notes – plays only a limited rôle. Examples are usually found in series (see below, ex. 8.17, sections A, B and C). Aside from the signals of closure represented by desinences on the one hand and cadenzas on the other, ornamentation of the kernel of the phrase is by the complementary techniques of interpolation and substitu-tion. The first consists in inserting a fragment in small note-values between the pitches of the original line written in longer note-values, while the second is the replacement of the original by a completely recomposed ornamental line. These two techniques are specific to different melodic and metrical contexts and hence are not interchangeable: interpolation, which demands great metrical flexibility, is preferred in cantabile and lyrical sections, while substitution is best suited to the strict scansion of fast movements. What both techniques have in common is to concentrate the listener's attention on a given passage within the melodic discourse, and in this sense they can be related to the *amplificatio*, or expansion of a point, in rhetoric. Both are used for reprises, whether simple, short-term phrase repetition or reprises of entire strophes, as well as for sections conceived as ornamented from the very outset (as is the case with the cabaletta of Pamyra's aria in *Le Siège de Corinthe*, ex. 8.17, section C).

The cantabile of Isabella's cavatina 'Cruda sorte' from *L'italiana in Algeri* presents several examples of interpolation (indicated in ex. 8.15 in small notation). Unlike figures of substitution (see below), interpolations can be removed from the principal melodic line. They consist primarily of stepwise *passaggi* whose structure is not geometric, that is, which cannot be broken down into repeated elements or cells, and in whose performance a certain irregularity is licensed. This kind of scalic flourish, the use of *tempo rubato* and nuances of timbre are features of the 'expression-orientated' singing

Example 8.15 *L'italiana in Algeri*, cavatina Isabella, 'Cruda sorte'

Example 8.16 (a) *Tancredi*, aria Amenaide, 'Giusto Dio'; (b) *Le Comte Ory*, *cavatine* Comte, 'Que les destins prospères'

traditionally held to be the most elevated form of the Italian lyrical art from the beginning of the eighteenth century onwards.

Another interpolated figure used very frequently by Rossini and his contemporaries is the arpeggiated leap, most often placed on the second beat of the bar. Whether followed by a *passaggio* descending towards resolution (ex. 8.16a) or not (ex. 8.16b), the effect is to move the melodic summit of the phrase upwards, to emphasise the off-beat and to let the voice (in falling off, as it were, both summit and syncopation) naturally vibrate. This simple but effective ornament is frequently to be found in singers' annotations, particularly those of sopranos and tenors. Originally, therefore, it would seem to have come from performance practice, but was subsequently integrated into the compositional vocabulary of Rossini and his epigones.

Substitution

In Pamyra's cabaletta, sections B and C mark a contrast with the sudden appearance of a new kind of melodic writing: substitution figures (ex. 8.17, bars 9–25). The line is embellished using reiterated ornamental cells: an in-tempo trill, b. 9; a series of in-tempo mordants, bb. 11–12; descending *volate*, bb. 13–15; a series of turns on a broken ascending arpeggio, bb. 17–18; a descending chromatic *volata*, b. 20; and a series of trills on an ascending arpeggio, bb. 21–24. Each of these basic cells could be replaced by an equivalent figure – a synonym, as it were – without either enriching or impoverishing it. The same melodic writing is used in the coda (section D,

Example 8.17 *Le Siège de Corinthe*, aria Pamyra, 'O patrie infortunée'

which follows C in the reprise), the equivalent of peroration in rhetorical discourse.

These sections, which provide good examples of Galeazzi's 'passo caratteristico' and 'periodo di cadenza', contrasting with the 'motivo principale' of the cabaletta (section A), treat the voice like an instrument, demanding from the singer agility, power and evenness of tone across the whole range. While this kind of 'performance-orientated' singing offers performers the greatest possible freedom to make their parts more interesting and show off their abilities, on the other hand it has been the object of a certain distrust on the part of theoreticians and pedagogues, who always attach to it a qualifying preference for 'expression-orientated' singing. Above and beyond a quite legitimate reaction against singer-worship, this distrust can be explained (to re-iterate a point made earlier) in the light of the rationalist prejudice against any form of artistic expression not subjected to the imitation of words. It is true that intelligibility takes second place during long vocalises, the text of the libretto serving as hardly more than a pretext for the kind of autonomous melodic organisation that was derided as 'mechanical' by nineteenth-century partisans of 'philosophical' music.[14] Yet vocal virtuosity and the exaltation of rhythm, both dear to Rossini, are means of

Example 8.18 (a) *Semiramide*, Andantino, 'L'usato ardir', in Act 2 Finale; (b) *La Cenerentola*, aria Clorinda, 'Sventurata'; (c) *La donna del lago*, cavatina Rodrigo, 'Eccomi a voi, miei prodi'; (d) *Il barbiere di Siviglia*, quintet, 'Don Basilio!'; (e) *Le Comte Ory*, duet Isolier–Comte, 'Une dame de haut parage'

expression capable of inducing in the listener (and the performer) an aesthetic pleasure such as to need no justification. This art, the vocal equivalent of the solo concerto, is indeed nothing less than dazzling when exercised by well-prepared singers.

Unlike cantabile phrases ornamented by interpolation, it is impossible to break down phrases containing substitution figures into a hierarchy of structural vs decorative notes. Furthermore, such phrases are characterised by a tendency towards continuous, non-hierarchical ornamentation (*coloratura minuta*), as well as by the generic and extremely variable nature of the basic cells used. As with cadenzas, recourse to passage-work and fragmentation of the melodic line into a succession of repeated cells is situated for preference on the resolving cadential chord-series I–IV–V–I – which is why descending contours, based on stepwise or arpeggiated patterns, predominate. The examples of one particular pattern, in which the cadential chord-series is confined to a single bar, give an idea of the great variety of ornamental formulations to be found in Rossini (ex. 8.18). By contrast, ascending contours (equivalent to ascending *passaggi* in cadenzas) are to be found over the chord-series II(or IV)–V(6/4) (ex. 8.19).

In each case, it may be observed that a combinatorial richness of 'geometric' ornamentation goes hand in hand not only with a relative poverty of harmonic framework, but also with a simplicity of basic cells: the more elementary the cells themselves, the more complex and varied their arrangement. A particular originality of Rossini's style is the use of substitution

Example 8.19 (a) *Il barbiere di Siviglia*, duet Rosina–Figaro, 'Dunque io son'; (b) *La Cenerentola*, *rondò* Cenerentola, 'Nacqui all'affanno e al pianto'; (c) *L'italiana in Algeri*, duet Lindoro–Mustafà, 'Se inclinassi a prender moglie'

Example 8.20 *Le Siège de Corinthe*, aria Pamyra, 'O patrie infortunée'

figures in slow movements, where they can be found in ternary subdivisions within bars of three or four beats, based on a stationary pattern – as in the cantabile of Pamyra's aria (ex. 8.20).

Singers' ornamentation

Contrary to received opinion – which seems to have come from a statement by Duprez, apparently confirmed in a letter written by the composer[15] – ornamentation of vocal parts by the singers themselves is completely legitimate in Rossini. That Rossini was one of the last *maestri* to cultivate such an art of singing – sustained partly by composer, partly by singer, and presuming the interaction of the two – is merely a historical contingency, one that we should be wary of interpreting as evidence of the composer's wishes, or, worse still, of the inevitable decline of that system. In the decades that followed Rossini's theatrical career the Italian art of *canto fiorito* passed from the domain of *opera seria* into *opéra comique* and subsequently into operetta, at the price of multiple technical and semantic evolutions. In any case, if excesses were always condemned, critics were at least careful to judge the appropriateness of ornamentation according to both context (i.e. by qualitative criteria) and extent (quantitative criteria). As in rhetoric, the same decoration may seem a figure or a fault – a device or just a vice – depending on whether it is used in a controlled and convincing manner or not.

Example 8.21 *Guillaume Tell*, *romance* Mathilde, 'Sombre forêt'; (a) Paris, Bibliothèque de l'Opéra, manuscript part of Mathilde; (b) Louis-Gilbert Duprez, *L'Art du chant* (Paris, 1845); (c) Laure Cinti-Damoreau, *Méthode de chant* (Paris, 1849)

The distinction between salon and theatre styles, fundamental to eighteenth-century aesthetics, still existed in Rossini's time. Consequently, the ornamentation performed on stage was not the same as that taught in singing classes, sung in concerts or published. The *variazioni* that were published were clearly much more elaborate than those heard in the theatre, as may be appreciated in the case of the cadenza 'mes secrets' from Mathilde's *romance* 'Sombre forêt' in *Guillaume Tell*. Laure Cinti-Damoreau, the first Mathilde, performed a more sober version than we might be led to believe by Duprez's published version of this cadenza, or even her own (ex. 8.21).[16]

Singers' annotations of their own copies reveal the order in which they went about ornamenting their parts: first the cadenzas, then the desinences and finally the substitutions for repeats, especially in cabalettas, which Rossini would leave to his singers' discretion. Passages with substitutions were often the object of multiple realisations, some merely sketched and then abandoned, in which different melodic cells were tried out (ex. 8.22).[17]

Example 8.22 *Moïse et Pharaon*, aria Anaï, 'Quelle horrible destinée', Paris, Bibliothèque de l'Opéra, manuscript part of Anaï

On the other hand, it is very rare to find manuscript annotations in cantabile sections. It can be deduced from this that singers actually did improvise in real time in slow tempos, where a flexible pulse and inter-polated, irregular *passaggi* would allow them to come together with the orchestra on the strong beats of the bar. The metrical rigour and rapid movement of the *canto fiorito* sections would render such improvisation extremely risky, which explains both why the singers took care to memo-rise those sections beforehand, and the existence of written traces of this preparation.

The performing material for Rossini's operas preserved in Paris gives a good overall idea of the arsenal of ornaments at his interpreters' disposal, and moreover shows that all their decorative figures descend from the composer's own hand, whether directly or by a kind of family resemblance. Indeed, singers' ornamentation is characterised by less audacity, as is typical of the work of imitators: the range of substitute melodic cells is narrower and the cadenzas tend to isolate the apex precisely where Rossini favours continuous arcs (see ex. 8.14). Generally, lines ornamented by the performers bear the traces of a hierarchy of scale-degrees – the seams showing, as it were – while Rossini's are characterised, on the contrary, by greater uniformity.[18]

According to the pecking order customary in Italian opera companies, only the parts of the principals carry annotated variations. The creative rights of secondary rôles were limited to the transposition of individual notes (*puntature*) in the case of difficulties with the register. Ornamentation of small ensembles is limited to the realisation of cadenzas in several voices at once, where *passaggi* are relayed between the different soloists. The possibility of a pair of exceptional singers playing improvisation games with each other live on stage should not be entirely ruled out, but the only trace of it is the testimony of the singers in question – testimony we may suspect of having itself been the object of a certain embellishment. In Paris, where the performing parts remained the property of the theatres, singers would pass on the copies they had used to their successors in the rôles, and hence their ornamentation too – a significant legacy if the outgoing singer in question was a figure of renown. In this way performance traditions, including ornamentation, cuts and transpositions, established themselves, traditions whose authority ended up supplanting that of the absent composer. Therefore it is important to keep in view on the one hand that the practice of ornamentation is by definition incompatible with the idea of an absolute point of reference, and, on the other, that only the text left by the composer can be invested with authority.

(translated by Cormac Newark)

9 Off the stage

RICHARD OSBORNE

Rossini's career as a stage composer spanned just nineteen years. His larger career, beginning with the six *Sonate a quattro* of 1804 and ending with the march *La corona d'Italia* in 1868, spanned sixty-four. The productivity of the operatic years was phenomenal, an Ixion's wheel of endeavour on which Rossini's fame and fortune rested. It was from this that dozens of additional commissions, the large and absorbingly diverse collection of non-operatic compositions, mainly flowed. The fate of both bodies of work has not been dissimilar, the byways neglected, the highways heavily trodden, but there the similarity ends. Formally and stylistically many of the non-operatic works have an individuality all their own.

Although Rossini was born into one revolution and lived through several others, and although his own early work revolutionised Italian opera, there was always something of the court composer about him. He wrote operas and secular cantatas for Bourbon court theatres in Naples and Paris and throughout his career accepted a string of lucrative private commissions from well-to-do patrons who had at their disposal grand and agreeable performing venues: a country villa (the six *Sonate a quattro*), a metropolitan cathedral (*Stabat mater*), a Parisian salon (*Les Soirées musicales*), a private chapel (*Petite messe solennelle*). In his final years in Paris he took the process to its logical conclusion. A *vieux rococo* (his own phrase) stranded in an age of Romantic individualism, he created his own private salon, becoming composer-in-residence to the court of which he himself was king.

Student works and cantatas

Memories of making music in Agostino Triossi's villa in Conventello near Ravenna probably stayed with Rossini all his life. It was there at the age of twelve in 1804 that he composed his six *Sonate a quattro* for two violins, cello and double bass in the canonical three-movement arrangement fast–slow–fast. The sonatas are not themselves operatic, but they look forward to the operas. Themes are briefly and vividly sketched, and a mordant wit goes hand in hand with a certain sensuous lyricism, short-breathed but sweet. The forms are simple, but the interplay of pitches and tonal volumes is a good deal more sophisticated.

Triossi also commissioned sacred music from Rossini, whose period of study with Padre Giuseppe Malerbi (Lugo, 1802–4) had provided him with an early and welcome exposure to the music of Haydn and Mozart. The Mass settings Rossini variously sketched and assembled between the years 1806 and 1810 during his time as a student at Bologna's Liceo Musicale share with the *Sonate a quattro* a certain unstoppable vitality, the writing for solo winds gracious and gay but also touched with a certain melancholy (one thinks of the 'Crucifixus' in the so-called *Messa di Milano*). What the music lacks is that discipline in development which the theatre would shortly impose on him.

Outstanding among the student pieces completed by Rossini for the Liceo Musicale is his *Il pianto d'Armonia sulla morte d'Orfeo* (1808). This short cantata to a somewhat stilted text by Girolamo Ruggia shows Harmony and a group of nymphs (male chorus) weeping over the death of Orpheus. Rossini took considerable trouble over the piece, submitting himself to correction by his teacher Padre Mattei and voluntarily rewriting the first chorus. The overture is enchanting, but it is the exquisite cello accompaniment to the recitative 'Ma tu che desti' which is most striking. As an invention, it would not seem out of place in *Guillaume Tell*.

Many of the works Rossini chose to call 'cantata' were theatrical in character: operatic offcuts pressed into public or private service. The restoration of European monarchies in the wake of the Napoleonic wars meant that there was once again a call from royal theatres for spectacular short stage shows, innocent of dramatic conflict but rich in vocal and scenic glitz. The cantatas *Le nozze di Teti e di Peleo* (1816) and *La riconoscenza* (1821) were both provided for performance in court theatres in Naples. A third, the virtuoso showpiece *La morte di Didone* (first performed in 1818) written for the soprano Ester Mombelli, bears many of the same stylistic characteristics, though the precise date of composition is not known.

Le nozze di Teti e di Peleo was written to celebrate the marriage of Ferdinand IV's granddaughter Princess Maria Carolina and the Duc de Berry, the second son of the future Charles X of France. (Rossini's *Il viaggio a Reims* was commissioned for Charles X's coronation in 1825. Although opera houses now claim it as their own, it is effectively the *ne plus ultra* of Rossini stage cantatas.) The librettist Angelo Maria Ricci, a local Neapolitan poetaster, based his pageant on the ancient Greek legend of Peleus and the sea-nymph, Thetis, fated to bear a son mightier than his father. The action is confined to Peleus's honouring Thetis in a love duet ('Costante al tuo fianco') and several tableaux in which the gods Jove, Juno and Ceres bless the nuptials and speculate on the events which might flow from this auspicious day. None of the music Rossini used in *Le nozze di Teti e di Peleo* was new, but it was carefully and expertly adapted: keys altered, vocal lines emended, orchestration revised. The number in *Le nozze di Teti e di Peleo* which it is difficult not to recognise is the central showpiece aria for Ceres, 'Ah, non potrian resistere'. Rossini used the aria, or parts of it, four times: (1) as Count Almaviva's aria 'Cessa di più resistere' in Act 2 of *Il barbiere di Siviglia*; (2) in *Le nozze di Teti e di Peleo*; (3) as an aria for Rosina in performances of *Il barbiere di Siviglia* in Bologna in the summer of 1816; (4) in the closing scene of *La Cenerentola*. Of the four, the Naples version is perhaps the most distinct by virtue of its colour, its manner and its positioning at the heart of the cantata.

Because *Le nozze di Teti e di Peleo* was itself an amalgamation of old materials, Rossini made no attempt to adapt it for use beyond the occasion for which it was commissioned. By contrast *La riconoscenza* was widely redeployed by him. The cantata was prepared for a benefit evening on 27 December 1821 to which Rossini was entitled under the terms of his Neapolitan contract. The text, by Giulio Genoino, concerns two pastoral lovers, Argene and Melania. Both are conscious of the blessings that surround them, but it is Argene who believes in the beneficence of the gods, a faith Melania longs to share. Argene takes her to an Arcadian grove where she encounters the white-haired philosopher-priest Elpino and where she is moved by the dances and sacrifices of the shepherds as they express their gratitude to the gods. It is one of Rossini's most beautiful scores, the music grave and measured yet guilefully paced. The cantata was revived, in slightly expanded form, at the Teatro del Fondo, Naples, in February 1822 and adapted as *Il vero omaggio*, text by Gaetano Rossi, for performance in the presence of European heads of state and their delegations at the Congress of Verona the following December. Music from this cantata later found its way into another cantata, *Omaggio pastorale*, which Rossini prepared for the unveiling of a bust of the sculptor Antonio Canova in Treviso in the spring of 1823, before the entire work resurfaced as the *azione pastorale Il serto votivo* in Bologna in 1829.

Rossini's only overtly political cantata, his *Cantata in onore del Sommo Pontefice Pio Nono*, was compiled in 1846 at the request of an influential banking and theatre-owning family in Rome, the Torlonias. The new Pope's decision, within a month of his election in June 1846, to grant an amnesty to all political prisoners inspired the belief that he had the capacity to heal wounds and unite Italy. Rossini, now in poor health, tried to reduce the scale of the commission, but the Torlonias, jealous of their reputation as powerbrokers and patrons within the Papal State, persuaded him to do otherwise. The cantata, to a text by Giovanni Marchetti, lasts forty-five minutes and is on a very grand scale indeed. The text does not shy away from sycophantic sentiments:

> Tanta di Pio clemenza
> una dolcezza inusitata e nova
> nel mio petto versò. Già da quel punto
> ch'egli cinse il gran serto, aura spirai
> oltre ogni dir soave; il ciel m'apparve
> più seren dell'usato,
> più florida la terra,
> del dì più lieti i rai;
> tutto dir mi sembrò: paga sarai.

[Pius's great clemency poured new and unaccustomed gentleness into my heart. From the very moment when he was crowned with laurel, I breathed air of a sweetness beyond words; the sky seemed more serene than usual, the earth more fertile, the sun's rays more propitious; all seemed to say to me: you will be satisifed.][1]

This kind of laudatory excess is confined to the recitatives, which are the only music composed anew – though Rossini again selects shrewdly and patches expediently, shaping the cantata in a series of interlocking tableaux. The first tableau (overture, chorus and Agorante's cavatina from *Ricciardo e Zoraide*) features the prisoners Pius has pardoned and Public Love, who praises Pius on their behalf. In the second, Hope engages the people (chorus from *Ermione*) before bringing together herself and the people's leader with Christian Spirit and Public Love in a vision of a new political order in which Rome will be more loved than feared (quartet from Act 1 of *Armida*). The concluding tableau (aria with chorus, 'Quel nuage sanglant', from *Le Siège de Corinthe*) is less benign, a call to arms by the Church Militant which proponents of the Risorgimento had no difficulty in hearing in more explicitly revolutionary terms.

If the choice of *Armida* (Christian knights) and *Le Siège de Corinthe* (doom-laden liberation music) seems merely expedient, the recycling of the powerful opening sequence from *Ricciardo e Zoraide* is something of a masterstroke. Such is the chameleon character of Rossini's music, the effect is both moving and inspiring, more so than in the dramatically vapid opera. The overture-cum-*introduzione*, with its 'compassionate' horn solo, skirling obbligato woodwinds and offstage *banda*, encapsulates in a single movement the cantata's idea of a great crusade, at once resolute and humane, in which the papacy and the people will be one.

The cantatas Rossini was occasionally persuaded to write for private consumption by well-to-do patrons bear little relation to these larger, public works. The cantata for soprano, contralto and piano *Egli ed Irene*, written for Princess Amelia Belgioioso in Milan in 1814, is run-of-the-mill salon music, famous now only for the old-fashioned 'echo' effect which Rossini redeployed to brilliant comic effect in the Act 2 trio of *Il barbiere di Siviglia*. Rossini's fondness for flattering and fleecing the great and the good did, however, produce a small cache of *pièces d'occasion* which is both diverse and diverting. In London in 1824 he wrote his *Duetto* for cello and double bass in honour of the great double bass virtuoso Domenico Dragonetti. He also obliged with a timely tribute to the late Lord Byron. His *Il pianto delle muse in morte di Lord Byron* was excoriated by the press, but as a song of mourning for tenor, six-voice three-part chorus and chamber ensemble it is as gracious as it is brief. It was a form Rossini would return to in his 'Quelques mesures de chant funèbre: à mon pauvre ami Meyerbeer' (Paris, 1864) written for four-part male chorus and drum. The light march rhythm, the text's gentle rhetoric ('Pleure, pleure, muse sublime'), the fine part-writing, the limpid modulations and the hieratic calm of the twice-uttered closing 'Requiem' make for something that is both exquisite and touching.

In Paris in July 1827 Rossini provided a cantata for six solo voices and piano for the baptism of the son of his friend and patron, the banker Alexandre-Marie Aguado. The following year he wrote his *Rendez-vous de chasse* for four horns and orchestra, a piece Weber or Schumann might have been proud to own. With its picturesque, *al fresco* mood it reads like an epigraph to *Guillaume Tell*. Rather more substantial than either of these is the cantata for soprano and piano *Giovanna d'Arco*, which Rossini composed in 1832 as a tribute to his mistress and future wife, Olympe Pélissier. Having contemplated but rejected the idea of writing an opera on the subject of Joan of Arc, he composed this fifteen-minute soliloquy instead. As Joan contemplates her departure, nothing stirs except for wind-ruffled waters and Joan's inner sense of destiny. In the central lyrical section she sentimentally contemplates her mother's sorrow upon discovering her daughter's departure. Both the Maestoso (Joan's vision) and the cabaletta (her anticipation of battle) are boldly, elaborately written in a style that is unapologetically operatic.

Messa di Gloria and *Stabat mater*

During his time as a professional opera composer Rossini wrote only one sacred work, the vivid and powerful *Messa di Gloria* in Naples in 1820. Unlike the *Stabat mater* and *Petite messe solennelle*, which are often wrongly accused of being persistently 'operatic', the *Messa di Gloria* draws on operatic forms and theatrical effects, whilst at the same time making token attempts to distance itself from these by reverting to older, quasi-ecclesiastical idioms – a stylistic mixture common to much nineteenth-century Catholic sacred music.

The most powerful movement is the Kyrie. Cogently shaped, with an unusual and far-from-obvious harmonic structure, this made little sense to the Neapolitans, who preferred the opening movement of the Gloria. Here the words 'Gloria in excelsis Deo, et in terra pax hominibus bonae voluntatis' are turned into what is generally taken to be a nativity sequence, a shepherds-and-angels narrative. The shepherds' theme, a lowly pizzicato building ebulliently through a typically Rossinian crescendo, takes us up towards the empyrean, where angel voices turn mundane matter into a swirling song of glory. The soprano's 'Laudamus' which follows is a bipartite aria of the kind familiar from the late Neapolitan operas. By contrast the two tenor arias revert to the older 'ritornello' form, in which vocal developments are confined within the melodic orbit of the introduction itself. Rossini composed the *Messa di Gloria* with two contrasting tenors in mind. The higher-lying 'Gratias' was written for Giovanni David, the more strenuously theatrical 'Qui tollis' for the darker-voiced Andrea Nozzari. It is probable, however, that the concise and skilful fugal setting of the concluding 'Cum sancto spiritu' is not the work of Rossini, but of the great *contrappuntista* Pietro Raimondi (1786–1853). Whether this collaboration with Raimondi came about through pressure of time or because of Rossini's own continuing doubts about his mastery of fugue it is impossible to say.

Rossini was certainly assailed by doubt when in 1831 he was invited by the Spanish cleric Francisco Fernández Varela to compose a new setting of the thirteenth-century Latin poem *Stabat mater*. Not the least of his problems in tackling such a commission was the fact that Pergolesi's *Stabat mater* (1736) remained extremely popular. The complex compositional history of Rossini's setting is examined in chapter 2 above. Suffice it to say that, after numerous alarums and excursions, the all-Rossini *Stabat mater* was first heard in Paris on 7 January 1842. It was a huge success, though it would soon fall foul of puritan opinion (in Anglo-Saxon countries in particular), which argues that the sacred works of composers whose principal trade is opera are almost invariably 'operatic', that is to say, tuneful, extrovert and spiritually insincere. Setting aside the problem of what is or is not appropriate for religious music, it should be pointed out that in such matters as the internal structuring of individual numbers, orchestration and deployment of the chorus, Rossini's *Stabat mater* is almost entirely unoperatic. That the work is *by* Rossini is everywhere apparent, but that is surely not in itself proof of spiritual mendacity.

Rossini's reputation for being indifferent to the texts he set (something we now know to be manifestly untrue) further muddied the waters. In the case of the *Stabat mater* we have no knowledge of the identity of the author of this medieval meditation on the Crucifixion. For years the name of Jacopone da Todi was given, but all we can reasonably say is that it is the work of an anonymous thirteenth-century Franciscan monk. The poem effectively falls into two parts, of which the first, the opening lines notwithstanding, is much less impressive than the second. The first tercet makes up the first movement of Rossini's setting. The words are impressive, not least for the harshness of the sound, particularly in the second line: 'Stabat mater dolorosa / iuxta crucem lacrimosa / dum pendebat filius'. What follows in the remainder of the first stanza, and in the next three stanzas, is merely a list of familiar facts and emotions about Christ on the Cross and his grieving mother. The words do not actually evoke anything. To a modern sensibility they give the impression of trundling mindlessly on.

Then, at the start of the fifth stanza, something remarkable happens. At the words 'Eia, Mater' the poem suddenly switches from recitation to prayer, and passionate prayer at that. It even takes on a certain quality of dramatic development as we move from the opening intercession to Christ's mother, through the drama of the Crucifixion and the Last Judgement, to the poem's ultimate resting-point in a vision of Paradise, where the words conjure their own verbal music, as lyrical and solemn as those of the opening lines were harsh and unyielding: 'Quando corpus morietur / fac ut animae donetur / paradisi gloria'. Rossini sets this final stanza as a meditation for unaccompanied choir, one of his most sublime inventions (praised by Wagner in the conversation he had with Rossini in Paris in 1860). The movements immediately before the 'Quando corpus morietur' are also impressive in their evocative force and expressive variety, even if our Victorian forebears did rather over-exploit Rossini's setting of the 'Inflammatus', the work's equivalent of the 'Dies irae'.

It is worth scrutinising the poem in this way because it throws up one interesting fact. Lines 4 to 24 of the original poem might seem to us a sequence of recycled images couched in unimaginative language. Is it, then, entirely coincidental that it was precisely these lines which Rossini initially farmed out to the composer Tadolini at the time of the original commission in 1832? Had Rossini simply run out of time or become bored with the piece, the probability is that he would have completed the first part of the poem and not the second. In practice, he worked first on those sections of the poem which most engaged him. In 1841, faced with replacing Tadolini's settings of those rather banal lines, Rossini fell back on a sequence of two arias and a duet, unpretentious, straightforward pieces which to some extent mirror the commonplace nature of the words themselves. The couplet 'Quae moerebat et dolebat / et tremebat, cum videbat' forms part of the tenor aria, the celebrated 'Cuius animam': with the poet on auto-pilot, Rossini obligingly chips in with one of his most memorable melodies. It is unfortunate that this aria, and the bass's 'Pro peccatis', come so early in the work, fixing in people's minds the idea, not of a text that is banal, but of music that might seem banal – or, as they usually choose to put it, 'operatic'.

Songs

Prior to his settling in Paris in 1824 Rossini's output of songs and vocal ensembles had been modest. The charming folk-song 'Se il vuol la molinara', about a love-lorn boy and his girl who works at the mill, has been attributed to 1801, but the finished composition is probably later. His earliest published song is the lilting, bitter-sweet 'Il trovatore' (Naples, 1818). The year 1821 brought a small rush of such compositions: a brilliant song in the Spanish style, 'En medio a mis dolores', the enchantingly sly 'La pastorella', and one of Rossini's own particular favourites, the magniloquent 'Beltà crudele'. That same year in Rome he and Paganini concocted a Carnival quartet for two tenors and two basses, 'Siamo ciechi, siamo nati'; and to mark his departure from Vienna in 1822 he wrote 'Addio ai viennesi', a song he later adapted for use in other cities.

It was not, however, until the operatic burden was laid down after the completion of *Guillaume Tell* in 1829 that Rossini began seriously to exercise his skill as a composer of chamber arias and songs designed to be performed to piano accompaniment in the salons of the well-to-do. In 1835 he gathered together twelve of these under the title *Les Soirées musicales*. By and large it is the more brilliant and extrovert songs – beginning with 'L'orgia', a flamboyant waltz-song about the joys of wine, women and song – which have caught the imagination of the public at large and composer-arrangers such as Liszt, Respighi and Britten. The dance-songs – a bolero, a yodelling *tyrolienne*, a barcarolle and a tarantella – are unashamedly demotic in manner, although the writing itself is full of courtly sophistication, harmonies and phrasing slyly redirecting our attention away from routine expectation. Among the duets the barcarolle 'La regata veneziana' stands out, a Venetian dialect song in which two coquettish girls urge a pair of gondoliers to put their backs into their punting. A somewhat grimmer maritime note is struck in 'Li marinari', a substantial duet for tenor and bass partly derived from music originally written for *Ricciardo e Zoraide*. Its brooding mood and lyrical-declamatory style attracted the attention of the young Wagner, who orchestrated it in 1838.

Rossini's so-called 'silent years' after the abandonment of opera were far from silent, although he himself liked to present them as such. Metastasio's aria 'Mi lagnerò tacendo' (from *Siroe*, 1726), suitably altered, became a leitmotif of these years:

Mi lagnerò tacendo
della mia sorte amara;
ma ch'io non t'ami, o cara,
non lo sperar da me.

Crudel! in che t'offesi?
Farmi penar, perché?[2]

[I shall lament in silence my bitter fate; but that I should not love you, my
dear, do not hope that from me. Cruel one! How have I offended you? Why
make me suffer?]

Over a period of more than a quarter of a century he prepared almost fifty
settings of the poem, sometimes with a new French or Italian text added
to the original words beneath, and often even dispensing with the original words altogether while clearly composing with them in mind. Some of
Rossini's finest songs come into one or other of these categories, among
them 'Aragonese', 'I gondolieri', 'La fioraia fiorentina', 'Le dodo des enfants'
and the 'complainte à deux voix' for tenor and baritone entitled 'Un sou'.
Most important of all, from Rossini's own personal point of view, was
his *Musique anodine*, a sequence of six settings of 'Mi lagnerò tacendo'
which he offered as a gift to his wife on 15 April 1857 as a mark of his
gratitude for her nursing him back to health after years of debilitating
illness.

Péchés de vieillesse

The *Musique anodine* marked the start of an extraordinary Indian Summer
in the 65-year-old Rossini's creative life, which led to the production of a
large number of small and not-so-small pieces to which he gave the collective
title 'Péchés de vieillesse', 'Sins of Old Age'. Vocal items are not preponderant
but the best are exceptional, ranging from the *a cappella* 'Cantemus' to the
diverting Offenbach-like 'Chanson du bébé' with its graphic cries of 'Atchi!'
'Papa' 'Pipi' 'Caca'. Only Rossini would have written an *a cappella* octet,
'Toast pour le nouvel an', which manages to celebrate champagne and the
Blessed Virgin at one and the same time. Yet not all the songs are amusing.
In 'L'ultimo ricordo' a dying man presses into his wife's hand the now faded
flower which she carried on their wedding-day. A swaying ostinato and the
rich, chromatic texturing underpin a vocal line of chiselled beauty which
reaches a declamatory climax similar in intensity to that of the 'Agnus Dei'
in the *Petite messe solennelle.* In one version of the song Rossini inserts his
wife's name into the text – 'This faded flower I leave to you, Olympe, as a
gift' – turning the song into his own private imaginary *Liebestod.* Equally

moving, with its despairing final cry of 'Ma mère, adieu!', is 'Elégie ('Adieux à la vie') sur une seule note'. In *Ciro in Babilonia* Rossini had written an aria on a single note as cruel prank. Here the effect is different: supported by an impassioned piano commentary, the monotone declamation gives the song a haunted, despairing quality as shifts of key, volume and pace articulate the text's changing perspectives.

Saint-Saëns was less than just when he talked of Rossini 'scribbling' these late pieces (the autographs are often beautiful calligraphic specimens), but most contemporaries seem to agree with his judgement that Rossini played the piano 'to perfection'. By all accounts Rossini's playing was precise without being dry, light-toned and sparely pedalled yet capable of considerable sensuous beauty, the hands gliding effortlessly across the keyboard. There is evidence of the neo-classical brilliance of his playing in pieces such as 'Prélude pétulant rococo' and 'Gymnastique d'écartement'. Few professional pianists have bothered to explore this repertory, though those who do will be surprised how strange much of it is to the touch, the fingerings often decidedly idiosyncratic.

In his earliest years Rossini had delighted in eighteenth-century Italian keyboard music (Clementi a particular favourite). Later the music of J. S. Bach was to leave its mark, clarifying and re-energising Rossini's writing and drawing from him a succession of wry tributes in pieces such as 'Prélude prétentieux' and the punningly named 'Prélude fugassé'. At the same time Rossini followed with interest the careers of leading contemporary composers. Ever the detached observer, he both appropriates and parodies their styles, hiding behind whimsical titles and defensive verbal epilogues lest we should be tempted to take the music too seriously. Thus we have a 'Thème naïf et variations idem', a 'Castor Oil Waltz' ('L'huile de Ricin') and a charmingly ruminative, rather Mendelssohnian piece entitled 'Ouf! les petits pois'. In the 'Petite caprice (style Offenbach)' the victim is openly named; the number – part jest, part parody – is said to have been Rossini's private response to Offenbach's guying the trio from *Guillaume Tell* in Act 3 of *La Belle Hélène* ('Lorsque la Grèce est un champ de carnage'). Marked 'Allegretto grotesco' and fingered in a decidedly novel way, the piece tiptoes its way through a harmonic minefield.

Rossini's relationship with the music of Chopin, Mendelssohn and Schumann is altogether more benign. 'Une caresse à ma femme', with its questioning Trio and a first subject of Eusebian wistfulness, could almost be by Schumann. Chopin may be gently chided in the title of the 'Prélude inoffensif' and made to wait upon tedious warming-up exercises in 'Mon prélude hygiénique du matin', but what follows pays generous tribute to a piano style noted for the elegance of its cantilenas, the brilliance of its sonorities and the quiet beauty of its modulations.

In the volume *Album de château* Rossini gives us specimens of the music of time past, time present and time to come. 'Spécimen de l'ancien régime' shines with its fine-grained melodic sense, its charming Biedermeierisch waltz and an exquisite short fugato in the Bach style. By contrast 'Spécimen de mon temps', despite some coursing pages in the manner of Schumann, seems to be parodying the four-square, robustly stated melodies all too familiar from many operas of the period. Cruellest of all is 'Spécimen de l'avenir', a wicked parody of the Lisztian method. Elaborate harmonic blueprints are laid down but lead nowhere; a huge accompaniment is set in motion but remains bereft of any covering melody; when a theme does finally appear towards the end of the piece, it is one of overwhelming banality.

If these pieces have a fault it is that some of them are too long, as discursive as the salon piece they sometimes deride. For all their good humour, grace and wit, there is also a sense in which they are the work of a man of complex moods, the humour occasionally morbid and coarse. In 'Un petit train de plaisir comico-imitatif' the train's progress is brought to an abrupt end by a fatal derailment. As the victims' souls soar heavenwards, the heirs of the more well-to-do victims cut a few celebratory capers. In 'Marche et reminiscences pour mon dernier voyage' Rossini writes his own requiem. The march is a funeral march after the manner of Beethoven or Chopin, if rather more broken-winded. Between the march fragments are quotations from several of Rossini's best-known operas. After a reference to the 'Goodnight' quintet from *Il barbiere di Siviglia* Rossini portrays himself: the theme is marked 'grazioso e leggiero'. Physically he was neither of these things, but, like Verdi's Falstaff, he believes himself possessed of a deftness of spirit which he defies the world to deny. The march continues to its grim close, at which point Rossini adds the single word 'Requiem'.

Petite messe solennelle

Rossini's real requiem, his true spiritual leave-taking, is the *Petite messe solennelle* (1863–4), the last of the important non-theatrical works and one of the finest of all his compositions. At a time when choral music was becoming ever grander and more bloated, the *Messe* is a singular achievement. Scored for twelve voices, two pianos and harmonium, it glances back to the music of Palestrina and forward to the music of Franck, Fauré and Poulenc. It has moments of airy joyfulness which suggest a spirit purged and liberated after deep gloom; yet it is also a work touched by doubt and riddled with anxiety.

The Kyrie immediately establishes this sense of spiritual bewilderment. The A minor–C minor–A minor framework contains tonal motion of unsettling fluidity, with Rossini's fondness for keys a third apart much in evidence – the moves to C major in the outer sections immediately darkening into C minor. Even more unsettling than the tonal motion is the actual sound of the music: harmony notes sustained by the eerie-sounding harmonium, while the pianos sketch out skeletal, asymmetrical ostinato figures which will later accompany the voices without in any real sense sustaining them.

The solo writing is particularly distinguished. The 'Qui tollis', a duet for soprano and contralto, clearly owes its inspiration to Rossini's artistic love-affair with the Marchisio sisters; this is music of tragic eloquence, long-breathed and gloomily beautiful. The A♭ major 'Crucifixus' is a strange piece: the piano's rhythm is lazily syncopated, and a drop back from C to B♮ in the repeated cry of 'Crucifixus' in bar 4 introduces a characteristic minor coloration, which Rossini will develop midway through the movement in an agonising sequence of rising minor thirds on a further fourfold repetition of the word 'Crucifixus'. The move to C♭ major at the words 'passus et sepultus est' has a sinking effect despite the major mode, and indeed Rossini recapitulates it in C major, hinting perhaps at the salvation which is the reason for Christ's passion. The double fugues at the end of the Gloria and Credo deploy a freely varied version of the *stile antico*. The 'Cum sancto spiritu', one of Rossini's happiest inventions, is based on a buoyant idea not unlike those in Haydn's masses. Yet the melancholy persists: the Agnus Dei sounds like late Schubert, the vocal line declamatory and intense, bordering on tragedy in the climactic cries of 'miserere'.

There are elements here which can be traced directly back to the sacred music Rossini was writing in Lugo, Ravenna and Bologna in his teenage years. What is different is the level of craftsmanship and, at a personal level, evidence of a life that has not been wholly merry and a mind-set that is not entirely serene. Which is why, if we wish fully to understand Rossini the man and the musician, it is to the non-stage works that we must eventually turn.

PART THREE

Representative operas

10 *Tancredi* and *Semiramide*

HEATHER HADLOCK

Tancredi and *Semiramide*, Rossini's first and last great Italian *opere serie*, bracket ten years of experimentation in the genre. Yet the two works do not fit into a 'progressive' developmental trajectory; rather, Rossini's Italian career seems to describe a loop, circling back to the elements and forms with which it had begun. Both works were written for Venice's Teatro La Fenice, *Tancredi* in 1813 and *Semiramide* in 1823. The prolific Gaetano Rossi wrote both librettos, basing each on a drama by Voltaire, *Tancrède* of 1760 and *Sémiramis* of 1748.[1] Formally both operas consist exclusively of arias, duets and full-cast ensembles – neither includes a trio (the Andantino for Semiramide, Arsace and Assur 'L'usato ardir' is part of the second-act Finale), quartet, etc. – and they employ almost the same array of voice-types, featuring soprano heroine, contralto hero *en travesti*, bass villain and tenor. Yet these similarities only highlight the differences between the two works, which reveal much about Rossini's development in the *seria* genre.

The invitation to compose a serious work for La Fenice came in 1812, after the success of the *farse* that Rossini had written for lesser Venetian theatres. *Tancredi*, which was premièred on 6 February 1813, catapulted the young composer to fame. The opera won praise for its magnificent sets and its cast, led by the company's *primo soprano assoluto* Adelaide Malanotte Montresor in the title rôle. But above all the success was due to Rossini's music, infused with the rhythmic vivacity and inventiveness that would become his trademark. A few days after the première the Venetian *Giornale dipartimentale* reported that 'the music of this opera in general offers a fragmented melodic style, with each step sprinkled with motives that are studied and brilliant at the same time'.[2] After the Venetian première the opera was quickly produced in Ferrara and then in Milan. For Ferrara Rossini revised the work rather drastically: he cut one of the two duets for the lovers Tancredi and Amenaide; reduced the tenor's rôle by omitting Argirio's Act 2 aria; and (most radically) replaced the Venetian happy ending with a tragic finale like that of the Voltaire source play.[3] For Milan he restored the lover's duet and the happy ending, and also returned Argirio's rôle to its original importance with two arias (both newly written for this version). Indeed, the revisions that *Tancredi* went through in its first season were extensive enough that we might consider the Venetian, Ferrarese and Milanese premières together as a kind of 'workshop' for the opera.[4] Only in Milan did it settle into something like a definitive form, and in this form it took Italy by storm. Within a few years of its première, *Tancredi* had become the modern classic of Italian serious opera, a model which new works would either imitate or – at greater risk – resist.

In the wake of *Tancredi*'s success, the impresario Domenico Barbaja invited Rossini to compose a new work for the Teatro San Carlo in Naples. *Elisabetta regina d'Inghilterra* (1815) established his reign in that theatre, where he served as music director for the next seven years. In the works that he wrote for Barbaja's company, Rossini faced the uncomfortable yet stimulating necessity of working against norms that he himself had established in *Tancredi* if he wanted to continue developing as an artist, and the nine Neapolitan *opere serie* are more experimental than either their predecessor *Tancredi* or their successor *Semiramide*.[5] Rossini and his librettists drew on such diverse literary sources as Tasso, Sir Walter Scott and the Bible, with settings that include Tudor England, the Scottish highlands, the quasi-legendary Holy Land of the Crusades and ancient Egypt. Working consistently with a company of outstanding singers, Rossini developed the florid vocal style that would culminate in *Semiramide*. Here he began writing for Isabella Colbran, the tempestuous Neapolitan prima donna who became his wife and for whom he composed, among others, the title rôles in *Elisabetta, Armida, Ermione, La donna del lago* and finally *Semiramide*. He also experimented with new uses of the conventional voice-types. Inspired by the talents of Giovanni David and Andrea Nozzari, he began composing heroic rôles for tenors, often favouring them over the female contraltos who had themselves begun to replace the castratos a generation earlier. *Otello* (1816), one of the most successful and durable of the Neapolitan works, actually features three tenors; *La donna del lago* (1819) is more curious still in that both a tenor and a female contralto *en travesti* (called a *musico* in contemporary parlance) vie for the heroine's affection and for the status of hero.

In his Neapolitan operas Rossini did not abandon the conventional forms that we now label with his name, but he began to stretch them. His music became more dramatically integrated, with mood and atmosphere sustained across multiple scenes and numbers, as in the brooding final act of *Otello* (1816). *La donna del lago* (1819) has a particularly magnificent opening scene-complex, a long duet for Elena and the tenor Uberto that grows seamlessly out of Elena's already unconventional opening barcarolle. Rossini stretched and blurred the contours of that duet to accommodate two choral interruptions and a scene-change, from the lake and forest of the *introduzione* to the hall of Elena's house. The duet's disparate movements, interrupted first by a hunters' chorus and then by women greeting Elena, are connected by the recurring barcarolle theme. In all the serious works composed for Naples one finds evidence of Rossini's concern for, and experimentation with, formal and structural elements.

Against this Neapolitan background, *Semiramide* looks deliberately classical, even regressive. For his return to Venice Rossini also returned to *Tancredi*'s traditional constellation of voices, and he retreated from formal experiments, packing his extravagant music into strict conventional forms that Marco Emanuele has described as 'grandiose but relatively simple geometries'.[6] Taking up those 'classic' forms again, this time inflating them to unprecedented proportions, Rossini was able simultaneously to yield to the overwhelming normative power of his first great success and rebel against it from within. If *Semiramide* represents a return to the composer's starting point c. 1813, it bears the stamp of his intervening years of exploration, both in the details of its construction and in its monumental, classicising approach to the *seria* archetypes.[7] (Indeed *Semiramide* seems to have exhausted those archetypes, and for the next generation they would represent a point of departure rather than a model.) Yet it would be a mistake to see *Semiramide* as a mere mannerist work; rather, its fascination lies in its paradoxical melding of conservative and progressive tendencies. If *Tancredi* and *Semiramide* do not quite bridge the gulf between eighteenth-century *opera seria* and nineteenth-century Romantic drama, they do show Rossini moving from the moral and aesthetic clarity of the classical tradition toward the more lavish, direct and morally ambiguous Romantic style.

From Voltairean tragedy to opera

The differences between the two operas begin with their source plays, two tragedies by Voltaire with colourful antique settings. *Tancrède* takes place in Syracuse, Sicily, at the time of the Crusades, while *Sémiramis* is set in the Babylon of the legendary Queen Semiramis, builder of the Hanging Gardens. Although both plots revolve around a question of crime and punishment, with a hero who must find a traitor and avenge the innocent, *Tancrède* is simpler and more straightforward than *Sémiramis* in its structure, focus and morality. When the heroine Amenaide is falsely accused of treason, her lover Tancrède must absolve her by defeating the real traitor, Orbassan, in a trial by combat. Never is there any ambiguity about her innocence or Orbassan's guilt. The tragic element resides in the hero's own limitations, for he is the only one who does not trust in the truth that his own victory has established; having saved Amenaide, he abandons her and only believes her innocence in the moment of his own death.

Where *Tancrède* centres on a hero, *Sémiramis* divides its focus between a hero's quest and an anti-heroine of Shakespearean moral complexity. The queen herself is the one whose criminal actions and desires must be purged for the redemption and renewal of the state. The drama relies on supernatural elements that had played no part in *Tancrède*'s more human drama, for the crime afflicting Babylon (Sémiramis's long-ago murder of her husband Ninus) is known only to the perpetrators, a ghost and the gods. Justice is served through divine revelation and accomplished with Arzace's unintentional killing of his mother, an error interpreted by all as divine retribution. Voltaire's *Sémiramis*, with its ghosts and oracles and its mingling of maternity and criminality, was intended by its author as a return to the classical values of ancient Greek tragedy, but in 1823 it also resonated with emerging Romantic tastes.[8]

Not surprisingly, Rossi adapted these two sources into librettos with strikingly different tones and dramatic styles. Following the example of earlier Italian librettists, he gave his *Tancredi* the traditional happy ending of *opera seria*.[9] Misunderstandings do happen in Syracuse (beginning with Amenaide's unsigned, intercepted letter to Tancredi), and individual villains like Orbazzano exploit them, but there is no pervasive corruption. The libretto's combination of moral clarity and dramatic irony makes the audience feel safe: although we pity the characters' confusion and unhappiness, we know the truth and expect that mysteries and misunderstandings will be resolved. Voltaire's *tragédie* became a *melodramma eroico*, in which political order and familial harmony ultimately prevail. Rossi's *Semiramide*, more faithful to Voltaire, is a real tragedy whose guilty yet sympathetic anti-heroine, unable to escape her own past actions, ultimately pays for her crimes and her hubris. We sympathise with her longing for happiness and for escape, but there can be no reconciliation. The action unfolds in a series of reversals, revelations and *coups de théâtre*, climaxing with Semiramide's death at her son Arsace's unwitting hands. No character consciously or intentionally punishes her; rather, her fate seems the inevitable work of a supernatural justice that leaves Arsace untainted by the usually unforgivable crime of matricide. This sacrificial purging cleanses the city and allows the new generation to start afresh with the blessing of the now-avenged father. *Semiramide*, with its guilty heroine, anticipates the tragic sensibility that will pervade operas of the 1830s, exemplified in Bellini's *Norma* and Donizetti's *Lucrezia Borgia*.

Voice types and rôles

Although the company of soprano, *musico*, tenor and bass required in these two operas would become obsolete a mere decade after *Semiramide*, it was still conventional in the 1810s and 1820s. *Tancredi* has the more balanced cast in that its main characters are given approximately equal importance, with similarly developed personalities and musical profiles. Of the three central characters the *musico* hero Tancredi dominates, followed by the soprano ingénue Amenaide and her tenor father Argirio. The most important secondary character is the bass villain, Orbazzano. *Semiramide*, ten years later, deploys these same voices in new ways that reflect the evolving tendencies in casting. Ingénue and tenor are demoted, while the bass villain is promoted to a new level of importance and the prima donna's rôle completely transformed. This cast is also curiously uneven, having two unusually complex characters in Semiramide and Assur; a rather conventional hero in Arsace (demoted from his central place in Voltaire's play); and two dramatic nonentities in Azema and Idreno.

The tenor rôle is more dramatically important in *Tancredi* than in *Semiramide*. In casting a tenor as Argirio, the father in *Tancredi*, Rossini followed the conventional use of this voice-type in the first two decades of the nineteenth century. Argirio is essential to the dramatic action, and his musical numbers grow out of and develop his relationships with the other protagonists: an aria addressed to Amenaide ('Pensa che sei mia figlia'), a prominent rôle in the Act 1 finale, and a dazzling martial duet with Tancredi ('Ah se dei mali miei'). Even in his most elaborate solo, the Act 2 soliloquy in which he wavers between severity and pity for Amenaide ('Ah! Segnar invano io tento'), his vocal flourishes and soul-searching are enmeshed in the opera's social fabric, being supported and punctuated by exhortations from the chorus.[10] Idreno, on the other hand, hovers on the margins of *Semiramide*'s plot and score. The only character not taken from Voltaire's play, he does not advance the action in his two elaborate arias and his function seems purely decorative. Idreno's rôle is symptomatic of the unsettled place of the tenor in the dramatic constellation of 1823: no longer a fatherly voice, it was not yet established as the proper or inevitable voice of the lover. Idreno thus represents a step back from Rossini's explorations of heroic tenor rôles and of tenor–soprano pairings in *La donna del lago* or *Otello*, and is one of *Semiramide*'s most regressive elements.

The bass villain Assur, on the other hand, represents a musical and dramatic advance from his counterpart in *Tancredi*. Like the earlier villain Orbazzano, Assur is the hero's rival and a corrupt general, a malicious schemer for political power. Yet Assur has an unusually complex psychology for an *opera seria* villain, for his place in the conventional love triangle involving himself, Arsace and Azema is overshadowed by the Shakespearean richness of his relationship with Semiramide. We see in their Act 2 duet how these two old accomplices in Nino's murder have become rivals for power, each distrusting and hating the other even as they are bound together by their guilty secret and political exigency. His mad scene in Act 2, where he seems to see the vindictive ghost of Nino even as he waits to ambush Arsace outside Nino's tomb, anticipates scenes of guilty delusion in operas of the Romantic generation and inspired some of the score's most intensely dramatic music.

While the villains and *musico* heroes of *Tancredi* and *Semiramide* are similar in voice and characterisation – in each case a sinister, scheming bass competes with an ardent young contralto rival for the love of a soprano ingénue – the heroines of the two operas could not be more different. Amenaide is a standard ingénue: innocent, loving, unjustly accused of wrongdoing, and at the mercy of the male order in which she lives. She is always subject to male authorities: her father, who threatens to disown her if she doesn't marry Orbazzano and win his military support for Syracuse; Orbazzano, who has her condemned to death on trumped-up charges of treason when she refuses him; and Tancredi, who loves her but believes Orbazzano's lies. She spends much of the opera being hectored, accused of crimes and incarcerated, praying always for outside forces to rescue her and clear her name. Her scenes emphasise her isolation and powerlessness, particularly the Act 1 Finale and the Act 2 prison scene, where she waits anxiously to learn the outcome of the off-stage trial by combat that will decide her fate.[11] She has no authority within the plot; not even Tancredi, who defends her, actually believes her story. Her power as a character comes from her sincerity and faith in the face of persecution, and even her most exalted moments, like the Act 2 prayer 'Giusto Dio, che umile adoro', move us through pathos rather than tragic grandeur. *Semiramide*, however, leaves behind this style of ingénue in favour of a new prima donna type, more socially powerful and psychologically complex.

There is no rôle analogous to Amenaide in *Semiramide*: Princes Azema's dramatic situation resembles Amenaide's in so far as she is secretly in love and dependent on powerful, hostile authorities to grant her happiness, but the opera reduces her to an absolute cipher. Although Azema had been a major character in Voltaire's play, and her scenes with the principals could easily have become musical numbers, Rossi and Rossini took none of these opportunities. Rather they focused their energies on Semiramide, who dominates the opera's action and moral landscape as well as its music. The near-elimination of Azema left the field clear for the title character's unchallenged dominance.

Rossini's Semiramide does differ from Voltaire's unrelievedly tragic queen in subtle but important ways, symptomatic perhaps of the transformation of Voltaire's self-consciously classical tragedy into an Italian opera. Rossini adds a sunny, flirtatious side to her original blend of melancholy and ferocity, as in the scene where she first appears with her ladies. Voltaire brought Sémiramis on fainting, clinging to her attendants for support, her first speech suggesting oppression of spirit if not outright delirium:

O voiles de la mort, quand viendrez-vous couvrir
Mes yeux remplis de pleurs, et lassés de s'ouvrir!
(*Elle marche éperdue sur la scène, croyant voir l'ombre de Ninus.*)
Abîmes, fermez-vous; fantôme horrible, arrête:
Frappe, ou cesse à la fin de menacer ma tête.
Arzace est-il venu?

[Oh veils of death, when will you cover my eyes, filled with tears and tired of being open! (*She staggers across the stage, believing she sees Ninus' ghost.*) Close up, oh abyss; horrid phantom, stop there: strike, or cease to threaten me. Has Arzace come?]

Rossini's Semiramide, on the other hand, describes the hopes that enliven her heart and mind in the brilliant coloratura aria 'Bel raggio lusinghier'. As in the play, she concludes by naming Arsace as the one who will ease her troubles, but her tone is different: her anxious 'Has Arzace come?' becomes the jubilant exclamation, 'Arsace has returned! Yes, he will come to me!' This aria, with the star supported by adoring female chorus, is also clearly designed to showcase Colbran's vocal gifts.

There is much more to Semiramide's character than this bravura optimism, however. While in *Tancredi* the *musico* hero had received top billing, Semiramide is second to no one in her cast, either in vocal brilliance or in dramatic complexity. In the subsequent course of the action her character gains depth and nuance as we see her torn between love and the will to power, tormented by guilt and denied redemption. She is a true tragic heroine, by turns imperious, guilt-ridden, amorous, optimistic and fatalistic. *Semiramide*'s most innovative and forward-looking character, then, is Semiramide herself, a prima donna ruling uncontested. Small wonder that Giuditta Pasta, Giulia Grisi and other divas of the post-Rossinian generation kept *Semiramide* in the repertoire long after the composer's other serious operas had fallen out of favour.

Musical structure and characterisation

Despite the similarities in their forms and vocal forces, *Tancredi* and *Semiramide* leave very different impressions, and this was true in their own time as well as in ours. *Tancredi* won praise for its clear harmonies (always subordinated to the singing melody), its formal purity and above all its melodic freshness. Giuseppe Carpani, answering an anonymous critic in Berlin who had wondered what was so remarkable about this 'so-called meteor of the modern Italian sky', this '*ne plus ultra* of the Italians of today', declared

Example 10.1 *Tancredi*, Allegro, 'Padre amato . . .', in Act 1 Finale

rapturously, 'it is *cantilena*, always *cantilena*, beautiful *cantilena*, new *cantilena*, magical *cantilena*, rare *cantilena*. Indeed, sir. This undiscoverable jewel, this rare if not exclusive merit of the Italians, this sun . . . shines again from its highest point in the music of Rossini.'[12] *Tancredi* thus seemed to restore an Arcadian past, a golden age of Italian song and musical spontaneity. The hero's entrance scene, with its pastoral orchestral introduction and unforgettable cabaletta 'Di tanti palpiti', was most frequently invoked as proof of this freshness and vigour, but examples occur throughout the score. The eight-bar melody for strings and winds that conveys Amenaide's mute distress to her father, lover and accuser in the Act 1 Finale, for example, inspired Stendhal to declare Rossini 'completely the master of those charming phrases of shapely and entrancing melody in the style of Cimarosa' (ex 10.1).[13] In *Tancredi* Italian opera seemed rejuvenated, bubbling up again from its original springs of inspiration, as Carpani concluded: 'The same nature that created a Pergolesi, a Sacchini, a Cimarosa and such, has now created a Rossini.'[14] Although *Semiramide*, ten years later, preserved the traditional forms found in *Tancredi*, Rossini now invested these forms with a musical language in every way more elaborate, and with new psychological and dramatic content.

Each opera begins with an *introduzione* for chorus and soloists that not only situates the action in place and time but also presents a characteristic 'sound-world' through orchestration, style and harmonic language. In *Tancredi* the curtain rises on a chorus of knights grouped casually in the courtyard of Argirio's palace. The sunny setting, an intermediate space between outdoors and indoors, suggests neither wild nature nor the oppressive or militaristic aspects of civilisation. Here nature and human order are in harmonious balance. The opening chords set the tone of pastoral simplicity and what Stendhal called the 'candeur virginale' that caused *Tancredi* to blow like a fresh breeze through the opera houses of its day. Philip Gossett, noting that English readers have often misconstrued Stendhal's phrase to mean that *Tancredi* represents Rossini's 'maiden effort' in the *seria* style, or (worse still) a naïve result of 'beginner's luck', rightly points out the sophisticated craftsmanship of *Tancredi*, emphasising the young composer's mature control of dramatic and musical forms.[15] Nevertheless, Stendhal's poetic locution does capture something of the opera's tone of sincerity and spontaneity. The knights in this opening chorus join in a light-hearted F major paean to 'Peace, honour, faith and love', vowing to devote their hearts to 'friendship most tender'. Although these utopian principles will be violated in the course of the action, the jaunty melody and diatonic harmonies of the *introduzione* give no foreshadowing of this.

In contrast with *Tancredi*'s cheerful, *al fresco* opening, *Semiramide* plunges us into a claustrophobic atmosphere of imminent crisis.[16] Rather than a sunlit chorus we see a High Priest and his attendants before the altar of a god who has apparently just promised 'a terrible moment of justice and revenge'. The very first words in the opera, Oroe's 'Yes, great god, I have heard thee', create a mystery, for there have been no witnesses to the priests' consultation with the god. Dread secrecy and divine retribution will be the guiding principles of this drama. When the priests are ready to open the doors, the people burst in with a festive chorus accompanied by on-stage military band, filling the stage with noise, light and splendour. Their exuberance does not dispel the ominous tone of the opening, however; rather it seems a vain attempt to overcome it with hysterical merriment. The men's trio and the exalted quartet with chorus that follow also have an edgy quality that seems to undermine the joyous solemnity of the occasion. The public grandeur of *Semiramide*'s *introduzione* is thus in constant tension with the private anxieties of the main characters. Although the libretto contains elliptical references to the central characters' guilty secrets and schemes, their anxiety is communicated most powerfully by the persistent agitation of the music. The vocal lines are full of fidgety turns, appoggiaturas and trills, over an equally frenzied orchestral texture. If Rossini's music has lost the clarity and spontaneity of *Tancredi* (as Stendhal complained), it serves the drama's difficult melding of mythic grandeur with the turbulent, all-too-human emotions of fear, guilt and personal ambition.

In *Semiramide*'s four grand duets, the traditional four-movement form that Rossini had all but codified likewise became the bearer of new psychological and dramatic content. The standard Rossinian duet has arioso passages of dramatic interaction alternating with more fully lyrical ones of private contemplation, a pattern exemplified in Tancredi and Argirio's 'Ah, se de' mali miei . . . Il vivo lampo' (Act 2). Twice in the course of this duet the participants turn away from each other to reflect on their situation: in the slow movement, father and lover lament their inability to hate the woman who seems to have betrayed them, while in the cabaletta they each swear revenge on the man who has accused her. Each lyric movement represents a doubled expression of a single emotion: sad love for 'the ungrateful woman' and a desire for revenge upon 'the traitor'. Tancredi and Argirio sing the same words, but they are not talking to each other – rather, each retreats into his own thoughts, contemplating the same absent object.

Although the duets in *Semiramide* follow the standard four-movement form, they tend to subvert or even abandon this habit of isolating characters during lyric movements. More subtly, they also chart the psychological nuances and the play of gendered qualities in the characterisations of the three central figures, particularly in the young hero Arsace and the queen Semiramide. The opera, following Voltaire, tacitly invokes the traditional androgyny of the legendary Sémiramis, an assassin, a warrior queen who dressed herself as a man, and a builder of mighty cities. Rossini's Arsace (*unlike* Voltaire's) becomes androgynous as well through the casting of a woman *en travesti*. If I may be forgiven an overly schematic use of the categories 'masculine' and 'feminine', traits associated with both genders are commingled in Semiramide and Arsace: their ambition and action are tempered with tender emotions, doubt and guilt. Assur, on the other hand, is unambiguously masculine: he is deep-voiced, single-minded, fierce and ambitious, a warrior and doer rather than a lover and dreamer. The extroverted, action-oriented traits of ferocity and ambition prevail in Assur's character, which lacks the more inward-facing emotions of love, ambivalence and anxiety.

As a masculine, active principle in the drama, Assur pushes Arsace and Semiramide out of their feminine absorption in feelings, their tendencies towards introspection and ambivalence. The slow movement of his Act 1 duet with Arsace ('Bella imago degli Dei') lays out this contrast. A tender flute melody introduces Arsace's declaration, 'You do not know what love is: of tender, true and constant love your fierce heart is incapable', while the accompaniment shifts into a 'feminine' triple metre, subdivided into lilting triplets. And indeed Arsace's mezzo-soprano voice is more at home in this delicate musical texture than Assur's bass. Nor does Assur defend himself as a lover – he only cares that Arsace's tender feelings are interfering with his own claims to the throne that Azema's husband will inherit. He refuses to be drawn into the contemplative style of a slow movement, but continues his taunts and threats: 'Renounce Azema, or fear for yourself!' The fierce

Assur never retreats into his own private thoughts, and does not give his antagonists time to do so either. When he is involved, conflict and dramatic interaction break in on traditionally introspective movements.

Assur thus seems to function as a kind of moving force that recasts the duet in a confrontational style. The *tempo di mezzo*, with its hammered chords and punctuating blasts from the brasses, brings the two antagonists back to Assur's masculine musical 'turf', and the cabaletta becomes a full-blown vocal duel. Assur has pushed Arsace into direct confrontation, and rather than turning aside to vent private feelings, the two characters hurl insults and challenges at each other: 'Go, arrogant one! I am ready to triumph in the royal palace.' The implicit competition between singers that energises any duet cabaletta here becomes an overt dramatic element. We see this merging of musical and dramatic contests in an 1827 review praising contralto Rosmunda Pisaroni for standing her ground against her bass rival: 'Now it is the little Arsace who overcomes the great Assur, Zucchelli.'[17]

In Assur's Act 2 duet with Semiramide ('Se la vita ancor t'è cara') the four-movement form carries even more complex dramatic content.[18] The *scena* begins with the two characters in similar psychological states, each angry and defying the other's anger. Semiramide tries to banish Assur, who in turn threatens to reveal her own part in her husband's murder. She claims that the gods have forgotten this long-ago crime, but Assur detects a note of uncertainty, and in the slow movement he preys on her emotions, drawing her into a disabling contemplation of her own guilt. The conventional slow tempo, quietly pulsing rhythm and reduced orchestration of the slow movement all underline his cruel insinuations, as stealthily treading middle voices are accompanied by a creeping bass line and anxious ascending gestures above. Weakening, she turns away from him to address her own 'treacherous heart' in an ever more neurotic G minor (ex. 10.2):

> Notte terribile!
> Notte di morte!
> Tre lustri corsero,
> e del consorte
> l'ombra sdegnosa,
> infra le tenebre,
> l'indegna sposa
> minaccia ognor!
>
> I miei spaventi . . .
> i miei tormenti,
> le angoscie, i palpiti,
> a tuo supplizio,
> gli Dei rivolgano
> perfido cor!

Example 10.2 *Semiramide*, duet Semiramide–Assur, 'Se la vita ancor t'è cara'

[Dreadful night! Night of death! Fifteen years have passed since then, yet my husband's angry ghost, from out the darkness, still menaces his unworthy consort! My fears, my suffering, my anguish and my agitation – let the gods turn them into a punishment for you, treacherous heart!]

The traditional introspection of a slow movement is present here, but it is one-sided: Semiramide alone is absorbed in private thoughts while Assur watches, feeding her distress with exhortations of 'Remember! Remember!' He takes advantage of the form itself in order to sap his antagonist's active energy.

Fortunately for Semiramide, a military band begins to play off stage, and its fanfares rally her spirits to resist Assur's manipulations. She escapes the trap of her own conflicted, guilt-ridden psyche and recovers a fierce masculine spirit like Assur's own, declaring, 'My heart regains its original force: as queen and warrior, I will know how to punish you!' This duet, like the earlier one for Assur and Arsace, ends with a cabaletta in which the two singers hurl threats and insults at each other. The distance between their vocal ranges intensifies the tension, pointing the way towards fiery male–female confrontations like the one between Lucrezia and Duke Alfonso in Donizetti's *Lucrezia Borgia*, and even beyond, to the soprano–baritone duets so central to Verdi's operas. Their encounters with Assur, then, compel both Arsace and Semiramide to access their 'masculine' energy, as he propels them into modern, action-oriented numbers.

By contrast, Arsace and Semiramide bring out each other's feminine-introspective sides in the two duets they sing together. The vocal style and emotional tone of these numbers are emphatically feminine, as each one features a lavish lyric movement that stops time in order to explore and express the characters' private feelings. Compared with the progressive style and drama of the opera's other duets, the Act 2 'Giorno d'orrore' sounds like a relic of the past. It exaggerates certain characteristic features of the traditional grand duet to the point of mannerism, particularly the luxuriant doubling of soprano sonorities and the exceptionally static slow movement. An oasis of suspended time in the midst of rapidly unfolding events, 'Giorno d'orrore' is both a culmination and an expansion of the Rossinian model. Yet paradoxically it too points towards the future, towards the presence of lush two-soprano duets like Bellini's 'Mira, o Norma' as a 'special effect' in operas of the 1830s.

Entrances (and departure) of the *musico* hero

Rossini's ability simultaneously to sum up and point beyond conventional *opera seria* forms and elements in *Semiramide* is also apparent if we compare the entrance scene for its contralto hero, Arsace, with the parallel scene in *Tancredi*. Formally, both *scena ed aria* complexes are similar and perfectly conventional: an opening recitative in which the hero comments on the landscape around him, followed by a slow movement in which he recalls the beginnings of his love for the heroine and an energetic cabaletta that celebrates their coming reunion. Through that conventional framework, however, Rossini creates two very different characters. Tancredi personifies an heroic ideal of chaste and elevated love; Rossini's defender Carpani, for example, links the character to the classical purity of Gluck in his response to a German critic who had derided the casting of a female *musico* hero, asking, 'Did not your Gluck himself compose Orfeo for a soprano?'[19] Tancredi is an unproblematic blend of civic virtue and individual devotion. Wrongly exiled from his native Syracuse, he has secretly returned with two objectives: to win both an end to his exile and the hand of Amenaide by defending his homeland against the Moors. In the lilting C major ritornello that ushers him onto the stage, we hear not only the lapping of the waves but also the purity of the hero's spirit and intentions.[20] The female performer, dressed as a warrior in helmet and tunic, evokes the traditional androgynous images of militant saints and angels. Tancredi's recitative monologue, 'O patria', blurs the line between civic and individual feeling as his apostrophe to the beloved country modulates towards the beloved woman:

> O patria! – dolce e ingrata patria! Alfine
> a te ritorno! – Io ti saluto, o cara
> terra degli avi miei: ti bacio. – È questo
> per me giorno sereno:
> comincia il cor a respirarmi in seno. –
> Amenaide! o mio pensier soave,
> solo de' miei sospir, de' voti miei
> celeste oggetto . . .

[Oh homeland! Sweet and ungrateful homeland, at last I return to you. I greet you, dear land of my ancestors: I kiss you. This is a blessed day for me: my heart begins to breath again within me. Amenaide! Oh sweet thought, bright object of my sighs and prayers.]

His rhetoric modulates just as effortlessly back again, and his concluding vow 'be worthy of you, or die' is addressed to both objects. Even the heady conclusion of 'Di tanti palpiti' remains faithful to the pure, pastoral style of the orchestral introduction, as Tancredi repeats his final line, 'I will nourish myself on your lovely glances' (ex. 10.3). As he anticipates a delight more spiritual than carnal, nothing disturbs our perception of this *musico* hero as chaste and exalted.

Example 10.3 *Tancredi*, cavatina Tancredi, 'Tu che accendi'

Like Tancredi, Arsace presents himself in a long solo *scena* and two-part cavatina, but his character is less angelic, less idealised. The distance travelled may be measured in the form of 'palpitar' that dominates Arsace's text, for the innocent *palpiti* (anxieties) of Tancredi's cavatina now become *palpitò*, Arsace's reminiscence of how the princess Azema once 'trembled' in his embrace.

> **Andante**
> Ah, quel giorno ognor rammento
> di mia gloria e di contento,
> che fra' barbari potei
> vita e onore a lei serbar.
> L'involava in queste braccia
> al suo vile rapitore;
> io sentia contro il mio core
> il suo core palpitar.

Schiuse il ciglio, mi guardò,
mi sorrise, e palpitò.

Allegro
Oh, come da quel dì
tutto per me cangiò!
Quel guardo mi rapì,
quest'anima avvampò:
Il ciel per me s'aprì,
amore m'animò . . .
D'Azema e di quel dì
scordarmi io mai saprò.

[Oh, I shall always remember that day of glory and happiness, when
among the barbarians I was able to preserve her life and her honour. Into
these arms I snatched her away from her vile abductor; I felt, against my
own heart, her heart beating. She opened her eyes, looked at me, smiled
and trembled. Oh, since that day, how everything has changed for me!
That gaze seized me, this soul burst into flame: the heavens opened for me,
and love so moved me that I shall never forget Azema and that day.]

Rossi's text for the Andante had ended with another, gentler verb: 'Schiuse
il ciglio, mi guardò . . . mi sorrise . . . sospirò' (She opened her eyes, looked
at me, smiled and *sighed*).[21] But when Rossini set this text, he substituted 'e
palpitò' (and *trembled*), introducing a more vibrant, more physical dimension to Arsace's recollection of the scene. The composer further emphasised
this couplet by setting it twice: Arsace sings it at the end of the Andante,
and then sings it again as a transition between the two statements of his
Allegro. Most significant is the way that Rossini intensified its second appearance. The first time we hear it the couplet is accompanied by an innocent
'sigh' motive (ex. 10.4a). But when Arsace returns to the memory midway
through the Allegro movement, gasping and palpitating orchestral effects
provide an erotic body for the hero that replaces the physical one on stage
(ex. 10.4b).

The passionate force of this aria creates a problem that drives the rest of
the opera: Rossini has taken the *musico* hero out of the chaste or sublime
realm of *Tancredi* and made him a new kind of lover, more fully imbued with
human sensuality. This sensuality in turn tested the limits of the convention
that allowed women to play lovers of female characters. Indeed, *Semiramide*'s
lurid plot of incestuous desire, paternal prohibition, last-minute revelation
and matricide may be read as an allegory about the proper relationship
between hero and soprano. The incest theme, in particular, both screens and
points towards the opera's real taboo – the soprano's desire for the newly
embodied contralto hero. The characterisation of the *musico* Arsace is part

Example 10.4 *Semiramide*, cavatina Arsace, 'Ah! quel giorno ognor rammento'

of *Semiramide*'s self-reflexive process of looking back on the *seria* tradition with the knowledge of its own obsolescence. We may read the *musico* Arsace's vexed relationships with the opera's two soprano characters, Semiramide and Azema, as a subtextual commentary on *opera seria*'s conventional yet increasingly dated practice of assigning heroic rôles to high voices.

To put it briefly, the prima donna Semiramide wants the wrong kind of love from her *musico* partner. When in their first duet Arsace stoutly and properly vows, 'I shall know how to die for my queen', she corrects him, 'No! you shall live for me' – accompanied by a new flute melody that flutters as flirtatiously as eyelashes. She wants Arsace's Eros, that palpitating and personal energy revealed in his first solo scene, rather than a more abstract or exalted devotion. But the opera demonstrates (in a series of implausible events that begins with an earthquake interrupting the announcement of their betrothal and culminates in the high priest's revelation that Arsace is Semiramide's long-lost son) that this Eros is impossible. In the slow movement of their final duet, 'Giorno d'orrore', the almost-lovers react to the revelation that they are mother and son with a mixture of horror at the crime and serene joy in the discovery of a proper channel for their mutual devotion.

What is that proper relation? Voltaire's play offers one answer when Arzace defends and defines his feelings for the queen to the jealous Princess Azema. Swearing that he loves Azema alone, he explains: 'Semiramis is dear to me, yes, I must declare it; your mouth and mine have praised her together. We have gazed upon her as a guardian deity, who watched over the sacred flame of our holy rites. Perhaps it is with such ardour, and with such pure vows, that the gods wish to be adored.'[22] The devotion Arsace describes is an infantile adoration of the goddess-queen who provides motherly care for her subjects. On one level, the revelation that Semiramide is Arsace's mother – and that he therefore cannot be the lover she desires – restores this relationship, made audible in the quasi-*religioso* quality of their duet, with its plain and perfectly parallel melodic lines. But the mother–son dynamic is complicated by the suggestion that even as the plot reveals Semiramide's maternal status, Arsace becomes her instructor and protector: the wise child, in teaching the mother how to be loved, himself moves into a maternal posture. The voice of the *musico* becomes in this duet the feminine voice of a mother – a beloved object of vocal imitation, a 'tutelary goddess' with whom the child prays. In the mannered exaltation of the slow movement, and in the subsequent cabaletta where Arsace 'leads' for the first time, Arsace and Semiramide become not hero and heroine, but rather two *women* in a reciprocally maternal relation to each other. This relation, purged of impossible Eros, returns them to the chaste and idealised love that had previously been possible between *musico* heroes and their soprano partners.

Yet even this purification of the relationship between *Semiramide*'s *musico* and prima donna cannot redeem the plot or the practice of casting women as men. Semiramide, the criminal mother, must be sacrificed in the final scene. More strikingly, the opera has so thoroughly demonstrated the impossibility of Eros between Arsace and another soprano that no musical place remains for Princess Azema. Despite her apparent importance as the object of obsession for all three of the male leads, Azema has no arias, and not even a recitative scene with Arsace, much less a duet. Azema is, in short, the 'blank spot' where Arsace's soprano object of desire should – but, according to the opera's internal logic, *cannot* – be. As if to emphasise this logic even further, Rossi and Rossini also invented the tenor prince Idreno, of whom Azema remarks, 'If Arsace did not have and deserve all my affections, I think I could love only Idreno' (recitative after no. 4 in Act 2). Perhaps Azema, in this brief recitative, sees opera's future.

Rossini did not take Italian opera into that future, of course. He moved to Paris, where he made over his earlier *opere serie Maometto II* and *Mosè in Egitto* as the French grand operas *Le Siège de Corinthe* and *Moïse* before proceeding to his final serious work, *Guillaume Tell*. Within a few years after the stylistic watershed of 1830, even the most successful of his Italian serious operas had come to sound old-fashioned. After hearing the contralto Rosmunda Pisaroni, the most celebrated Arsace of Rossini's era, sing his Act 2 aria in 1833, a critic noted, 'Arsace's *rondò*, as sung by la Pisaroni, is a delicious thing which must intoxicate even the insensitive listener, and which does not allow even the most eloquent to describe their feeling of inebriation. But more moderate tastes now dominate the Italian stages.'[23] To those new tastes, the once-dazzling Rossinian vocalism seemed fussy and tedious. And as vocal styles and training changed to meet the demands of Donizetti, Bellini and Verdi, Rossinian *bel canto* ceased to be generally singable.

Nevertheless, *Tancredi* and *Semiramide* each enjoyed a notable 'after-life', thanks to the popularity of particular numbers and to the advocacy of certain singers. Long after *Tancredi* had fallen out of the operatic reper-toire, the hero's famous 'Di tanti palpiti' lived on in concert performances, instrumental arrangements and variations of all kinds.[24] As a favourite inter-polation for the 'Lesson Scene' in *Il barbiere di Siviglia*, the 'palpiti' aria trav-elled through history on the coattails of Rossini's comic style, which never lost favour. While no single number in *Semiramide* enjoyed this degree of popularity and familiarity, its title rôle remained a favourite of prima donnas who could handle its unusual combination of coloratura virtuosity and dramatic authority. Throughout the nineteenth century *Semiramide* proved irresistible to those few sopranos who could both sing it and per-suade impresarios to revive it. Giulia Grisi kept the piece in the repertory at the Théâtre Italien from 1841 to 1847 and then took it to London, where it played annually until 1851. Carlotta Marchisio, partnered by her sister Barbara as Arsace, revived it at Paris's Salle Le Peletier in a French four-act version in 1860. Later in the century, Adelina Patti performed it every year in London between 1878 and 1885, and Nellie Melba brought it to New York's Metropolitan Opera in the 1890s. Thus it was by far the longest-lived of all Rossini's serious operas, albeit in heavily cut and rearranged forms.

Semiramide also left subtler traces on Italian serious opera, which was poised on the threshold of great changes when Rossini left it. While *Semiramide* did not in itself establish a new paradigm, I have tried to sketch some of the ways in which it pointed to later developments. Its moral complexity and the psychological depth of its soprano and bass protagonists anticipated Romantic tastes, as did its destabilising of the old-fashioned contralto hero type. It foreshadowed the next generations' incorporation of dramatic action and development in lyric movements that had traditionally been static. Its monumental construction, particularly the spectacular tableaux of its *introduzione* and ensemble Finales, made it a model for later, more grandly conceived, operas. Its exotic *mise en scène* proved especially important for later Biblical and Orientalist opera, beginning a lineage that would extend through *Nabucco* and *Aida* to *Turandot*. Although audiences regarded it as old-fashioned just ten years after its première, it may be that they saw only half the picture; nearly two hundred years later, we can discern *Semiramide*'s resonances with Italian opera's future as well as its past.

11 *Il barbiere di Siviglia*

JANET JOHNSON

Le Barbier de Séville, ou La Précaution inutile has been on the boards of the Comédie Française almost continuously since its première there on 23 February 1775. But outside Paris and professional literary circles the play by Beaumarchais has long been virtually synonymous with Rossini's *opera buffa* on a libretto by Cesare Sterbini, given its first performance in Rome on 20 February 1816 as the third opera of the Teatro Argentina's Carnival season.[1] Rossini's most frequently staged work, *Il barbiere di Siviglia* was one of only two or three still being performed when the 'renaissance' of his music began in the twentieth century. It is also the first for which a critical edition was prepared,[2] and has continued to be anthologised as the composer's representative work.

Yet despite the accolades of Italians like Verdi, who at the end of the nineteenth century pronounced it 'the finest opera buffa ever written',[3] *Il barbiere di Siviglia* has not commanded anything like the prestige enjoyed by Mozart's *Le nozze di Figaro* (1786), based on Beaumarchais's sequel play, *Le Mariage de Figaro* (1784). Rossini scholars have generally attributed the work's mixed critical reception to its performance 'traditions', a snowballing accumulation of cuts, substitutions and mutations in vocal casting and orchestral disposition, made with or without Rossini's consent to accommodate specific performers and local preferences, beginning with its very first season. Such 'corruptions', Alberto Zedda has argued, echo traits of earlier, Neapolitan intermezzi, turning what he supposes to be a modern 'comedy of character' into farce, and its 'psychologically deepened' personae into two-dimensional stereotypes.[4]

Even more fundamentally problematic, however, are the entrenched assumptions about genre underlying such claims, assumptions conditioned by Mozart's reading of *Le Mariage de Figaro* and the universalising claims that have been made for it. The tendency in the Beaumarchais literature has been to read *Le Barbier de Séville* in terms of *Le Mariage de Figaro*, and the latter in terms of its posthumous reputation as proto-Revolutionary. This tendency has been carried to an extreme in the musicological literature owing both to the prestige of Mozart's work and to the chronologically later, post-Revolutionary position of Rossini's. When the characters of *Il barbiere di Siviglia* turn out to be nothing like their 'older' counterparts, we blame either Rossini or his performers. But the two sets of characters are the dramatic and musical equivalent of *faux amis*, the plays two very different kinds of comedy.[5] A brief exploration of Beaumarchais's play will therefore help us to reassess Rossini's opera in terms more appropriate to its own pedigree.

Le Barbier de Séville, a comedy of intrigue

Le Barbier de Séville is not a comedy of character, but a comedy of intrigue and words. Its effectiveness depends upon its rapid pace, its accumulation of imbroglios, and its sustained and virtuosic combination of literary wit and linguistic invention. Its origins lie in Spanish-inspired French farce and Fair theatre opera.[6] The comedy of intrigue had fallen into disrepute in France in the aftermath of Molière, whose serious comedies had developed character over intrigue by probing 'blocking' comic types like the miser and the misanthrope. As August Wilhelm Schlegel pointed out in the lectures he delivered at the University of Vienna in 1808, however, the older genre had 'become new again by force of having been neglected'. He defended it against 'what French critics called the *pièce de caractère*', asking: 'What kind of invention cannot be found in a work of this genre [the *pièce d'intrigue*]? Is it not an amusement for our intellect [esprit] to see a display of such acuteness and ingenuity, and don't the wonderful tricks and contrivances which are practised have a great charm for the fancy? This is at least what the example of many a Spanish piece has sufficiently proved.'[7] The Spanish connection has usually been presumed to have been only a source of local colour (sets and costumes, and musical *décors* like serenades and guitar accompaniment). In fact, it was crucial to the playwright's choice of comic genre, which in turn reflects the formative influence on Spanish theatre of the *commedia dell'arte*.

The play's carnivalesque themes (disguise and the reversal of a repressive moral order) as well as its setting in a Franco-Spanish 'never-never land'[8] suited this concentration on intrigue, opening it up to the theatrical interplay of comic character types, conventions and modes from both Spanish and French dramatic and literary genres. These included the *entremés*, a farcical genre with music and dance performed between the acts of a *comedia*. It satirised risqué topics like divorce and cuckoldry and featured a stock type unknown in French and Italian theatre, the barber go-between. As is now known, though it has gone unacknowledged in the musicological literature, the earliest incarnation of *Le Barbier de Séville* was an 'intermède imité de l'espagnol' modelled on the *entremés*. Entitled *Le Sacristain*, it appears to have been performed in a double bill with one of the pseudo-populist *parades* that launched Beaumarchais's dramatic career sometime between 1765 and 1772.[9]

Also at play was the Spanish picaresque tradition from which the *entremés* derived the figure of the barber. Both the satiric chronicle of recent escapades that Figaro relates to the Count (Act 1, scene 2) and the play's subtitle, which alludes to a seventeenth-century *nouvelle* by Paul Scarron set in Spain, reveal that he is a *pícaro* – a witty and peripatetic rogue. His name may in fact derive from that word.[10] The picaresque narrative had been popularised by French works like Le Sage's novel *L'Histoire de Gil Blas de Santillane* (1715–35), which traces its hero's life from his beginnings as a barber to his remarriage, including his surgical internship with Doctor Sangrado and his commissions for various nobles. Influential, too, especially from the point of view of narrative technique, was Diderot's tale *Jacques le fataliste et son maître*, written and read in Paris around 1772 and published two decades later. These works were themselves influenced by Rabelais and Cervantes, and, in the case of Diderot's tale, the novels of Sterne (*The Life and Opinions of Tristram Shandy, Gentleman*, 1759–67, and *A Sentimental Journey through France and Italy*, 1768), which were to be translated and adapted for the French theatre in the early nineteenth century. Their heroes became prototypes for the Romantic grotesque, the revived, romanticised form of the carnivalesque that survived as a literary and artistic mode and countered the classical aesthetics of the beautiful and the sublime. They inherited the rôle of carnival's main representative in the eighteenth century, Harlequin, hero of the *commedia dell'arte*, one of the only forms in which the original folkloric traditions of carnival had survived.[11] Since its demise in the middle of the eighteenth century, explains Stendhal in his analysis of *Il barbiere di Siviglia*, 'the little true comedy still left in Italy is found in marionette shows'.[12] In the play, the first words out of the Count's mouth on seeing Figaro are 'I know that man. That grotesque shape. I believe that's that rascal Figaro.'

When the Italian playwright and librettist Carlo Goldoni purged comedy of its 'filthy Harlequinades' in order to make it more moral and realistic, he turned the carnivalesque into a 'cautious bourgeois festivity' characterised by 'a certain spirit of civic happiness and honesty that amuses greatly and doesn't offend'.[13] Even his overtly fantastic 'reverse-world' librettos like *Il paese della Cuccagna* were meant to illustrate the dangers of carnivalesque vice already satirised in his mid-century reform plays. In *Il tutore*, for example, Pantalone warns his charge that women who go out into the disorder that reigns beyond the domestic sphere may leave wearing a 'mask of indifference' but are bound to return wearing a 'mask of diminished reputation'.[14] 'Espagna' is indeed the reverse world of carnival, as Beaumarchais's own antagonist, Doctor Bartholo, suggests indirectly when he unconvincingly tells his ward Rosine that 'this isn't France, where women always get their way; but to rid you of that fantasy, I'll close the door' (Act 2, scene 15).[15]

In an open letter published in 1775 with the first edition of his play, Beaumarchais reminded stodgy critics that its characters in fact go all the way back to the archetypal ones of classical New Comedy: 'An amorous old man intends to marry his pupil tomorrow; a young, more adroit lover forestalls him and that very day makes her his wife under the nose of her tutor and in his own house.' Progressive, though, was the inclusion of the eponymous character conspicuously missing from this scenario, Figaro, who according to Beaumarchais specialises in 'shaves, *romances* and marriages'.[16] As Figaro himself explains, he has left the whole 'republic of letters' behind in Madrid and traded in his pen for a razor with which to 'faire la barbe à tout le monde' – a pun on 'barbe' (a shave or the quill of a pen), meaning 'to take people by the beard', or to 'exercise one's superiority over people'. The idiom also plays on the then influential definition of laughter that Hobbes gave in *Leviathan* (1651), as the 'sudden glory' caused by 'the unexpected sight of our superiority over someone'.[17]

Another progressive feature was the play's shift of focus away from old Doctor Bartholo, who it should be noted is neither a pedant nor a charlatan like Molière's doctors but an enemy of the French Enlightenment drawn 'a little less stupid than those tutors usually deceived in the theatre' (hence the indignity of the Count's *parade*-like wordplay on his name: Barbaro, the Italian word for 'barbarian', and Balordo, or 'numskull', a bastardisation of 'Baloardo', Bartholo's 'unevolved' ancestor from the *commedia dell'arte*).[18] Emphasis was displaced from Bartholo onto the youthful, romantic protagonists, both of 'noble extraction', although in order to be loved truly the Count disguises himself as the poor student 'Lindor', enveloped in a brown ecclesiastical cape. Lindor was also the hero of *Le Sacristain*, whose title refers to the sexton responsible for a church's sacristy and for ringing bells and digging graves. As 'the indispensable hero of the majority of the *entremeses* and *sainetes* of the Spanish repertory', the *sacristán* was also 'a seducer *par excellence*, who even obtained preference over the military in the hearts of the fair sex', playing a rôle 'similar to that of the monk in our old farces'.[19] In this *intermède*, Lindor woos Pauline, wife of the impotent Bartholo, by disguising himself first as a drunken soldier with a billeting warrant, then as the *sacristán* supposedly sent by the organist of the local convent, Dom Bazile, to give her a music lesson. 'Figuaro' did not actually figure in the story until 1772, when Beaumarchais recast his material as an *opéra comique*. The character's job will be to mediate between Beaumarchais and his audience as well as between 'Lindor' (now 'Le Comte' in disguise) and 'Rosine' (now Bartholo's ward, not his wife).

The Count's two further disguises afford pretexts for their meetings (Act 2, scenes 12–14, and Act 3, scenes 2–13). These are as in the *intermède* except that for the music lesson he is disguised as 'Alonzo', supposedly sent by Don Bazile, who is busy spreading rumours about Count Almaviva. Each meeting includes dialogue spoken openly 'in character' by the dissimulating lovers as well as stolen, 'out of character' asides, with the additional complication that while 'out of character' as the soldier or 'Alonzo', the Count is still 'in character' as 'Lindor'. Moreover, Rosine imagines herself to be playing the heroine's rôle in the fictional opera of the play's subtitle, a cliché of the Fair theatres.[20] At the dénouement (Act 4, scene 6) when, believing 'Lindor' to be Almaviva's procurer, she is about to abandon herself to Bartholo, he tears off his cape to reveal that he is Almaviva himself. This clears the way for their marriage and Figaro's pronouncement of the play's cautionary maxim: 'When youth and love unite to deceive an old man, everything he does to prevent it can rightly be called *The Useless Precaution*.'

The first version of the work to bear its present title was the lost *opéra comique* rejected by the Comédie Italienne reportedly because the Spanish and Italian airs Beaumarchais had allegedly composed or adapted were thought inadequate and his situations considered too close to those of a sentimental one-act *opéra comique* by Monsigny and Sedaine, *On ne s'avise jamais de tout* (1761). Unusually for the Comédie Française, the play as performed in 1775 still included four vocal numbers, published separately in orchestrations provided by the theatre's *chef d'orchestre*, Antoine Laurent Baudron, who also contributed the storm music between the third and fourth acts (see Table 11.1).

The lovers also sang snatches of four tunes from contemporary *opéras comiques – vaudevilles* whose original texts, replaced by Beaumarchais, would have suggested themselves to contemporaries as subtexts. Rosine's two-line response to 'Lindor's' serenade, ostensibly from *La Précaution inutile* but actually from an *opéra comique mêlée d'ariettes et de vaudevilles* about another, famously amorous Lindor, betrayed her dreams of yielding to his desire. The two rowdy songs sung by the Count in the billeting scene evoked even bawdier counterparts and audibly reinforced his disguise.[21] Significantly, in every case but Figaro's song, which is *composed*, the character in question is *performing* a preexistent, or supposedly preexistent piece. As in popular French lyric theatre, this performative inclination distanced the audience from the illusion of reality produced on stage, reminding them of the other contexts in which they had heard the same melody.

The grotesque carnival of *Il barbiere di Siviglia*

Giovanni Paisiello's opera based on Beaumarchais's play, *Il barbiere di Siviglia, ovvero La precauzione inutile* (St Petersburg, 1782), had turned carnival into the kind of decorous celebration found in Goldoni's reform

Table 11.1 Source texts for *Il barbiere di Siviglia*

Number in *Il barbiere di Siviglia*	Principal passage in *Le Barbier de Séville*
Sinfonia	* =**musical number**
ACT 1	**ACT 1**
1: Count's cavatina, 'Ecco ridente in cielo', included in *introduzione*	MONOLOGUE: Count Almaviva, sated with the pleasures of court in Madrid (1: 1)
2: Figaro's cavatina, 'Largo al factotum della città!'	**IMPROVISATION*: Figaro, 'Bannissons le chagrin' on the good life (1: 2) (guitar)
	TIRADE: Figaro, literary travelogue (1: 2 and 6)
3: 'Lindoro's' *canzone*, 'Se il mio nome saper voi bramate' (two strophes)	**ROMANCE*: Lindor, 'Vous l'ordonnez, je me ferai connaître' (1: 6) (serenade in three couplets, text improvised at Rosine's request to tune 'from *La Précaution inutile*', with guitar)
(Rosina's 2- and 3-bar inverted echoes after the strophes of No. 3)	**VAUDEVILLE*: Rosine, 'Tout me dit que Lindor est charmant' (1: 6) ('from *La Précaution inutile*', words and music from Monsigny and Lemonnier's *opéra comique Le Maître en droit*, 1760)
	ACT 2
4: Recitative and duet for Figaro and the Count, 'All'idea di quel metallo'	DIALOGUE: (Rec.: 1: 6; 4: 8; Duet: 1: 4; 2: 6)
5: Rosina's cavatina, 'Una voce poco fa'	MONOLOGUE: Rosine, epistolary scenes (writing to Lindor, reading his letter to her) (2: 1; 2: 16)
6: Basilio's aria, 'La calunnia è un venticello'	*TIRADE*: Don Bazile, calumny speech (2: 8)
7: Recitative and duet for Figaro and Rosina, 'Dunque io son . . . tu non m'inganni?'	DIALOGUE: (2: 2)
8: Bartolo's aria, 'A un dottor della mia sorte'	*TIRADE*: Bartholo to Rosine on writing covert letters (2: 11)
9: Finale (Marziale movement), 'Ehi di casa . . . buona gente . . .'	DIALOGUE: (2: 12–14 plus 15), including **VAUDEVILLES* for Count Almaviva: 'Réveillons-la' (a well-known *réveille*); 'Le Chef branlant, la tête chauve' ('Ici sont venus en personne', an erotic song from a lost *opéra comique, Le Contrat de mariage*, 1742); and 'Non, docteur, je ne prétends pas' ('Vive le vin', from Monsigny and Sedaine's *drâme mêlé de musique Le Déserteur*, 1769, sung by a mock-serious drunken dragoon)
ACT 2	**ACT 3**
10: Duet for Bartolo and 'Don Alonso', 'Pace e gioia sia con voi'	DIALOGUE: (3: 2)
11: Rosina's music lesson aria, 'Contro un cor che accende amore'	**ARIETTE* (Séguedille): Rosine, 'Quand dans la plaine' (3: 4) ('from *La Précaution inutile*')
12: Bartolo's music lesson aria, 'Quando mi sei vicina'	**[AIR WITH] RITOURNELLE*: Bartholo, 'Veux-tu, ma Rosinette?' (3: 5) (strings only)
13: Quintet for all the principals, 'Don Basilio! . . .'	DIALOGUE: (3: 11–12 – *scène de stupéfaction*)
14: Berta's aria, 'Il vecchiotto cerca moglie'	DIALOGUE: (2: 6)
15: *Temporale*	**ORAGE POUR L'ENTR'ACTE DU 3.e AU 4.e*
	ACT 4
16: Recitative and trio for Rosina, Figaro and the Count, 'Ah, qual colpo inaspettato!'	DIALOGUE: (4: 6)
17: Accompanied recitative and Count's aria, 'Cessa di più resistere'	*TIRADE*: Count Almaviva to Bartholo on abuse of authority (4: 8)
18: *Finaletto* II, 'Di sì felice innesto'	DIALOGUE: (4: 8 – Figaro's maxim: 'La Précaution inutile')

comedies. His Figaro, for example, dares not discuss on stage the necessity of the Count's appearing drunk when he arrives at Bartolo's disguised as a soldier-veterinarian. By contrast Rossini's opera, performed in the midst of Roman Carnival, embodies the world of early Romantic grotesque realism, where the picaresque meets the *parade*.[22] His Count lives up to his name, meaning 'lively soul' – one reason the opera was presented during its first season under the title *Almaviva, ossia L'inutile precauzione*. The official reason given in the *Avvertimento al pubblico* issued with the libretto – 'the sentiments of respect and veneration which animate the author of the music of the present *dramma* towards the so celebrated Paisiello, who has already treated this subject under its original title' – simply put a polite (and politic) construction on Rossini's radically different aesthetic sensibilities.[23]

In order to introduce the choruses 'essential to the musical effect in a theatre of considerable capacity', and also to bring out the play's two-fold identity as a romantic fantasy with *parti serie* and a gallery of grotesques, he and his librettist parodied yet another Spanish genre suggested by the play: the cloak and sword comedy, with its emphasis on reputation and masculine honour always on the verge of erupting into violence (though rarely with serious consequences). Their sword-wielding Count overplays his rôle in the opening movement of the Finale as a soldier spoiling for a fight. Reverting to type, he provokes the arrival of the entire cast as well as an added men's chorus (as 'la forza') – a send-up of the Goldonian requirement that first-act Finales achieve maximal comic confusion. In Mozart's central Finale, it will be recalled, it is Antonio, a mere gardener, who turns up drunk, not a Spanish grandee. The Count's feigned drunkenness, however, restored carnival's 'temporary suspension of all hierarchic distinctions and barriers among men and of certain norms and prohibitions of usual life'.[24]

It is this carnivalesque context that will make the exercise of privilege so shocking, facilitating large-scale effects like the 'quadro di stupore' (the Finale's *largo concertato*, 'Fredda ed immobile'), produced when with a word to the head officer the Count averts arrest. At the end of the opera, when Rossini's Count cannot persuade Basilio to sign his marriage certificate with either his rank or his wealth, he is forced to offer him 'two bullets through your head' as a more effective incentive. Since nobility still has its obligations, he also lectures the doctor on his own, far more serious abuses of power (in the aria with chorus 'Cessa di più resistere'). In fact, all of the 'new situations for musical pieces' which Sterbini says were contrived to satisfy 'modern theatrical taste, so much altered since the epoch in which the renowned Paisiello wrote his music', involve either the Count or Rosina, or both. The poet's contention that he 'would not otherwise have dared to introduce the slightest change into the French product, already consecrated by theatrical applause throughout all of Europe' thus needs to be understood partly as a reference to the early Romantic revival of the carnivalesque.

Although the contexts for understanding the Count's *vaudevilles* would have been less accessible outside Paris, Sterbini facilitated Rossini's recreation of the spirit in which they are sung by rendering them in *versi lirici* as part of the Finale. The preponderance of arias in the opera, moreover, is directly attributable to the play. With only two exceptions, these derive from essentially the same songs, *tirades* and monologues adapted in Paisiello's *Barbiere di Siviglia*, which had been pronounced an 'exact translation' bereft of 'the epigrams, the sallies and the original features of the play'.[25] Yet all but one of these, the one-movement *aria di sorbetto* added for the *seconda donna* who played Bartolo's harassed old housekeeper, Berta, emulate the performativity and virtuosity of their source texts.

'Cessa di più resistere', the other exception, is the only aria the Count sings *in propria persona*, heard only in recitatives up to the trio (the first number in which we see his costume as a Spanish grandee). His earlier arias are relatively modest serenades – which is not to say that his florid cavatina, 'Ecco ridente in cielo' (part of the *introduzione*), is modest at all; sung before dawn, this rousing double aria is accompanied by full orchestra including brass, plus guitar and sistrum, the Count having hired musicians to cover his own musical inexperience. By contrast the later aria, paired with the opera's only accompanied recitative, opens with an added *primo tempo* inspired by his imperious *tirade*. Its slow movement is addressed to Rosina, and its fast concluding movement is a theme and two increasingly ornate variations with choral *pertichini* and repeated cadential extensions, audible proof that his heart is 'the most joyful, the happiest of all loving hearts'.[26]

It is Figaro, however, who was perceived from the beginning as the embodiment of the Romantic grotesque.[27] His ironically distanced perspective gives the opera its status as a piece of 'metatheatre' representing the world as a stage and life as a dream. This distanced perspective is especially apparent during the 'quadro di stupore', a pseudo-canon in the relaxed key of A♭ unfolding at an Andante tempo in the 'suspended time' of 12/8 metre, all the more effective because it appears in the midst of a series of dramatic *péripéties éclairs* – lightning-fast turning points marking the shift of advantage from one group of characters to another. As all profess to be 'cold and motionless like a statue', having 'hardly the breath to breathe', Figaro can barely restrain his laughter, cuing ours in a contrasting phrase, where he tells us, 'Guarda Don Bartolo, sembra una statua!' ('Look at Don Bartolo, he seems like a statue!'). It is by means of this laughter 'at the second degree' that Figaro forges the social alliance with the audience required by comedy. For an age as individualistic as the nineteenth century, when audiences preferred tears to laughter and turned for comedy to novels, Figaro thus solved a problem which the simulated laugh-track on television situation comedies solved for twentieth-century at-home audiences.[28] He was a prototype for a new kind of hero, whose invention was to be the first step in the Romantic era's reconception of laughter as individual and distanced rather than direct and collective, and as biting rather than benign, to be accomplished with heroes like the young artist of Berlioz's *Symphonie fantastique* and the jester Triboulet of Victor Hugo's *Le Roi s'amuse*.

Figaro as machinist

Figaro's part is a double one: he is both character and author. Beaumarchais called the barber his 'machinist' – in eighteenth-century theatrical parlance, 'the one who weaves the intrigues and leads the theatrical action', a 'machine', according to the *Dictionnaire de l'Académie*, being 'an invention, an intrigue, a ruse used in some situation'.[29] This had been the function of Harlequin and the other scheming valets of French and Italian comic tradition. Figaro, of course, is Count Almaviva's *former* valet, though in the later plays he returns to the Count's service and stays on for another twenty years, following the family even when it renounces its title and emigrates to Revolutionary Paris. But barbers as a class were freelance valets, and Figaro retains this dramaturgical function, expanded to include compositorial duties both literary and musical.

It is Figaro's rôle as machinist that Rossini and Sterbini celebrate in the duet 'All'idea di quel metallo', which is precipitated by the Count's insistence that he is 'delirious, on fire' and must see Rosina 'at all costs'. In the first movement, Figaro hatches the play's intrigues in two modulatory passages employing *parole sceniche* and *parlante* and then, urged on by the Count's bravos, congratulates himself on his own 'invenzione prelibata' (exquisite invention). His opening statement of the movement's theme employs the musical equivalent of what Freud calls 'ideational mimicry'[30] to spoof the effect that the 'idea' of gold has had on generations of valets past. A hushed Maestoso phrase made of dotted rhythms and rising sixths sequentially interlocked with descending sevenths sinking under the imaginary weight of 'portentous, omnipotent' gold is followed by a 'volcanic eruption' (marked Vivace) into fast, florid triplets for the extended cadential phrase group.

The cabaletta plays on Julien Offroy de La Mettrie's materialistic interpretation of psychic phenomena (*L'Homme machine*, 1747), as if to prove the philosopher Henri Bergson's theory that laughter is animated by some 'psychic automatism' – the mechanical element in our personality resembling 'a piece of clockwork wound up once for all and capable of working automatically'.[31] Against the orchestra's statement of the main and crescendo themes, Figaro declaims a description of his boutique entailing seventy-three iterations of the common tone D. He metronomically replicates the beat as if he were the musical machinery driving the opera, shifting into high gear at the *rinforzando*, where quavers split into semiquavers. Then he throws his ironic patter over the Count's effusively elaborated statement of the vitalistic theme, parodying the heroic part in the manner of the *gracioso* (the Spanish counterpart of the machinist familiar from Leporello in Mozart's *Don Giovanni*). This illustrates another of Bergson's points – that the art of comedy lies in either 'lulling sensibility to sleep and providing it with dreams' or, as in this case, in 'throwing a wet blanket upon sympathy at the very moment it might arise' so that 'the situation, though a serious one, is not taken seriously'.[32]

Early versions of the play and the *opéra comique* that preceded it included a similar scene in which Figaro not only boasts that he has written two *opéras comiques*, but imitates an orchestra playing an 'ariette de bravoure' from one of them.[33] Like Beaumarchais's Figaro, Rossini's is one of those *fourbes* who, 'unlike the *serious* rogues such as . . . Figaro in *Le Mariage de Figaro*, give the impression, either by their excessive theatricality or by their detached attitude, less of *being* tricksters than of playing the part'. His main rôle is to act as 'surrogate dramatist' – as a kind of 'puppeteer . . . manipulating the other characters on the playwright's behalf',[34] thus fulfilling one of comedy's chief purposes: 'to show people for the puppets of their needs and desires that they are' (though Figaro too will be made to dance to the control of 'a superior hand').[35] He literally 'stages' the intrigue, distancing himself from the action. This creates the illusion that he is 'actively engaged behind the scenes in furthering the desired outcome of the plot'.[36] Thus he incarnates the inner workings of both play and opera, giving them the raised-up 'metatheatrical' dimension missed by the early critic who called the play a 'superbly acted carnival farce',[37] and by his later counterparts who treated the opera like a Neapolitan intermezzo.

Figaro's one-movement cavatina, 'Largo al factotum', establishes him in this rôle. He enters during the orchestral prelude, with his guitar strapped bandolier-style to his back as in the play, singing 'la ran la lera'. The implication (and here as elsewhere Sterbini could count on his audience's sensitivity to intertextual references) is that he has just composed the song worked out in the play, where he tells his critics, 'just wait until there is an orchestra behind it, and we'll see . . . if I don't know what I'm talking about'. Improvisatory vocalise is also interpolated within and between the aria's twelve quatrains, which are loosely arranged according to the musical scheme A (q. 1–3) B (q. 4–7) A' (q. 2) Coda (q. 8–12+3). The text (taken together with that of the following recitative) combines the essential ideas of his picaresque *improvisation* about pleasure and leisure, 'Banissons le chagrin' (accorded a separate aria by Paisiello) and two first-act *tirades*: the long one on Madrid and his travels through Spain, emphasising his mobility (the basis for Paisiello's buffo catalogue aria), and some virtuosic later lines in which he explains to the Count how with the 'force of his art', he will 'with a single wave of his wand, put vigilance to sleep, awaken love, mislead jealousy, foil intrigue, and overturn all obstacles'.

These qualities are represented musically by Figaro's tossed-off octave leaps, which serve as the springboard for continuous chains of turns around the axial pitches C, G and D, a kind of musical juggling embodying his claim to be 'always on the go around here' – except when he is dallying 'colla donnetta . . . col cavaliere', as the tonal intensification and insinuating colour chords in the central section suggest. Contributing to the sense of accelerating verbal momentum are also dynamic and rhythmic transitions from *pianissimo* to *fortissimo* within the outer sections and overall, and from articulated eight-bar phrases to one-bar phrases in perpetual quaver motion.

The placement of the words 'bravo, bravissimo' and 'pronto, prontis-simo' so that, in effect, he applauds himself at the end of both the A section and the oversized coda points once again to Figaro's double rôle and suggests his identification with the crescendo as a kind of avatar of laughter. His words comment on his song, not the other way around, and in this respect Rossini's handling of crescendos is symptomatic of his comic technique overall in the opera. The text for Basilio's calumny aria is based closely on Beaumarchais's *tirade* likening slander to a crescendo, and Rossini built the aria up from a crescendo he had already composed for *Sigismondo*. Also emulating a crescendo is the ruckus stirred up by the Count's hired musicians in the *stretta* of the *introduzione* after they are paid off in the *tempo di mezzo* by their leader, the Count's servant, Fiorello, for accompanying his cavatina (and singing the obligatory opening chorus). Reversing his usual procedure, Rossini makes the *stretta* theme itself the crescendo; the transitional passage separating statements of the theme becomes a decrescendo, its initial *forte* dynamic being suppressed by the Count's repeated cry 'basta'.

If in each case the crescendo represents a kind of laughter, that inspired by the *stretta* of the Finale represents the kind encountered in dreams, which as Bergson notes is the only form of lunacy compatible with healthy laughter: 'Not infrequently do we notice in dreams a particular *crescendo*, a weird effect that grows more pronounced as we proceed'. Having been flummoxed by 'la forza' in the Vivace section (a fast pseudo-canon), mesmerised by the Count in the *quadro di stupore* and silenced in the *tempo di mezzo*, the characters are prisoners of their thoughts, which simulate the 'mechanism of illusion in dreams'.[38] As Sterbini's onomatopoeic verses suggest, they sound like 'deafening anvils in a dreadful forge, the din ceaselessly growing and making the very walls resound with a barbarous harmony, reducing our poor stunned and confounded brains, in confusion and without reason, to insanity'. This collective madness is evidenced by the repeat of the *stretta* theme in the wrong key – E♭ instead of C, a kind of false recapitulation. At the last possible moment, this 'mistake' is corrected: the theme's third phrase is foreshortened and the harmony wrenched downward, destabilising the moment of arrival in the home key and the ensuing repeat of the crescendo theme.

The quintet, 'Don Basilio! . . .', on the other hand, inspires the Dionysian kind of laughter Stendhal described as 'a roar as rollicking and irrepressible as the mirth of the gods'.[39] Based on Beaumarchais's own 'scène de stupéfaction' (Act 3, scenes 11–12), the number brings into the lesson scene the one character no one wants to see, each for his own reasons: Basilio, who is supposedly ill in bed. The other characters form an unlikely alliance to urge him there in order to prevent him from revealing either his machinations on behalf of Bartolo (which would anger Rosina) or that 'Don Alonso' is not his student (which would compromise the Count, the plausibility of whose disguise plays ironically on the literary tradition of the *sacristán* sent by the local organist). Basilio lets himself be persuaded that he has scarlet fever with the help of a purse from the Count, which he accepts with perfect *sang-froid*. When Bartolo overhears the Count and Rosina plotting during the *tempo di mezzo* and realises he has been the instrument of his own deception, he explodes in anger. But his brief *stretta* theme is completely overwhelmed by the crescendo – the laughter of the others who tell him he is crazy. Stendhal reports that Figaro defended himself against Bartolo's indignation by slashing at him with a towel in a production involving the buffo Luigi Bassi, who played the scene with such art that the audience took pity on the poor tutor.[40] Fairy-tale-like in its sustained improbability, the scene was recognised in its own time as one of the funniest ever written.

Rosina's cunning masks

The ambiguity of Beaumarchais's Rosine has much perplexed commentators, beginning with the anonymous one who noted, on an early draft manuscript of *Le Barbier de Séville*, that her character has 'two nuances': on the one hand she is 'a woman carried away by confinement and passion'; on the other, 'she is a small, timid person'.[41] Although this has partly to do with her literary origins, it seems also to reflect a deliberately anti-sentimental comic strategy, since Beaumarchais emphasises her *sensibilité* only to have Figaro mock it. Paisiello nonetheless made her a sentimental heroine and omitted the ironic comments Figaro makes when she 'accidentally' drops a note to Lindoro from the balcony (Act 1, scene 4); when she says her letter to Lindoro was inspired by 'friendship' (Act 2, scene 2); and when she faints at Lindoro's revelation of his identity (Act 4, scene 6). Paisiello emphasised her 'naturalness' by locating her first musical number (part of a duet with Bartolo) on the balcony, where she steals some fresh air (Act 1, scene 3), and by providing as her lesson aria a da capo setting of Metastasio's pastoral canzonetta 'La Primavera' with a contrasting, minor-mode section in the sentimental style. The earlier aria 'Giusto ciel', which she sings after reading Lindoro's letter giving instructions for their escape (Act 2, scene 16), is an invocation for grace of the sort to which the tragically virtuous heroine of Richardson's second epistolary novel, *Clarissa* (1748), is prone.

Rossini's Rosina, however, is a force to be reckoned with. An embodiment of the ambiguity inherent in Beaumarchais's Rosine, she is a contralto, a vocal type associated with the travesty roles of *opera seria*. In the same monologue from which Paisiello derived 'Giusto ciel', Sterbini found the line 'But an unjust man will make a schemer [rusée] out of innocence itself.' Fusing it with her earlier letter-writing monologue, he produced the cavatina 'Una voce poco fa', in the first movement of which she resolves to have Lindoro *before* Figaro gives her any intelligence about him. Then in the cabaletta, 'Io sono docile', she aggressively vows to resist Bartolo's designs with 'a hundred viper's tricks'. The repeat of the cabaletta theme includes only the music uncorked after the fermata with her staccato 'ma' ('but'). In the first half (whose opening bars were borrowed, appropriately enough, from another character's *rondò* in *Aureliano in Palmira*) Rossini reins in her registral, figural and rhythmic resources and fits an obedient pair of antecedent–consequent phrases to a patterned accompaniment so as to suggest innocence and docility. She puts on modesty like a social mask, bringing to mind Stendhal's observation in his treatise on love, *De l'amour*, that 'for women, to be frank would be like going out without a shawl'.[42]

Indeed, in the recitative before Lindoro's *canzone*, when she emerges from Bartolo's house and drops the note from the balcony, Figaro calls her a 'furba' (sly one). In their duet, 'Dunque io son . . . tu non m'inganni?', following a recitative in which he teasingly reveals that Lindoro loves her, he concludes (portentously) that she could give him lessons in cunning. The compact number contains three movements in one (marked Allegro), but conversation takes place only during the central section (beginning with the words 'Senti, senti, ma a Lindoro') and in two further places: during the initial phrase of each character's statement of the first theme, and the few bars between statements of Rosina's closing theme (again from 'Senti, senti, ma a Lindoro'). Otherwise, the duet's outer sections are sung as asides, Figaro's pattered ironising about the unfathomability of women serving as the comical antidote to Rosina's sentimental raptures in the last section.

Stendhal, whose feminine ideal was the divine Clarissa, reported that the Romans thought Rossini had transformed an ingénue into a 'virago', and he privately suspected him of being jaded by late nights with 'les grandes dames romaines'. Rosina's campaign, he argued, might suit a 'widow of twenty-eight', but no girl, even a Roman, could be so devoid of 'melancholy' and of 'a certain flower of delicacy and timidity'; against such resolution there could be no contest. For all his perspicacity in love, he could not appreciate Rossini's ironic play of musical modes because he thought that 'music can no more render an affected tone than painting can portray a mask'.[43] This, however, is precisely what Rossini and Sterbini did, taking their cue from Beaumarchais himself. Indeed, it may have been such rôle-playing that inclined Marie Antoinette, Queen of France, to take the rôle of Rosine in a court production at the Trianon in 1785.

Rosina's lesson aria, 'Contro un cor che accende amore', a concatenation of *esercizi*, was almost always replaced in performance with an aria of the *prima donna*'s choice. But as part of the imaginary opera *La precauzione inutile*, it parodies a serious aria about a heart 'inflamed with love' and burning with an 'unquenchable fire'. Falling out of character and into conversation with the Count when Bartolo dozes off during the *tempo di mezzo* (and later between statements of the cabaletta theme), Rosina implores the Count to save her from her 'cane di tutore' (dog of a tutor), employing a repeated, melodically overextended cadential passage that suggests she is still playing the heroine of a *dramma semiserio*, the rôle Bartolo thinks she is rehearsing.

This melodramatic tendency is at its most pronounced in the recitatives framing the *temporale*, the ostensible counterpart of the *orage* separating the third and fourth acts of Beaumarchais's play. In the play, however, the storm is a representation of Bartholo's fury in the aftermath of the 'scène de stupéfaction'; in the scenes framing the *orage* (Act 3, scene 14 and Act 4, scenes 1–2), he conspires with Bazile, intent on collecting Rosine's dowry, and in Act 4, scene 3 he persuades an uncharacteristically ingenuous Rosine that Don Alonzo/Lindor was only out to 'diminish her reputation' (as Pantalone would put it). In the opera, on the other hand, the *temporale* takes the place of the play's ensuing scene (Act 4, scene 4), in which the vengeful Rosine 'abandons herself to tears' then steels herself for the arrival of Figaro and Lindoro (in scene 5). Sterbini and Rossini thus made the *temporale* a musical metaphor for the sudden barrage of unexpressed thoughts and feelings that contend for mastery of Rosina's spirit. In the play Rosine reacts to the Count's unmasking (Act 4, scene 6) with what Figaro insinuates is a counterfeit swoon, and is scarcely to be heard from again after she comes to, confesses her breach of faith, and runs to the arms of her Lindor, her heart too full to think as he does of punishing the avaricious Bartholo. Given

```
ANDANTE, F major, common time
  Theme A (asides, contrasting texts):
    Rosina                                          I     (Ah, qual colpo inaspettato!)
        Figaro: transitional patter               vi–V      (Son rimasti senza fiato)
    Count                                           V     (Qual trionfo inaspettato!)
        Figaro: transitional patter               V₇-        (Son rimasti senza fiato)
    Figaro: partial statement                       I     (Guarda, guarda il mio talento)
    parlante conversation: Rosina–Count            I-V    Mio signor! . . . Ma . . . voi . . .
                                                            ma . . . io

  Theme B (to love, shared text):                        Dolce nodo avventurato
    Rosina ⎫   with Figaro's                        I        Figaro: Nodo. Andiamo.
    Count  ⎭   mocking echoes                        V        Figaro: Nodo. Presto
                                                              andiamo. Paghi. Vi sbrigate.
  cadential phrase, a due: Rosina–Count            V₇-I   Alla fin de' miei martiri
    Figaro: patter                                        Via lasciate quei sospiri
  cadenza no. 1: Rosina–Count, a due                I₆₄-  [Amor pie]tà
        ironic continuation a due for Count–Figaro
    no. 2: Rosina–Count, a due
        Figaro: patter                                    Se si tarda, i miei raggiri
                                                              fanno fiasco in verità

  transition: Figaro then Count, Rosina: patter   vi-vi-V
ALLEGRO, F major, cut time
  Cabaletta Theme: Count                            I     Zitti, zitti, piano, piano
            Rosina, with Count                      V
            Figaro, with Rosina and Count           I
  continuation, a tre
  repeat of Theme: Rosina, with Count and Figaro    I
  continuation, a tre
  cadences                                          I
```

Figure 11.1 Trio, 'Ah, qual colpo inaspettato'

the cunning character of Rosina (justified, we suspect, by the lively Count's potential for philandering), this moment of discovery is even more fraught with implications in the opera. Will she, too, have her destiny decided, by men? How will she feel when Lindoro proves to be other than what she dreamed?

Rossini and Sterbini turn the moment into the deliriously ecstatic 'Ah, qual colpo inaspettato!' Nominally a trio, this number is actually an ironic love duet 'composed', with critical commentary, by Figaro. Still reacting in asides, the surprised lovers sing parallel statements of two different themes (see Figure 11.1), both led off by Rosina, who takes her place as the Count's equal. In the meantime, Figaro boasts to the audience of his romantic coup, then gets on with the dramatic and musical business at hand, trying to force the number to a conclusion before their escape ladder disappears. He usurps the conventional lovers' echoes of theme B and exasperatedly joins the Count on the end of his staggered statement of the first cadenza *a due* so that, in effect, the passionate Count finds himself making love to Figaro. This turns the lovers' second attempt at a cadenza and the threefold statement of the comically quick cabaletta theme into an unlikely *ménage à trois*. That the barber must still endure a further repeat of the theme while the lovers play out the scene is nothing less than Rossini's musical joke on his own machinist.

At the end of the opera, though, it is Figaro who leads off the strophic *Finaletto*, a French *vaudeville final* addressing the opera's cautionary maxim directly to the audience. As cast and chorus join in on the first of the number's three refrains, the factotum of the town blows out his lantern, declaring, 'I have nothing more to do.'

12 *Guillaume Tell*

CORMAC NEWARK

Guillaume Tell was first performed, to great acclaim, on 3 August 1829 at the Académie Royale de Musique in Paris. It was put on in London and Berlin in 1830; performances in New York and not one but two Italian translations (by Luigi Balocchi and Calisto Bassi) came the following year. Victor-Joseph Etienne de Jouy, a senior and respected member of the Académie Française, had written the libretto, and Pierre-Luc-Charles Cicéri, the Opéra's chief designer, mounted a lavish production. It seemed the pinnacle of Rossini's career. Yet the composer's largest-scale, most monumental work for the stage was also his last: he wrote no more operas, preferring to retire, at the age of thirty-seven, to a more leisurely life in Italy (Bologna and Florence) and then, from 1855, Paris. *Tell* on its own would have represented a substantial legacy: it was to prove a foundational example of French *grand opéra*, that handful of massive, four- and five-act historical spectaculars that held sway at the Paris Opéra from the 1820s almost throughout the rest of the nineteenth century. By the time it dropped out of the repertory there in the 1930s, *Tell* had clocked up over 900 performances.[1]

After that time *Tell*, along with other *grands opéras*, virtually disappeared from the stage. In twentieth-century America and Great Britain, the best-known music from the opera was a section of the overture made famous by the Lone Ranger.[2] For later generations of Rossini's compatriots, on the other hand, it was a more meaningful passage from the other end of the opera (ex. 12.1).[3] The scene is alpine Switzerland, the rocky heights above Lake Lucerne to be precise, in the year 1308: the villain defeated and the fatherland freed, Tell and his band survey the landscape as the storm clears and the sun comes out.

An instrumental arrangement of this chorus was used for two decades by Italian state television (RAI) at the beginning and end of transmission. The screen showed swirling clouds that gradually cleared to reveal a transmitter giving off dynamic-looking pulses of light. First aired in 1954, the sequence broadcast an obvious metaphor: RAI's mission was enlightenment. Those zigzags of light were the knowledge and technological progress RAI was disseminating; the clouds, of course, were various sorts of ignorance driven back and dispersed.

It is easy to see why RAI chose this music (apart from its having been written by a famous Italian composer, that is): not only did it originally

Example 12.1 *Guillaume Tell*, Allegro maestoso in Act 4 Finale, orchestral theme

accompany a story of clouds clearing and subsequent illumination, but the scene in the opera had a similarly symbolic aspect. It is clear that throughout *Tell* light represents political freedom and darkness oppression. This idea is indeed expounded at such length that the opera sometimes seems about the weather. Especially bad weather: how powerful the storm is; how it is permanently on the way; how it both mirrors and inspires the feelings of the community. The mountain people that make up most of its dramatis personae live closer to the sky than the rest of us, both geographically and mentally; they are constantly looking upward, as shepherds will, to know what is coming their way. While almost all inhabitants of French *grand opéra* are fond of exclaiming 'O heavens!', these people mean it literally.

An opera about the weather

Though it opens with Swiss peasants celebrating a beautiful day, the rest of the first act of *Tell* is full of meteorological portents to contradict the first words, 'what a serene day the sky foretells'. Sure enough, as the halcyon scene widens over the course of the drama to include representations of Swiss subjugation by the evil Austrian governor, Gesler, so the weather deteriorates. Storms threaten from shortly after the beginning, as a fisherman sings a piece of stage music about the secret of love that controls the weather over the lonely lake. Tell, resentful of such carefree behaviour, complains about the political situation; Tell's wife Hedwige and son Jemmy express, with heavy significance, their worry that defying the storm only invites shipwreck. A village elder, Melcthal, is invited to bless three marrying couples, which he is happy to do, again in the name of the beautiful day. His one regret is that his own son, Arnold, has shown no signs of such virtuous attachment. But Arnold does have a lover; unfortunately, it is Mathilde, princess of the Austrian royal family, whose life he has saved in an avalanche. Apart from causing him intense discomfort, his inner conflict makes his behaviour rather suspect – at least to Tell, who feels it necessary to demand from him an assurance of patriotic loyalty. As if to make Arnold more miserable – and to keep up the metaphor – everyone goes on to sing of the couples' tenderness being like the bright sky (No. 3). Nevertheless, the irony of the peasants making merry while under the Austrian yoke is increasingly painful to Tell, who hopes that the noise of their celebration is disguising that of the gathering protest: 'Let it keep the noise of the tempest from the ears of the tyrants.'

Yet it is the tyrants' anger we experience first. A herdsman arrives, fleeing the Austrian soldiers. He has killed one of them in defence of his daughter's virtue, and can only escape if a skilled pilot will take him across the torrent. Tell heroically does so, to the frustration of the soldiers and especially their leader Rodolphe. Melcthal enjoins the villagers not to betray Tell's name, and is promptly arrested. The villagers retreat, muttering darkly about storms rumbling overhead. Meanwhile Arnold has slipped away to meet Mathilde, who has managed to separate herself from an Austrian hunting party. In her famous Act 2 aria, 'Sombre forêt' (No. 9), she tells us that it is not in splendid palaces but rather in the mountains, in the dwelling-place of the storm, that she can find peace. She likens Arnold's gentle presence to the light of a shepherd star. After their tryst, Mathilde hurries away, but is spotted by Tell and Walter arriving, and they confront Arnold over his apparently treacherous liaison. His protestations are silenced by the news that his father has been executed by the Austrians. Arnold pledges allegiance to the rebellion Tell and Walter are planning, and, joined by representatives of the Swiss cantons, they all swear a stirring oath as dawn breaks: tomorrow will be their day of vengeance; to any traitor among them, let the sun refuse its light.

At the beginning of Act 3, Arnold breaks the news of his father's murder to Mathilde and they bid one another a last farewell. Then the scene shifts to the main square of Altdorf, where Gesler is celebrating 100 years of Austrian domination. He commands everyone to bow before his hat; only Tell refuses, which leads to Rodolphe recognising him as the rebel pilot and to Gesler forcing him to shoot an apple from the top of his son's head. Amid mutinous grumbling from the crowd, Tell is arrested, to be taken across the lake to prison. Jemmy is saved only by Mathilde granting him her protection; he takes with him Tell's instruction to light a hill-top fire as a signal for the insurrection. Back in the village for the final act, Arnold is lamenting his loss before his father's empty chalet when news of the arrest reaches him. He resolves to act, and arms the rebels. Mathilde arrives in the village to return Jemmy to Hedwige and offer herself as a hostage for Tell. She is gratefully compared to the heavens after bad weather has cleared; in fact the storm, or rather the even more awesome 'hurricane' is at that moment breaking over the lake. But Tell, his chains loosened because only he can steer the governor's boat in such conditions, succeeds in jumping ashore, leaving his captors behind. By the time they manage to land, Tell has reached the village and claimed his crossbow: with a single bolt he slays Gesler leading soldiers towards the village, even before Walter and his companions arrive, alerted by Jemmy's fiery beacon. When Arnold and the rest of the Swiss conspirators return, having secured Altdorf, it seems victory is theirs. The storm passes over to reveal the landscape in all its luminous glory.

The metaphor equating light and liberty was by no means new, even if Rossini's opera explored it extraordinarily thoroughly. Nor, of course, was the Tell legend: Paris was already more than familiar with its crossbow-wielding protagonist. To tell the truth, both had been little short of ubiquitous ever since the Revolution.

From legend to libretto

Though the story probably originates in Nordic myth, written versions begin with an early-fourteenth-century Tell mentioned in the so-called *White Book of Sarnen* (1470). The narrative was picked up in the *Chronicon Helveticum* (first published 1734–6) of a seventeenth-century historian, Aegidius Tschudi, and the *Geschichten schweizerischer Eidgenossenschaft* (1786) of Johannes Müller. In 1797 Goethe visited Switzerland and formed a plan to write an epic poem on the Tell fable, but it came to nothing. It was his friend Schiller who, in the early years of the nineteenth century, developed the idea into a verse drama, *Wilhelm Tell*, first performed on 17 May 1804 at Weimar, and for the first time in French translation in 1818 in Geneva. Schiller never went to Switzerland himself; local colour in his play comes from Tschudi and Müller and from maps and travel literature. In Paris, a generation before Rossini, there had been an opera on the subject, André-Ernest-Modeste Grétry's *Guillaume Tell* of 1791 (libretto by Michel-Jean Sedaine, based on Antoine-Marin Lemierre's tragedy of 1767). Schiller's play was widely read in translation, Jean-Pierre Claris de Florian's prose drama *Guillaume Tell ou la Suisse libre* (1805) was reprinted frequently, and there were numerous Tell poems in circulation.[4]

But the narrative of the Swiss uprising – oppression, popular revolt, freedom – had proved irresistible in particular to the revolutionaries of

1789, images of Tell often standing in for the proto-Jacobin messages the basic story was taken to contain. Abstractions such as Liberty carrying her torch were the stock-in-trade of revolutionary iconography; equally, among human paragons of Republican conduct, Tell was perhaps the most popular with the Jacobin régime. One can see why: not only was his reputation based on suitably radical acts, but his distinctive props (crossbow, apple, etc.) brought the added advantage of making him clearly identifiable, as in this description of decorations for a Revolutionary festival in 1796: 'Beyond the line of bayonets, the statue of Liberty, seated on military trophies. With one hand, she is leaning on the constitution, and in the other she is holding a stick on which is mounted William Tell's hat.'[5] So clearly identifiable, then, that his hat, the least of his accessories, was capable of representing him on its own. And such was the longevity of the Jacobin Tell that Rossini's opera, though forty years after the Revolution, with Empire and Restoration already water under the bridge, still relied heavily on it and associated symbols. To take a minor example, the staging manual for *Tell* stipulates that the tenor Arnold (though not initially committed to the cause of liberty) should from the opening wear his hair 'à la Titus', which is to say in the manner of Roman citizens, to connote democracy and civic virtue.[6] This convention had been so firmly established during the Revolution that Rossini's audience must have known the tenor would come through for his fellow Swiss in the end: his haircut gave him away.

Naturally enough, after the end of the Terror and the death of Robespierre in 1794, and above all after Napoleon was proclaimed Emperor in 1804, the potential for objects to signify the Revolution was (to put it mildly) not valued quite as much. Therefore what Tell stood for was not as unambivalently endorsed – but he did not disappear from view, merely trod more carefully. Schiller agonised over his social responsibilities while writing a play he realised might be taken to advocate assassination and popular insurrection. For him Tell had to be a peaceable character, acting only under the most extreme personal provocation. For the French, on the other hand, representing revolution – let alone the Revolution – was positively traumatic. To illustrate this, here is part of one Parisian account of Schiller's play, written in the first decade of the nineteenth century:

> Tell is not party to the conspiracy . . . Stauffacher, Walther Fürst and Arnold Melcthal prepare the revolt. Tell is its hero but not its author; he does not think about politics at all, he only worries about tyranny when it disturbs his peaceable life: he pushes it away with both hands when he feels its touch; he judges it, he condemns it at his own private hearing; but he does not conspire.[7]

The author of this commentary had more reason than most to remember the Terror with a shudder: she had lived at its epicentre. Germaine de Staël was the daughter of Charles Necker, the reforming minister whose removal from office by Louis XVI precipitated the storming of the Bastille. De Staël needed a whole chapter to talk about *Wilhelm Tell*, though she ostensibly had the canon of German literature to get through, and it is easy to guess why. In it she is confronting her fear of being implicated, along with the rest of French society, in the murder of the king and the atrocities of the Terror. The era of the Jacobins was for De Staël and many like her a time of dangerous chaos, a perversion of reforms begun with the best liberal intentions: it is thus not surprising that she, even more than Schiller, should feel a need to stress the personal drama over the ideological. Jouy's libretto is similarly ambivalent: though Schiller is the principal basis (Florian is another, but secondary), in it Tell is once again a political activist; the opera, however, is as shy of violence as the play. Even if there is an armed mob of aspiring sans-culottes in the final act, they perform off stage whatever bloody coup is necessary to overcome Altdorf. It is indeed unclear whether there is need for reprisals other than Gesler's assassination. The reason for this, of course, is censorship: the Viscount Sosthène de La Rochefoucauld, minister for the arts, would not have allowed any such bad example to appear on stage – the restored monarchy of Charles X, it need hardly be pointed out, was opposed to popular insurrection as a matter of principle.

Grand opéra, on the other hand, was from the beginning obsessed with just that. The major works of the genre (*La Muette de Portici* by Auber, 1828; *La Juive* by Halévy, 1835; Verdi's *Don Carlos*, 1867; and the four Meyerbeer operas, *Robert le diable*, 1831, *Les Huguenots*, 1836, *Le Prophète*, 1849, and *L'Africaine*, 1865) contain a great deal of mob action, frequently suggesting violence, with a correspondingly important musical rôle for the chorus. Rossini's own adaptation for the Opéra, *Le Siège de Corinthe* (1826), helped establish the pattern.[8] The collective musical presence of the doomed Greeks made a profound impression, especially as the Greek struggle for independence was just then catching the public imagination. Writers were inspired to fables of successful resistance, and Tell was the perfect subject; in 1828, once word got around that Rossini was working on the subject, there was a particular flurry of interest: Pixérécourt's *mélodrame* at the Théâtre de la Gaîté and Grétry's opera revived (with revisions by Pellissier) at the Opéra Comique.[9]

In order to respond to these circumstances, the young dramatist Hippolyte-Louis-Florent Bis was given the job of revising Jouy's *Tell* to Rossini's satisfaction. He introduced important changes, but the libretto remained substantially Jouy's work – and though Marrast, Crémieux and Barateau, friends of the composer, have all been listed as co-authors, there is no hard evidence to support their claim.[10] The only other possible contributor is Adolphe Nourrit, the tenor playing Arnold, an unusually literary singer who habitually took a close interest in the texts he performed. Whoever wrote it, the finished product was sharply criticised for being unbalanced: the third and fourth acts in particular are an uncomfortable mixture of stasis and frantic action, while the first appears long and bland by comparison. In contrast to the usual stories of hopeless librettos being transformed by more dramatically sensitive composers, however, it seems that here Rossini may be to blame: the changes made at his instigation are responsible for some of the problems.[11] His motivation was apparently a desire to echo the ideals of liberal opposition to his employer, King Charles X, by increasing the importance of the ordinary people in the opera (represented by the chorus) and reducing the dramatic weight of the soloists. Only one of the major changes to Jouy's libretto scored a success in its own right: the hymn to liberty, striking in more ways than one, and pure Bis.

Chorus and soloists: revisions in musical dramaturgy

This is not to say that the opera was poorly received, as claimed by later commentators seeking to explain either Rossini's retirement or the impact of *Tell* in 1837, when Gilbert Louis Duprez's début as Arnold was said (above all by Duprez himself) to have rescued the work from decline. Instead of leaving Paris for the summer as was the custom, many of the *beau monde* stayed to be present; demand for tickets was high. The choruses, which Rossini had considered so important, were appreciated as a cut above the average, even if some critics found them too numerous. The opera is certainly well provided with choral numbers, Act 1 above all, but more than quantity it is the variety that is striking: some sort of hunting chorus would be standard for a wooded setting, but the rhythmic and harmonic élan of No. 8, 'Quelle sauvage harmonie', is anything but standard: 'What wild harmony', ostensibly the hunting horns, sounds very much as if Rossini intended a pun. No. 4 (a danced chorus, 'Hyménée, ta journée') is an exceptionally poised piece, whereas No. 15 (a Tyrolean chorus, 'Toi que l'oiseau ne suivrait pas!'), which serves as the music for a *pas de trois*, is unique in the genre: unaccompanied, vocally challenging, and very long. More dramatically integrated moments for the chorus include No. 12, the Finale of Act 2, in which three groups of men, representing the oath-takers of the Swiss cantons (Unterwalden, Schwyz and Uri respectively), sing subtly differentiated – but all suitably patriotic – promises to defend the fatherland. The Finale of Act 3 even contains an ensemble that could be straight out of *opera buffa*, in which Gesler and his soldiers promise Tell an ugly fate in prison, and Mathilde, Jemmy, Tell and the crowd of Swiss in the town square protest: No. 17-V, 'Quand l'orgueil les égare', is joyful kitsch until Gesler draws his dagger, a shocked Tell curses him, and seriousness is restored.

The première came later than La Rochefoucauld wanted: he had hoped that *Tell* might be produced late in 1828, but various delays beset the project. Nothing could be discussed concerning the sets, for example, until the designer, Cicéri, had returned from his quest for *couleur locale* in Altdorf;[12] then the reading committee complained that the scene where Jemmy climbs the rocks to light the beacon in Act 4 was superfluous and scenically too difficult; then the soprano, Laure Cinti-Damoreau, was pregnant; then Rossini himself withdrew the score twice over contractual disputes with the administration. Though the composer had chosen the libretto by the spring of 1828 (and had earlier in his career been in the habit of finishing operas in no more than two or three months), by the beginning of November not much more than the vocal parts of the first two acts were done and the scene painting had not started. Models of the costumes were not ready when requested by La Rochefoucauld in January 1829; full cast stage rehearsals began only on 23 June 1829. Orchestral rehearsals got under way on 5 July, and the dress rehearsal took place two days before the première, on 1 August.[13]

As preparations entered their final phase, slow progress was also partly due to a perennial problem of *grand opéra*: once it was rehearsed on stage, it became clear that *Tell* was far too long, and cuts would need to be made. A solo for Melcthal was removed from Act 1 and a prayer for Hedwige from Act 4;[14] six months after the première the whole of the first scene of Act 3, between Mathilde and Arnold, would also be jettisoned. The two large set-pieces for the ballet (village festivities in Act 1 and Gesler's anniversary celebration in Act 3) remained largely intact, however, leading to accusations that its rôle was being privileged against the interests of the singers and perhaps the drama as a whole. Whether or not the *maître de ballet* exercised undue influence behind the scenes, as some critics suspected, the revisions made at this late stage are especially revealing of the differences between practices in the aria-culture of Rossini's earlier Italian works and what was now required at the Opéra. None of the principals' rôles escaped untouched, with Jemmy losing an aria in Act 3 and Tell some stirring declamation in Act 1; in fact, the old structure of lengthy, multipartite solos and duets for the principals and filling-in for everybody else was so far left behind in *Tell* that the eponymous hero (played by Henri-Bernard Dabadie, whose performance was by all accounts a dramatic tour de force) had no such formal aria at all, only the short solo 'Sois immobile' in Act 3. Even without considering the fashionability of the Tell story and the qualities of the chosen libretto, this emphasis on choral and danced episodes would in itself be ample testimony to how much in tune Rossini was with contemporary Parisian opera aesthetics. Though critics sometimes complained about one or both of these features, they remained fundamental to the genre right up until the end.[15]

In some ways more traditional are the two main pieces for the lovers, Mathilde and Arnold. Mathilde's 'Sombre forêt' is a classic soprano entrance aria in terms of positioning (beginning of Act 2) and technical weight (substantial). It also sounds very Italianate, with bel canto much in evidence, and displays the slight chromatic tendency that characterises some of her other music (e.g. 'Sur la rive étrangère', No. 13). More than anything else, however, it establishes Mathilde as a vocal presence – indeed, as a presence more or less solely vocal. One of the handful of criticisms that were repeatedly levelled against the opera when first produced was that Mathilde was weak dramatically. There is no opportunity for her relationship with Arnold to develop, and her one definite action, that of taking Jemmy under her wing, is overtaken by the accelerating storyline: the quick succession of Gesler's nastiness, Tell's removal and return, Hedwige's grief and Jemmy's insurrectionary behaviour means that there is no time for her to impose herself other than by briefly expressing sympathy with the Swiss (No. 18bis). As in Schiller (where she is called Berta von Bruneck), she is mostly just the standard love-interest, with a standard *vocalità* (soprano, serious, showy) to match. Though *grand opéra* continued to pair off the principal sopranos and tenors as other lyric traditions did, its historical precepts and the breadth of its canvas combined to bring to the fore other characters to compete with the obligatory lovers – above all their parents: Eléazar in *La Juive*, Fidès in *Le Prophète*, Philippe in *Don Carlos*, and of course Tell himself.

Arnold's scene and aria at the beginning of Act 4, where impassioned recitative about revenge ('Ne m'abandonne point, espoir de la vengeance!') precedes his lament on the loss of his father ('Asile héréditaire'), is less well known nowadays, but in 1829 it was at the cutting edge of the tenor repertoire. Though also reminiscent of Italian prototypes in scale and rhetoric, there is a peculiarly French declamatory quality to it, and, in proper *grand opéra* style, the chorus joins in to bring it to a rousing close. It is a much more dynamic piece than 'Sombre forêt', in more ways than one: obviously Arnold's decision finally to act in the cause of Switzerland is momentous, even if it is Tell's heroism that we see on stage; there is also the sense that Arnold too is wrestling with (and here defying) a generic structure that wants to push him into the background. Alphonse before him (in *La Muette de Portici*) and Léopold after (*La Juive*) were fatally weak lover-tenors;[16] Arnold, like Don Carlos, manages to shake off his inaction, at least for the last few scenes. 'Asile héréditaire' is significant also in performance history: it is one of the places where Nourrit may have made some kind of authorial contribution, thus helping to define the generic figure of which he was (and would for the next eight years continue to be) the principal exponent.[17]

Lastly, it is the rôle of Arnold, and 'Asile héréditaire' in particular, that figured in the controversy surrounding the 'do di petto', or chest-voice high C,
made famous by Duprez.[18]

The fact that in July and August 1829 Cinti-Damoreau was below par
after her pregnancy but Nourrit as fit and pro-active as ever may also be
relevant to the complexion of the finished opera; whatever their precise
influence, it seems clear that Rossini's association with the cast that created
Tell (which had begun with preparations for *Le Siège de Corinthe* several
years earlier) was one of reciprocal learning: Rossini brought with him to
Paris an unrivalled overview of singing technique, gathered from all the
major opera centres in Italy; conversely, work on *Siège* (and also *Moïse et
Pharaon*, first performed at the Opéra in 1827) was for the composer a
necessary learning experience preparatory to embarking on *Tell*.[19] Many
influential critics thought *Tell* combined new departures (to be expected
from a composer of genius) with a solid understanding of the local tradition:
François-Joseph Fétis found the opera extraordinarily well adapted to the
demands of French lyric theatre,[20] and Berlioz, after initial reservations,
thought it sublime, especially 'Asile héréditaire' and the whole of Act 2.[21]
The authors of the libretto, in an advertisement for *Tell* published on the
eve of the première, pronounced their judgement that with this immense
work Rossini had at last become French.[22]

Tell and the aesthetics of spectacle in 1820s Paris

But *Tell* differs from every other *grand opéra* (wherever you draw the boundaries of the genre) in one unmissable way: it has an almost completely happy
ending. The only fly in the ointment is Melcthal's execution – as Arnold says,
Switzerland's happiness lacks only his presence – but that seems a long time
ago. The clearing of the storm abruptly cuts short discussion following the
death of Gesler, and a truly magical shift of perspective is announced by
Tell: 'The whole place is changing, growing.' As the staging manual tries
hard to convey, Switzerland is experiencing a new dawn, one hinted at in
the auguries near the beginning of the opera: 'The storm having entirely
cleared, the horizon brightens sharply to reveal a part of Switzerland in all
its beauty. Boats decked out with flags drift on the lake, everything comes
to life, and the curtain falls on this tableau.'[23] And to round it all off, an
echo from *Tell*'s revolutionary past: the chorus 'A nos accents religieux', with
which I began, is very much in the mould of hymns to Liberty enthusiasti-
cally performed under the Jacobins.[24] What makes the scene doubly unique,
though, is how static the final tableau is. Certainly the hymn staged a kind
of contemplation completely foreign to participants in other *grand opéra*

Finales, where the general rule was, on the contrary, frantic acceleration towards disaster, heralded by a record- (and often bank-)breaking *coup de théâtre*. The year before *Tell*, *La Muette de Portici* had ended with the eruption of Mount Vesuvius, the heroine throwing herself into the crater; *Robert le diable* was to go with a similarly fiery bang as the villain descended, Don-Giovanni-style, into hell. *La Juive* would serve up another cooked heroine, this time in boiling oil, *Les Huguenots* disposing of its principals more prosaically, by firing squad. The indigenous characters in *L'Africaine* were to be shown committing suicide with the aid of a poisonous tree, while for *Don Carlos*, in other ways a more serious work, was reserved the high camp of Emperor Charles V, risen from the dead in full imperial costume, snatching his stricken grandson from the clutches of the Inquisition.

Yet for an 1820s audience, with most of those apocalypses still to look forward to, such awestruck gazing would have been nothing strange: then, and for some time afterwards, the aesthetic of contemplation was a big part of the experience of opera. The stage tableau (from *mélodrame* and boulevard theatre, where the Opéra borrowed a great many new optical effects) and the diorama were in everyone's eyes;[25] premières of new productions were as much visual gratification as aural; and Cicéri's name was included (in letters of the same size) on posters for the première alongside those of Jouy, Bis, Aumer (*maître de ballet*) and Rossini. The sunrise at the end of Act 2, for example, which was achieved with gas lighting (still relatively new at the Opéra in 1829) and which entranced the public almost as much as the final panorama, was only the latest step in a continual march of technological progress – it would be trumped only by the electric sunrise in *Le Prophète* in 1849. To conclude, therefore, the music for RAI's transmitter was doubly well chosen: not only did it sing 'let there be light', in all its senses, metaphorical and literal; it also had an aura of technology that was just right for the dawn of national television. And it was, first and foremost, an injunction to watch. Now that productions of *Tell* and those other operas are so rare, and that in any case their visual aspect is forever lost, there could be no more appropriate reminder of the essence of *grand opéra*.

PART FOUR

Performance

13 Singing Rossini

LEONELLA GRASSO CAPRIOLI

What were Rossini's opinions on singing and its expressive capacities? What was his relationship to the Italian traditional school of singing? How did he relate to and interact with performers? Which voices and singers did he prefer? How did these personal views affect his style? Answering these questions means trying to understand not only how Rossini's works were performed when they first appeared, but also how we might achieve historically and aesthetically aware performances today. The many-faceted nature of Rossini's position can be seen, on the one hand, in his nostalgia for a bygone age and his taste for a singing style glorified as 'antico', and, on the other, in his fundamental innovations, which gave singing new life during a period when it was considered in a state of crisis. What unifies these different traits is the consistent privileging of the voice as a means of conveying emotion. Keeping this key aesthetic principle in mind, we need to consider the historical context in which Rossini worked, particularly with regard to the system of operatic production and the nature of the artistic rôles within it.

There is little explicit first-hand evidence from which to glean Rossini's relationship with the art of singing. His letters contain occasional remarks, but, although these are sometimes of significance, they lack an explicitly 'authorial' viewpoint, any attempt at sketching a system. Because of this relative lack of sources, and of the fact that Rossini rarely made public comments on the state of contemporary music, the writings of biographers who had the opportunity to note Rossini's opinions become particularly important.[1] However, to gain a fuller picture of Rossini's opinions on singing, his relationship with singers, and the developments in his vocal writing in different genres and periods, we need to look at his scores.[2] The composer also left us a collection of singing exercises – *Gorgheggi e solfeggi, vocalises et solfèges pour rendre la voix agile et pour apprendre à chanter selon le goût moderne* (Paris, 1827) – which, along with his assiduous work in advising the 'Liceo Musicale' (conservatoire) of Bologna during the 1840s, demonstrates a particular interest in teaching and a desire to preserve traditional vocal education, albeit in revised and updated form. In this chapter I will briefly outline Rossini's relationship with singers, especially those for whom he wrote rôles in his operas; then I will turn to the composer's ideas on the art of singing and on how to acquire it; and finally I will place these ideas in the context of the theory and pedagogy of singing in early-nineteenth-century Italy.

Rossini and his singers

Rossini's connections with singing were deep-rooted. His mother was a singer; he himself took up the profession before becoming a composer; he was married to one of the greatest singers of the period, Isabella Colbran; and he was a friend and patron of many vocal performers. Indeed, his entire biography could be filtered through the lens of an intense and idiosyncratic relationship between man and artist on the one hand, and singing on the other. Demonstrating early on an extraordinary inclination for music, the young Rossini possessed a marvellous voice, and his musical training began, as was usual at the time, with a serious vocal apprenticeship. Talent and a natural technical ability allowed him to make successful appearances as a soloist in public concerts of sacred music and some operatic performances. The idea of directing their son towards a vocal career seems to have been discussed seriously in the family, primarily because they would soon need to decide whether he should be a castrato. Notwithstanding the insistence of his maternal uncle, Rossini was saved from mutilation by his mother's fierce opposition, and the notion of a serious career as a singer was gradually replaced by the study of composition, and then laid aside permanently once his voice had broken. One should remember, however, that he completed his musical training in Bologna, home to one of the most well-established and famous schools of Italian singing.

Rossini worked during a period in which the entire operatic industry revolved around singers. He basically accepted this situation, and more often than not found himself writing for a voice rather than choosing a singer to suit what he had written. While taking into account the particular capabilities, vocal limitations and characteristics of his singers was part of the game, Rossini did not let himself be inhibited by such working conditions. His most explicit statement on this issue is found in a letter of 1851:

> So I say to you that the good singer, to fulfil his rôle, must be none other than the skilful *interpreter* of the designs of the master composer, seeking to express them with the appropriate efficacy and show them in the appropriate light. The players too must be no more than accurate *executants* of that which is on the page before them. In the end the composer and the poet are the only real *creators*. Some able singer or other will usually want to parade his accomplishments from time to time in the form of decorative ornamentation – and if that is to be called creation, so be it. By no means seldom is it the case, however, that the results of such

creation are less than happy, often even marring the composer's inspiration and robbing it of that simplicity of expression which it ought to have. The French use the phrase *créer un rôle* (to create a rôle), and it is a vain Gallicism, used by the singers who first perform a leading part in a new opera, who want to imply that they have created a model, to be imitated by other singers later required to perform the same part. Even in this case, however, the word 'create' seems hardly apt, in as much as create means *extract from nothing*; the singer certainly works from something, the Poetry and the Music, which are not of his creation.[3]

We must remember, however, that these words were written long after Rossini had abandoned the stage. In practice, when he was active as an operatic composer, it seems that he found a compromise between total control of singers and total submission to them. On the one hand, he often reserved for himself the right to compose embellishments and cadenzas, proclaiming and defending the originality of his own creations; his feelings were offended more by unwarranted liberties taken by singers than by the restriction of having to write to suit the voices of the cast. On the other hand, Rossini always treated the human voice with loving sensitivity, and acted as a fatherly guide to many of his performers, at the same time benefiting from their insights, including on a pedagogical level. He was a close friend of such singers as Geltrude Righetti Giorgi, Domenico Donzelli, Luigi Pacini and Giovanni Battista Rubini; he taught Marietta Alboni, cultivating her voice and career with pride and passion. He even became a sort of adoptive-father-cum-agent to Nicola Ivanoff, taking him in as a boarder in his own house for seven years. To Maria Malibran he paid this extraordinary tribute:

> That marvellous creature! She surpassed all her imitators by her truly disconcerting musical genius, and all the women I have ever known by the superiority of her intelligence, the variety of her knowledge, and her flashing temperament, of which it is impossible to give any idea . . . When she was to appear in *Semiramide*, *La gazza ladra*, *Cenerentola*, *Il barbiere*, above all in *Otello*, nothing could have kept me from going to hear her. The fact was that each time her creative genius inspired her in a stupefying, always different way with unexpected effects, both vocal and declamatory . . . Each time, too, she taught me how I could have done *better* than I had done.[4]

Rossini had a particularly close artistic tie to his first wife, the soprano Isabella Colbran. Born in 1785 in Madrid, Colbran was a pupil of Francisco Pareja, Gaetano Marinelli and Girolamo Crescentini. She met Rossini in Naples in 1815, on the occasion of *Elisabetta regina d'Inghilterra*, and they married at the height of her fame. The composer wrote for her the rôles of Desdemona (*Otello*, 1816), Armida (*Armida*, 1817), Elcia (*Mosè in Egitto*, 1818), Zoraide (*Ricciardo e Zoraide*, 1818), Ermione (*Ermione*, 1819), Elena

(*La donna del lago*, 1819), Anna (*Maometto II*, 1820) and Zelmira (*Zelmira*, 1822). Well-versed in the tragic genre and gifted with an impressive stage presence, Colbran's talents included a range of almost three octaves (from g to e‴), great agility, beauty of tone and the ability to sustain phrases of *canto spianato*. Her voice changed a great deal over the course of the years, as Rossini's scores attest; it began to decline as early as 1816, and she was forced to quit the stage in 1824, after her London tour, by which time her voice was seriously compromised.

The relationship between Rossini and his singers was bound to be intense: in many respects he was the greatest vocal expert of his time, and the situation whereby an opera was created or re-staged in his presence involved periods of study and rehearsal during which the composer contributed his own advice and technical opinions. A cult of 'Rossinian singing' and 'the Rossinian voice' was diffused widely in didactic circles by means of the teaching activities of singers who had had first-hand experience of his training (see the annotated list at the end of the chapter).[5]

Rossini particularly loved the contralto voice, a register which recalled the rich, broad resonance of the castratos. He spoke about the contralto on only one occasion, and, what is more, with no intention of leaving a testimony about his compositional dramaturgy. However, beyond the general interest of this passage, note that Rossini conceives the contralto as the norm:

> The contralto is the norm against which the other voices and instruments must be gauged. If you want to do without the contralto you can push the *prima donna assoluta* as high as the moon, and the *basso profondo* right down to the bottom of the well. And this will leave you with nothing in the middle. One should concentrate on the central register in order to be always in tune; at the extreme ends, what you gain in force you often lose in grace, and by this abuse you paralyse the throat, resorting as a remedy to *canto declamato*, that is, out-of-tune shouting. Then it becomes necessary to give the orchestration more body in order to cover the excesses of the voice, to the detriment of good musical colour.[6]

Soft, dark timbre; broad range; natural flexibility; expressivity; powerful agility; versatility across different genres: these were the characteristics that inspired the composer to create many of his most successful characters: Ernestina (*L'equivoco stravagante*, 1811), Clarice (*La pietra del paragone*, 1812), the title rôle of *Ciro in Babilonia* (1812), Isabella (*L'italiana in Algeri*, 1813) and Sigismondo (*Sigismondo*, 1814), all sung for the first time by Maria Marcolini; Siveno (*Demetrio e Polibio*, 1812) for Anna Mombelli; the title rôle of *Tancredi* (1813) for Adelaide Malanotte Montresor; Rosina (*Il barbiere di Siviglia*, 1816) and Angelina (*La Cenerentola*, 1816) for Geltrude Righetti Giorgi; Zomira (*Ricciardo e Zoraide*, 1818), Andromaca (*Ermione*,

1819) and Malcom (*La donna del lago*, 1819) for Rosmunda Pisaroni; Falliero (*Bianca e Falliero*, 1819) for Carolina Bassi; Calbo (*Maometto II*, 1820) for Adelaide Comelli Rubini; and Arsace (*Semiramide*, 1823) for Rosa Mariani.

Bel canto = voice + technique + style

Rossini's predilection for 'cantare che nell'anima si sente'[7] (singing that you can feel in your soul) seems to relate to a musical ideal from a time gone by, a past world graced by vocal heroes called castratos. This expression, so dear to him, echoes the typically powerful rhetoric used for these singers, who, thanks to their 'singing to the heart', realised the typically Italian ideal of expression through pure voice. The passing of such a world was due 'to the disappearance of the *castratos*. One can form no notion of the charm of voice and consummate virtuosity – which, lacking something else, and by a charitable compensation – those best of the best possessed.'[8] Although Rossini had very few occasions to work directly with castratos (they were already disappearing by the time he became a composer), he retained an indelible memory of them from his early days. This could not fail to have an effect on his conception of the voice and of music for it: 'I have never forgotten them. The purity, the miraculous flexibility of those voices and, above all, their profoundly penetrating accent – all that moved and fascinated me more than I can tell you.'[9] This, then, is the starting point for any discussion of Rossini's attempt to compose in a way that would prolong an illustrious period of Italian art – to develop a personal code, rooted in tradition, which suited the different vocal means available to him.

Rossini evaded any definition of his own rôle within the history of music, stubbornly avoiding the heated artistic-aesthetic debates going on around him; but he obviously found the subject of vocal discipline stimulating. On one occasion – a small gathering of friends at his house in 1858 – he abandoned his usual reserve and commented at length on the technical facility that a cultivated voice should command before it was fit for the demands of bel canto. According to Rossini, 'bel canto is made up of three elements: 1. The instrument – the voice – the *Stradivarius*, if you like; 2. Technique – that is to say, the means of using it; 3. Style, the ingredients of which are taste and feeling'.[10] His approach to the subject effectively insists on didactic issues: to Rossini, the equation 'end of a school (with all that an old tradition involves in terms of pedagogical customs and methods) = decline of a style' is the heart of the issue. 'Ah yes, in those days the formation of the voice, the instrument, was an ungrateful labour. It began with work exclusively on the pure and simple emission of sound. Homogeneity of timbre, equalisation of the register – that was the basis of the apprenticeship upon which all later study was based. That practical instruction filled up at least three years of exercises.'[11]

From his niche of privileged isolation, Rossini listened to and judged the new generation of singers; and he did not always appreciate their approach to performance, or even think that they had a vocal training worthy of the name. Two new effects, in particular, were disagreeable: the 'canto di forza' espoused by the tenor Duprez; and excessive vibrato. He thought both an attack on the senses used by certain singers as if they were valid expressive effects. 'I always found it disagreeable', he wrote, 'when they obliged me to have my music performed by singers who, following the *progress* fashionable today, think they have to illustrate every note with a sort of convulsive *tremolio* in their voice (it seems more like an attack of epilepsy), or those who work up a sweat producing the painful chest-voice high C, or even, God forbid, the chest-voice high C#, which I would never ever have dreamed of!'[12]

The point, in Rossini's opinion, is that one could not seriously talk of singing, and particularly its expressive possibilities, outside a highly professional context based on the acquisition of elaborate vocal techniques. Vocal mastery, however much aided by natural gifts, was acquired by means of advanced study over many years: 'Without that first discipline, aimed at developing equality of timbre over the whole range of the organ, a voice, no matter how richly endowed by nature it may be, always will remain completely defective.'[13] The idea that only the naturally gifted could aspire to a singing career was strongly contested by traditional Italian singing teachers. A good teaching method was thought capable of resolving even the most serious problems, and there were tried and tested strategies that a student in difficulties could, with the help of such a guide, attempt with realistic hopes of success: 'Upon certain pupils, whose emission was functionally faulty, often as the result of a not very appropriate development of the voice, the teacher imposed special gymnastics of guttural contractions that the patient, I must say, had to practise without emitting the tiniest sound; that purely aphonic gymnastic sound could go on for months and months.'[14]

After the first phase of vocal training was completed, the student began advanced study: the art of embellishment. 'When the voice finally had acquired the desired suppleness and equality – that is to say, when the future singer was in possession of his Stradivarius – only then did he begin to learn *the way to use it*! THE TECHNIQUE, which included placement, the holding of sound, and all the exercises in virtuosity: *vocalises*, *gruppetti*, trills, etc.'[15] Once vocal homogeneity had been acquired (equality of registers and smoothness of timbre), students progressed to correct vowel sounds and the precise articulation of syllables. The ultimate end was to make words intelligible to the listener, and it was not enough, indeed downright wrong, merely to try to produce a beautiful sound.

The placement of the sound and the *vocalises* were practised from the first on the vowels, one at a time, a, e, i, o, u; then all five of them were produced alternatively on the same held tone or same figure . . . The aim was to reach the point at which, as much as possible, the sound would not vary in timbre or intensity in spite of movements of the tongue and displacements of the lips caused by the succession of vowels, sometimes open, sometimes closed. In that way, one obtained *o*s that did not resemble the noise of a rattle, and *i*s that were not mixed *à la vinaigrette*. That was one of the subtlest parts of teaching.

The study of the vowels was followed by that of diphthongs, consonants, articulation, breathing, etc. Special attention was paid, above all, to the sound created with the help of the roof of the mouth. In fact, it is the transmitter *par excellence* of beautiful sounds. And in that regard one must agree that the Italian language really seems privileged to favour the evolution of bel canto. Amâre . . . bêllo . . . Those mâs and bêlls, placed in the roof of the mouth and sounded thus – isn't that already a sort of music? . . .

The third phase of the training consisted of putting into practice as a whole everything that had been studied in detail over a period of not less than five years for women, seven for men. Then, at the end of a final year, the teacher could say proudly to that student – who had scarcely tried out a cavatina in class: 'Go now, get on with you. You can sing whatever you wish.'[16]

It is interesting to note that the stages of vocal training Rossini proposes do not correspond chronologically to those usually followed in other methods. In particular the exercises on vowels, which elsewhere constitute the central material (formation and development of the voice, unification of registers, pronunciation and correct placement), are in Rossini located after exercises for embellishments, which were usually the final stage of training. This does not mean that the placement of vowels did not at all times constitute a fundamental aspect of correct singing, but the relaxation of such systematic study (which seems to have been a constant of Rossini's thought) is a shift of perspective that places increased emphasis on the importance of correct pronunciation within the total pedagogical picture. An advanced student could benefit from experience, established methods of study and a developed vocal organ, and was therefore capable of performing this type of exercise to maximum effect.

This difficult, multi-stage training was merely the foundation on which a real singer would build. The cycle completed, only personality and experience would make a singer into a performer:

Style is traditions, and the secrets of those traditions could be surmised by the young novice only among great singers, the perfect models consecrated by fame. Those traditions, on the other hand, elude scholastic instruction.

Only the *performing model*, taken from life, can inculcate and transmit them. So that if those who possess the great, true tradition disappear without leaving disciples on their level, their art vanishes, dies. *De profundis!* . . . In my time, there were numerous incomparable virtuosos in whose presence the new adepts could initiate themselves into taste, elegance, the judicious use of all the vocal effects – into *style*, that is.

As for the qualities of expression, feeling, grace, charm, stage insight: that is an affair of the individual temperament.[17]

The picture painted by Rossini outlines the essential elements of a traditional way of training whereby the pupil, after being formed by 'study of the voice', as a professional singer maintained his or her vocal organ by means of a large number of exercises, *solfeggi* and vocalisations. Rossini's allegiance to the past, however, should be considered alongside his significant personal contributions to the updating of a centuries-old tradition with a glance to the new institutional context of the conservatoires.

The theory and pedagogy of singing in early-nineteenth-century Italy

The chance to engage with issues of teaching within an institutional context occurred in 1839 with Rossini's nomination by the Bologna city council to the post of 'Consulente onorario perpetuo' (permanent honorary adviser) of the Liceo Musicale. Rossini was not new to teaching: he had frequently given private singing lessons to professionals and to society dilettantes. Indeed, during certain periods (his time in London in particular) this activity constituted the major part of his income. The composer lived in Bologna until 1848 and advised the management of the Liceo assiduously. Among his numerous successes during his time as adviser, he instituted a chair of *Accompagnamento*, and a division of the singing chair into two, *Solfeggio e Vocalizzo* and *Canto Perfezionato*.

The institution of a class specifically for teaching advanced singing, while simultaneously stressing the importance of a class entirely dedicated to the basics of reading vocal music, says much about the priorities of an opera composer become teacher. With this opportunity to manage a school personally, Rossini tried as far as he could to adapt vocal training to the realities of a new institutional system. But a conservatoire of music – a public institution in which Rossini demonstrated firm faith by both word and deed – could not compensate for a unique, exclusive and personal course of study of the type received by previous generations. Rossini spoke out on this issue during an interview with Wagner:

> They [the *castratos*] were also incomparable teachers. The teaching of
> singing in the master schools attached to the churches and supported at
> the churches' expense generally was confided to them. Some of those
> schools were famous. They were real singing academies. The pupils flocked
> to them, and some of them abandoned the choir loft to devote themselves
> to theatrical careers. But after a new political regime was installed
> throughout Italy by my restless contemporaries, the master schools were
> suppressed, being replaced by some *conservatories* in which, though good
> traditions existed, absolutely nothing of *bel canto* was conserved.[18]

But the conservatoires were the reality of Rossini's time, and, leaving aside
his reservations, he did not shun the chance of acting from within them,
evidently in the hope that he might be able to do some good.

Rossini's rôle in shaping singing pedagogy at the Bologna Conservatoire is better understood in the context of vocal pedagogy in early-
nineteenth-century Italy. The system of vocal education in Italy, above all
the seventeenth- and eighteenth-century professional model experienced
by castratos, and in general by pupils destined from infancy for a singing
career, was administered exclusively through a strict and prolonged relationship between student and teacher.[19] In other words, the Italian school
of singing was handed down and developed in the first centuries of its
history exclusively by means of an oral tradition. In the eighteenth century,
thanks to the fundamental work of Pier Francesco Tosi – *Opinioni de' cantori
antichi e moderni* (1723) – and Giambattista Mancini – *Riflessioni pratiche
sul canto figurato* (1777) – it became acceptable to fix and then disseminate
in printed form the pedagogical heritage that had previously been enclosed
within the educational system. These two important treatises, written by two
singers turned teachers, address an advanced student capable of profiting
from their instructions on the basis of knowledge already acquired under
the direct guidance of a teacher.

The first decades of the nineteenth century brought notable developments in the number and type of publications dedicated to singing. First
of all there were 'methods' intended for both beginning and advanced students, which offered exercises and vocalisations with reduced theoretical
indications, or even none at all. There were also more wide-ranging treatises, using a great many musical examples, which approached the problem
of vocal training and singing style according to a systematic method, even
discussing such matters as the physiology and hygiene of the voice. Some of
these works were written by composers and singing teachers who worked
in the conservatoires, and were used primarily by their students. Finally
there were numerous pamphlets, memoirs and essays written by singers,
composers and non-professional music-lovers, for the most part bemoan-
ing the decline of Italian singing. The exchange between French and Italian

theoretical models was intense: works dedicated to Italian singing were published first in France and then disseminated widely, being imported into Italy in translation (primarily published by Ricordi in Milan) some years later. Other publications included editions of manuscript collections of *solfeggi* and *vocalizzi* from great composers of the past: Davide Perez, Nicolò Porpora, Pasquale Cafaro, Francesco Feo, Leonardo Leo and others – for example, *Solfèges d'Italie avec la basse chiffrée composés par Léo, Durante, Scarlatti, Hasse, Porpora, Mazzoni, Caffaro, David, Perez, etc* (Paris, 1768; many reprints). Composers directly connected to Rossini in one way or another also wrote *solfeggi* and *vocalizzi* for various uses: Ferdinando Paer, *24 exercises pour voix de soprano ou tenore* (Leipzig, c. 1822); Giuseppe Catrufo, *Vocalizzi o studi per la voce secondo la Scuola d'Italia* (Milan, 1819); Nicola Vaccaj, *Metodo pratico di canto italiano per camera* (London, 1832);[20] Auguste Panseron, *Méthode de vocalisation, en deux parties, pour soprano ou ténor* (Paris, 1839).[21] That these composers felt it necessary to write and publish material seemingly so ungratifying from a compositional point of view testifies to the importance of these preparatory exercises within the system of vocal production as a whole.

The typology of books on singing theory broadened to include different levels of competence and different types of sources and readers. Many interesting volumes, in the form of either the simple method or the broader treatise, were solely concerned with purely vocal issues, for example, Anna Maria Pellegrini Celoni, *Grammatica, o siano regole per ben cantare* (Rome, 1810); Marcello Perrino, *Osservazioni sul canto* (Naples, 1810); Antonio Benelli, *Regole per il canto figurato* (Dresden and Leipzig, 1814); Ambrogio Minoia, *Lettera sopra il canto* (Milan, 1812). Among the works produced within the context of the conservatoires, the most important and influential was the *Méthode* of the Paris Conservatoire.[22] In Italy this context produced, among others, the works of Francesco Florimo of the Naples Conservatoire – *Metodo di canto* (Naples, n.d., c. 1840; several reprints) – and Lauro Rossi of the Milan Conservatoire – *Esercizi per canto a complemento dello studio dei solfeggi e dei vocalizzi come preparazione allo studio complessivo delle partiture di opere teatrali* (Milan, 1864). With regard to the relationship between France and Italy, and without forgetting the dissemination of the Italian singing tradition in England, we might also cite François-Joseph Fétis's *Méthode des méthodes de chant, basée sur les principes des écoles les plus célèbres de l'Italie et de la France* (Paris, 1869), a sort of compendium of both the French and Italian traditions, and the works of Giacomo Gotifredo Ferrari – *A Concise Treatise on Italian Singing* (London, 1818)[23] – and Domenico Crivelli, son of the Rossini tenor Gaetano – *L'arte del canto* (London, 1841). Finally, many famous singers, having turned to teaching at the end of their careers, published collections of *vocalizzi* and *solfeggi*: the best examples from the generation preceding Rossini are those by two castratos active at the end of the eighteenth and the beginning of the nine-teenth centuries, Giuseppe Aprile – *The Modern Italian Method of Singing* (London, c. 1795) – and Girolamo Crescentini – *Raccolta di esercizi per il canto all'uso del vocalizzo (Recueil d'Exercises pour la vocalisation musicale)* (Paris, n.d., c. 1810; several reprints).

The treatise of Manuel García – *Ecole de Garcia: Traité complet de l'art du chant en deux parties* (Paris, 1840–7) – constitutes a very special case, since it was without doubt the most important publication on singing of the whole nineteenth century in terms both of very broad diffusion and of strong influence – it was soon translated into Italian, English and German, in part or in full.[24] The son and pupil of the tenor Manuel García (Rossini's first Almaviva in *Il barbiere di Siviglia*), brother of Maria Malibran, and himself a singer, García taught at London's Royal Academy of Music from 1850 to his death, and invented the laryngoscope. His intention was to pass on the teaching method he had learned directly from his father, but he also added a completely modern view of the vocal mechanism and its physiology. A fundamental influence on the whole next generation of both Italian and French treatises, *The School of Garcia* presents many examples drawn from Rossini's scores, whose memory it helped to preserve even when they had disappeared from the stage.[25]

An annotated list of Rossinian singer-teachers

Moving on to teaching after retiring from the stage was (and still is) a natural course for a singer. Numerous Rossinian singers followed this tradition, devoting the second part of their lives to perpetuating a vocal aesthetic close to the composer's own principles. The following list is a selection of singers, chosen among the first performers of Rossini's operas, whose teaching activities are known and relatively well documented. Many of them published their own methods of singing; in other cases it seems to be the parents' teaching which is immortalised in print by their children. To these singers I have added others who are particularly important from the didactic point of view and who, although they may not have participated in Rossini premières, were admired and known personally by the composer. The list includes information (when known) on the teachers with whom the singers themselves studied, the rôles Rossini wrote for them (or the Rossini rôles in their repertory), the place and period of their teaching activities, their students and their published works. Even such a brief list reveals the close relationships among singers of the period from the point of view of teaching. While certainly not exhaustive, the list emphasises the importance of the didactic activity of Rossini's singers as a fundamental means for the diffusion of a Rossinian aesthetic and pedagogy of singing.

Eliodoro Bianchi (1773–1848), tenor. Rossini wrote for him the rôles of Baldassare in *Ciro in Babilonia* and Carlo in *Eduardo e Cristina*. He taught in Milan after 1835; his students included Cesare Badiali, Nicola Ivanoff, Elisa Orlandi, Joséphine Fodor-Mainvielle and Enrico Crivelli. He wrote *12 studi di canto (in chiave di sol) sopra varii caratteri della musica per voce di soprano o tenore* (posthumous publication: Milan, 1863), dedicated to Rossini.

Marco Bordogni (1788–1856), tenor. A pupil of Giovanni Simone Mayr, he made his début in Italy and in 1819 moved to Paris, where he sang until 1833. He performed in almost all Rossini's Paris premières, primarily taking rôles which had been David's and Nozzari's (see below). Rossini wrote for him the rôle of Conte di Libenskof in *Il viaggio a Reims*. He taught at the Paris Conservatoire from 1820; his students included Henriette Sontag, Laure Cinti-Damoreau and Mario. His numerous collections of *solfeggi* and *vocalizzi* are still used today, including the *Méthode de chant* (Paris, 1840).

Laure Cinti-Damoreau (1801–63), soprano. A pupil of Angelica Catalani and Marco Bordogni, she premièred Rossini's French works (Contessa di Folleville in *Il viaggio a Reims*, Pamyra in *Le Siège de Corinthe*, Anaï in *Moïse et Pharaon*, Comtesse de Formoutiers in *Le Comte Ory*, Mathilde in *Guillaume Tell*). She taught at the Paris Conservatoire between 1834 and 1856, and wrote the *Méthode de chant composée pour ses classes du Conservatoire* (Paris, 1849).

Gaetano Crivelli (1768–1836), tenor. He completed his studies in Naples with Andrea Nozzari and Giuseppe Aprile. In 1822 he premièred the rôle of Genio dell'Austria in the cantata *Il vero omaggio*. He taught Domenico Donzelli, and launched his children's singing careers: his son Domenico (1793–1857), having moved in 1817 to London to teach singing, published a bilingual treatise, *L'arte del canto ossia corso completo d'insegnamento sulla coltivazione della voce* (London, 1841).

Giovanni David (1790–1864), tenor. He created rôles in eight works by Rossini written between 1814 and 1822 (Don Narciso in *Il turco in Italia*, Peleo in the cantata *Le nozze di Teti e di Peleo*, Rodrigo in *Otello*, Ricciardo in *Ricciardo e Zoraide*, Oreste in *Ermione*, Corifeo in the *Cantata da eseguirsi la sera del dì 9 maggio 1819*, Giacomo V in *La donna del lago*,

Ilo in *Zelmira*). He was taught by his father Giacomo, and he ran a singing school in Naples between 1840 and 1844.

Domenico Donzelli (1790–1873), tenor. He was a pupil of Antonio Bianchi and then, in Naples, of Giuseppe Viganoni and Crivelli. Rossini wrote for him the rôle of Torvaldo in *Torvaldo e Dorliska* in 1815, and in 1825 the Cavalier Belfiore in *Il viaggio a Reims*. Duprez was among his pupils. He published a collection of *Esercizi giornalieri di canto basati sulla esperienza di molti anni* (Milan, c. 1840).

Louis-Gilbert Duprez (1806–96), tenor. He studied first at the Institution Royale de Musique directed by Alexandre-Etienne Choron, then in Italy with Donzelli. He sang much Rossini to great acclaim, including the rôles of Arnold in *Guillaume Tell* and Almaviva in *Il barbiere di Siviglia*. He taught singing at the Paris Conservatoire between 1842 and 1849, and in 1853 founded his own Ecole Spéciale de Chant. His pupils included Carolina Carvalho, Marie Battu, the Devriès sisters and his children Caroline and Léon. He published various works, including a treatise dedicated to Rossini, *L'Art du chant* (Paris, 1845).

Joséphine Fodor-Mainvielle (1789–1870), soprano. A pupil of Eliodoro Bianchi and Caterino Cavos, her repertory included numerous Rossini rôles, notably in *Elisabetta regina d'Inghilterra*, *La gazza ladra*, *Il barbiere di Siviglia*, *Otello* and *Zelmira*. She left the stage in 1833 and dedicated herself to teaching, publishing *Réflexions et conseils sur l'art du chant* (Paris, 1857).

Filippo Galli (1783–1853), bass (1801 début as a tenor, as a bass in 1813). Rossini wrote for him no fewer than nine rôles between 1812 and 1823: Batone in *L'inganno felice*, Conte Asdrubale in *La pietra del paragone*, Mustafà in *L'italiana in Algeri*, Selim in *Il turco in Italia*, Duca d'Ordowo in *Torvaldo e Dorliska*, Fernando Villabella in *La gazza ladra*, Maometto II (title rôle), Elpino in the cantata *Il vero omaggio*, Assur in *Semiramide*. In 1842 he moved to Paris, where he became 'Maestro di declamazione' at the Conservatoire.

Manuel García (1775–1832), tenor. He studied with Giovanni Ansani, and was the first Norfolk in *Elisabetta regina d'Inghilterra* and Almaviva in *Il barbiere di Siviglia*. From 1829 he dedicated himself to teaching in Paris, publishing *Exercises and Method for Singing* (London, 1824). His students included Nourrit, Henriette Méric-Lalande, and his children Maria Malibran, Manuel (author of the *Ecole de Garcia*; see above) and Pauline Viardot, who taught at the Paris Conservatoire between 1871 and 1875 and published *Ecole classique du chant* (Paris, 1861) and *Une heure d'étude: exercises pour voix de femme* (Paris, c. 1880).

Italo Gardoni (1821–82), tenor. He performed in the première of the *Petite messe solennelle*, and published *15 Vocalises calculées sur la formation du style moderne et le perfectionnement de l'art du chant* (Paris, n.d.).

Giacomo Guglielmi (1782–1820), tenor. Rossini wrote for him the rôle of Don Ramiro in *La Cenerentola*. He taught in Bologna, among others Giulia Grisi and Enrico Tamberlick. The library of the Milan Conservatoire owns a manuscript entitled *Avvertimenti. Principj per solfeggio, e vocalizzo per voce di basso del M.tro Giacomo Guglielmi*.

Luigi Lablache (1794–1858), bass. A pupil of Giovanni Ansani and Saverio Valente at the Conservatorio dei Turchini, Naples, he had enormous success in the comic rôles in *La Cenerentola* (Dandini) and *Il barbiere di Siviglia* (Figaro, Bartolo and Basilio), but also serious ones such as Elmiro in *Otello* and Assur in *Semiramide*. He wrote the *Méthode complète de chant, ou analyse raisonnée des principes d'après lesquels on doit diriger les études pour développer la voix* (Paris, 1840), whose authorship was however doubted by some of his contemporaries.

Nicolas Prosper Levasseur (1791–1871), bass. Active at the Théâtre Italien and the Opéra in Paris, he was the first Don Alvaro in *Il viaggio a Reims*, Moïse in *Moïse et Pharaon*, Gouverneur in *Le Comte Ory* and Walter Furst in *Guillaume Tell*. From 1841 until 1870 he taught at the Paris Conservatoire.

Barbara Marchisio (1833–1919), contralto. Together with her sister Carlotta, she was highly thought of by Rossini, and performed at the première of the *Petite messe solennelle* in 1864. She retired from the stage in 1876 and taught singing at Mira (near Venice) and later, from 1892 until 1911, at the Naples Conservatoire. She published various didactic works, including *Solfeggi per mezzo soprano della scuola classica napoletana* (Milan, 1892) and *Esercizi vocali* (Milan, c. 1895).

Domenico Mombelli (1751–1835), tenor. The first to commission an opera from Rossini, *Demetrio e Polibio*, he also premièred the rôle of Demetrio. Shortly thereafter he retired to Bologna where he dedicated himself to teaching. He had already taught his own children Ester, Anna and Alessandro (who was chosen by Rossini to teach advanced singing at the Bologna Liceo musicale).

Adolphe Nourrit (1802–39), tenor. He created Néoclès in *Le Siège de Corinthe*, Aménophis in *Moïse et Pharaon*, the title rôle in *Le Comte Ory* and Arnold in *Guillaume Tell*. A student of García (the father), he taught at the Paris Conservatoire from 1827 to 1837.

Andrea Nozzari (1775–1832), tenor. He was a pupil of Giacomo David and Giuseppe Aprile. In Naples between 1815 and 1822 Rossini wrote ten rôles for him: Leicester in *Elisabetta regina d'Inghilterra*, Giove in the cantata *Le nozze di Teti e di Peleo*, the title rôle in *Otello*, Rinaldo in *Armida*, Osiride in *Mosè in Egitto*, Agorante in *Ricciardo e Zoraide*, Pirro in *Ermione*, Rodrigo in *La donna del lago*, Paolo Erisso in *Maometto II*, Antenore in *Zelmira*. From 1825 he turned to teaching in Naples; his pupils included Giovanni Basadonna and Rubini.

Luigi Pacini (1767–1837), bass. He studied at the Naples Conservatoire with Giacomo Tritto, and was the first Parmenione in *L'occasione fa il ladro* and Geronio in *Il turco in Italia*, and also admired by Rossini as Taddeo in *L'italiana in Algeri*. From 1821 he taught singing at the Liceo musicale of Viareggio, founded by his son, the composer Giovanni.

Felice Pellegrini (1774–1832), bass. He was the first Don Profondo in *Il viaggio a Reims*. From 1819 until 1827 he sang in various Rossini performances at the Théâtre Italien, Paris, and from 1830 he taught at the Paris Conservatoire, publishing *Solfèges pour la vocalisation musicale* (Paris, n.d.).

Rosmunda Pisaroni (1793–1872), contralto. She made her début as a soprano, but on Rossini's advice shifted to contralto. She completed her studies with the famous castratos Gaspare Pacchierotti, Giambattista Velluti and Luigi Marchesi, and created the rôles of Zomira in *Ricciardo e Zoraide*, Andromaca in *Ermione* and Malcom (Rossini's spelling of Malcolm) in *La donna del lago*. She taught at the Paris Conservatoire from 1829.

Giovanni Battista Rubini (1794–1854), tenor. A pupil of Nozzari, he was the first Araldo in the *Cantata da eseguirsi la sera del dì 9 maggio 1819* and Fileno in *La riconoscenza*. Extremely well thought of by Rossini, whose lighter tenor rôles he frequently performed (such as Don Ramiro in *La Cenerentola*), he dedicated himself to teaching mainly after 1847; his students included the tenor Mario. He published *Douze leçons de chant moderne, pour voix de ténor ou sopran* (Paris, n.d.).

Nicola Tacchinardi (1772–1859), tenor. His repertory included many Rossini operas (*Tancredi, Aureliano in Palmira, Ciro in Babilonia, Otello, Semiramide, La donna del lago, Il barbiere di Siviglia, La Cenerentola*). He left the stage in 1831, turning to teaching at the Florence Conservatoire, his students including Erminia Frezzolini and his daughter Fanny. He wrote *Dell'opera in musica e de' suoi difetti* (Florence, 1833) and published many collections of vocal exercises.

(*translated by Laura Basini*)

14 Staging Rossini

MERCEDES VIALE FERRERO

Staging conventions and practices in Italy

The visual realisation of Rossini's operas – *décors*, costumes and props – was at first directly dependent on a system of theatrical production and management rooted in the last years of the *ancien régime*. Two staging practices coexisted in Italy: these were not strictly separate, but, on the contrary, often interrelated. Smaller theatres had a stock of about eight or ten sets, called 'di dotazione' (literally, 'dowry'), which could be used for the majority of scene changes asked for in the librettos; more could be added if necessary. Major opera houses (La Scala in Milan, the San Carlo in Naples, La Fenice in Venice, the Teatro Regio in Turin and a few others) provided new sets each season only for *opere serie*; if *opere buffe* were staged, their sets were not updated quite so frequently. Statistically the 'dotazione' system prevailed, as can be seen from the *Indice de' teatrali spettacoli* published annually in Milan, from which we discover that in the year 1790 opera seasons took place in eighty different Italian cities and towns and an even larger number of theatres (some cities had more than one theatre).

The importance of productions in major opera houses which employed the most famous stage designers and offered the novelties of the season is obvious; these were the operas which, if successful, would be taken to other venues, thus supplying this massive operatic circuit. This constant need for new works was partly satisfied by the circulation of a large number of comic operas, while the serious repertoire remained much more limited. Not many titles recurred between 1800 and 1812, with a few *drammi per musica* possibly owing their popularity to a political interpretation (e.g. Cimarosa's *Gli Orazi e i Curiazi* and Nicolini's *Trajano in Dacia*). With *Tancredi* and the operas that immediately followed, Rossini came to occupy the privileged position available to a composer who could successfully meet the expectations and needs of those who looked on opera as an essential element of social life. If anything changed after the Restoration it was the increased tempo of theatrical activity, with the building of new theatres and hence a multiplication of opera seasons – in which what could be called 'the Rossinian repertoire' was constantly present.

In theory this situation should have caused the recurrence of set types – in other words, a repertoire of images relative to specific operas. In practice, however, things went differently. The scenarios (i.e. the sequence of set changes described in the libretto) of Rossini's early operas presented no particular structural problems and could have been adapted from the stocks in storage. For instance, the view of Mount Etna in *Tancredi* could be easily painted on a backdrop; in *Elisabetta regina d'Inghilterra* a wall needed to collapse during the action, but this was a fairly common and relatively basic scenic trick known as 'diroccata' (literally, 'dilapidated'). Problems arose for a different reason: the principle, unquestioned at the time, of historically accurate sets. Accordingly, *Ciro in Babilonia* and *Semiramide* required the visual representation of ancient Babylon – with very little supporting archaeological evidence; *Mosè*, of ancient Egypt; *Tancredi*, of the early middle ages; *Otello*, of Renaissance Venice. And if a generic knowledge of classical monuments could seem sufficient for *Aureliano in Palmira*, in Milan the historically fastidious Paolo Landriani reconstructed on the stage the temple of Bacchus in Baalbek.[1]

Milan seems indeed to have been the focal point where Rossinian scenic types were in some cases established, and in others re-established by altering the original sequence and/or description of sets. The history of these alterations is sometimes complex, as for example with *Otello*. The sequence of sets for the première at the Teatro del Fondo, Naples, on 4 December 1816 read: 'A hall in the Senate, with a view of the shore; Room in Elmiro's Palace; Public hall; Elmiro's room; Bedroom'. *Otello* arrived at La Scala, Milan, on 3 September 1823, preceded (in 1818) by a ballet with the same title by Salvatore Viganò – which Stendhal found more dramatic and moving than Rossini's opera.[2] For this production of Rossini's opera Alessandro Sanquirico changed the first set into 'A room in the Doge's palace' looking out on the Riva degli Schiavoni with a view of the island of San Giorgio in the background, and he also added a 'Garden' taken wholesale from the sets for Viganò's ballet. In other theatres the set for the opening scene of Viganò's ballet, 'Piazzetta San Marco', was also transferred to Rossini's *Otello*. In Turin (Teatro Regio, 31 January 1825, sets by Luigi Vacca and Fabrizio Sevesi) and in Venice (La Fenice, 31 January 1826, sets by Francesco Bagnara) the set sequence became: 'Piazzetta San Marco; Elmiro's rooms; Public hall; Gallery (only in Turin); Garden; Bedroom'. The 'Garden' was no longer in Act 1, as in Milan, but in Act 2; in 1834 at La Fenice it disappeared altogether and was replaced by 'A loggia overlooking the lagoon'; in Giuseppe Bertoja's designs for the 1846 production, again at La Fenice, both 'Loggia' and 'Garden' were present. Meanwhile in Alessandria (1835, with the Deleonardi brothers as designers) the first set had been changed to 'Magnificent pavilion in Piazzetta San Marco', while at the San Carlo, Naples, in 1838, Antonio Niccolini had revived the original sequence of sets.

Tancredi presents a less complicated case, which affects more the evocative function of its sets than their sequence. For its première at La Fenice (6 February 1813) the designer Giuseppe Borsato kept scrupulously to the scene directions in the libretto, producing results of great spatial and stylistic complexity: his 'Prison', for example, resonates with echoes of Piranesian *Carceri* (plate 14.1). In Naples in 1818 Pasquale Canna transformed this prison into a kind of Gothic courtyard (albeit closed at either end by gates); at the Teatro Carcano, Milan, in 1829 Sanquirico imagined it as the hall of an ancient crumbling palace. Similarly, the 'Public square' in Act 1 was variously interpreted: it was a spooky place, guarded by animal-like sculptures and dominated by a horse statue, in Venice in 1813, while at the Carcano in 1829 Sanquirico turned it into a cold and almost metaphysical square framed by symmetrical classical arches. A few years earlier, for a production at La Scala in 1823, Sanquirico himself had summed up the scene with the only image truly essential to the action, 'Before a temple' (the church where Amenaide's nuptials will *not* take place). Recently Pier Luigi Pizzi has interpreted this scene in similar terms – naturally with a very different stylistic language – for a co-production between the Schwetzinger Festspiele and La Scala (1992–3). Milan also left its mark on *La Cenerentola*: at La Scala in 1817 Sanquirico slipped in a 'Cellar' between the 'Cabinet' and the 'Delightful place [deliziosa] in the gardens of Don Ramiro's palace', a more appropriate location for Don Magnifico's drunkenness. Francesco Bagnara revived it almost exactly at La Fenice in 1835, and it has made the rounds of modern opera houses in the very successful 1973 production by Jean-Pierre Ponnelle, which originated at La Scala.

This fluidity of sets in Italian productions of Rossini's operas may seem surprising, especially since it did not last – the sets for Bellini's *Norma* (1831) and *Beatrice di Tenda* (1833), for example, were not substantially modified, even though the places represented were differently interpreted. The presence of such variants is partly due to a continuous search for historical and geographical precision: the 'Piazzetta San Marco' in Venice, unchanged for centuries, was historically correct, and therefore preferable to an unidentified hall from the presumed time of *Otello*; it also had a connotative function, allowing the spectator to identify immediately the location where the dramatic action takes place, thus increasing its plausibility (plate 14.8). The technical necessity of changing sets in full view of the audience ('a vista') remained a determining factor, imposing the alternation between so-called 'long' or 'half-stage' scenes and 'short' or 'very short' ones. From this point of view the set sequence for *Otello* did not change: the opera opened with a long scene ('A hall in the Senate', 'Hall', 'Square', or whatever) in front of which the backdrop for 'Elmiro's room' (a short set) descended, while behind this the following 'Public hall' (long) or 'Garden' (half-stage) were prepared, and so on, in order to finish with the obligatory 'Bedroom' (short). The rhythm of set changes remained the same, even though the locations where the action took place might differ.

Reproduction and circulation of images

Other needs determined the adoption of normative models for sets. This adoption was made possible by the circulation of replicable reproductions, as either engravings or lithographs – a practice which, at the initial stages of Rossini's career, had no clearly defined purpose in the theatre. For some time, collections of scene reproductions, generally promoted by engravers rather than by the artists who created them, offered images of sets unrelated to any current production. They were intended rather as ideal set types, adaptable to different dramatic situations: their destination was then the 'dotazione' of stock productions.[3] Only later, from 1816 onwards, did their objective become the representation of scenes from specific operas, intended as records of past productions but also as examples for future ones. A few collections were promoted by music publishers and aimed at a larger usage.[4] With a few exceptions, such material was published in Milan and privileged the set designers who worked there; those who worked in theatres elsewhere quite simply lacked the same circulation opportunities. An exception seems to be the *Raccolta di Disegni . . . da Pasquale Canna Direttore ed Esecutore delle Scene del Real Teatro di S. Carlo*, published in Naples and edited by the artist himself, who came from La Scala (where he had worked alongside Landriani, Perego and Sanquirico), perhaps with the intention of exporting Milanese initiatives to Naples.[5]

The situation described above produced a curious and long-lasting dichotomy: even to this day our knowledge of the sets for Rossini's operas in the first half of the nineteenth century depends on two main kinds of sources, which present totally different characteristics. The valuable body of set designs by Giuseppe Borsato, Francesco Bagnara and Giuseppe Bertoja for the Rossinian repertoire of the Venetian theatres is entirely made up of projects and sketches of sets planned before performance.[6] For this reason this material did not circulate at the time; rediscovered not many years ago, only recently has it become the object of systematic research.[7] The documentation for productions in Milan, on the contrary, consists mainly of prints – some issued at the time of actual productions, others years later – based on drawings by the various authors active there – Paolo Landriani, Pasquale Canna, Luca Gandaglia and Alessandro Sanquirico. What these prints transmit, then, is not the initial conception of a scene, but its final image as realised in the theatre, sometimes even including the action taking place on stage (plates 14.3 and 14.4).

How faithful are these reproductions? Today nobody can say for sure. We can only attempt to see them through the eyes of their contemporary audiences by consulting newspaper reviews, which generally paid detailed attention to the *mise en scène* (plate 14.9). There are no reasons to doubt the freedom of opinion of the reviewers: since the Napoleonic era, even when toeing the establishment line on political matters, journalists had been able to express themselves on artistic and theatrical matters without restriction. After the Restoration, censorship, however strict and fastidious, did not limit the critical freedom of reviewers discussing a performance. Freedom of judgement does not necessarily mean objectivity, however, and it may not be by mere chance that Pasquale Canna, for instance, was extremely popular in Milan and frowned upon in Venice and Naples.[8] We cannot take for granted the objectivity of even such an exceptional spectator as Stendhal, who considered Alessandro Sanquirico to be the ideal set designer, but was far less generous towards his colleagues. Stendhal was an attentive observer, at any rate, and discussed aspects of the *mise en scène* that we cannot surmise from drawings or prints alone. Coming from Milan – where at La Scala 'there are no lamps in the auditorium, which is illuminated only by the light reflected from the sets' – in 1817 Stendhal arrived at the Teatro San Carlo in Naples, where he was dazzled by the magnificence of the new chandelier, 'stupendous, shining with lights', while the sets appeared to him 'of the worst kind'. Until, that is, he realised that it was the chandelier that 'killed them', as it remained lit during the show.[9] In 1821 La Scala also adopted a chandelier that lit the auditorium during the performance. A fiery controversy followed; but from the images of Rossinian sets that we have it is not possible to make out any difference between 'before' and 'after'.

Costumes

Another aspect of Rossinian *mise en scène* to which Stendhal paid substantial attention is the costumes. In his *Life of Rossini* he stated that for the Naples première of *Elisabetta regina d'Inghilterra* (4 October 1815) 'an Englishman . . . had had sent out from England a set of extremely accurate drawings, which made it possible to reproduce exactly, and in every detail, the costume of the severe-minded Elizabeth. These sixteenth-century dresses turned out to be exquisitely becoming to the figure and features of the beautiful Colbran.'[10] Here Stendhal mixes reality and invention (as he often does): the extremely accurate drawings did exist, but they came from only as far as Milan and the costume designer of La Scala, Giacomo

Pregliasco – who was about to move to Naples, where he would design the costumes for the première of *Otello* and a revival of *Tancredi*.[11] One might argue that the generous *décolleté* in the costume for Elisabetta showed off Isabella Colbran's curves rather than the presumed austerity of the British sovereign. But, as Stendhal agreed, what really mattered was the artist's intention rather than the results: the search for historical precision, authenticated by contemporary sources (plate 14.2).

It was not by chance that Naples chose a designer from La Scala: not only because Barbaja, the impresario of the San Carlo, came from Milan, where he had been able to appreciate the quality of Pregliasco's creations, but also because it was in Milan that a new collaboration between theatre and academia had started to emerge. It was not unheard of for a set designer to operate also as a professor at an academy.[12] What was new was for a designer to check the details of each production against authoritative historical and iconographical sources with the help of illustrious scholars. The eight volumes of costume sketches for operas and ballets performed at La Scala between 1818 and 1823, now kept in the Biblioteca Nazionale Braidense, Milan,[13] are the combined efforts of Alessandro Sanquirico and his colleagues in collaboration with Robustiano Gironi, the learned librarian at Brera, and Giulio Ferrario, scholarly polygraph and co-author and editor of the monumental work *Il costume antico e moderno*, published in Milan between 1815 and 1827.[14] These two scholars examined the drawings and annotated them in the margins, pointing out possible historical imprecisions, stating which sources they had used, suggesting alternatives and commenting on the appropriateness of the choices made. This collection includes costume sketches for *L'italiana in Algeri*, *Otello*, *Tancredi*, *Zoraide* (*Ricciardo e Zoraide*), *La donna del lago* and *Matilde di Shabran*. Some were reproduced by the engraver Stanislao Stucchi in the *Raccolta di figurini ad uso dei teatri*, which was meant to accompany the *Raccolta di scene teatrali* published by the engraver himself.[15] Another source for the *Raccolta di figurini* was the tables of the *Galerie dramatique* published in Paris.[16] We know that these engravings were actually used as models thanks to annotations on some of them by theatre tailors and dressmakers (about fabrics, the number of costumes needed for extras, etc.).[17] Costume sketches circulated as drawings as well as prints, however, as demonstrated by two collections which should be explored comparatively: Edoardo Viganò's sketches from the Cellini Collection, Turin, and Carlo Martini's from the Théâtre Italien, Paris.[18] The Rossinian titles present in both collections are *Elisabetta regina d'Inghilterra*, *Otello*, *La donna del lago*, *Le Comte Ory* and *Guillaume Tell*. And both collections include costumes derived from French models, such as Maria Taglioni's attire for the *tyrolienne* in *Guillaume Tell*, copied from the *Petite galerie dramatique* published by Martinet.[19]

Paris: the Théâtre Italien and the Opéra

There was a great deal of further contact between Italy and France: Alessandro Sanquirico, who was enormously prestigious, was often consulted by French artists and theatre personalities.[20] However, when in 1824 an Italian artist, Giulio Cesare Carnevali, applied for the post of set designer at the Théâtre Italien, he was rejected because 'the Italian way of painting sets has nothing to do with the French way: preparation, technique, effect, everything is different'.[21] What sounded like a technical or stylistic issue was in fact an eminently financial one: it would have been impossible to re-use the elements of the scenes 'confectionnées à la française' from the house stock; new (and costly) ones for each opera would have to be made, as was the practice in Italy.[22] A few years later, in 1829, the Théâtre Italien recruited an Italian artist, Domenico Ferri, on Rossini's recommendation. Since Rossini was (like Verdi later) respectful of specialist theatrical competence, this personal intervention in matters of scenography could be of great significance, especially considering the local aversion towards 'la manière italienne'. A question remains, however: were the negative comments by French reviewers (with Théophile Gautier at their head) regarding the sets of the Théâtre Italien grounded in reality, or were they motivated by a more generic dislike for their foreign character?[23] In 1837 Ferri published a collection of engravings, *Choix de décorations du Théâtre Royal Italien par Domenico Ferri*, following the example of the Milanese publishers – who had ceased to issue theatrical prints after Sanquirico's retirement from the stage in 1832. If we compare images of the Rossinian repertoire in Ferri's *Choix de décorations* with images of the same repertoire from the Paris Opéra, we do not perceive a significant difference in quality – apart from details of a designer's personal style, which is inevitable. And yet there must have been a difference, since in the nineteenth century the *décorations* for the Paris Opéra were considered by many superior to those in any other theatre: even Verdi, who was extremely critical of the 'grande boutique' (his disparaging name for the Opéra), appreciated them.[24] It is easier to highlight differences and analogies with the Italian sets than to identify the distinctive character of the superior achievements of the Opéra's scenes.

As for the administration, in 1827 the Opéra instituted a 'Comité de mise en scène', of which Rossini was a member. The function of the committee was to examine, discuss and approve (or reject) set and costume designs. This was not a unique case; there was a similar committee at La Scala.[25] The practice of re-using stock material was also common at the Opéra, as in Italy, though it was done differently there, by painting new *décors* on old canvases.[26] What is considered peculiar to the French administration is the employment of a number of specialists, each working on a different aspect of set design (architecture, landscape, decor, etc.). This division of labour had been present in Italy as early as the seventeenth and eighteenth centuries, however. On the other hand, during the Restoration both in Italy and in France two artists dominated dictatorially in their theatres – Sanquirico in Milan, Pierre-Luc-Charles Cicéri in Paris – leaving little room for their colleagues.

The Opéra made large use of practicables and pieces of ground-scenery, generally avoided in Italy because they made scene changes in full view of the audience more problematic. These changes were not frequently adopted in Paris: the 1875 revival of *Guillaume Tell* made use of only one, to judge from the *maquettes* of Charles Cambon, Philippe Chaperon, Joseph Chéret, Edouard Despléchin, Antoine Lavastre and Auguste Rubé. The use of 'maquettes construites' – that is, model theatres to visualise the scene's final effect – was peculiarly French, but it became established relatively late. Despite the systematic preservation of documents to illustrate sets and costumes (the latter regularly circulated in the form of prints, mainly by the publisher Martinet), the flexibility of Rossinian set sequences as observed in Italy was also present at the Opéra when Rossini's Italian operas were performed: in the 1844 *Othello* the only remainder of the original scenario was the unavoidable 'Chambre de Desdémone'. In 1860 *Sémiramis* was to have only four scene changes, as opposed to the ten of the Venice première (1823).[27]

The expressive language of set design differed, naturally, from designer to designer. Compare, for example, Cicéri's 'Tente de Mahomet' for *Le Siège de Corinthe*, reproduced in watercolour by Auguste Caron, with Sanquirico's 'Padiglione di Maometto' for *L'assedio di Corinto*, lithographed in Ricordi's *Nuova raccolta*: the distance between a vision of exquisitely ornate exoticism with a tendency towards *dépaysement* and the conception of a panoramic view that aimed at descriptive verisimilitude is striking (plates 14.5 and 14.6). In fact, Sanquirico generally confined himself to a certain structural sobriety which tended to limit decorative effusions: if we compare the lithograph of his 'Room in Elmiro's palace' for *Otello* with the engraving of Domenico Ferri's 'Salon' for the same opera, we find an amazing divergence between the prominence of architectonic invention in the former, and of invasive ornamentation in the latter, which Ferri seems to derive from Cicéri – albeit with less sophistication.

The *livrets de mise en scène*

One essential difference from Italian productions can be found in France (and not only at the Opéra) in the use of *livrets de mise en scène*, which would reach Italy only in 1856 (thanks to Verdi). The *livrets de mise en scène* (staging manuals) were printed or handwritten brochures which contained notes relative to the various aspects of a performance in its different stages: the exact placing of the groundplans of settings and anything needed to make them; costumes; tools and props; stage directions, including movements for singers, chorus and extras; the relationship between their gestures and voices and the orchestral score; and ways of expressing visibly a dramatic situation. The immediate aim was to provide a blueprint for subsequent performances and revivals so that they would conform to the ideal model of the première.[28] An example may help clarify the difference between information on the *mise en scène* provided by librettos (time and place of action, visual aspect of sets, entries and exits of actors, special effects such as storms and fires) and that provided by the *livrets*. In the libretto of *Guillaume Tell*, Act 1 scene 1, there is a lengthy and detailed description of everything that the spectator is supposed to see: Tell's house, a stream, a bridge, a boat, and Tell, Hedwige and Jemmy in significant postures. The *livret de mise en scène* specifies that the house must be 'in the foreground', that the little boat 'must be placed between two streams of water and must move easily from one side to the other and even on a slope', and that the bridge must be practicable, as it will be crossed by the villagers.[29] In other words, the libretto describes *what* is to be seen, the *livret* explains *how* to achieve the desired result.

There was also a more ambitious reason for the use of *livrets* alongside the practical one, however: to make 'the author's thoughts clear and evident', as Eugène Scribe wrote to Louis Palianti, compiler of numerous *livrets*.[30] Ideally, then, these appear to be authorised interpretations of a dramatic creation which, once established as conforming to the 'author's thoughts', could not, and in fact must not, be altered. At least in theory; in practice, different *livrets* for the same opera could co-exist, sometimes showing considerable differences. In the case of Rossini's works, often handled rather freely, the *livrets* relative to the first productions could provide important clues, if not exactly to the 'author's thoughts', then at least to his consent to the scenic interpretation they described. In any case, it is fascinating to be able to read a good thirty-three *livrets* dated or datable between 1826 and 1933 for a limited number of operas: *Le Barbier de Séville*, *Le Comte Ory, Guillaume Tell, Moïse, Sémiramis, Le Siège de Corinthe*.[31] This material deserves detailed research, with accurate analyses and comparisons, the more so since the *livrets* mirror the changing fortunes of Rossini's operas, which, following the raving successes scored in opera houses everywhere, were subsequently subjected to a slow eclipse that only a few titles survived.

All late examples of *livrets* refer to *Le Barbier de Séville* (1907, 1909, 1919, 1930 and 1933, the last an autograph by Albert Carré, a creative and talented stage director). For *Guillaume Tell* there is a printed *livret* dated 1892; for *Moïse*, one dated 1902. In fact, *Guillaume Tell* was still performed at the Opéra in 1899; at La Scala this opera enjoyed four productions between 1860 and 1899, while more or less at the same time (1861–1905) there had been seven for *Il barbiere di Siviglia* and only one for *Mosè*. *Guglielmo Tell* and *Mosè* are the only Rossini titles in the huge catalogue of sketches for the most important Italian set designer of the second half of the nineteenth century, Carlo Ferrario. He encountered with *Tell* the same difficulty experienced many years earlier by Giuseppe Bertoja: that of performing a heroic drama in a rustic setting – but Bertoja solved the problem much better than Ferrario, who paid too much attention to *couleur locale*.[32]

My discussion of the staging of Rossini's operas has dealt with Italy and France, a rather telling fact about the present state of research on the subject. Up to now there has been only sporadic interest in productions that took place in England (mainly regarding the activity of the Grieve family; plate 14.10),[33] while those in such a major operatic centre as Vienna have been hardly touched upon,[34] to say nothing of other European capitals such as Brussels, Amsterdam, Lisbon and Madrid. At present it is not yet possible to have a panoramic view of Rossinian stage design, even if our knowledge of the materials still available is incomparably more extended than it was twenty years ago. The number of studies devoted to individual set designers,[35] as well as to theatres where his operas were performed,[36] has increased; stage and costume designs have been reproduced in biographical and musicological studies.[37] Until all the available images related to Rossini's operas in Italian collections were recently collected, described and reproduced in *Rossini sulla scena dell'Ottocento*,[38] the specific topic 'staging Rossini' had been addressed directly only in a handful of useful but brief essays.[39] This impressive and invaluable work raises hopes that similarly extensive research will be undertaken for other countries, leading to new discoveries that will surely provoke new thinking.

Six set designers for Rossini

Giuseppe Borsato (Venice 1771–1849). He devoted only a few years of over half a century of artistic activity to set designing: from 1809 to 1823. These dates encompass a crucial period of Rossini's career, however, including, among other things, the premières of *Tancredi*, *Sigismondo* and *Semiramide* at La Fenice. Borsato worked in a transitional period that witnessed the softening of neo-classical rigour: it is therefore extremely difficult to apply a stylistic label to his scenic compositions, characterised by a dramatic intensity that borders at times on the visionary (plate 14.1).[40]

Antonio Niccolini (San Miniato 1776 – Naples 1850). Following initial work in Tuscany, he was selected by the choreographer Gaetano Gioja for the Teatro San Carlo. In Naples he enjoyed such success that he eventually limited his designing activity to the supervision and artistic direction of productions. His impetuous style and fruitful 'creative freedom' (in Franco Mancini's words) had enormous influence. However, no documents regarding the few Rossini works for which he made sets – *Elisabetta regina d'Inghilterra, Ermione, Le nozze di Teti e di Peleo*, the cantata *Omaggio umiliato* (for which he wrote the text), a revival of *Otello* – have been identified among the surviving rich corpus of his designs.[41]

Alessandro Sanquirico (Milan 1777–1849). After studying at the Accademia di Brera, he began his designing career at La Scala, collaborating with Giovanni Pedroni, Paolo Landriani and Giovanni Perego. When Landriani retired from the theatre in 1815, and Perego died prematurely in 1817, Sanquirico became sole arbiter of the Milanese stage until 1832, when, following disputes with the management, he resigned and devoted himself to painting. Among set designers for Rossini he was perhaps the most remarkable, even though he worked for only two prèmieres: *La gazza ladra* and *Bianca e Falliero* (the sets for *La pietra del paragone* and *Aureliano in Palmira* were by Landriani; those for *Il turco in Italia* by Canna). Sanquirico nonetheless designed a great number of Rossini's operas, and in multiple versions; moreover, systematic reproduction of his sets in engravings and lithographs disseminated views of evocative intensity that became a fundamental component of the 'Rossini phenomenon' – for instance, the 'Trial court' in *La gazza ladra*, or the 'Tomb of Nino' in *Semiramide* (plates 14.3–14.5).[42]

Pierre-Luc-Charles Cicéri (Saint-Cloud 1782 – Saint-Chéron 1868). He was active from 1805 at the Opéra in Paris, where, after a meteoric rise, he earned the title of 'peintre en chef' in 1816. He also worked in other theatres in Paris (Théâtre Italien, Comédie Française, Odéon, etc.) and in other cities. In 1827 he went to Milan to consult Sanquirico. In 1831 disputes began with the new management of the Opéra, where his position was threatened, but he remained in his job until 1848. Among his productions were *Le Comte Ory, Guillaume Tell, Moïse, Le Siège de Corinthe* at the Opéra, and *Zelmira* at the Théâtre Italien. He showed remarkable evocative ability, both in his ambiances and in his weather effects, which were always functional to the dramatic situation. A versatile talent, he also worked as landscape painter and decorator (plate 14.6).[43]

Francesco Bagnara (Vicenza 1784 – Venice 1866). He worked in Venice, initially in the theatres of San Moisè and San Benedetto, the latter for the prèmiere of *Eduardo e Cristina*. Succeeding Borsato at La Fenice, he worked there until 1840, designing many of Rossini's operas, developing a variety of ingenious inventions with a particular predilection for sets based on panoramic views.[44]

Giuseppe Bertoja (Venice 1804–73). An artist of great pictorial and imaginative quality, Bertoja had an extremely busy theatrical career: he worked in Venice, Turin, Trieste, Vicenza and Bologna. In Venice and Trieste he was the set designer for six of Verdi's premières; he was less involved with Rossini, on account of the decline in number of Rossinian productions. His sets for *Guglielmo Tell* in Turin (1840) and Venice (1856) and for *Otello* in Venice (1846) remain nonetheless memorable (plates 14.7–14.8).[45]

(*translated by Rosa Solinas*)

Plate 14.1 Giuseppe Borsato, *Prison*, stage design for the first performance (Venice, La Fenice, 1813) of *Tancredi* (Bibliothèque de l'Opéra, Paris)

Plate 14.2 Giacomo Pregliasco, *Elisabetta d'Inghilterra*, costume sketch for the first performance (Naples, San Carlo, 1815) of *Elisabetta regina d'Inghilterra* (Biblioteca Civica, Turin)

Plate 14.3 Alessandro Sanquirico, *Nino's Tomb*, stage design for *Semiramide* (Milan, La Scala, 1824 or 1825) in *Nuova raccolta di scene teatrali inventate da Alessandro Sanquirico e pubblicate da Giovanni Ricordi* (Milan, 1827–32)

Plate 14.4 Sanquirico, *Hall in Argirio's Palace*, stage design for *Tancredi* (Milan, Carcano, 1829) reproduced in *Nuova raccolta di scene teatrali inventate da Alessandro Sanquirico e pubblicate da Giovanni Ricordi* (Milan, 1827–32)

Plate 14.5 Sanquirico, *Maometto's Tent*, stage design for *L'assedio di Corinto* (Milan, La Scala, 1829) in *Nuova raccolta di scene teatrali inventate da Alessandro Sanquirico e pubblicate da Giovanni Ricordi* (Milan, 1827–32)

Plate 14.6 Pierre-Luc-Charles Cicéri, *Mahomet's Tent*, stage design for the first performance (Paris, Opéra, 1826) of *Le Siège de Corinthe* (Bibliothèque de l'Opéra, Paris)

Plate 14.7 Giuseppe Bertoja, *The Lake of the Four Cantons*, stage design for *Guglielmo Tell* at the Teatro Regio, Turin in 1840 (Civico Museo Correr, Venice)

Plate 14.8 Giuseppe Bertoja, *Piazzetta S. Marco*, stage design for *Otello* at La Fenice, Venice in 1846 (Civico Museo Correr, Venice)

Plate 14.9 Anonymous, *Scene from "Matilde di Shabran" as performed at the Italian Opera in London* reproduced in *Panorama universale*, 16 June 1855, p. 80 (Biblioteca Civica, Turin)

Plate 14.10 Thomas Grieve, *The Acropolis of Corinth*, stage design for *The Siege of Corinth* at Drury Lane, London in 1836 (University of London Library, Grieve Collection, London)

15 Editing Rossini

PATRICIA B. BRAUNER

The *Edizione critica delle opere di Gioachino Rossini*

At its simplest, a critical edition of music presents a printed score that reflects as accurately as possible the composer's concept and provides the user with information about how the editor arrived at this form of the score and with the tools to interpret it. An immediate qualification is necessary. To speak of the composer's concept as something that is fixed, that can be expressed in a score and that can be recovered through study of the sources raises the issues of authorship and the nature of an opera as a work of art. These topics have been much discussed by textual critics and musical scholars. In some senses an opera has multiple authors: we consider the composer to be the principal author, but the work of the librettist with whom he collaborates can also be seen as authorial. Censors and financial controls can affect the final form of the opera. An opera, furthermore, needs a theatre directorship, stage director, set and costume designers, musicians and stage hands to realise it in performance.

Nonetheless, the Rossini critical edition, like the critical editions of other nineteenth-century Italian opera composers, generally regards the original score as reflecting the composer's intention – much as that intention may have been modified by the entire social setting in which an opera is composed, produced and published or otherwise disseminated – and takes the autograph as the principal source for the edition. As adjunct sources the editor uses the librettos, manuscript copies, published scores, performing materials and designs for sets and costumes for the première and subsequent authentic productions (defined as those that Rossini directly supervised), reviews, letters and whatever else may exist. In the critical edition the poetic text as found in the score is given preference over that of the printed libretto; no edition of the text as a literary entity is attempted, nor is the libretto printed separately from the music.[1] A critical edition of a Rossinian work, therefore, is an interpretation of a score, characterised by careful study and evaluation of all the materials available to the editor and making clear the editorial interventions in the principal source. How this happens in the Rossini edition is explained later in this chapter.

The first modern critical editions of music were the *Gesamtausgaben* (complete editions) of the great German and Austrian composers: Bach (begun in 1851), Handel (1858), Beethoven (1862), Mozart (1877) and so on. Until the 1960s the prevailing view of the American and European academy (except for Italy) was that nineteenth-century Italian composers, who were largely opera composers, were not valid subjects for serious study. It was Philip Gossett's ground-breaking investigation of the sources for Rossini operas (in his 1970 dissertation) that made musicologists aware of the necessity of applying textual criticism to nineteenth-century Italian opera.[2] When Gossett catalogued the extant sources for fourteen Rossini operas, identifying the various versions of a work as they are represented by the sources and presenting the work as recoverable through its sources, others were encouraged to consider Italian opera in the same light.

In the next decade the Fondazione Rossini of Pesaro established the critical edition of the works of Rossini. In 1974 the editorial committee – Bruno Cagli, Philip Gossett and Alberto Zedda – published the criteria for the edition,[3] and in 1979 the first volume, *La gazza ladra*, appeared.[4] These criteria became the model for subsequent editions of Italian opera composers, and the impulse given by the Rossini critical edition to succeeding ones was supported by the publishing house of Ricordi in Milan, continuing its historic role in opera publication: the first volume of the Verdi critical edition, *Rigoletto*, was published in 1983 (University of Chicago Press and Ricordi),[5] the Donizetti edition made its début in 1990 with *Maria Stuarda* (Ricordi),[6] and in 2000 Ricordi and the Teatro Massimo 'Bellini' of Catania established the Bellini critical edition.

The need for a complete edition of a composer as well known as Rossini may not seem obvious. But only a handful of his works – mainly the comic operas – remained continuously in the repertory, and largely in versions so transformed by additions and subtractions, even of whole numbers, as to bear little resemblance to their originals. Although full scores of several of his operas were published in the nineteenth century – *L'inganno felice, Il barbiere di Siviglia, Mosè in Egitto, Ricciardo e Zoraide, Matilde di Shabran, Semiramide, Le Siège de Corinthe, Moïse, Le Comte Ory* and *Guillaume Tell* – most circulated only in manuscript form. On the other hand, excerpts in reduction for voice and piano were often printed at the time of the première of an opera, and in many cases complete piano-vocal scores were published by such houses as Lucca and Ricordi in Milan; Breitkopf & Härtel and Schott in Germany; Carli, Janet et Cotelle, Pacini and Troupenas in Paris. In the 1850s Ricordi undertook a new, complete edition of Rossini's operas in piano-vocal reductions, the 'Nuova Compiuta Edizione di tutte le opere teatrali edite ed inedite, ridotte per Canto e Piano, del celebre Maestro Gioachino Rossini'. (Rossini himself was not pleased with the publication, fearing his numerous self-borrowings would become too apparent.) The

Ricordi scores remained the standard edition until the critical edition began to replace them.

The current critical edition divides Rossini's compositions into eight sections:

  I Operas (42 volumes, 18 published to date)
 II Incidental Music and Cantatas (7 volumes, 5 published to date)
III Sacred Music (6 volumes)
 IV Hymns and Choruses (1 volume)
  V Vocal Music (4 volumes)
 VI Instrumental Music (6 volumes, 1 published to date)
VII *Péchés de vieillesse* (9 volumes, 3 published to date)
VIII Other Works

The editorial board in 2003 consists of Philip Gossett (director of the edition), Patricia Brauner and Bruno Cagli.

For the Rossini critical edition, as for most editions of nineteenth-century Italian opera, the main score usually represents the work as it was first performed (although there may be reasons to choose another version as the principal text). Whether this can be said to represent the composer's intent is a problematic notion, particularly for a repertory in which it was customary for the author to revise the operas for revivals in new cities with new casts. Even the first version of an opera was composed for a specific opera company, of course. Rossini knew who the singers would be and what their vocal abilities were; he followed the custom of the particular theatre in matters such as size of orchestra, presence of male or mixed chorus, use of secco or accompanied recitative. Choosing the first version of an opera as the basic text unavoidably gives an impression of privilege: that this is the way the composer envisaged the composition, and that subsequent changes were made from necessity, not from artistic motivation. The twentieth-century reception of *Tancredi* illustrates the opposite perspective: the 'tragic finale', written as an alternative to the original happy ending, was unsuccessful but is now perceived as dramatically and musically more satisfying and has become the standard version performed in today's opera houses.

To counterbalance the false primacy suggested by the selection of a main text, the Rossini edition makes it possible to perform all the recoverable authentic versions of a piece. It reports cuts and substitutions made in authentic performances; it provides vocal ornamentation by Rossini or by Rossinian singers as models for performers; in sum, it seeks to affirm the flexibility of performance practice in the nineteenth century and to encourage contemporary directors, conductors, singers and players to approach the work with a freedom grounded in knowledge of Rossini's style.

Rossini sources: what, where and why

If a critical edition develops from a text-critical study of the sources, in order to edit Rossini we must first know what the sources are. Unlike editors of earlier music, in most cases those who edit nineteenth-century opera are fortunate to have the composer's autograph score. Although the original scores of Rossini's first five operas, as well as those of many of his youthful instrumental works, have vanished, many scores were in the composer's possession at the time of his death. He left them to his widow, Olympe Pélissier, who presented a few to friends; the remainder then passed to the Fondazione Rossini of Pesaro. Some of those gifts, along with other surviving manuscripts, are found in the collections of the Opéra and the Paris Conservatoire (now in the Bibliothèque Nationale), of Ricordi in Milan, the Naples Conservatoire and other libraries. Of the non-operatic works, the single greatest repository is Pesaro, where the *Petite messe solennelle* and the thirteen albums of the *Péchés de vieillesse* are preserved. But significant works are found elsewhere: the autograph of the *Stabat mater* is in the British Library, while masses, cantatas, songs and instrumental pieces are found in Paris, New York, Brussels, Washington D.C. and even Russia, as well as, of course, in Italy.

In this age of facsimile, photocopy and digital image, why not perform from Rossini's autographs? In every case problems arise from the nature of a Rossinian score that require the intervention of an editor. Every musical autograph poses questions: they are particularly numerous in those of early-nineteenth-century operas, both because of the rapidity with which the works were composed and because the manuscript was prepared for performance and not for the press. The existence of an autograph score does not mean that an editor can simply transcribe it, or that no other sources need be consulted, as we shall see in more detail later. Here we will consider the general problems associated with using an autograph score as the basis for a critical edition of an opera or cantata by Rossini.

The present physical condition of the autograph often no longer reflects the work's initial content and order. The duet 'Ai capricci della sorte' from *L'italiana in Algeri* is in the collection of La Scala while the rest of the score is in the Ricordi archives; Rossini himself removed the chorus 'Dall'oriente' from the score of *Ermione* to re-use it in an 1823 revision of *Maometto II*; Gernando's flashy aria from *Armida* and the particularly complex history of *Il viaggio a Reims* will be discussed in the section 'Case studies' below. Rossini wrote his operas on oblong-format paper, varying from approximately 30 × 23 cm to 35 × 27 cm, with ten to twenty staves. For numbers with five or six soloists, chorus and full orchestra, even twenty staves are not enough: Rossini's procedure was to transfer excess orchestral parts – percussion, trombones, trumpets, horns – to a *spartitino* or short score, which would be used by the copyists preparing the parts but would not be present in the conductor's score (i.e. Rossini's score, for his contract usually required him to be at the keyboard for rehearsals and the first few performances). The *spartitini* were not always reunited with the rest of the autograph, thus there are often missing passages in the winds and percussion for which there is no autograph source. The parts may be recovered from manuscript copies or early printed editions of the score, if indeed they are present there, but even these sources are suspect, for they themselves may have been composed to fill the gap already existing in their exemplar.

Even as the author was still writing an opera, copyists would prepare parts for the use of the singers and scores for the use of the theatre. These copies of the score might in turn serve as models for scores for other impresarios, composers and cognoscenti. Twenty-one manuscript copies were consulted for the critical edition of *La Cenerentola*, a work that never completely left the repertory but for which no full score was ever printed, and this is not the entire number surviving. Copies of the score may help solve ambiguities in the autograph, although the copyists tended not to correct problems they encountered. The manuscripts also expand our knowledge of the work's performance history.

Early publications are also important secondary sources for the editors of the critical edition. Vocal scores, made for purchase and continued use, took care to be at least functionally error-free. The exemplar for a vocal score was normally not the autograph, but rather a manuscript copy of it, and of course the piano reduction can serve only as a suggestion of the orchestral accompaniment; however, the early vocal scores usually reflect the form of the opera at the first performance. In some cases they are the only musical source for pieces indicated in the printed libretto, and thus presumably performed, but now missing from the autograph and surviving manuscript copies.

Non-musical sources are also important for understanding Rossini's compositions, since they can preserve information not indicated by a score. Librettos printed for the original and subsequent productions help to establish the different versions of an opera, especially when the autograph is disturbed or incomplete. The music of the *Scena ed Aria* for Zomira from *Ricciardo e Zoraide* is known only from secondary sources – two copies of the score and the first Ricordi vocal score – but the poetic text appears in the original libretto, establishing this number as part of the earliest version of the opera. The libretto from a Roman revival of *Otello* shows that Rossini, submitting to the censors' bidding, changed the tragic ending to one in which Otello believes Desdemona's protestations of innocence and they live happily ever after, closing the opera with the duet 'Amor, possente nome' from *Armida*. Contemporary newspaper reviews may give clues about what was actually sung or how the music was interpreted. The autograph of the overture to *Il signor Bruschino* has a peculiar notation that appears as four double-stemmed minims in a 4/4 bar, but the only indication that Rossini intended the string players to beat their bows on their candleholders comes from a review of the première.

For non-operatic works the autograph scores present a different set of problems. The largest group consists of small-scale salon pieces, primarily piano compositions and songs for solo or few voices with piano accompaniment. They derive largely from the last decade of Rossini's life, after his return to health (marked by the dedication of *Musique anodine*, 15 April 1857, 'to my dear wife Olympe . . . for the affectionate, intelligent care she lavished on me during my too long and terrible illness'). The composer did not permit these pieces to be published but rather collected dozens of them into thirteen albums that he called *Péchés de vieillesse* ('Sins of old age'). He apparently intended this collection of unpublished pieces to be a form of insurance policy for his wife, to be sold should he precede her in death.

Many of these compositions were not among his last in a strict sense, however, since they were revisions or recompositions of earlier works. During his life Rossini composed nearly fifty settings of a sort of 'template' poetic text drawn from Metastasio's *Siroe* (1726), 'Mi lagnerò tacendo', slightly modified by the composer.[7] Often he requested a poet to write a new text to the music he had already composed. Many songs in the *Péchés de vieillesse* were originally written as a 'Mi lagnerò tacendo' setting: thus they exist in other versions, in which musical details as well as the text may differ. Are they the same work? Do they both deserve a critical edition, or does one become an appendix to the other or even just a critical note? In some cases Rossini did not choose to include the latest manuscript in his albums: which version has priority? Further complicating the array of sources is Rossini's practice, in composing the salon pieces, of having a copyist at hand to make fair copies of the drafts, which the composer then edited: does the edited copy then supplant the autograph? In the 'Case studies' section of this chapter we will examine a situation in which an extraordinary paper trail reveals eight levels of composition in a single piece.

Criteria for the Rossini edition

The edition aims to provide a musical text that satisfies the needs of scholars and performers alike. Musicologists want to know what the original text is and what the editor's interventions, whereas musicians require clear, coherent scores without an excess of extraneous signs. The Rossini edition does not rigidly apply the rule of some other critical editions (such as that of Verdi) that demands that every editorial intervention be clearly indicated. It extends to identical parts or to repeated figuration those signs of dynamics and articulation for which Rossini provided clear models, limiting graphic distinction to added or modified signs that may be interpreted in different ways and giving the alternative readings in the commentary. Distinguishing only the problematic editorial interventions means not only that the editor must be very cautious in his or her use of automatic extension, but also that he or she must document any possible doubts in the critical notes. Editorial decisions take into account the conventions of early-nineteenth-century notation in general and Rossini's style and habits of writing in particular. Readings from secondary sources are reported when they support the editor's choice or offer other valid solutions.

The criteria of the edition set out the following basic tenets for practical application of the editorial philosophy:[8]

Extensions. Interpretative indications present in one or more instrumental parts but obviously common to others rhythmically or melodically identical are extended without brackets or critical notes. If the evidence is unusually sparse or found only in a repetition of the passage (so that the extension is backward), there should be a critical note.

Equalising essentially identical passages. If two or more essentially identical passages have contradictory interpretative indications, the editor must decide if there is a logical reason for the differences that might be intentional. If the passages are made to conform to each other, a critical note explains the alternative readings suggested by the autograph and the reasons for the editorial choice. Vocal parts are allowed more diversity than instrumental parts, since incongruent indications may reflect Rossini's alternative ideas about performance.

Additions. The rare editorial additions that seem indispensable for coherence and clarity are graphically distinguished in the score (brackets, dotted slurs, smaller noteheads, etc.). The intervention may be discussed in the critical notes, especially when the reading is derived from secondary sources.

Correction of errors. When the autograph (or principal source) presents an error that can be corrected only one way, it is done without indication in the score. Where the reading is less clearly a real error, or where different solutions are possible, the editor's choice is signalled in the score. All errors are cited in the notes. This principle is also adopted when the autograph is obscure or confused, or has lacunae. In the same way, vertical inconsistencies in the instrumental parts – differences in dynamics, articulation or rhythm between analogous parts – are regularised and the alternative readings indicated in the notes. The vocal parts are not forced into consistency with the orchestra.

Case studies in editing Rossini

Armida

Armida (Naples, San Carlo, 1817) had a relatively limited performance history in Rossini's lifetime, thus avoiding multiple revisions for revivals.[9] The autograph score is largely intact, but two choruses and an aria were separated from it. The autograph of the bravado aria for the crusader Gernando, 'Non soffrirò l'offesa', apparently found its way into the possession of Giulio Marco Bordogni, a tenor among Rossini's circle of friends, perhaps to serve him as a showpiece. In the score of *Armida* it was replaced by a different aria, in a copyist's hand, which does not seem to be by Rossini. The substitute aria, 'Sopportar non sa l'offesa', has only the vocal and bass lines.

The problem is intriguing. The physical evidence suggests that the disturbance of the autograph occurred at an early stage. Contrary to the original, the substitute is notated for bass rather than tenor. Claudio Bonoldi, who sang the tenor rôles of Gernando and Ubaldo at the première, was a tenor with an extended lower range; he sang tenor and baritone rôles (including Don Giovanni in Milan in 1813) and presumably could have sung either aria. Both Giovanni David and Giovanni Battista Rubini, who replaced Bonoldi in the rôle in later seasons, were high tenors, however, and neither would have sung the substitute in preference to the original; this means that the substitute could not have been written for the later Neapolitan productions. The original aria is found in all but one manuscript copy, the one belonging to the impresario of the Teatro San Carlo (now in the library of the Naples Conservatoire), but this copy lacks the substitute aria as well; the text of the original version is in all the librettos, including that of the première.

The end of the preceding recitative was revised in Rossini's own hand, to lead to the new key of B♭ rather than the A of the autograph aria. However, the original recitative after Gernando's aria is in B♭, the key of the substitute aria; Rossini's normal practice is to begin the recitative following a number in the key of the number or in a closely related one. Complicating the story even further is the fact that Rossini wrote the aria and following recitative on a type of paper used nowhere else in the opera. What happened in Gernando's scene? One hypothesis is that the substitute was a last-minute replacement during the first season (possibly because Bonoldi would not or could not, in fact, sing the original) made too late to appear in the libretto and then suppressed. Another less likely possibility is that the substitute was supplied for the première because Rossini's own aria was actually not ready. Neither hypothesis explains the key of the recitative after the aria. Whatever occurred, the critical edition uses the autograph aria since it is attested to by the libretto and is in Rossini's hand; the substitute is given as an appendix.

Il viaggio a Reims

The sources for *Il viaggio a Reims*, performed in Paris on 19 June 1825 to celebrate the coronation of Charles X of France, are in an extremely compli-cated state.[10] Because *Il viaggio* was an occasional piece, Rossini withdrew it from the theatre after only a few performances; apparently he already had it in mind to use much of the music for *Le Comte Ory* (première 20 August 1828). And he did literally use the music: the autograph of *Il viaggio a Reims* physically lacks all the numbers that were adapted for *Le Comte Ory*, leaving only four numbers and five recitatives. Of *Le Comte Ory* little autograph remains, Rossini's score – including the modified portions from *Il viaggio* – presumably having been disposed of by the publisher Troupenas, who printed the full score of *Ory* in 1828. To complete the critical edition of *Il viaggio* the editor had to rely on secondary sources. These primarily con-sist of performing material from an 1848 Parisian revision of *Il viaggio* under the title of *Andremo a Parigi?*, some parts clearly derived from the 1825 material, some heavily rewritten. The printed full score of *Le Comte Ory* also served as a source for the orchestral parts. There is performing material from a revision for Vienna in 1854, *Il viaggio a Vienna*, that must have been derived from the *Viaggio/Andremo* parts. Finally, a chorus missing from the autograph of the Finale was identified as deriving from *Maometto II*; the autograph of that opera is in Pesaro, but the detached chorus is in the New York Public Library. The reconstruction of *Il viaggio a Reims* is a major philological accomplishment.

'Choeur de chasseurs démocrates'

The 'Choeur de chasseurs démocrates', one of the *Péchés de vieillesse*, is a brief composition for two tenors, baritone and bass, with two snare drums and a tam-tam at the end, written as a 'fanfare' for a visit by the Emperor Napoleon III to the Rothschild château at Ferrières in December 1862.[11] It has survived in a series of scores and parts that were created successively by various copyists, each manuscript subjected to Rossini's intervention before the next was prepared.[12] From this remarkable series we are able to identify eight different stages in the compositional process. In the following discussion the multiple sources are designated by abbreviations representing their structure (s = score, p = parts), their location (Harvard, Pesaro) and Harvard's number indicating the item in the folder.

We have no autograph manuscript for the 'Choeur de chasseurs', as it was first titled. Rossini had a copyist (copyist A) prepare a textless score (sH12), presumably derived from the missing autograph, which may have had a different text or perhaps was instrumental. Rossini asked his friend Emilien Pacini to write a text to fit the music, and the composer himself entered it in the copyist's manuscript. At the same time, Rossini revised the dynamic markings and made some musical changes (Level I). A set of parts (pH14) was made by copyist B from this revised score (sH12). Rossini, reviewing them, made some changes in both parts (pH14) and score (sH12) simultaneously (Level II). Some time after the second level of correction (and most likely after the performance at the Rothschild château), Rossini made major revisions in sH12 (Level III), also expanding the title by the addition of 'démocrates'.

A new score reflecting these revisions (sP) was made by a third copyist (C). Rossini then again significantly altered the chorus (Level IV), apparently using the already revised first score (sH12) as a working copy and transferring the revisions into the new copy (sP). Nonetheless the changes are not always identical in the two scores, suggesting that he was constantly recomposing and not just copying. A fifth level of adjustment to sP alone preceded the copying of a new set of parts (pH15), probably including the part for drums and tam-tam (pH16), some of which are by copyist C, the others by two secondary copyists. These parts, like the earlier set, underwent revision, and Rossini modified both them and their source (sP) simultaneously (Level VI). In the seventh level Rossini corrected sP alone prior to having a fair copy (sH13) made by copyist C. Finally Rossini reviewed both of these scores (sP and sH13) and the set of vocal parts (pH15), making similar emendations in all of them (Level VIII).

To summarise:

Level I: creation of the texted version (sH12; text and musical modifications added by Rossini to textless copy);

Level II: correction of score (sH12) and parts (pH14);

Level III: compositional changes, presumably made after the first performance (sH12 revised and recopied as sP);

Level IV: revisions in both the old and new scores (sH12 and sP);

Level V: massive revisions in sP requiring a new set of parts (pH15) for another performance;

Level VI: emendations made in sP and pH15;

Level VII: changes in sP in preparation for the fair copy (sH13), presumably after performance from pH15 parts;

Level VIII: emendations made in sP, sH13 and pH15 during the final review of the three sources.

Interestingly, Rossini chose sP rather than the fair copy sH13 to include in the *Album français*, and the critical edition uses it as the base source for the principal version. sP embodies a process impossible to reconstruct without the other scores and parts, however. The version represented by the first set of parts is given as an appendix, assuming that the parts were used for an authentic performance under the auspices of the composer. All the modifications are described in the critical notes.

Almost every page of the first two scores of the 'Choeur de chasseurs démocrates' shows erasures and additions in Rossini's hand. Similar series of corrections are present in other pieces in the *Péchés de vieillesse* that have left only a single source, but the erasures have often obliterated the earlier layers. Our case study is unusual not in that it has undergone so much reworking, but in that it has left such a complete documentation of its history – three scores and two sets of parts associated with at least two performances – revealing for us the entire compositional process. The opera scores, produced in haste for immediate performance, do not usually show much rewriting at all, although some surviving sketches for *Semiramide* prove that the operas did not spring fully formed from Rossini's brow.

From editor to user

A functional preliminary edition, based on the autograph or other principal source, the libretto and the more significant secondary sources, is the first milestone in a volume's journey to print. The work will have taken a plausible form – not necessarily the final one – substantiated by basic textual and documentary research; all issues that would cause problems in performance have been resolved; a preliminary critical commentary has been prepared. The score and commentary are submitted for review to the editorial committee, who proofread the score and compare it with the principal source. Most of the editions of theatrical works are prepared with a specific performance in mind – the Rossini Opera Festival of Pesaro normally mounts the first production of a new edition – so the score is sent to Ricordi in Milan, which produces the performing material. The standard vocal score is modified where necessary to make it conform to the critical edition in the structure of the work, in the vocal lines and in major aspects of the accompaniment such as harmony, rhythm and dynamics.

The Rossini critical edition has been fortunate in its long collaboration with the Rossini Opera Festival. Given that an editor must interpret a score and often reconstruct parts of it, the opportunity to experience the edition in the theatre before making final decisions is invaluable. Aside from discovering the odd wrong note (inevitable), the editor can hear how a reconstructed part functions; a conductor may propose a different approach to problematic dynamics; an experienced Rossini singer may suggest that the reading chosen for an ambiguous note or ornament lies badly in the voice.

After incorporating into the edition what has been learned from the performances, the editor must complete the work of critical analysis of all the relevant sources. The score – revised as necessary – is set on computer; the editor completes the critical notes and source descriptions for the commentary and writes the historical introduction. The editor, a member of the editorial committee and the director of the edition read first proofs of the score along with the completed commentary. In the next stage the editor and the committee refine the preface and commentary (translating them if necessary) and send them to the typographer. The last stages are carried out by the editorial committee and staff of the Fondazione Rossini: reading second and third proofs of the score and two or three sets of proofs of the preface and commentary (with its musical examples) and following the progress of the volumes through the bindery and into distribution.

The Rossini edition aspires to be well crafted as well as philologically sound. In addition to painstaking accuracy in the music, this means conscientiously minding one's p's and q's: font size, alignment of elements of the score, consistency in capitalisation and punctuation of the poetic text and critical apparatus are among items for editorial scrutiny. The time needed to review the editor's work, let alone to proofread hundreds of pages of music and a volume of small-type commentary, limits the number of titles that can be printed to no more than two a year, while additional volumes are always in various stages of preparation. It can be several years between the first performance of a preliminary edition and its publication. Once an edition is in print, Ricordi must revise all its performance material to correspond to the final version of the score. Only then can work begin on a piano-vocal reduction for the sales market.

The decisions an editor makes influence those who use the edition. The Rossini Renaissance has produced conductors who are eager to use critical editions and singers who study the style of vocal production and ornamentation practised by those for whom Rossini composed. Scholars, performers, critics and audiences who encounter the critical edition may be liberated from the clichés handed down by the generations who did not know Rossini's music as he directed it.

Two final caveats are in order. First, returning to the original version of the score does not make a historically accurate performance. The modern lyric theatre does not accept all the conventions of Rossini's time, particularly the use of head tones rather than chest tones for high notes, nor is Rossini normally performed with historical instruments: for example, natural horns and trumpets, smaller trombones, timpani with less definite pitch. Staging, even when 'traditional', is very far from nineteenth-century stagecraft. Second, by printing a principal text, by removing inconsistencies and filling lacunae, the critical edition gives its interpretation an authority that may offset its attempt to return to the performers the expressive freedoms of bel canto. A text is a version, an interpretation that represents a composition at one moment of its existence. Each new performance must use what the edition provides to make the music live.

Notes

1. Introduction: Rossini's operatic operas

1. Stendhal, *Life of Rossini*, trans. Richard N. Coe (London, 1970), 3 (translation modified).
2. Philip Gossett, 'Rossini, Gioachino (Antonio)', *The New Grove Dictionary of Music and Musicians*, rev. edn, ed. Stanley Sadie and John Tyrrell, 29 vols. (London, 2001), vol. XXI, 734–68: 738.
3. Stendhal, *Life of Rossini*, 37 (translation modified).
4. Leigh Hunt, review of *Il barbiere di Siviglia* at London's King's Theatre, *The Examiner* (22 March 1818), in *Leigh Hunt's Dramatic Criticism*, ed. Lawrence Huston Houtchens and Carolyn Washburn Houtchens (New York, 1949), 189.
5. 'Lord Mount Edgcumbe's Musical Reminiscences' (1835), in *The Works of Thomas Love Peacock*, ed. H. F. B. Brett-Smith and C. E. Jones, vol. IX, *Critical and Other Essays* (London and New York, 1926), 223–52: 244.
6. See Paolo Gallarati, 'Per un'interpretazione del comico rossiniano', *Gioachino Rossini, 1792–1992. Il testo e la scena*, ed. Paolo Fabbri (Pesaro, 1994), 3–12. See also his 'Dramma e *ludus* dall'*Italiana* al *Barbiere*', *Il melodramma italiano dell'Ottocento. Studi e ricerche per Massimo Mila*, ed. Giorgio Pestelli (Turin, 1977), 237–80.
7. Gianni Ruffin, 'Drammaturgia come auto-confutazione teatrale: aspetti metalinguistici alle origini della comicità nelle opere di Rossini', *Recercare* 4 (1992), 125–63.
8. Alessandro Baricco, *Il genio in fuga. Due saggi sul teatro musicale di Gioachino Rossini*, 2nd edn (Turin, 1997), 33.
9. Carl Dahlhaus, *Nineteenth-Century Music*, trans. J. Bradford Robinson (Berkeley and Los Angeles, 1989), 59.
10. *Ibid.*, 64.
11. *Ibid.*, 59.
12. Heinrich Heine, *Über die französische Bühne* (1837), in Heine, *Historisch-kritische Gesamtausgabe der Werke*, vol. XII, ed. Jean-René Derré and Christiane Giesen (Hamburg, 1980), 227–90: 275.
13. Letter to Giovanni Pacini, 27 January 1866, in Gioachino Rossini, *Lettere*, ed. Enrico Castiglione (Rome, 1992), 250.
14. As reported in Antonio Zanolini, *Una passeggiata in compagnia di Rossini* (1836), cited and translated in Paolo Fabbri, 'Rossini the Aesthetician', *Cambridge Opera Journal* 6 (1994), 19–29: 20.
15. See Fabbri, 'Rossini the Aesthetician', 28–9.
16. See especially Edmond Michotte, *Richard Wagner's Visit to Rossini (Paris 1860) and An Evening at Rossini's in Beau-Sejour (Passy 1858)*, ed. and trans. Herbert Weinstock (Chicago, 1968), 73–4, 105–21.
17. See Luca Zoppelli, 'Intorno a Rossini: sondaggi sulla percezione della centralità del compositore', *Il testo e la scena*, ed. Fabbri, 13–24.
18. For a case study of this phenomenon, see Emanuele Senici, ' "Adapted to the Modern Stage": *La clemenza di Tito* in London', *Cambridge Opera Journal* 7 (1995), 1–22.
19. This letter, dated 9 December [1816], is part of a group of c. 250 mostly unpublished letters by Rossini and his wife Isabella Colbran to the composer's parents, recently sold at auction by Sotheby's, London, and acquired by the Fondazione Rossini, Pesaro, for future publication in GRLD. My summary is based on the one in Sotheby's Sale Catalogue, London, 7 December 2001, item no. 175, 115–22: 119.
20. Herbert Lindenberger, *Opera in History: From Monteverdi to Cage* (Stanford, 1998), 99.
21. *Ibid.*, 100.

2. Rossini's life

1. Leigh Hunt, *Autobiography* (London, 1928), 433.
2. Ferdinand Hiller, 'Plaudereien mit Rossini (1856)', BCRS 32 (1992), 63–155: 79.
3. Facsimile in Alfredo Casella, *Rossiniana* (Bologna, 1942), 37–9.
4. GRLD, vol. I, 5.
5. Edmond Michotte, *Richard Wagner's Visit to Rossini (Paris 1860) and An Evening at Rossini's in Beau-Sejour (Passy) 1858*, ed. and trans. Herbert Weinstock (Chicago, 1968), 109.
6. Lady Morgan, *Italy* (London, 1821), vol. III, 278.
7. For the correspondence on the opening of Pesaro's theatre, see GRLD, vol. I, 244–306.
8. *Ibid.*, 334.
9. *The Quarterly Musical Magazine* 6 (1824), 49–50.
10. Henry Chorley, *Thirty Years' Musical Recollections* (London, 1926; first published 1862), 27.

[229]

11. *The Original Staging Manuals for Ten Parisian Operatic Premières, 1824–1843*, ed. H. Robert Cohen (Stuyvesant, NY, 1998), 205.

12. Herbert Weinstock, *Rossini: A Biography* (New York, 1968), 379.

13. *Ibid.*, 258.

14. *Rossini à Paris*, ed. Jean-Marie Bruson (Paris, 1992), 151; trans. in Weinstock, *Rossini*, 269.

15. *Rossini à Paris*, 165.

16. Luigi Rognoni, *Gioacchino Rossini* (Turin, 1968), 333–6.

17. *Rossini à Paris*, 173; trans. in Weinstock, *Rossini*, 373.

3. Rossini and France

1. An engraving from a photograph of the event is reproduced in *Rossini à Paris*, ed. Jean-Marie Bruson (Paris, 1992), 174.

2. Giuseppe Radiciotti, *Gioacchino Rossini. Vita documentata, opere ed influenza su l'arte*, 3 vols. (Tivoli, 1927), vol. II, 553–4. Radiciotti provides a full account of the return of Rossini's body to Florence, and the celebrations that took place there. For a summary in English see Herbert Weinstock, *Rossini: A Biography* (New York, 1968), 373–4.

3. Maurice Cristal, *Le Correspondant* (25 November 1868), 701.

4. *Le Gaulois* (27 April 1887).

5. Stendhal, *Life of Rossini*, trans. Richard N. Coe (London, 1970), 3 (translation modified).

6. *Giacomo Meyerbeer: Briefwechsel und Tagebücher*, ed. Heinz Becker (Berlin, 1960), vol. I, 360; the letter is quoted in Weinstock, *Rossini*, 89–90. Meyerbeer's informant was Jean-Jacques Grasset, leader of the orchestra at the Théâtre Italien in Paris.

7. See Jean Mongrédien, *French Music from the Enlightenment to Romanticism, 1789–1830*, trans. Sylvain Frémaux (Portland, OR, 1996), 131, and Bruson, *Rossini à Paris*, 26.

8. The sequence of premières runs as follows: 1819, *L'inganno felice* (13 May), and *Il barbiere* (26 October); 1820, *Il turco in Italia* (23 May) and *Torvaldo e Dorliska* (21 November); 1821, *La pietra del paragone* (5 April), *Otello* (5 June), *La gazza ladra* (18 September) and *L'italiana in Algeri* (27 November); 1822, *Tancredi* (23 April), *La Cenerentola* (8 June), *Elisabetta regina d'Inghilterra* (10 September) and *Mosè in Egitto* (20 October). Rumours of Paer's resentment and even of his deliberate sabotage of Rossini's works appeared most prominently in Stendhal's *Life of Rossini*, and the older composer's machinations after Rossini's appointment as director of the Théâtre Italien have been documented by Bruno Cagli in 'Rossini a Londra e al Théâtre Italien di

Parigi: documenti inediti dell'impresario G. B. Benelli', BCRS 21 (1981), 7–53. However, the extent to which Paer acted against Rossini in earlier years remains unproven; in his defence, see Richard N. Coe, 'Stendhal, Rossini and the "Conspiracy of Musicians"(1817–23)', *Modern Language Review* 54 (1959), 179–93.

9. See, for example, the background to the vicious and sustained attacks on Rossini by Charles Maurice in *Le Courrier des théâtres* between 1824 and 1826, as described by Janet Johnson, an author who has done more than anyone to bring to light the underground world of Restoration music criticism: 'Rossini, Artistic Director of the Théâtre Italien, 1830–1836', *Gioachino Rossini, 1792–1992. Il testo e la scena*, ed. Paolo Fabbri (Pesaro, 1994), 599–622, especially 601–4. For a survey of Rossini and musical criticism in Paris under the Restoration see Fiamma Nicolodi, 'Rossini a Parigi e la critica musicale', *Studi e fantasie. Saggi, versi, musica e testimonianze in onore di Leonardo Pinzauti*, ed. Daniele Spini (Florence, 1996), 193–219. Summaries of reception for each opera performed in Paris can also be found in Radiciotti, *Gioacchino Rossini* and Alexis Azevedo, *G. Rossini, sa vie et ses oeuvres* (Paris, 1864).

10. See Joseph d'Ortigue, *De la Guerre des dilettanti, ou de la révolution opérée par M. Rossini dans l'opéra français; et des rapports qui existent entre la musique, la littérature et les arts* (Paris, 1829), 23. On contemporary meanings for the word dilettante see Janet Johnson, 'The Musical Environment in France', *The Cambridge Companion to Berlioz*, ed. Peter Bloom (Cambridge, 2000), 25.

11. 'De la musique mécanique et de la musique philosophique', *L'Abeille* 3 (May–June 1821), 149–56, 195–206, 292–8; the reprint, published by Alexis Eymery (Paris, 1826), included Berton's *Lettre à un compositeur français*, addressed to Boieldieu.

12. Berton, 'De la musique mécanique', 294.

13. *La Pandore* (9 September 1823), 2.

14. See Berton's articles in *L'Abeille* 4 (August–September 1821), 86–9, 174–8, 267–74.

15. Stendhal, *Racine et Shakespeare* (Paris, 1970; first published 1823), Part 1, Chapter 3, 'Ce que c'est que le romanticisme', 71. For a complete survey of Stendhal's writings on Rossini see Stéphane Dado and Philippe Vendrix, 'Stendhal e Rossini: uno studio documentario', BCRS 39 (1999), 21–69.

16. On García's rôle in the decision to mount *Il barbiere* see Azevedo, *G. Rossini*, 134.

17. *La Pandore* (11 November 1823), 3. Azevedo claimed that Rossini had learnt to speak French while in Bologna (Azevedo, *G. Rossini*, 199).

18. See for example *La Quotidienne* (2 December 1823), quoted in Azevedo, *G. Rossini*, 183–4.

19. *La Pandore* (16 November 1823), 3.

20. Rossini's friend Boieldieu wrote in a letter to Pierre Crémont that 'the French Rossinistes would like to place us completely under the feet of their idol'. Quoted in Arthur Pougin, *Rossini: Notes–Impressions–Souvenirs–Commentaires* (Paris, 1871) 18.

21. Rossini attended the dress rehearsal of the play by invitation on 28 November. Anti-Rossini reviews can be found in predictable papers: *Le Courrier des théâtres* (1 December 1823), *La Gazette de France* and *La Quotidienne* (both 2 December).

22. 'Timon' in *La Minerve littéraire* (undated; probably 5 November 1820). In 1821 Eugène Delacroix produced a caricature of the Opéra as an ageing dancer on crutches, together with a companion print of Rossini as an embodiment of the Théâtre Italien; for descriptions and an assessment of their place in the Stendhal–Berton dialogue see Johnson, 'The Musical Environment in France', 30–7.

23. Rossini was officially the director of the Théâtre Italien from December 1824 to October 1826. In practice his influence at the theatre began even before his arrival in Paris, and continued well into the 1830s. See Bruson, *Rossini à Paris*, 65.

24. For a list of the works in translation and *pasticci* that used bits of Rossini at the Odéon see Bruson, *Rossini à Paris*, 103–4. The main translator and arranger for the theatre, Castil-Blaze, had originally been commissioned to translate *Mosè* and *Tancredi* into French for possible performance at the Opéra in 1821. His versions of Rossini operas also introduced many other towns in France to the composer's works; on the production of *Il barbiere* for Lyon see Mark Everist, 'Lindoro in Lyon: Rossini's *Le Barbier de Seville*', *Acta musicologica* 64 (1992), 50–85.

25. Ortigue, *De la Guerre des dilettanti*, 39.

26. See the chapter on *Le Siège de Corinthe* in Benjamin Walton, 'Romanticisms and Nationalisms in Restoration France' (Ph.D. dissertation, University of California, Berkeley, 2000).

27. See Anselm Gerhard, *The Urbanization of Opera*, trans. Mary Whittall (Chicago, 1998), 76–8.

28. On Rossini's extreme noisiness see Jean-Toussaint Merle, *Du marasme dramatique en 1829* (Paris, 1829). Another pamphleteer, Amédée de Tissot, suggested a need for the evolution of ear-lids that could work on the same principle as eyelids to block out the 'insupportable hullabaloo' generated by Rossini's orchestra; *Deux mots sur les théâtres de Paris* (Paris, 1827), 10.

29. On *Il viaggio* see Janet Johnson, 'A Lost Rossini Opera Recovered: *Il Viaggio a Reims*', BCRS 23 (1983), 5–57, as well as the critical introduction to Johnson's edition of the work in GREC (1999), xxi–lii.

30. The lithograph is reproduced in *Hommage an Rossini*, ed. Reto Müller (Leipzig, 1999), 58.

31. Paris, Archives Nationales, AJ13.130; reprinted in Bruson, *Rossini à Paris*, 61.

32. Quoted in Weinstock, *Rossini*, 195.

33. See Johnson, 'Rossini, Artistic Director of the Théâtre Italien', 599–622.

34. G. B., *Rossini* (n.d.), 16; part of *Les Grands et les petits personnages du jour par un des plus petits*. On Balzac and Rossini see Pierluigi Petrobelli, 'Balzac, Stendhal and Rossini's *Moses*', *The Barber of Seville/Moses*, English National Opera Guide 36 (London, 1985), 99–108; Matthias Brzoska, 'Mosè und Massimilla: Rossinis *Mosè in Egitto* und Balzacs politische Deutung', *Oper als Text: Romanistische Beiträge zur Libretto-Forschung*, ed. Albert Gier (Heidelberg, 1986), 125–45; Pierre Brunel, 'Mosè dans Massimilla Doni', *L'Année balzacienne* 15 (1994), 39–54; Klaus Ley, *Die Oper in Roman: Erzahlkunst und Musik bei Stendhal, Balzac und Flaubert* (Heidelberg, 1995).

35. [Antonio Zanolini], 'Une Promenade en société de Rossini', *Rossini et sa musique* (Paris, 1836), 13–16.

36. Dumas, *Un Dîner chez Rossini* (Paris, n.d., probably 1849), 305–14; Janin, *Voyage en Italie* (Paris, 1839), 230–43.

37. See Ferdinand Boyer, 'Stendhal, les biographes de Rossini et la presse musicale à Paris en 1858', *Stendhal Club* 14 (1962), 164–9.

38. Fétis, *Biographie universelle des musiciens et bibliographie générale de la musique*, 2nd edn (Paris, 1864), vol. VII, 329; [Escudier brothers], *La France musicale* (6 June 1858).

39. A. Fiorentino, 'Rossini à Beauséjour', *Le Moniteur universel* (6 June 1856); reprinted in *Comédies et comédiens* (Paris, 1866), vol. I, 327–44.

40. *La Revue et gazette musicale* (23 May 1858).

41. Fiorentino, 'Rossini et ses biographes', *La Revue des deux mondes* (15 August 1854); reprinted in *Comédies et comédiens*, 197–215.

42. Fiorentino, 'Rossini et ses biographes', 207.

43. Boyer, 'Stendhal', 167.

44. For a partial list of famous visitors to Rossini's *samedi soirs* see Weinstock, *Rossini*, 467.

45. Maurice Serval, 'Une Enigme balzacienne: la Foedora de la *Peau de Chagrin*', *Bulletin de la*

société historique et archéologique des VIIIème et XVIIème arrondissements de Paris 5 (1925–6), 387–403: 402.

46. *The Times* (16 November 1868); Saint-Saëns, *Echo de Paris* (19 March 1911); reprinted in *Regards sur mes contemporains*, ed. Yves Gérard (Arles, 1990), 155–60.

47. *Le Journal de Paris* (29 November 1868); see also *Le Figaro* for the same date.

4. The Rossini Renaissance

1. I have consulted the published annals of the following opera houses: La Scala, Milan (supplemented by its website); San Carlo, Naples; La Fenice, Venice; Maggio Musicale, Florence; Metropolitan Opera, New York; Covent Garden, London; Staatsoper, Vienna. See also the articles by Antolini and Sala cited below.

2. Emilio Sala, 'Di alcune "rossiniane" novecentesche', *La recezione di Rossini ieri e oggi*, Atti dei convegni Lincei 110 (Rome, 1994), 81–99: 81.

3. Fedele D'Amico, who was present, has observed that this production 'had nothing to do with Rossini or with *Semiramide*': 'Questo compleanno', BCRS 31 (1991), 9–19: 10.

4. '*Opere serie*' will refer to the Italian serious operas; when I wish to include the French operas I will use 'Rossini *serio*' or 'serious operas'.

5. Nothing quite matched the Metropolitan Opera's dedication to *Lucia*: thirty-two consecutive seasons (1918–50) and frequent presentations before and after.

6. A French opera (*Le Siège de Corinthe*), based on the Neapolitan *Maometto II* and like *Mosè* translated back into Italian, often presented in a hybrid form with elements of *Maometto*.

7. A complete list of post-war productions of Rossini's *opere serie* (including *L'assedio di Corinto* but not the other French operas *Moïse/Mosè* and *Guillaume/Guglielmo Tell*) up to 1990 may be found in '"L'altro" Rossini serio nel mondo (1949/88 [*sic*, *recte* 1949/90])', ed. Alberto Bottazzi and Giorgio Gualerzi, *Ricciardo e Zoraide*, Rossini Opera Festival programme book (Pesaro, 1990), 92–110. The *opere semiserie* are listed in 'Il Rossini "semiserio" nel mondo (1949–1988)', ed. Bottazzi and Gualerzi, *La gazza ladra*, Rossini Opera Festival programme book (Pesaro, 1989), 117–19. The authors do not provide the number of performances, and they count separately the same production produced at different venues.

8. See Bianca Maria Antolini, 'Rappresentazioni rossiniane e dibattito critico in Italia nel decennio 1860–70', *La recezione di Rossini ieri e oggi*, 121–48, especially 128–35.

9. Francesco D'Arcais, *L'opinione* (14 October 1861), in Antolini, 'Rappresentazioni rossiniane', 133.

10. 'The Rossini Centenary', *The Illustrated London News* (5 March 1892), reprinted in *Shaw's Music*, ed. D. H. Laurence (London, 1981), vol. III, 562.

11. 'Rossini Redivivus', *The World* (9 March 1892); *Shaw's Music*, vol. III, 568.

12. Particularly in Germany; see, for example, the review of *Otello* in the *Allgemeine musikalische Zeitung* 21 (1819), cols. 124–6, and, for an overview, Josef Loschelder, 'Rossinis Bild und Zerbild in der allgemeinen musikalischen Zeitung Leipzig', BCRS 13/1 (1973), 23–42; 13/2 (1973), 23–42; 17/3 (1977), 19–40; Italian translations follow each part.

13. Costantin Phiotadès, *La Revue de Paris* (1 July 1929), in Sala, 'Di alcune "rossiniane"', 81.

14. 'Some Reasons Why a "Futurist" May Admire Rossini', *The Chesterian* 2 (December 1920), 321–4: 323.

15. See Sala, 'Di alcune "rossiniane"', 83, n. 8.

16. *Gioacchino Rossini. Vita documentata, opere ed influenza su l'arte*, 3 vols. (Tivoli, 1927–9).

17. See, for example, vol. I, 252 and 331.

18. *Rossini: A Study in Tragi-Comedy* (London, 1934).

19. *Shaw's Music*, vol. I, 59–60.

20. A. J. B. Hutchings, 'The Nineteenth Century', *The Pelican History of Music*, ed. Alec Robertson and Denis Stevens (Harmondsworth, 1968), vol. III, 114–15.

21. Andrew Porter's essays in the *New Yorker* have been published in a series of volumes: *Music of Three Seasons: 1974–1977* (New York, 1978); *Music of Three More Seasons: 1977–1980* (New York, 1981); *Musical Events, a Chronicle: 1980–1983* (New York, 1987); *Musical Events, a Chronicle: 1983–1986* (New York, 1989).

22. No unthinking fan of bel canto, Taubman wrote of *Lucia di Lammermoor*, 'it is futile to pretend that this music of Donizetti's is emotionally convincing today' (4 December 1956).

23. For example, Fedele D'Amico, *Il teatro di Rossini* (Bologna, 1992), 135.

24. Essentially the same rôle as Neocle. Rossini turned Neoclès/Neocle into a tenor, but later performances of the Italian translation retransformed him into a mezzo-soprano.

25. Marilyn Horne with Jane Scovell, *Marilyn Horne: My Life* (New York, 1983), 170.

26. Published as *Vincenzo Bellini und die italienische Opera Seria seiner Zeit: Studien über Libretto, Arienform und Melodik*, Analecta musicologica 6 (Cologne and Vienna, 1969).

27. 'C'è modo e modo (*I Capuleti e i Montecchi* di Bellini nella revisione di Claudio Abbado)', *Nuova rivista musicale italiana* 1 (1967), 142.

28. On the rôle of this production for the founding of the critical edition, see Philip Gossett, *Divas and Scholars: On Performing Italian Opera* (Chicago, forthcoming). Gossett's review of the related recording appeared in *The Musical Quarterly* 61 (1975), 626–38.

29. See the Festival's website: www.rossinioperafestival.it, as of April 2001.

30. Matthew Gurewitsch, 'Poking Holes in Verdi to Let Audiences In', *The New York Times* (4 March 2001).

31. Arrigo Quattrocchi, 'La Rossini Renaissance', *Musica e Dossier* (July–August, 1989).

5. Librettos and librettists

1. Stendhal, *Life of Rossini*, trans. Richard N. Coe (London, 1970), 74.

2. Documents read out in the opera in a speaking voice, such as the promissory note in *La cambiale di matrimonio* (scene 2) and the parchment that Rosina lets fall in *Il barbiere di Siviglia* (Act 1, scene 4), are exceptions to this rule.

3. At the time of Rossini Italian versification generally made use of all metres from *quadrisillabo* to *endecasillabo* (except *novenario*, very rare). Three types of line endings commonly occur, *piano*, *tronco* and *sdrucciolo*; occasionally, the metre is repeated within a line, creating a 'double' (*doppio*) metre. It is best to work out the metre on the basis of the strong accents in the line; the last always falling on the penultimate syllable. Therefore, if the strong accent falls on the fifth syllable, the verse is *senario*, independent of the fact that the verse may have five, six or more syllables, given that it could be *senario tronco*, *piano* or *sdrucciolo* respectively. On versification, see Pietro G. Beltrami, *La metrica italiana* (Bologna, 1991). A history of metrical issues can be found in my 'Istituti metrici e formali', *Storia dell'opera italiana*, ed. Lorenzo Bianconi and Giorgio Pestelli, vol. VI (Turin, 1988), 165–233, and in *Libretti d'opera italiani dal Seicento al Novecento*, ed. Giovanna Gronda and Paolo Fabbri (Milan, 1997). For the nineteenth century in particular, see Friedrich Lippman, *Versificazione italiana e ritmo musicale. I rapporti tra verso e musica nell'opera italiana dell'Ottocento* (Naples, 1986).

4. *Indice dei teatrali spettacoli di tutto l'anno dal carnovale 1808 a tutto il carnovale 1809* (Venice, 1809), ix. The whole collection is reprinted anastatically in Roberto Verti's edition *Un*

almanacco drammatico. L'indice de' teatrali spettacoli (Pesaro, 1996).

5. For a multi-century panorama, see Fabrizio Della Seta, 'The Librettist', in *Opera Production and Its Resources*, ed. Lorenzo Bianconi and Giorgio Pestelli (Chicago, 1998), 229–89.

6. On this, see my 'Il conte Aventi, Rossini e Ferrara', BCRS 34 (1994), 91–157: 108ff. Aventi had already written a *dramma giocoso*, *Voglia di dote e non di moglie*, staged at the Comunale in Ferrara in the Carnival season of 1809 with music by Coccia.

7. See Claudio Toscani, 'Politica culturale e teatro nell'età napoleonica: i concorsi governativi', in *'L'aere è fosco, il ciel s'imbruna'. Arti e musica a Venezia dalla fine della Repubblica al Congresso di Vienna*, Atti del Convegno internazionale di studi, Venezia, Palazzo Giustinian Lolin 10–12 aprile 1997, ed. Francesco Passadore and Franco Rossi (Venice, 2000), 71–98.

8. See Alessandro Roccatagliati, 'Derivazioni e prescrizioni librettistiche: come Rossini intonò Romani', *Gioachino Rossini, 1792–1992. Il testo e la scena*, ed. Paolo Fabbri (Pesaro, 1994), 163–82. On the two versions of *Il turco*, see my 'Caterino Mazzolà e l'opera italiana a Dresda' (forthcoming).

9. See my 'Due boccon per Mustafà', in *L'italiana in Algeri*, vol. IV of *I libretti di Rossini*, ed. Paolo Fabbri and Maria Chiara Bertieri (Pesaro, 1997), 9–47.

10. The impresario's autobiography is partially published in Alberto Cametti, *Un poeta melodrammatico romano. Appunti e notizie in gran parte inedite sopra Jacopo Ferretti e i musicisti del suo tempo* (Milan, 1897), edited by Francesco Paolo Russo in *Recercare* 8 (1996), 185–6.

11. Cited in Emilio Sala, 'Ascendenti francesi della "farsa moderna" ', in *I vicini di Mozart*, vol. II, *La farsa musicale veneziana (1750–1810)*, ed. David Bryant (Florence, 1989), 551–65: 552.

12. These are described in Bruno Cagli, 'Le farse di Rossini', *La farsa musicale veneziana (1750–1810)* (see note 11 above), 633–40.

13. See Paolo Gallarati, *Musica e maschera. Il libretto italiano del Settecento* (Turin, 1984).

14. See Cesare Questa, *Il ratto dal serraglio. Euripide, Plauto, Mozart, Rossini* (Urbino, 1997), 134–5.

15. See, again, Questa, *Il ratto dal serraglio*, 110ff., on how Anelli's libretto exhibits precise debts to the comedies and tragedies of Plautus and Euripides.

16. See for example Sabine Henze-Döhring, 'La tecnica del concertato in Paisiello e Rossini', *Nuova rivista musicale italiana* 22 (1988), 1–23.

17. See my 'La farsa *Che originali* di Mayr e la tradizione metamelodrammatica', in *Giovanni Simone Mayr. L'opera teatrale e la musica sacra*, ed. Francesco Bellotto (Bergamo, 1997), 139–60.

18. Around 1810 he had written *Il naso in pericolo ovvero Il disinganno*, but it was not set to music and did not reach the stage (see Toscani, 'Politica culturale', 83–4).

19. The prosodic conventions of French verse are summarised in the *Commento critico* accompanying M. Elizabeth C. Bartlet's critical edition of *Guillaume Tell* (Pesaro, 1992), 14–15. For a more general discussion, see Jean-Michel Gouvard, *La Versification* (Paris, 1999).

20. See Anselm Gerhard, 'La "liberté" inadmissible à l'Opéra', in *Le Siège de Corinthe (Maometto II), L'avant-scène Opéra* 81 (November 1985), 69–71; also GRLD, vol. II, no. 604 (note).

6. Compositional methods

1. The letter entered the Rossini literature through its publication by Lodovico Silvestri, in his *Della vita e delle opere di Gioachino Rossini* (Milan, 1874), 61, whence it became part of the collection edited by Giuseppe Mazzatinti, *Lettere di G. Rossini* (Florence, 1902), 342–3. Silvestri affirms that he obtained it from an article by one 'signor De Mirandel' in the '*Pall-Mall Gazzetta*'.

2. Geltrude Righetti-Giorgi, Rossini's first Rosina in *Il barbiere di Siviglia* (1816) and Cenerentola in *La Cenerentola* (1817), describes just such a scene in her *Cenni di una donna già cantante sopra il Maestro Rossini* (Bologna, 1823), 52.

3. That is the attitude of Stendhal, who tells a version of the anecdote in his *Life of Rossini*, trans. Richard N. Coe (London, 1970), 413–14, referring it specifically to *Il Signor Bruschino*.

4. See, for example, Reto Müller, 'Rossini e Hiller attraverso i documenti e gli scritti', and Guido Johannes Joerg, ed., 'Gli scritti rossiniani di Ferdinand Hiller', BCRS 32 (1992), 33–62 and 63–155 respectively. The comment appears in Hiller's 'Plaudereien mit Rossini', first published serially in the *Kölnische Zeitung* in 1856 and then in the second volume of Hiller's *Aus dem Tonleben unserer Zeit* (Leipzig, 1868), 1–84. In Joerg's transcription the remarks are printed on 92–3.

5. The codicil is printed in Giuseppe Radiciotti, *Gioacchino Rossini. Vita documentata, opere ed influenza su l'arte*, 3 vols. (Tivoli, 1927–9), vol. II, 531.

6. For complete details concerning the history of these works, see the facsimile editions of their autograph manuscripts, with introductions by Philip Gossett: *Il barbiere di Siviglia* (Rome, 1993) and *La Cenerentola* (Bologna, 1969).

7. 'I am now writing for the Teatro dei Fiorentini an *opera buffa*, whose title is *La gazzetta*. The Neapolitan dialect, which I don't know very well, forms the dialogue and the development of the plot; heaven will help me.' The letter is deposited at the Fondazione Rossini. This is an opera heavily dependent on self-borrowing, however, as we shall see.

8. See Rossini's letter to Romani of 31 August 1819, in which he expresses approval of the 'sogetto' of the new opera, by which he presumably means the outline of its contents, in GRLD, vol. I, 393.

9. For a consideration of Verdi's working methods, see Philip Gossett, 'Der kompositorische Prozeß: Verdis Opernskizzen', *Giuseppe Verdi und seine Zeit*, ed. Markus Engelhardt (Laaber, 2001), 169–90.

10. The sketch first came to light when it was auctioned at Sotheby's (London) on 28–29 May 1992 (lot no. 635, 310–11 of the catalogue, with the recto of the leaf reproduced in facsimile on 310). The leaf was purchased by Lord St Davids, from whom it was acquired by the Fondazione Rossini of Pesaro in 2000. See the catalogue of this collection, *Rossini. Musica da vedere* (Pesaro, 2000), 62 (item 391).

11. The *Semiramide* sketches are preserved in the Raccolte Piancastelli of the Biblioteca Comunale in Forlì, near Bologna. For a complete transcription, prepared by Philip Gossett, see Gioachino Rossini, *Semiramide*, ed. Philip Gossett and Alberto Zedda, 4 vols., GREC (Pesaro, 2001), vol. IV, 1421–41. In Forlì there is also a sketch for the concluding section of the duet for Pamyra and Mahomet from *Le Siège de Corinthe*, the only part of the duet completely rewritten from the original version of the opera (*Maometto II*).

12. These sketches are in the Fonds Michotte of the Brussels Conservatoire: no transcription has been published.

13. For further details, see Philip Gossett, 'Gioachino Rossini and the Conventions of Composition', *Acta musicologica* 42 (1970), 48–58.

14. See Gioachino Rossini, *Edipo Coloneo*, ed. Lorenzo Tozzi and Piero Weiss, GREC (Pesaro, 1985).

15. See chapter 7 of the present volume.

16. See Scott L. Balthazar, 'Rossini and the Development of the Mid-Century Lyric Form', *Journal of the American Musicological Society* 41 (1988), 102–25, as well as chapter 8 of the present volume.

17. For further details, see Gossett, 'Gioachino Rossini and the Conventions of Composition', 56–7.

18. For further information about the reception of the opera, see the preface to *Il turco in Italia*, ed. Margaret Bent, GREC (Pesaro, 1988), xxiv–xxvii.

19. See Mazzatinti, *Lettere*, 284.

20. I exclude *Demetrio e Polibio*, probably written before 1810, and two other very early works, *La cambiale di matrimonio* (1810) and *L'equivoco stravagante* (1811).

21. That Rossini stopped composing operas, however, does not mean he prepared no new music between 1829 and 1858, witness the *Stabat Mater* and his many songs and cantatas.

22. The remark is attributed to Rossini by the Italian critic Filippo Filippi; see Radiciotti, *Gioacchino Rossini*, vol. II, 370 (note).

23. For further details, see chapter 15 of the present volume.

24. See Philip Gossett, 'Rossini's *Petite messe solennelle* and its several versions', forthcoming in a book of essays in memory of William Holmes.

7. The dramaturgy of the operas

1. For an overview of the standard traits of the genre as a whole, Carl Dahlhaus's discussion remains fundamental; see his 'Drammaturgia dell'opera italiana', *Storia dell'opera italiana*, ed. Lorenzo Bianconi and Giorgio Pestelli, vol. VI (Turin, 1988), 77–162.

2. See chapter 5 of the present volume.

3. Stendhal, *Life of Rossini*, trans. Richard N. Coe (London, 1970), 339 (translation modified).

4. Letter to Cesare De Sanctis, 7 February 1856, *Carteggi verdiani*, ed. Alessandro Luzio, 4 vols. (Rome, 1935–47), vol. I, 32.

5. Stendhal, *Life of Rossini*, 112 (note).

6. Carlo Ritorni, *Ammaestramenti alla composizione d'ogni poema e d'ogni opera appartenente alla musica* (Milan, 1841), 40.

7. Jacopo Ferretti, *Alcune pagine della mia vita* (1835), in *La Cenerentola*, ed. Marco Mauceri, vol. VI of *I libretti di Rossini* (Pesaro, 2000), ix–x.

8. The structures of the *introduzione* and Finale are thoroughly examined in Daniela Tortora, *Drammaturgia del Rossini serio. Le opere della maturità da 'Tancredi' a 'Semiramide'* (Rome, 1996); on duets, see Scott L. Balthazar, 'Mayr, Rossini, and the Development of the Opera Seria Duet: Some Preliminary Conclusions', *I vicini di Mozart*, vol. I, *Il teatro musicale tra Sette e Ottocento*, ed. Maria Teresa Muraro (Florence, 1989), 377–98, and Balthazar, 'The Primo Ottocento Duet and the Transformation of the Rossinian Code', *Journal of Musicology* 7 (1989),

471–97. On the different types of solo arias see Marco Beghelli, 'Tre slittamenti semantici: cavatina, romanza, rondò', *Le parole della musica III. Studi di lessicologia musicale*, ed. Fiamma Nicolodi and Paolo Trovato (Florence, 2000), 185–217.

9. Ferretti, *Alcune pagine*, x (I have corrected the obvious error where Ferretti speaks of a 'duet for the *prima donna* and soprano').

10. On the genre of the *buffa* aria, one of the few musico-dramatic aspects distinguishing *opera buffa* from *opera seria* in Rossini, see John Platoff, 'The Buffa Aria in Mozart's Vienna', *Cambridge Opera Journal* 2 (1990), 99–120.

11. Then as now, 'Largo', 'Adagio', 'Adagio cantabile' were all common labels for the first section of the musical number, unrelated to the real tempo indication (Largo, Larghetto, Adagio, Andante, etc.) placed at the start of the piece. Similarly, the *stretta* is called 'Allegro' or, more frequently, 'cabaletta', a term which, as we will see, more accurately corresponds to the melodic theme of the *stretta* only. See Marco Beghelli, 'Alle origini della cabaletta', *'L'aere è fosco, il ciel s'imbruna'. Arte e musica a Venezia dalla fine della Repubblica al Congresso di Vienna*, ed. Francesco Passadore and Franco Rossi (Venice, 2000), 593–630.

12. The first to interpret the Rossinian musical number in terms of the alternation between static and kinetic moments was Philip Gossett; see his 'The "candeur virginale" of *Tancredi*', *The Musical Times* 112 (1971), 326–9.

13. See Carl Dahlhaus, 'Zeitstrukturen in der Oper', *Die Musikforschung* 34 (1981), 2–11.

14. In the absence of established terms from the period, musicologists have recently turned a discursive phrase used by a mid-nineteenth-century Verdi critic, Abramo Basevi, into a technical term. He outlined how a certain duet veered away 'from the usual form of duets, that is a *tempo d'attacco*, the *Adagio*, the *tempo di mezzo* and the cabaletta'; see Harold S. Powers, ' "La solita forma" and the "Uses of Convention" ', *Acta musicologica* 59 (1987), 65–90. The labels 'tempo d'attacco' and 'tempo di mezzo', less common than 'Adagio' and 'cabaletta', are also drawn from this context and extended retroactively to Rossini. It is with these historical-linguistic limits in mind that the terms are used here.

15. See Marco Beghelli, 'Die (scheinbare) Unlogik des Eigenplagiats', *Rossinis 'Eduardo e Cristina'. Beiträge zur Jahrhundert-Erstaufführung*, ed. Reto Müller and Bernd-Rüdiger Kern (Leipzig, 1997), 101–22, and chapter 6 in the present volume.

16. Ritorni, *Ammaestramenti*, 46.

17. See the letter from the impresario Angelo Petracchi, who, in anticipation of a revival of *Mosè in Egitto* at La Scala, suggested to Rossini that they should substitute a musico for the 'amorous' tenor (GRLD, vol. I, 135).

18. Stendhal, *Life of Rossini*, 169.

19. Ritorni, *Ammaestramenti*, 43.

20. For the melodic structure of single formal sections, see Scott L. Balthazar, 'Rossini and the Development of the Mid-Century Lyric Form', *Journal of the American Musicological Society* 41 (1988), 102–25; Steven Huebner, 'Lyric Form in Ottocento Opera', *Journal of the Royal Musical Association* 117 (1992), 123–47; Giorgio Pagannone, 'Mobilità struturale della *lyric form*. Sintassi verbale e sintassi musicale nel melodramma italiano del primo Ottocento', *Analisi* 20 (1996), 2–17. Other structural mechanisms of the period, typical of the famed Rossinian crescendo and certain *larghi concertati*, are examined in Lorenzo Bianconi, ' "Confusi e stupidi": di uno stupefacente (e banalissimo) dispositivo metrico', *Gioachino Rossini, 1792–1991. Il testo e la scena*, ed. Paolo Fabbri (Pesaro, 1994), 129–61.

21. Honoré de Balzac, 'Massimilla Doni' (1839), *Sarrasine. Gambara. Massimilla Doni* (Paris, 1995), 157–228: 195.

8. Melody and ornamentation

1. For Rossini's aesthetic pronouncements on melody, see Paolo Fabbri, 'Rossini the Aesthetician', *Cambridge Opera Journal* 6 (1994), 19–29.

2. On the immanence of Rossinian melody, see Friedrich Lippmann, 'Per un'esegesi dello stile rossiniano', *Nuova rivista musicale italiana* 2 (1968), 813–56.

3. It is interesting to observe this structure in Rossini's French operas, where it has been transplanted from Italian opera; see *Le Siège de Corinthe*, Pamyra's aria 'Du séjour de la lumière' or Ory's *cavatine* in *Le Comte Ory*, 'Que les destins prospères'.

4. See John Platoff, 'The Buffa Aria in Mozart's Vienna', *Cambridge Opera Journal* 2 (1990), 99–120.

5. The term 'open' is from Lippmann, 'Per un'esegesi dello stile rossiniano', 817.

6. For example, *Aureliano in Palmira*, duet Arsace–Aureliano 'Pensa che festi a Roma'; *L'italiana in Algeri*, Isabella's *rondò*, 'Pensa alla patria'; *Elisabetta regina d'Inghilterra*, Norfolk's aria, 'Deh! troncate i ceppi suoi'; *Il barbiere di Siviglia*, Count's aria, 'Cessa di più resistere', and related figures such as those in *Otello*, duet Desdemona–Otello, 'Non arrestar il colpo'.

7. 'In that which I would call *melodic verse*, on the contrary, there reigns the most complete regularity. There rhythmic instinct has absolute sovereignty. To fulfil the conditions for melodic verse, complete symmetry is established between the different parts of the melody and they are enclosed within certain limits of duration, marked by easily-noticeable rests: in this way, the ear may recognise each element of the phrase without any uncertainty, just as in the verse it recognises the stresses, the caesura, the rhyme, etc.'; Manuel García, *Traité complet de l'art du chant* (Paris, 1840), 15.

8. Jean-Jacques Rousseau, 'Unité de mélodie', *Dictionnaire de musique* (1767) (first definition): 'There is in music a sequential unity with the subject, by virtue of which all the parts, closely linked, make up a single whole, in which one may perceive at once the ensemble and all its internal interrelationships.' This is a modern version of the ancient principle of the necessary relationship of the parts to the whole, outlined in the first section of the present chapter.

9. The pattern of choice in Bellini is a a' b a''; see Friedrich Lippmann, 'Vincenzo Bellini e l'opera seria del suo tempo. Studi sul libretto, la forma delle arie e la melodia', in Maria Rosaria Adamo and Friedrich Lippmann, *Vincenzo Bellini* (Turin, 1981), 313–429: 363–429; and Scott L. Balthazar, 'Rossini and the Development of the Mid-Century Lyric Form', *Journal of the American Musicological Society* 41 (1988), 102–25.

10. See Francesco Galeazzi, 'Articolo III (Della melodia in particolare, e delle sue parti, membri e regole)', *Elementi teorico-pratici di musica*, 2 vols. (Rome, 1791–6), and the commentary of Renato Di Benedetto, 'Lineamenti di una teoria della melodia nella trattatistica italiana fra il 1790 e il 1830', *Analecta musicologica* 21 (1982), 421–43.

11. For more detailed analysis of the morphological properties of desinences, cadenzas and ornamentation of the melodic kernel in Rossini, see Damien Colas, 'Les Annotations des chanteurs dans les matériels d'exécution des opéras de Rossini à Paris (1820–1860). Contribution à l'étude de la grammaire mélodique rossinienne', 4 vols. (doctoral dissertation, Université de Tours, 1997).

12. In this context the word 'cadenza' has a sense distinct from the usual one in English, i.e. a relatively long improvised passage at the end of an aria or a concerto movement [translator's note].

13. This is how Gesualdo Lanza distinguishes 'ornamenti' (metrical) from 'cadenze'

(ametrical) in his *Elements of Singing* (London, 1809), 160.

14. See Henri-Montan Berton, *De la musique mécanique et de la musique philosophique* (Paris, 1826).

15. 'But when third- or fourth-rate artists, with the aim of imitating their first-rate colleagues, substitute bad-taste, badly-executed *passaggi* for the written melodies, it is an abuse that must be among the greatest dangers to the reputation of the *maestri*. It was probably for this reason that Rossini was inspired with the idea of ornamenting and embellishing his music himself. For, both singer and composer as he was, he had a perfect right to impose upon his performers *passaggi* and flourishes according to his own taste'; Gilbert-Louis Duprez, *L'Art du chant* (Paris, 1845), 109; the letter in question (from Rossini to Ferdinando Guidicini, 12 February 1851), in *Lettere di G. Rossini*, ed. Giuseppe Mazzatinti (Florence, 1902), 191, is quoted at length in chapter 13 of the present volume.

16. Cadences published by M. Elizabeth C. Bartlet in the *Commento critico* of her critical edition of *Guillaume Tell* (Pesaro, 1992), 147–9.

17. All the annotations in this part, as well as in all of those relating to rôles in Rossini's operas produced at the Opéra and Théâtre Italien, are transcribed in Colas, *Les Annotations des chanteurs*, vol. IV.

18. On the particular problem of mono- and bi-stratification of the vocal line, see Colas, *Les Annotations des chanteurs*, vol. II, 324ff.

9. Off the stage

1. *Cantata in Onore del Sommo Pontefice Pio Nono*, ed. Mauro Bucarelli, GREC (Pesaro, 1996), 115–77.

2. An alternative reading for the last line (one of those modified by Rossini from the original text) is 'farmi penar così?' ('make me suffer so much?'), which is however syntactically problematic. See Gioachino Rossini, *Album français, Morceaux réservés*, ed. Rossana Dalmonte, GREC (Pesaro, 1989), xviii.

10. *Tancredi* and *Semiramide*

1. On early-nineteenth-century librettists' use of Voltaire's dramas, see Sabine Henze-Döhring, ' "Combinammo l'ossatura": Voltaire und die Librettistik des frühen Ottocento', *Die Musikforschung* 36 (1983), 113–27.

2. *Giornale dipartimentale* (9 February 1813), quoted in the Preface to *Tancredi*, ed. Philip Gossett, GREC (Pesaro, 1984), xxv.

3. This Finale, never published, was considered lost until its rediscovery and publication in the

1970s; see Philip Gossett, *The Tragic Finale of 'Tancredi'* (Pesaro, 1977).

4. For details of the revisions and substitutions made in Ferrara and Milan, see *Tancredi*, ed. Gossett, xxviii–xxxiii and Appendices 3 and 4.

5. On the librettos and large-scale musical planning of these works, see Daniela Tortora, *Drammaturgia del Rossini serio. Le opere della maturità da 'Tancredi' a 'Semiramide'* (Rome, 1996), and Philip Gossett, 'History and Works That Have No History: Reviving Rossini's Neapolitan Operas', *Disciplining Music: Musicology and its Canons*, ed. Katherine Bergeron and Philip V. Bohlman (Chicago, 1992), 95–115. See also Marco Emanuele, *L'ultima stagione italiana. Le forme dell'opera seria di Rossini da Napoli a Venezia* (Florence and Turin, 1997).

6. Emanuele, *L'ultima stagione italiana*, 9.

7. Alberto Zedda and Marco Emanuele have offered contrasting views of the relationship between *Tancredi* and *Semiramide*. Zedda considers *Semiramide* a return to the 'Apollonian' values manifest in *Tancredi*, following Rossini's 'Dionysian' explorations in Naples: its Apollonian qualities include 'the luminous transparency of the melodic line', 'the rational organisation of the musical structure', and the avoidance of 'veiled sentiments and ambiguous expressive polyvalence'; see Alberto Zedda, 'Rossini a Napoli', Raffaele Ajello et al., *Il Teatro di San Carlo*, 2 vols. (Naples, 1987), vol. I, 119–40: 127. Emanuele attempts to reconcile this opposition between the two strains in Rossini's *seria* output, proposing that *Semiramide* represents not an escape from or rejection of the aesthetic values explored in Naples, but the composer's more complex response to his own awareness that that period had come to an end; see Emanuele, *L'ultima stagione italiana*, 11.

8. As Romantic dramatists like Victor Hugo would do in the 1830s, Voltaire invoked Shakespeare to justify the more extreme elements in his drama, particularly the appearance of Ninus's ghost. See Voltaire, 'Dissertation sur la tragédie ancienne et moderne' (Preface to *Sémiramis*, 1748), in *Théâtre de Voltaire* (Paris, n.d.), 461–3.

9. The tragic Finale that Rossini composed for the Ferrara première in 1813 adheres to Voltaire's original plot, ending with the hero's death.

10. The social fabric is most complicated in the original, Venetian version of this scene, where Argirio is backed by two choruses – one led by Isaura implores him to take pity on his daughter, while the other led by Orbazzano urges him to fulfil the law and sign her death warrant. The substitute aria introduced in Milan ('Al campo

mi chiama') expresses the same ambivalence, but the chorus's rôle is reduced and simplified. (In Ferrara, Argirio's aria was omitted and he simply signed the order at the end of a brief secco recitative.)

11. For a discussion of Amenaide's prison scene in light of similar scenes in Rossini's other *opere serie*, see Daniela Tortora, 'Il personaggio recluso: un *topos* drammaturgico dello scioglimento', in *Gioachino Rossini, 1792–1992. Il testo e la scena*, ed. Paolo Fabbri (Pesaro, 1994), 278–82.

12. Giuseppe Carpani, 'Risposta all'anonimo autore dell'Articolo sul *Tancredi* di Rossini, inserito nella Gazzetta di Berlino, N 7., 1818', in *Le Rossiniane, ossia, Lettere musico-teatrali* (Padua, 1824), 74–5.

13. Stendhal, *Life of Rossini*, trans. Richard N. Coe (London, 1970), 63.

14. Carpani, 'Risposta', 75.

15. Philip Gossett, 'The "candeur virginale" of *Tancredi*', *The Musical Times* 112 (1971), 326–9.

16. For a formal analysis and discussion of this *introduzione*'s poetry and musical sections, see Tortora, *Drammaturgia del Rossini serio*, 97–101. The composer seemed to have been inspired by his own earlier work in this scene, rather than by the dramatic source. Tortora notes that while this *introduzione* has no corresponding scene in Voltaire's *Sémiramis* (which begins with Arzace's arrival at Ninus's tomb), it is similar in form and content to the opening two-scene complex of *Mosè in Egitto* (1818): in both cases the action begins with a grand scene involving all but one of the characters, and climaxes with a manifestation of divine wrath. The multi-movement opening scene of Romani's and Meyerbeer's *L'esule di Granata*, written a year before *Semiramide*, is another likely model: in a letter dated 28 October 1822, Rossi even describes *Semiramide*'s *introduzione* as 'alla Meyerbeer' (GRLD, vol. II, no. 347).

17. *The Harmonicon* 5/7 (July 1827), 143.

18. For an analysis of this duet's unusual formal qualities in the context of Rossini's *oeuvre*, see Scott L. Balthazar, 'Evolving Conventions in Italian Serious Opera: Scene Structure in the Works of Rossini, Bellini, Donizetti, and Verdi, 1810–1850' (doctoral dissertation, University of Pennsylvania, 1985), 144–7.

19. Carpani, 'Risposta', 87.

20. A similar 'water music' topos accompanies Elena's entrance *en bateau* in *La donna del lago*. There may even be a distant allusion to the C major tonality and prominent flutes of the Elysian Fields in Gluck's *Orfeo*.

21. *Tutti i libretti di Rossini*, ed. Marco Beghelli and Nicola Gallino (Milan, 1991), 723.

22. Voltaire, *Sémiramis*, Act 4, scene 1, lines 1115–20.

23. *Il censore universale dei teatri* 30 (4 April 1833), 120.

24. See Daniela Tortora, 'Fortuna dei "palpiti" rossiniani nella musica strumentale a stampa dell'Ottocento', BCRS 28 (1988), 7–25.

11. *Il barbiere di Siviglia*

1. The formal contract, dated 26 December 1815, obliged Rossini to accept whatever libretto was provided by the impresario (Duke Francesco Sforza Cesarini) by the beginning of January for a performance on or around 5 February. In the event, Sterbini delivered a rough outline of the libretto on 17 January, promising to deliver its two acts by 25 and 29 January respectively (GRLD, vol. I, 124–6 and 135–6). See Philip Gossett, 'The Operas of Rossini: Problems of Textual Criticism in Nineteenth-Century Opera' (doctoral dissertation, Princeton University, 1968), 272–309, and Gossett's introduction to the facsimile reprint of the autograph score of *Il barbiere di Siviglia* (Rome, 1993), where he notes (25) that despite this tight schedule, 'Rossini borrowed only a few themes from other operas, and in almost every case either rewrote them extensively or placed them in a new context.' The exception was the celebrated Sinfonia, which was actually composed for *Aureliano in Palmira*. He used collaborators only to compose the secco recitatives between musical numbers.

2. *Il barbiere di Siviglia*, ed. Alberto Zedda (Milan, 1969); citations here are from the 'Introduzione' to the piano-vocal reduction issued the same year.

3. Letter of 1898 to Camille Bellaigue, in *Copialettere di Giuseppe Verdi*, ed. Gaetano Cesari and Alessandro Luzio (Milan, 1913), 415.

4. Zedda, 'Introduzione', viii.

5. Not the least of the differences concerns the influence of the moralising mid-century bourgeois *drame* on both the sequel play and Mozart's opera. See Stefano Castelvecchi, 'Sentimental and Anti-Sentimental in *Le nozze di Figaro*', *Journal of the American Musicological Society* 53 (2000), 1–24.

6. The Parisian Fair theatres at St Germain and St Laurent (which operated, in turn, during Lent and from late July or early August through September) were known from 1714 as the Opéra Comique, which in 1762 merged with the Comédie Italienne.

7. Schlegel's influential lectures were translated into French by Albertine-Adrienne Necker de Saussure as *Cours de littérature dramatique*, 3 vols. (Paris, 1814), into English, by John Black, in 1815 (as *A Course of Lectures on Dramatic Art*

and Literature), and into Italian, by Giovanni Gherardini (the librettist of Rossini's *La gazza ladra*), in 1817 (as *Corso di letteratura drammatica*). My translation here is from the French (vol. II, 307 and vol. I, 363), but draws for the second passage on Black's as revised by A. J. W. Morrison in 1846 (reprint, New York, 1965), 182.

8. John Dunkley, *Beaumarchais: 'Le Barbier de Séville'* (London, 1991), 62.

9. The fragmentary, undated manuscript, forming probably one third of *Le Sacristain*, was first published in 1974. See J.-P. de Beaumarchais, 'Un Inédit de Beaumarchais: *Le Sacristain*', *Revue d'histoire littéraire de la France* 74 (1974), 976–99; and, for a critical edition of the first layer of the text and fragments relating to a planned revision (either as a *parade* or as an *opéra comique*), Beaumarchais, *Oeuvres*, ed. Pierre Larthomas (Paris, 1988), 1138–45 and 1655–6. Other fragments relating to the project's various versions are in E. J. Arnould, *La Genèse du 'Barbier de Séville'* (Dublin and Paris, 1965), 100–13.

10. Another candidate is '*fils* (pronounced "fi") Caron (Beaumarchais's family name)'. De Beaumarchais was the assumed name of Pierre-Augustin Caron.

11. On Romantic theorising about grotesque realism, see, for example, Nina Maria Athanassoglou-Kallmyer, *Eugène Delacroix: Prints, Politics, and Satire, 1814–1822* (New Haven, 1991), 100–10 ('The Comic as Dissent and Modernity'). Mikhail Bakhtin's famous critique of Romantic theories is in his *Rabelais and His World*, trans. Helene Iswolsky (Cambridge, MA, 1965), 36–45. In identifying Rossini's comic style with Bakhtin's grotesque realism and Mozart's comic style with an 'everyday realism' that developed entirely outside the influence of the carnivalesque, Paolo Gallarati – in his 'Per un'interpretazione del comico rossiniano', *Gioachino Rossini, 1792–1992. Il testo e la scena*, ed. Paolo Fabbri (Pesaro, 1994), 3–12 – dismisses the possibility that either the Romantic grotesque or Beaumarchais's play influenced the opera; rather, he stresses its relationship to Molière's comedies and Goldoni's reverse-world librettos, arguing that all the opera's principals (including Figaro and Rosina, but not the Count) are 'colossal' representatives of the rising, post-Napoleonic bourgeoisie. Bakhtin claims that 'the essential principle of grotesque realism is degradation, that is, the lowering of all that is high, spiritual, ideal, abstract; it is a transfer to the material level, to the sphere of earth and body in their indissoluble unity' (19–20). But Gallarati asserts

quite the opposite, namely, that 'the denigration of caricature is in fact completely absent from the expressive system of *L'italiana in Algeri*, *Il barbiere di Siviglia* and *La Cenerentola*' (342). In his perceptive study of the *Barber*s of Paisiello and Rossini, David Kimbell points out – see his *Italian Opera* (Cambridge, 1991), 363–87 – many of the features of the Romantic grotesque (without ever naming it), but concludes that Rossini's characters 'are closer to their origins in the *commedia dell'arte* than they had been in Paisiello's opera or in Beaumarchais's play' (380). Neither Gallarati nor Kimbell appears aware of the play's origins in *Le Sacristain*.

12. Stendhal, *Life of Rossini*, trans. Richard N. Coe (London, 1970), 191 (translation emended).

13. Jacques Joly, 'La festa nelle commedie goldoniane di chiusura di carnevale', *Studi goldoniani* 5 (1979), 46, cited in Ted Emery, *Goldoni as Librettist: Theatrical Reform and the 'drammi giocosi per musica'* (New York, 1991), 94 and 102.

14. Emery, *Goldoni as Librettist*, 102 and 105.

15. French spellings of characters' names refer to the play, Italian to the opera.

16. 'Lettre modérée sur la chute et la critique du *Barbier de Séville*', in Beaumarchais, *Oeuvres*, 274 and 277.

17. Stendhal paraphrases it thus in the first part of *Racine et Shakespeare* (Oxford, 1907; first published 1823), 13.

18. Beaumarchais, *Oeuvres*, 277. It is precisely Bartholo's worthiness as an opponent that Rossini had in mind when he cast the concluding movement of Bartolo's aria ('A un dottor della mia sorte') as a dynamic, modulatory sonata, accompanied by violins *sul ponticello* (on the bridge, where the strings have the least play).

19. Beaumarchais, 'Un Inédit de Beaumarchais', 993.

20. An *opéra comique* called *Les Précautions inutiles*, by Anchard, Anseaume and Chrétien, for example, was performed in 1760.

21. See Philip Robinson, *Beaumarchais et la chanson. Musique et dramaturgie des comédies de Figaro* (Oxford, 1999), 28–47.

22. The play's first stage set explicitly evokes the festive setting in which *parades* were originally performed: on a balcony outside the Fair theatres to lure the crowd inside.

23. The *Avvertimento* is translated in Herbert Weinstock, *Rossini: A Biography* (New York, 1968), together with Rossini's letter of 22 March 1860 to a French admirer named Scitivaux giving an account of the opera's conception and première and recalling that he had written to the seventy-six-year-old Paisiello, 'declaring to him that I had not wanted to enter into a contest

with him, being aware of my inferiority, but had only wanted to treat a subject that delighted me, while avoiding as much as possible the exact situations in his libretto' (58–9). Rossini's efforts notwithstanding, the première of his opera proved to be one of the great theatrical fiascos.

24. Bakhtin, *Rabelais and His World*, 15.

25. Julien-Louis Geoffroy, *Cours de littérature dramatique*, 2nd edn, 6 vols. (Paris, 1825), vol. V, 455 and 457.

26. Appropriated for a Bolognese revival by the first Rosina, Geltrude Righetti Giorgi, the aria was dropped when Rossini himself reworked it as part of the *rondò*-Finale of *La Cenerentola*.

27. See, for example, Eugène Delacroix's famous caricature of Rossini published with Stendhal's commentary on 13 August 1821 in *Le Miroir des spectacles*. It shows the youthful composer 'singlehandedly supporting the Italian Opera', represented by the singers who created the rôles of Otello, Isabella and Figaro in Paris. Whereas the first two are realistic and statuesque, the latter is a *portrait-charge* (cartoon) depicting Figaro's caricature of Bartolo's galant minuet during the music lesson scene, a grotesque parody of a grotesque parody. See the quotation from Bakhtin in note 11 above.

28. On this double dramatic discourse, see Gabriel Conesa, *La Trilogie de Beaumarchais. Ecriture et dramaturgie* (Paris, 1985), 173, and Schlegel, *Cours de littérature dramatique*, vol. I, 359 and 365–8.

29. Beaumarchais, *Oeuvres*, 274 and 1308.

30. Sigmund Freud, *Wit and Its Relation to the Unconscious*, trans. A. A. Brill (London, 1916; reprint, 1993), 308–12.

31. Henri Bergson, 'Laughter' ('Le Rire', 1899) in *Comedy*, ed. Wylie Sypher (Baltimore and London, 1956), 156–7.

32. Bergson, *Comedy*, 150–1.

33. 'J'aime mieux être un bon barbier'. See Arnould, *La Genèse du 'Barbier de Séville'*, 94–5, 148 and 330–2; and Beaumarchais, *Oeuvres*, 1302.

34. Jean Emelina, *Le Comique: essai d'interprétation générale* (Paris, 1991), 36, cited in William Howarth, *Beaumarchais and the Theatre* (London and New York, 1995), 144, the source of the second quotation.

35. Melveena McKendrick, *Theatre in Spain, 1490–1700* (Cambridge, 1989), 169.

36. Dunkley, *Beaumarchais: 'Le Barbier de Séville'*, 20.

37. *Le Journal encyclopédique* (1 April 1775), cited in Arnould, *La Genèse du 'Barbier de Séville'*, 484.

38. Bergson, *Comedy*, 180–3.

39. Stendhal, *Life of Rossini*, 198.

40. *Ibid.*, 198–9.

41. These 'Observations' are reprinted in Arnould, *La Genèse du 'Barbier de Séville'*, 97.

42. Stendhal, *De l'amour* (Paris, 1965; first published 1822), 92.

43. Stendhal, *Life of Rossini*, 177, 186 and 188–91 (translation emended).

12. *Guillaume Tell*

1. This and other impressive *grand opéra* performance figures may be found in Stéphane Wolff, *L'Opéra au Palais Garnier (1875–1962): les oeuvres, les interprètes* (Paris, 1962).

2. This prolific Wild West hero conducted his daring exploits (first broadcast in 1938 and reprised in the 1940s, 1950s and 1960s) to the Allegro vivace.

3. All references to the score will be to the critical edition by M. Elizabeth C. Bartlet, (Pesaro, 1992); all translations are my own.

4. See Claudine Lacoste-Veysseyre, *Les Alpes romantiques. Le thème des Alpes dans la littérature française de 1800 à 1850*, 2 vols. (Geneva, 1981), vol. II, 746–7.

5. Description of an engraving by Bertaut after a drawing by Girardet, quoted in Marie-Louise Biver, *Fêtes révolutionnaires à Paris* (Paris, 1979), 107. For more on Revolutionary festivals, see also Mona Ozouf, *Festivals and the French Revolution* (Cambridge, MA, 1988).

6. 'Quelques indications sur la mise en scène de *Guillaume Tell*', reprinted in *The Original Staging Manuals for Twelve Parisian Operatic Premières*, ed. H. Robert Cohen (Stuyvesant, NY, 1986), 227.

7. Anne-Louise-Germaine de Staël, *De l'Allemagne*, 3 vols. (Paris, 1958; first published 1810), vol. III, 8–9.

8. See the section entitled 'Rossini and the Revolution' in Anselm Gerhard, *The Urbanization of Opera: Music Theater in Paris in the Nineteenth Century*, trans. Mary Whittall (Chicago, 1998), especially 82–90.

9. For more detail on the sources, see Gilles de Van, 'Les Sources littéraires de *Guillaume Tell* de Rossini', *Chroniques italiennes* 29 (1992), 7–24, and Andrea Baggioli, 'Le fonti letterarie di *Guillaume Tell*', BCRS 37 (1997), 5–50. For discussion of the Parisian tradition of theatrical parody, in which each major production inspired numerous other versions of the same story, see Sarah Hibberd, 'Magnetism, Muteness, Magic: Spectacle and the Parisian Lyric Stage c. 1830' (doctoral dissertation, University of Southampton, 1999).

10. See Bartlet's 'Prefazione' to the critical edition of the opera, where she carefully weighs up these and other questions concerning the

genesis of *Tell*; xxvi–xxvii for a table
summarising modifications to Jouy's text.

11. This is Gerhard's theory; see his ' "Sortire
dalle vie comuni"? Wie Rossini einem
Akademiker den *Guillaume Tell* verdarb', in *Oper
als Text: Romanistische Beiträge zur
Libretto-Forschung*, ed. Albert Gier (Heidelberg,
1986), 185–219. Jouy's original is reproduced in
a supplement to the critical commentary on
Bartlet's edition, *Commento critico. Testi*,
17–105.

12. Some of the sketches Cicéri made there are
reproduced in M. Elizabeth C. Bartlet,
*'Guillaume Tell' di Gioachino Rossini. Fonti
iconografiche* (Pesaro, 1996).

13. For the details, see Bartlet, 'Prefazione',
xxii–xxxviii.

14. On the latter, see Anselm Gerhard, ' "La
prière qui nous parait être d'un pittoresque
achevé": Ein Plädoyer für Hedwiges Solo im
vierten Akt von Rossinis *Guillaume Tell*', in *D'un
opéra à l'autre. Hommage à Jean Mongrédien*, ed.
Jean Gribenski, Marie Claire Mussat and
Herbert Schneider (Paris, 1996), 287–94.

15. For more on the considerable rôle of dance
at the Opéra, see Marian Smith, *Ballet and Opera
in the Age of 'Giselle'* (Princeton, 2000), and
Maribeth Clark, 'Understanding French Grand
Opéra Through Dance' (doctoral dissertation,
University of Pennsylvania, 1998).

16. See Gerhard's consideration of this idea,
'L'eroe titubante e il finale aperto: un dilemma
insolubile nel *Guillaume Tell* di Rossini', *Rivista
italiana di musicologia* 19 (1984), 113–30, and
The Urbanization of Opera, 81.

17. For Nourrit's important rôle in the
composition of *La Juive*, see chapter 1 of Diana
Hallman, *Opera, Liberalism, and Antisemitism in
Nineteenth-Century France: The Politics of
Halévy's 'La Juive'* (Cambridge, 2002).

18. See Marco Beghelli, 'Il "do di petto":
dissacrazione di un mito', *Il saggiatore musicale* 3
(1996), 105–49.

19. See M. Elizabeth C. Bartlet, 'Rossini e
l'Académie Royale de Musique a Parigi', in
Rossini 1792–1992. Mostra storico-documentaria,
ed. Mauro Bucarelli (Perugia, 1992), 245–66. For
a discussion of how Rossini's vocal writing
changed in Paris, see Giancarlo Landini,
'Riflessioni su alcuni aspetti della vocalità
francese di Rossini', *Chigiana* 34 (1981),
153–72.

20. *Revue Musicale* 6/4 (22 August 1829), 34–46.

21. His analysis was for the time unusually long
and detailed; see Hector Berlioz, '*Guillaume Tell*
de Rossini', *Gazette Musicale de Paris* 41–4
(1834), 326–7, 336–9, 341–3 and 349–51. A later
version of the article, edited by Gérard Condé, is

reprinted in *L'Avant-Scène Opéra* 118 (1989),
81–95.

22. For the full text of the 'avertissement', see
Bartlet's critical commentary, 51–2.

23. Cohen, *The Original Staging Manuals*, 225.

24. See Bartlet, *Fonti iconografiche*, 17.

25. For more, see Alison Gernsheim and
Helmut Gernsheim, *L.-J.-M. Daguerre: The
History of the Diorama and the Daguerreotype*
(London, 1956).

13. Singing Rossini

1. Especially interesting in this context is
Edmond Michotte, *Une soirée chez Rossini à
Beau-Séjour (Passy) 1858. Exposé par le Maestro
des principes du 'Bel Canto'* (Bruxelles, n.d.,
c. 1910?); see *Richard Wagner's Visit to Rossini
(Paris 1860) and An Evening at Rossini's in
Beau-Sejour (Passy) 1858*, trans. and ed. Herbert
Weinstock (Chicago, 1968). Rather than merely
dismissing this text as unreliable, as some have
done, we should consider it in so far as it agrees
with Rossini's thoughts as we can glean them
through his letters.

2. For a more specifically technical examination
of Rossini's vocal writing, see chapter 8 in the
present volume. An essential and specific
bibliography of studies on Rossini singing
includes Rodolfo Celletti, 'Origine e sviluppi
della coloratura rossiniana', *Nuova rivista
musicale italiana* 2 (1968), 872–919; Celletti, 'Il
vocalismo italiano da Rossini a Donizetti. Parte
I: Rossini', *Analecta musicologica* 5 (1968),
267–93; Austin Caswell, 'Vocal Embellishment
in Rossini's Paris Operas: French Style or
Italian?', BCRS 15 (1975), 5–21; Caswell, 'Mme
Cinti-Damoreau and the Embellishment of
Italian Opera in Paris: 1820–1845', *Journal of the
American Musicological Society* 28 (1975),
459–92; Giancarlo Landini, 'Riflessioni su alcuni
aspetti della vocalità francese di Rossini',
Chigiana 34 (1981), 153–72; Landini,
'Gilbert-Louis Duprez ovvero l'importanza di
cantar Rossini', BCRS 22 (1982), 29–54; Giorgio
Appolonia, *Le voci di Rossini* (Turin, 1992);
Marco Beghelli, 'Il "do di petto": dissacrazione
di un mito', *Il saggiatore musicale* 3 (1996),
105–49.

3. Letter of 12 February 1851 to Ferdinando
Guidicini, quoted in Luigi Rognoni, *Gioacchino
Rossini* (Turin, 1968), 301. Note Rossini's use of
'interpreter' ('interprete') to designate what
until shortly before everyone had called simply
'singer' ('cantante').

4. Michotte, *Richard Wagner's Visit*, 121–2 and
127.

5. The number of biographies in English of
singers who enjoyed a close working relationship

with Rossini is small; for a recent and richly documented volume, see James Radomski, *Manuel García (1775–1832): Chronicle of the Life of a Bel Canto Tenor at the Dawn of Romanticism* (Oxford, 2000).

6. Letter from the end of 1852 (or beginning of 1853) to Luigi Crisostomo Ferrucci, in Rognoni, *Gioacchino Rossini*, 306.

7. Letter from June 1851 to the Marquis Torquato Antaldi, in Rognoni, *Gioacchino Rossini*, 302.

8. Edmond Michotte, *Souvenirs personnels. La visite de R. Wagner à Rossini (Paris 1860)* (Paris, 1906); trans. in Michotte, *Richard Wagner's Visit*, 73.

9. Michotte, *Richard Wagner's Visit*, 109. Rossini dedicated four letters sent to the Latinist Luigi Grisostomo Ferrucci (in Rognoni, *Gioacchino Rossini*, 322ff.) to the question of castratos and their disappearance, judged to be ruinous for opera and sacred music alike.

10. Michotte, *Richard Wagner's Visit*, 108.

11. *Ibid.*, 110–11.

12. Edmond Michotte, 'Autobiografia Rossiniana', *Fanfulla della Domenica* (29 May 1887), 1, and (24 July 1887), 1–2: 1. The few scholars who have paid attention to this article have mistakenly identified it as a translation of *Une soirée chez Rossini à Beau-Séjour*, whereas the 'Autobiografia' is effectively a different and autonomous text, evidently drawn from Michotte's memoirs.

13. Michotte, *Richard Wagner's Visit*, 112.

14. *Ibid.*, 113. This practice is not mentioned in any other sources I have consulted.

15. *Ibid.*

16. *Ibid.*, 114–17.

17. *Ibid.*, 118. For a recent study of expressive singing in the English context at the time of Rossini, see Robert Toft, *Expressive Singing in England, 1780–1830* (Oxford, 2000).

18. Michotte, *Richard Wagner's Visit*, 73–4.

19. On the system of singing teaching in Italy, see John Rosselli, *Singers of Italian Opera: The History of a Profession* (Cambridge, 1992), and Sergio Durante, 'The Opera Singer', in *Opera Production and Its Resources*, ed. Lorenzo Bianconi and Giorgio Pestelli (Chicago, 1998), 354–417.

20. This work was particularly successful; reprinted many times, it is still known and used today in a new edition based on the autograph, ed. Elio Battaglia (Milan, 1990). Rossini himself voiced a favourable opinion of it (see his letter of June 1851 to the Marquis Torquato Antaldi, in Rognoni, *Gioacchino Rossini*, 302).

21. Auguste Panseron (1796–1859), a French composer, was for a brief period Rossini's fellow student at Bologna. Singing teacher at the Opéra Comique, he became chorus master at the Théâtre Italien during Rossini's directorship.

22. *Méthode de chant du Conservatoire de Musique* (Paris, 1803); Italian translation, *Metodo di canto del Conservatorio di Parigi* (Milan, n.d., 1825?). The work was a team effort in which Bernardo Mengozzi, student of the castrato Bernacchi and singing teacher at the Conservatoire, probably took the leading rôle.

23. See Leonella Grasso Caprioli, 'L'opera teorica sul canto di G. G. Ferrari (1763–1842) e la tradizione didattica italiana', *Giacomo Gotifredo Ferrari, musicista roveretano in Europa* (Lucca, forthcoming).

24. It has been republished recently in an edition by Louis Jacques Rondeleux (Geneva, 1985).

25. For a thorough study of nineteenth-century Italian vocal treatises, see Marco Beghelli, 'I trattati di canto italiani dell'Ottocento' (doctoral dissertation, University of Bologna, 1995).

14. Staging Rossini

1. Donald Oenslager, *Four Centuries of Scenic Invention* (Washington, 1974), 92 and 94.

2. Stendhal, *Life of Rossini*, trans. Richard N. Coe (London, 1970), chapters 18–19.

3. Such are the set designs engraved in Reggio Emilia by Ercole Montavoci, Carlo Zucchi and Lodovico Pezzetti, or the *Dodici vedute* by Pietro Gonzaga engraved by Luigi Rados and published in Milan by Gaspare Galliari.

4. Sets for Rossini's operas can be found in the following collections: (a) *Fasti del Regio Teatro alla Scala di Milano*, published in Milan by Sonzogno in 1816, issue no. 3 (*L'inganno felice*); (b) *Raccolta di scene teatrali eseguite o disegnate dai più celebri Pittori Scenici in Milano*, published in Milan by the engraver Stanislao Stucchi (c. 1822–9; 300 prints, about 100 of which are of sets for operas, a third of them by Rossini); (c) *Raccolta di varie Decorazioni Sceniche inventate, ed eseguite, da Alessandro Sanquirico Architetto, Pittore scenico del'I.I.R.R.T.T. di Milano*, c. 1824–32, a luxury publication of water-colour-tinted engravings endorsed by Sanquirico himself, which contains sets for *Ciro in Babilonia, La gazza ladra, Otello, Semiramide*; (d) *Nuova raccolta di scene Teatrali Inventate da Alessandro Sanquirico e pubblicate da Giovanni Ricordi*, launched in 1827 and continued until Sanquirico's retirement from the theatre (1832), and consisting of single fascicles, each reproducing in lithograph all the sets for a specific Milanese production (among them,

Tancredi, Otello, Elisabetta regina d'Inghilterra, L'assedio di Corinto, Semiramide, Il conte Ory).

5. *Raccolta di Disegni Alla Sacra Real Maestà D[onn]a M[a]ria Cristina Borbone Regina di Spagna e delle Indie Da Pasquale Canna Direttore ed Esecutore delle Scene del Real Teatro di S. Carlo*. Two of the sets are for operas by Rossini: 'Prison' (*Tancredi*) and 'Sepulcral vault' (*Zelmira*).

6. The drawings are dated or dateable between 1813 and 1856. Those by Borsato are in the Bibliothèque Nationale, Paris; those by Bagnara and Bertoja in the Civico Museo Correr, Venice.

7. See Elena Povoledo, 'Les Premières représentations des opéras de Rossini et la tradition scénographique de l'époque', *Anatomy of an Illusion: Studies in Nineteenth-Century Stage Design. Lectures of the Fourth International Congress on Theatre Research, Amsterdam 1965* (Amsterdam, 1969), 31–4; Mercedes Viale Ferrero, 'Per Rossini: un primo tentativo di iconografia scenografica', BCRS 22 (1982), 5–28; Maria Ida Biggi, *Giuseppe Borsato scenografo alla Fenice dal 1809 al 1823* (Venice, 1995); Maria Ida Biggi, *Francesco Bagnara scenografo alla Fenice, 1820–1839* (Venice, 1996); Maria Teresa Muraro and Maria Ida Biggi, *Giuseppe e Pietro Bertoja scenografi alla Fenice, 1840–1902* (Venice, 1998). Many drawings of the Venetian repertoire are included in the iconographic documentation provided by Margherita Antonelli and Maria Ida Biggi for Giovanni Carli Ballola, *Rossini* (Milan, 1992). For a comprehensive repertoire (drawings and prints) of nineteenth-century Rossinian stage designs and costumes, see *Rossini sulla scena dell'Ottocento. Bozzetti e figurini dalle collezioni italiane*, ed. Maria Ida Biggi and Carla Ferraro (Pesaro, 2000).

8. See Elena Povoledo, 'Le prime esecuzioni delle opere di Rossini e la tradizione scenografica del suo tempo', *Rossini 1792–1992. Mostra storico-documentaria*, ed. Mauro Bucarelli (Perugia, 1992), 285–313: 291 and 297.

9. Stendhal, *Voyages en Italie*, ed. Victor Del Litto (Paris, 1973), 6, 33 and 35.

10. Translation modified from Stendhal, *Life of Rossini*, 162.

11. For Pregliasco's costume designs in Turin's Biblioteca Civica, see Mercedes Viale Ferrero, 'Giacomo Pregliasco al Teatro di S. Carlo in Napoli', *Studi piemontesi* 16 (1987), 293–300.

12. Paolo Landriani taught at the Accademia di Belle Arti di Brera in Milan, of which Alessandro Sanquirico was 'Consigliere Ordinario''. Giuseppe Borsato was professor of drawing and Francesco Bagnara of landscape at the Accademia di Belle Arti in Venice. Luigi Vacca taught at the Accademia Albertina in Turin.

13. *Costumi del teatro alla Scala in Milano . . . dal 1818 al 1823*. The drawings are by at least four different artists and are of uneven quality: some, particularly well executed, could be ascribed to Sanquirico himself; others are the work of his collaborators.

14. *Il Costume antico e moderno ovvero storia del governo, della milizia, della religione, delle arti, scienze ed usanze di tutti i popoli antichi e moderni provata coi monumenti dell'antichità e rappresentata con analoghi disegni dal dottore Giulio Ferrario*, 2nd edn (Florence, 1823–37). The lengthy title is indicative of the ambitious aims of this publication.

15. See note 4 above, item b, for the complete title. A series of lithographs of costume designs was also published by Giovanni Ricordi to accompany the *Nuova raccolta* of set designs (item d).

16. The Brera costume designs have been discussed by Fernando Mazzocca, *Neoclassico e troubadour nelle miniature di Giambattista Gigola* (Florence, 1978), 221. A study of the sources for the drawings is Franco Ricci, 'La precisione storica nei costumi teatrali del primo Ottocento: un esempio italiano', *Quindici* (December 2000), 12–17.

17. Traditionally male tailors were in charge of costumes for male characters, and female dressmakers of the ones for female characters.

18. For Viganò's costume designs (Turin, Biblioteca Musicale Andrea Della Corte), see *Da Rossini a Verdi. Immagini del teatro romantico*, Catalogue of the exhibition, Turin, Villa Tesoriera, December 1981–January 1982 (Turin, 1982); for Martini's (Paris, Bibliothèque de l'Opéra), see Nicole Wild, *Décors et costumes du XIXe siècle*, 2 vols. (Paris, 1987–93), vol. II, 106–16.

19. See *Da Rossini a Verdi*, 24–7; Wild, *Décors et costumes*, vol. II, 106.

20. Wild, *Décors et costumes*, vol. II, 93.

21. *Ibid.*, 92.

22. *Ibid.*

23. *Ibid.*, 94.

24. There were a few exceptions, however, among them *Guillaume Tell*, which at the Opéra 'is performed crippled and in an unworthy *mise en scène*' (Verdi to Chiarina Maffei, 2 March 1854).

25. The committee at La Scala, much less cumbersome than the one at the Opéra, consisted of two painters, Francesco Hayez and Luigi Bisi, who signed the minutes of the meetings; from 1832 to 1849 Sanquirico acted as consultant.

26. This convention was still alive in 1883 if Giulio Ricordi could announce to Verdi, as an

exceptional piece of news, that the sets for *Don Carlo* at La Scala would be painted 'on new canvases'; see the *Carteggio Verdi–Ricordi, 1882–1885*, ed. Franca Cella, Madina Ricordi and Marisa Di Gregorio Casati (Parma, 1994), 157.

27. Wild, *Décors et costumes*, vol. I, 199 and 247. The set sequence for *Othello* read 'La piazzetta à Venise / Riche galerie dans le palais de Brabantio / Un vestibule dans les palais d'Othello / Chambre de Desdémone'.

28. *Cent ans de mise en scène lyrique en France (env. 1830–1930)*, ed. H. Robert Cohen and Marie-Odile Gigou (Stuyvesant, NY, 1986). The surviving *livrets* are listed under opera titles.

29. *The Original Staging Manuals for Twelve Parisian Operatic Premières*, ed. H. Robert Cohen (Stuyvesant, NY, 1991), 211–29.

30. Scribe to Palianti, 2 December 1849, in Cohen and Gigou, *Cent ans de mise en scène*, xxv.

31. In addition to these, there is at least a *livret* for *Elisabeth reine d'Angleterre*, mentioned in Brigitte Labat-Poussin, *Archives du Théâtre National (AJ13/1 à 1466). Inventaire* (Paris, 1977).

32. See Carlo Ferrario, *500 bozzetti scenografici*, ed. R. Ferrario, 5 vols. (Milan, 1919): for *Guglielmo Tell*, vol. II, nos. 193–4, and vol. V, nos. 486–90; for *Mosè*, vol. III, nos. 212–13. For Bertoja's sets, see Mercedes Viale Ferrero, 'Guglielmo Tell a Torino (1839–40) ovvero una "procella" scenografica', *Rivista italiana di musicologia* 14 (1979), 378–94.

33. Sybil Rosenfeld, 'The Grieve Family', *Anatomy of an Illusion*, 139–44.

34. Hellmuth Christian Wolff, *Oper: Szene und Darstellung von 1600 bis 1900*, vol. IV/1 of *Musikgeschichte in Bildern* (Leipzig, 1968), 148–9.

35. Catherine Join-Diéterle, 'Cicéri et la décoration théâtrale à l'Opéra de Paris pendant la première moitié du XIXe siècle', *Victor Louis et le théatre. Scénographie, mise en scène et architecture théâtrale aux XVIIIe et XIXe siècles* (Paris, 1982), 141–51; Franco Mancini, *Scenografia napoletana dell'Ottocento. Antonio Niccolini e il Neoclassico* (Naples, 1980); Biggi, *Giuseppe Borsato*; Biggi, *Francesco Bagnara*; Muraro and Biggi, *Giuseppe e Pietro Bertoja*.

36. Mercedes Viale Ferrero, *La scenografia della Scala nell'età neoclassica* (Milan, 1983); Franco Mancini, *Le scene, i costumi*, vol. III of *Il teatro di San Carlo (1737–1787)*, 3 vols. (Naples, 1987); Wild, *Décors et costumes*; Catherine

Join-Diéterle, *Les Décors de scène à l'Opéra de Paris à l'époque romantique* (Paris, 1988).

37. An ample and useful collection of images is the one assembled by Biggi and Antonelli for Carli Ballola, *Rossini*; see also *La casa di Rossini. Catalogo del museo*, ed. Bruno Cagli and Mauro Bucarelli (Modena, 1989).

38. Biggi and Ferraro, *Rossini sulla scena dell'Ottocento*.

39. See Povoledo, 'Les Premières Représentations'; Viale Ferrero, 'Per Rossini: un primo tentativo'; Povoledo, 'Le prime esecuzioni'.

40. See Biggi, *Giuseppe Borsato*.

41. See Mancini, *Scenografia napoletana*; Mancini, *Le scene, i costumi*, 63–88.

42. See Mario Monteverdi, *Scene di Alessandro Sanquirico nelle collezioni del Museo Teatrale alla Scala* (Alessandria, 1968); Viale Ferrero, *La scenografia della Scala*, 77–138 and 148–53.

43. See Join-Diéterle, 'Cicéri'; Wild, *Décors et costumes*, vol. II, 296–304.

44. See Biggi, *Francesco Bagnara*.

45. See Muraro and Biggi, *Giuseppe e Pietro Bertoja*.

15. Editing Rossini

1. The Fondazione Rossini does publish, however, a series treating the historical antecedents of each libretto, *I libretti di Rossini*, printing in facsimile the libretto of the opera's première along with significant precursors and authentic revivals. Another series, *Iconografia rossiniana*, began in 1996 with a sumptuously illustrated volume on the iconography of *Guillaume Tell*.

2. Gossett illuminates the perspective of critical editions in his book *Divas and Scholars: Performing Italian Opera* (Chicago, forthcoming), especially chapter 5, 'The Romance of the Critical Edition'.

3. 'Criteri per l'edizione critica delle opere di Gioachino Rossini', BCRS 14 (1974), with English translation. An addendum was published as 'Opera omnia di Gioachino Rossini. Norme editoriali integrative per i curatori', ed. Patricia B. Brauner, BCRS 32 (1992), 157–69.

4. GREC, I/21, ed. Alberto Zedda (Pesaro, 1979).

5. *The Works of Giuseppe Verdi*, I/17, ed. Martin Chusid (Chicago and Milan, 1983).

6. *Edizione critica delle opere di Gaetano Donizetti*, ed. Anders Wiklund (Milan, 1990).

7. See the full text in chapter 9 of the present volume.

8. 'Criteri dell'edizione', xiv, in each volume of the critical edition.

9. GREC, I/22, ed. Charles S. Brauner and Patricia B. Brauner (Pesaro, 1997).

10. GREC, I/35, ed. Janet L. Johnson (Pesaro, 1999).

11. *Album français*, no. 12, GREC, VII/2, ed. Rosanna Dalmonte (Pesaro, 1989). 'Rossini's fanfare, announced for the imperial hunt at Ferrières, has been transformed into a chorus of hunters and the trumpeters into choristers from the Opéra, under the direction of M.Victor Massé'; *Le Ménestrel* (21 December 1862), 23.

12. Cambridge, MA, The Houghton Library, Harvard University, fMS Mus 153(12–16) and Pesaro, Fondazione Rossini, *Album français*, no. 12.

List of works

Operas

Title, genre, acts	Librettist(s)	First performance
Demetrio e Polibio Dramma serio, 2	V. Viganò Mombelli	Rome, Teatro Valle, 18 May 1812
La cambiale di matrimonio Farsa comica, 1	G. Rossi	Venice, Teatro San Moisè, 3 Nov. 1810
L'equivoco stravagante Dramma giocoso, 2	G. Gasbarri	Bologna, Teatro del Corso, 26 Oct. 1811
L'inganno felice Farsa, 1	G. Foppa	Venice, Teatro San Moisè, 8 Jan. 1812
Ciro in Babilonia, ossia La caduta di Baldassare Dramma con cori, 2	F. Aventi	Ferrara, Teatro Comunale, 14 March 1812
La scala di seta Farsa comica, 1	G. Foppa	Venice, Teatro San Moisè, 9 May 1812
La pietra del paragone Melodramma giocoso, 2	L. Romanelli	Milan, Teatro alla Scala, 26 Sep. 1812
L'occasione fa il ladro Burletta per musica, 1	L. Prividali	Venice, Teatro San Moisè, 24 Nov. 1812
Il signor Bruschino, ossia Il figlio per azzardo Farsa giocosa, 1	G. Foppa	Venice, Teatro San Moisè, 27 Jan. 1813
Tancredi Melodramma eroico, 2	G. Rossi and L. Lechi	Venice, Teatro La Fenice, 6 Feb. 1813
L'italiana in Algeri Dramma giocoso, 2	A. Anelli	Venice, Teatro San Benedetto, 22 May 1813
Aureliano in Palmira Dramma serio, 2	F. Romani	Milan, Teatro alla Scala, 26 Dec. 1813
Il turco in Italia Dramma buffo, 2	F. Romani	Milan, Teatro alla Scala, 14 Aug. 1814
Sigismondo Dramma, 2	G. Foppa	Venice, Teatro La Fenice, 26 Dec. 1814
Elisabetta regina d'Inghilterra Dramma, 2	G. Schmidt	Naples, Teatro San Carlo, 4 Oct. 1815
Torvaldo e Dorliska Dramma semiserio, 2	C. Sterbini	Rome, Teatro Valle, 26 Dec. 1815
Il barbiere di Siviglia Commedia, 2	C. Sterbini	Rome, Teatro Argentina, 20 Feb. 1816
La gazzetta Dramma, 2	G. Palomba	Naples, Teatro dei Fiorentini, 26 Sep. 1816
Otello, ossia Il moro di Venezia Dramma, 3	F. Berio di Salsa	Naples, Teatro del Fondo, 4 Dec. 1816
La Cenerentola, ossia La bontà in trionfo Dramma giocoso, 2	J. Ferretti	Rome, Teatro Valle, 25 Jan. 1817
La gazza ladra Melodramma, 2	G. Gherardini	Milan, Teatro alla Scala, 31 May 1817
Armida Dramma, 3	G. Schmidt	Naples, Teatro San Carlo, 9 Nov. 1817

(cont.)

(*cont.*)

Title, genre, acts	Librettist(s)	First performance
Adelaide di Borgogna Dramma, 2	G. Schmidt	Rome, Teatro Argentina, 27 Dec. 1817
Mosè in Egitto Azione tragico-sacra, 3	A. L. Tottola	Naples, Teatro San Carlo, 5 March 1818
Adina, o Il califfo di Bagdad Farsa, 1	G. Bevilacqua- Aldobrandini	Lisbon, Teatro Saõ Carlos, 12 June 1826
Ricciardo e Zoraide Dramma, 2	F. Berio di Salsa	Naples, Teatro San Carlo, 3 Dec. 1818
Ermione Azione tragica, 2	A. L. Tottola	Naples, Teatro San Carlo, 27 March 1819
Eduardo e Cristina Dramma, 2	G. Schmidt	Venice, Teatro San Benedetto, 24 April 1819
La donna del lago Melodramma, 2	A. L. Tottola	Naples, Teatro San Carlo, 24 Oct. 1819
Bianca e Falliero, ossia Il consiglio dei tre re Melodramma, 2	F. Romani	Milan, Teatro alla Scala, 26 Dec. 1819
Maometto II Dramma, 2	C. Della Valle	Naples, Teatro San Carlo, 3 Dec. 1820
Matilde di Shabran, ossia Bellezza e cuor di ferro Melodramma giocoso, 2	J. Ferretti	Rome, Teatro Apollo, 24 Feb. 1821
Zelmira Dramma, 2	A. L. Tottola	Naples, Teatro San Carlo, 16 Feb. 1822
Semiramide Melodramma tragico, 2	G. Rossi	Venice, Teatro La Fenice, 3 Feb. 1823
Il viaggio a Reims, ossia L'albergo del giglio d'oro Dramma giocoso, 1	L. Balocchi	Paris, Théâtre Italien, 19 June 1825
Le Siège de Corinthe Tragédie lyrique, 3	L. Balocchi and A. Soumet	Paris, Opéra, 9 Oct. 1826
Moïse et Pharaon, ou Le Passage de la Mer Rouge Opéra, 4	L. Balocchi and E. de Jouy	Paris, Opéra, 26 March 1827
Le Comte Ory Opéra, 2	E. Scribe and C.-G. Delestre-Poirson	Paris, Opéra, 20 Aug. 1828
Guillaume Tell Opéra, 4	E. de Jouy and H.-L.-F. Bis	Paris, Opéra, 3 Aug. 1829

Church music

Five masses, plus various liturgical and non-liturgical pieces, the most important of which are:

Title, genre	Performing forces	First performance
Messa di Gloria	Solo vv, chorus, orch	Naples, 24 March 1820
Stabat mater	2S, T, B, chorus, orch	Madrid, Good Friday 1833 (2nd version Paris, 7 Jan. 1842)
Petite messe solennelle	12 solo vv, 2 pf, harmonium	Paris, 14 March 1864 (2nd version Paris, 24 Feb. 1869)

Occasional compositions

About twenty cantatas and various incidental music, hymns and choruses, including:

Title, genre	Performing forces	First performance
Il pianto d'Armonia sulla morte di Orfeo, cantata (text by G. Ruggia)	T, male chorus, orch	Bologna, 11 Aug. 1808
La morte di Didone, cantata	S, chorus, orch	Venice, 2 May 1818
Inno dell'indipendenza, hymn (text by G. Giusti)	Chorus	Bologna, 15 April 1815
Le nozze di Teti e di Peleo, cantata (text by A. M. Ricci)	3S, 2T, chorus, orch	Naples, 24 April 1816
Edipo a Colono, incidental music (text by G. Giusti)	B, male chorus, orch	Before 1817
La riconoscenza, cantata (text by G. Genoino)	S, A, T, B, chorus, orch	Naples, 27 Dec. 1821
Il pianto delle muse in morte di Lord Byron, canzone	T, chorus, orch	London, 11 June 1824
Cantata per il battesimo del figlio del banchiere Aguado	6 solo vv, pf	Paris, 16 July 1827
Giovanna d'Arco, cantata	S, pf	Paris, 1832
Cantata in onore del Sommo Pontefice Pio Nono (text by G. Marchetti)	4 solo vv, chorus, orch	Rome, 1 Jan. 1847
Hymne à Napoléon III et à son vaillant peuple (text by E. Pacini)	Bar, chorus, orch, military band	Paris, 1 July 1867

Miscellaneous songs

Around fifty, many based on settings of Metastasio's 'Mi lagnerò tacendo', of which the following represents a small sample:

Title	Performing forces	First performance
Se il vuol la molinara	S, pf	1801?
Il trovatore	T, pf	1818
Beltà crudele	S, pf	1821
La pastorella	S, pf	c. 1821
Canzonetta spagnuola	S, pf	1821
Les Soirées musicales (collection of 12)	1 or 2 vv and pf	c. 1830–5

Instrumental music

About two dozen pieces for orchestral or chamber performance, among which are:

Title	Performing forces	First performance
6 Sonate a quattro	2 vn, vc, db	c. 1804
Rendez-vous de chasse	4 corni da caccia, orch	1828
La corona d'Italia	military band	1868

Péchés de vieillesse (1857–68)

Thirteen volumes of songs (some based on settings of Metastasio's 'Mi lagnerò tacendo'), choruses, dances and piano pieces:

I	*Album italiano*
II	*Album français*
III	*Morceaux réservés*
IV–VIII	*Un peu de tout: recueil de 56 morceaux semi-comiques pour le piano*
IV	*Quatre mendiants et quatre hors-d'oeuvres*
V	*Album pour les enfants adolescents*
VI	*Album pour les enfants dégourdis*
VII	*Album de chaumière*
VIII	*Album de château*
IX	*Album pour piano, violon, violoncelle, harmonium et cor*
X	*Miscellanée pour piano*
XI	*Miscellanée de musique vocale*
XII	*Quelques riens pour album*
XIII	*Musique anodine*

Bibliography

The most complete and up-to-date bibliography on Rossini is Denise P. Gallo, *Gioachino Rossini: A Guide to Research* (London and New York, 2002). A more selective list is found in Philip Gossett, 'Rossini, Gioachino (Antonio)', *The New Grove Dictionary of Music and Musicians*, rev. edn, ed. Stanley Sadie and John Tyrrell, 29 vols. (London, 2001), vol. XXI, 734–68. The following list, more selective still, does not include articles published in BCRS (an index of its contents from 1955 to 1991 is found in the 1992 issue) and *La gazzetta: Zeitschrift der Deutschen Rossini Gesellschaft* (Leipzig, 1991–).

Source materials

Lettere inedite di Gioacchino Rossini, ed. Giuseppe Mazzatinti (Imola, 1890); 2nd edn, as *Lettere inedite e rare di G. Rossini* (Imola, 1892); 3rd edn, as *Lettere di G. Rossini*, with Fanny and Giovanni Manis (Florence, 1902; reprint: Bologna, 1975)

Quaderni rossiniani (Pesaro, 1954–76)

'*La Cenerentola'. Riproduzione dell'autografo*, ed. Philip Gossett (Bologna, 1969)

Il barbiere di Siviglia, ed. Alberto Zedda (Milan, 1969)

Edizione critica delle opere di Gioachino Rossini (Pesaro, 1979–) (see chapter 15 for details)

Early Romantic Opera, series of facsimile editions of manuscripts (mostly autograph) or early printed scores (New York, 1978–81): vol. VII, *Elisabetta regina d'Inghilterra*; vol. VIII, *Otello*; vol. IX, *Mosè in Egitto*; vol. X, *Ricciardo e Zoraide*; vol. XI, *Maometto II*; vol. XII, *Zelmira*; vol. XIII, *Semiramide*; vol. XIV, *Le Siège de Corinthe*; vol. XV, *Moïse et Pharaon*; vol. XVI, *Le Comte Ory*; vol. XVII, *Guillaume Tell*

The Original Staging Manuals for Twelve Parisian Operatic Premières, ed. H. Robert Cohen (Stuyvesant, NY, 1991) (*Guillaume Tell*)

Tutti i libretti di Rossini, ed. Marco Beghelli and Nicola Gallino (Milan, 1991)

Gioachino Rossini. Lettere, ed. Enrico Castiglione (Rome, 1992)

Gioachino Rossini. Lettere e documenti, ed. Bruno Cagli and Sergio Ragni, 3 vols. to date (Pesaro, 1992–)

'*Il barbiere di Siviglia'. Facsimile dell'autografo*, ed. Philip Gossett (Rome, 1993)

I libretti di Rossini (Pesaro, 1994–), 8 vols. to date (I: *Tancredi*; II: *La gazza ladra*; III: *Otello*; IV: *L'italiana in Algeri*; V: *La scala di seta, L'occasione fa il ladro, Il signor Bruschino*; VI: *La Cenerentola*; VII: *Armida*; VIII: *Edipo coloneo*)

Iconografia rossiniana, 2 vols. to date (Pesaro, 1996–) (see Bartlet and Biggi in 'iconography', below, for separate volumes)

Un almanacco drammatico. L'indice de' teatrali spettacoli, 1764–1823, ed. Roberto Verti, 2 vols. (Pesaro, 1996)

Rossini. Tutti i libretti d'opera, ed. Piero Mioli (Rome, 1997)

Fanan, Giorgio, *Drammaturgia rossiniana. Bibliografia dei libretti d'opera, di oratori, cantate ecc. posti in musica da Gioachino Rossini* (Rome, 1997)

Iesuè, Alberto, *Rossini rivoltato. Incipitario testuale della musica vocale di Gioachino Rossini* (Rome, 1997)

The Original Staging Manuals for Ten Parisian Operatic Premières, 1824–1843, ed. H. Robert Cohen (Stuyvesant, NY, 1998) (*Moïse et Pharaon* and *Le Siège de Corinthe*)

Biographies and studies published before 1900

Azevedo, Alexis, *G. Rossini: sa vie et ses oeuvres* (Paris, 1864)

Carpani, Giuseppe, *Le rossiniane, ossia lettere musico-teatrali* (Padua, 1824)

Edwards, H. Sutherland, *The Life of Rossini* (London, 1869)

Escudier, Léon and Marie, *Rossini: sa vie et ses oeuvres* (Paris, 1854)

Hiller, Ferdinand, *Plaudereien mit Rossini*, ed. Guido Johannes Joerg (Stuttgart, 1993; first published 1868); also in BCRS 32 (1992), 63–155

Michotte, Edmond, *Richard Wagner's Visit to Rossini (Paris 1860) and An Evening at Rossini's in Beau-Sejour (Passy) 1858*, trans. and ed. Herbert Weinstock (Chicago, 1968; first published 1906 and after 1893 respectively)

Mordani, Filippo, *Della vita privata di Gioacchino Rossini. Memorie inedite* (Imola, 1871)

Pougin, Arthur, *Rossini. Notes, impressions, souvenirs, commentaires* (Paris, 1871)

Righetti Giorgi, Geltrude, *Cenni di una donna già cantante sopra il maestro Rossini* (Bologna, 1823; also in Rognoni, *Rossini*, below)

Stendhal, *Life of Rossini*, trans. Richard N. Coe (London, 1956; 2nd edn, London, 1970; first published 1824)

Wendt, Amadeus, *Rossinis Leben und Treiben* (Leipzig, 1824); also in BCRS 40 (2000), 5–147, with Italian translation and commentary by Reto Müller

Zanolini, Antonio, *Biografia di Gioachino Rossini* (Bologna, 1875)

Biography and general studies

Appolonia, Giorgio, *Le voci di Rossini* (Turin, 1992)

Baricco, Alessandro, *Il genio in fuga. Due saggi sul teatro musicale di Gioachino Rossini*, 2nd edn (Turin, 1997)

Bini, Annalisa and Franco Onorati, eds., *Jacopo Ferretti e la cultura del suo tempo* (Rome–Milan, 1999)

Bruson, Jean-Marie, ed., *Rossini à Paris*, Exhibition catalogue (Paris, 1992)

Bucarelli, Mauro, ed., *Rossini 1792–1992. Mostra storico-documentaria*, Exhibition catalogue (Perugia, 1992)

Rossini e Firenze. Immagini e note, Exhibition catalogue (Florence, 1993)

Cagli, Bruno, 'Al gran sole di Rossini', *Il Teatro di San Carlo, 1737–1987*, 3 vols., vol. II: *L'opera, il ballo*, ed. Bruno Cagli and Agostino Ziino (Naples, 1987), 133–78

Cagli, Bruno and Mauro Bucarelli, eds., *La casa di Rossini. Catalogo del museo* (Modena, 1989)

Carli Ballola, Giovanni, *Rossini* (Florence, 1992)

Chigiana 34 (1981), special issue, 'Rossini: edizioni critiche e prassi esecutiva'

Collisani, Amalia, 'Umorismo di Rossini', *Rivista italiana di musicologia* 33 (1998), 302–49

Della Croce, Vittorio, *Una giacobina piemontese alla Scala. La primadonna Teresa Belloc* (Turin, 1978)

Engelhardt, Markus and Wolfgang Witzenmann, eds., *Convegno italo- tedesco 'Mozart, Paisiello, Rossini e l'opera buffa'* (Laaber, 1998)

Fabbri, Paolo, 'Rossini the Aesthetician', *Cambridge Opera Journal* 6 (1994), 19–29
   Rossini nelle raccolte Piancastelli di Forlì (Lucca, 2001)

Fabbri, Paolo and Sergio Monaldini, 'Delle monete il suon già sento! Documenti notarili relativi a Gioachino Rossini, possidente', *Una piacente estate di San Martino. Studi e ricerche per Marcello Conati*, ed. Marco Capra (Lucca, 2000), 77–115

Fabbri, Paolo, ed., *Gioachino Rossini, 1792–1992. Il testo e la scena* (Pesaro, 1994)
   Di sì felice innesto. Rossini, la danza e il ballo teatrale in Italia (Pesaro, 1996)

Ferrari, Luigi, ed., *Viaggio a Rossini*, Exhibition catalogue (Bologna, 1992)

Gossett, Philip, 'Rossini in Naples: Some Major Works Recovered', *The Musical Quarterly* 54 (1968), 316–40
   'Le fonti autografe delle opere teatrali di Rossini', *Nuova rivista musicale italiana* 2 (1968), 936–60
   'The Operas of Rossini: Problems of Textual Criticism in Nineteenth-Century Opera', Ph.D. dissertation, Princeton University (1970)
   'Becoming a Citizen: The Chorus in *Risorgimento* Opera', *Cambridge Opera Journal* 2 (1990), 41–64
   'History and Works that Have No History: Reviving Rossini's Neapolitan Operas', *Disciplining Music: Musicology and its Canons*, ed. Katherine Bergeron and Philip V. Bohlman (Chicago, 1992), 95–115
   'The Rossini Thematic Catalogue: When Does Bibliographical Access Become Bibliographical Excess?', *Music Reference Service Quarterly* 2 (1993), 271–80

Grempler, Martina, *Rossini e la patria: Studien zu Leben und Werk Gioachino Rossinis vor dem Hintergrund des Risorgimento* (Kassel, 1996)

Henze-Döhring, Sabine, '"Combinammo l'ossatura . . ." Voltaire und die Librettistik des frühen Ottocento', *Die Musikforschung* 36 (1983), 113–27

Johnson, Janet, 'The Théâtre Italien and Opera and Theatrical Life in Restoration Paris', Ph.D. dissertation, The University of Chicago (1988)
   'Rossini in Bologna and Paris during the Early 1830s: New Letters', *Revue de musicologie* 79 (1993), 63–81

Kendall, Alan, *Gioacchino Rossini, the Reluctant Hero* (London, 1992)

Kern, Bernd-Rüdiger and Reto Müller, eds., *Rossini in Paris: Tagungsband* (Leipzig, 2002)

Lindenberger, Herbert, 'Rossini, Shelley, and Italy in 1819', in his *Opera in History: From Monteverdi to Cage* (Stanford, 1998), 81–106

Lippmann, Friedrich, *Versificazione italiana e ritmo musicale. I rapporti tra verso e musica nell'opera italiana dell'Ottocento*, trans. Lorenzo Bianconi (Naples, 1986)

Mitchell, Jerome, *The Walter Scott Operas* (University, AL, 1977)

Müller, Reto, ed., *Hommage an Rossini*, Exhibition catalogue (Leipzig, 1999)

Osborne, Richard, *Rossini* (London, 1986; 2nd edn 1993)

Radiciotti, Giuseppe, *Gioacchino Rossini. Vita documentata, opere ed influenza su l'arte*, 3 vols. (Tivoli, 1927–9)

Radomski, James, *Manuel García (1775–1832): Chronicle of the Life of a Bel Canto Tenor at the Dawn of Romanticism* (Oxford, 2000)

Rescigno, Eduardo, *Dizionario rossiniano* (Milan, 2002)

Roccatagliati, Alessandro, *Felice Romani librettista* (Lucca, 1996)

Rognoni, Luigi, *Rossini* (Parma, 1956; 2nd edn Turin, 1968; 3rd edn Turin, 1977)

Rosselli, John, *The Opera Industry in Italy from Cimarosa to Verdi: The Role of the Impresario* (Cambridge, 1984)

Ruffin, Gianni, 'Drammaturgia come auto-confutazione teatrale: aspetti metalinguistici alle origini della comicità nelle opere di Rossini', *Recercare* 4 (1992), 125–63

Russo, Francesco Paolo, ed., *Rossini a Roma, Rossini e Roma* (Rome, 1992)

Il teatro di Rossini a Roma, 1812–1821. Debutti musiche artisti librettisti teatri, Exhibition catalogue (Gaeta, 1992)

Toye, Francis, *Rossini: A Study in Tragi-Comedy* (London, 1934)

Verdi, Luigi, ed., *Rossini a Bologna. Note documentarie*, Exhibition catalogue (Bologna, 2000)

Walton, Benjamin, 'Romanticisms and Nationalisms in Restoration France', Ph.D. dissertation, University of California, Berkeley (2000)

Weinstock, Herbert, *Rossini: A Biography* (New York, 1968)

Zedda, Alberto, 'Rossini a Napoli', in Raffaele Ajello et al., *Il Teatro di San Carlo*, 2 vols. (Naples, 1987), vol. I, 119–40

Musical studies

Balthazar, Scott L., 'Evolving Conventions in Italian Serious Opera: Scene Structure in the Works of Rossini, Bellini, Donizetti, and Verdi, 1810–1850', Ph.D. dissertation, University of Pennsylvania (1985)

'Rossini and the Development of Mid-Century Lyric Form', *Journal of the American Musicological Society* 41 (1988), 102–25

'The *Primo Ottocento* Duet and the Transformation of the Rossinian Code', *Journal of Musicology* 7 (1989), 471–97

'Ritorni's *Ammaestramenti* and the Conventions of Rossinian Melodramma', *Journal of Musicological Research* 8 (1989), 281–311

'Mayr, Rossini, and the Development of the Early Concertato Finale', *Journal of the Royal Musical Association* 116 (1991), 236–66

Beghelli, Marco, 'I trattati di canto italiani dell'Ottocento', doctoral dissertation, Università di Bologna (1994)

'Il "do di petto": dissacrazione di un mito', *Il saggiatore musicale* 3 (1996), 105–49

Bernardoni, Virgilio, 'La teoria della melodia vocale nella trattatistica italiana (1790–1870)', *Acta musicologica* 62 (1990), 29–61

Caswell, Austin, 'Mme Cinti-Damoreau and the Embellishment of Italian Opera in Paris, 1820–1845', *Journal of the American Musicological Society* 28 (1975), 459–92

Caswell, Austin, ed., *Embellished Opera Arias* (Madison, WI, 1989)

Celletti, Rodolfo, 'Origine e sviluppi della coloratura rossiniana', *Nuova rivista musicale italiana* 2 (1968), 872–919

'Il vocalismo italiano da Rossini a Donizetti. Parte I: Rossini', *Analecta musicologica* 5 (1968), 267–93

Colas, Damien, 'Les Annotations des chanteurs dans les matériels d'exécution des opéras de Rossini à Paris (1820–1860). Contribution à l'étude de la grammaire mélodique rossinienne', doctoral dissertation, Université de Tours (1997)

D'Amico, Fedele, *Il teatro di Rossini* (Rome, 1992)

DeMarco, Laura E., 'Rossini and the Emergence of Dramatic Male Roles in Italian and French Opera', Ph.D. dissertation, Columbia University (1998)

Di Benedetto, Renato, 'Lineamenti di una teoria della melodia nella trattatistica italiana fra il 1790 e il 1830', *Analecta musicologica* 21 (1982), 421–43

Emanuele, Marco, *L'ultima stagione italiana. Le forme dell'opera seria di Rossini da Napoli a Venezia* (Florence and Turin, 1997)

Gerhard, Anselm, *The Urbanization of Opera: Music Theater in Paris in the Nineteenth Century*, trans. Mary Whittall (Chicago, 1998)

Gossett, Philip, 'Gioachino Rossini and the Conventions of Composition', *Acta musicologica* 42 (1970), 48–58

'The Overtures of Rossini', *19th-Century Music* 3 (1979–80), 3–31; enlarged Italian edition as 'Le sinfonie di Rossini', BCRS 19 (1979), 5–123

'Rossini's *Ritornelli*: A Composer and His Orchestral Soloists', *Musique–signe–image. Liber amicorum François Lesure*, ed. Joel-Marie Fauquet (Geneva, 1988), 133–41

Henze-Döhring, Sabine, 'La tecnica del concertato in Paisiello e Rossini', *Nuova rivista musicale italiana* 22 (1988), 1–23

Huebner, Steven, 'Lyric Form in *Ottocento* Opera', *Journal of the Royal Musical Association* 117 (1992), 123–47

Lamacchia, Saverio, '"Solita forma" del duetto o del numero? L'aria in quattro tempi nel melodramma del primo Ottocento', *Il saggiatore musicale* 6 (1999), 119–44

Lippmann, Friedrich, 'Per un'esegesi dello stile rossiniano', *Nuova rivista musicale italiana* 2 (1968), 813–56

'Il "Grande Finale" nell'opera buffa e nell'opera seria: Paisiello e Rossini', *Rivista italiana di musicologia* 27 (1992), 225–55

Pagannone, Giorgio, 'Mobilità strutturale della *lyric form*: sintassi verbale e sintassi musicale nel melodramma italiano del primo Ottocento', *Analisi* no. 20 (May 1996), 2–17

'Tra "cadenze felicità felicità felicità" e "melodie lunghe lunghe lunghe": di una tecnica cadenzale nel melodramma del primo Ottocento', *Il saggiatore musicale* 4 (1997), 53–86

Tortora, Daniela, *Drammaturgia del Rossini serio. Le opere della maturità da 'Tancredi' a 'Semiramide'* (Rome, 1996)

I vicini di Mozart, vol. I, *Il teatro musicale tra Sette e Ottocento*, ed. Maria Teresa Muraro; vol. II, *La farsa musicale veneziana (1750–1810)*, ed. David Bryant (Florence, 1989)

Zoppelli, Luca, '"Stage Music" in Early-Nineteenth-Century Italian Opera', *Cambridge Opera Journal* 2 (1990), 29–39

Studies on individual works

Aldrich-Moodie, James, 'False Fidelity: *Othello*, *Otello*, and Their Critics',
   Comparative Drama 28 (1994), 324–47

Le Barbier de Séville, *L'Avant-scène opéra* 37, 3rd edn (March 1996)

Bolin, Norbert, 'Gefangenschaft und Freiheit: Topoi in Gioachino Rossinis *La
   gazza ladra*', '*Aspetti musicali*': *Musikhistorische Dimensionen Italiens 1600 bis
   2000. Festschrift für Dietrich Kämper zum 65. Geburtstag*, ed. Norbert Bolin,
   Christoph von Blumröder and Imke Misch (Cologne, 2001), 161–74

La Cenerentola, *L'Avant-scène opéra* 85 (March 1986)

Conati, Marcello, 'Between Past and Future: The Dramatic World of Rossini in
   Mosè in Egitto and *Moïse et Pharaon*', *19th-Century Music* 4 (1980–81),
   32–47

Gallarati, Paolo, 'Dramma e *ludus* dall'*Italiana* al *Barbiere*', *Il melodramma italiano
   dell'Ottocento. Studi e ricerche per Massimo Mila*, ed. Giorgio Pestelli (Turin,
   1977), 237–80

Gerhard, Anselm, 'L'eroe titubante e il finale aperto: un dilemma insolubile nel
   Guillaume Tell di Rossini', *Rivista italiana di musicologia* 19 (1984), 113–30
   '"Sortire dalle vie comuni"? Wie Rossini einem Akademiker den *Guillaume Tell*
   verdarb', *Oper als Text: Romanistische Beiträge zur Libretto-Forschung*, ed. Albert
   Gier (Heidelberg, 1986), 185–219

Goldin, Daniela, 'Il *Barbiere di Siviglia* da Beaumarchais all'opera buffa' and 'Vita,
   avventure e morte di Semiramide', in her *La vera fenice. Librettisti e libretti tra
   Sette e Ottocento* (Turin, 1985), 164–89, 190–229

Gossett, Philip, 'The *candeur virginale* of *Tancredi*', *The Musical Times* 112 (1971),
   326–29
   The Tragic Finale of '*Tancredi*' (Pesaro, 1977)
   'Rossini e i suoi *Péchés de vieillesse*', *Nuova rivista musicale italiana* 14 (1980),
   7–26

Grondona, Marco, *La perfetta illusione.* '*Ermione*' *e l'opera seria rossiniana* (Lucca,
   1996)
   '*Otello*', *una tragedia napoletana* (Lucca, 1997)

Grondona, Marco and Guido Paduano, eds., *I quattro volti di Otello: William
   Shakespeare, Arrigo Boito, Francesco Berio di Salsa, Jean-François Ducis* (Milan,
   1996)

Guillaume Tell, *L'Avant-scène opéra* 118 (March 1989)

Isotta, Paolo, 'I diamanti della corona. Grammatica del Rossini napoletano', *Mosè
   in Egitto/Moïse et Pharaon/Mosè*, ed. Paolo Isotta (Turin, 1974), 145–346

L'Italienne à Algier, *L'Avant-scène opéra* 157 (Jan.–Feb. 1994)

John, Nicholas, ed. '*La Cenerentola*', ENO Opera Guides (London and New York,
   1980)
   '*Il barbiere di Siviglia*' – '*Moïse et Pharaon*', ENO Opera Guides (London and
   New York, 1985)

Lamacchia, Saverio, 'Recezione e ideologia *ancien régime* da *Zelmira* a *Bianca e
   Fernando*', *Vincenzo Bellini nel secondo centenario della nascita*, ed. Graziella
   Seminara and Anna Tedesco (Catania, forthcoming)

Lippmann, Friedrich, 'Rossini 1815: *Elisabetta regina d'Inghilterra*', *Analecta
   musicologica* 30 (1998), 741–66

Marinelli, Carlo, ed., *Almaviva, o sia, L'inutile precauzione/Il barbiere di Siviglia*, discography (Rome, 1991)

Mauceri, Marco, '*La gazzetta* di Gioachino Rossini: fonti del libretto e autoimprestito musicale', *Ottocento e oltre. Scritti in onore di Raoul Meloncelli*, ed. Francesco Izzo and Johannes Streicher (Rome, 1993), 115–49

Müller, Reto and Bernd-Rüdiger Kern, eds., *Rossinis 'Eduardo e Cristina'* (Leipzig, 1997)

La Pie voleuse, *L'Avant-scène opéra* 110 (June 1988)

Poriss, Hilary, 'Bartolo's Naps and Rosina's Reactions: The Lesson Scene of *Il barbiere di Siviglia*', in 'Artistic License: Aria Interpolation and the Italian Operatic World, 1815–1850', Ph.D. dissertation, The University of Chicago (2000), 46–95

Porter, Andrew, 'A Lost Opera by Rossini', *Music and Letters* 45 (1964), 39–44

Questa, Cesare, *Semiramide redenta. Archetipi, fonti classiche, censure antropologiche nel melodramma* (Urbino, 1989)

   Il ratto dal serraglio. Euripide, Plauto, Mozart, Rossini, 2nd edn (Urbino, 1997)

Sémiramis, *L'Avant-scène opéra* 184 (May–June 1998)

Le Siège de Corinthe, *L'Avant-scène opéra* 81 (Nov 1985)

Spada, Marco, '*Elisabetta regina d'Inghilterra* di Gioachino Rossini: fonti letterarie e autoimprestito musicale', *Nuova rivista musicale italiana* 24 (1990), 147–82

Tammaro, Ferruccio, 'Ambivalenza dell'*Otello* rossiniano', *Il melodramma italiano dell'Ottocento. Studi e ricerche per Massimo Mila*, ed. Giorgio Pestelli (Turin, 1977), 187–236

Tartak, Marvin, 'The Two "Barbieri"', *Music and Letters* 50 (1969), 453–69

Teske-Spellerberg, Ulrike, *Die Klaviermusik von Gioacchino Rossini* (Tutzing, 1998)

Le Turc en Italie, *L'Avant-scène opéra* 169 (Jan.–Feb. 1996)

Le Voyage à Reims; Le Comte Ory, *L'Avant-scène opéra* 140 (July–Aug. 1991)

Walton, Benjamin, '"Quelque peu théâtral": The Operatic Coronation of Charles X', *19th-Century Music* 26 (2002–3), 3–22

Staging

Barbero, Luca B., '"Ho sbagliato: la testa va chinata dall'altra parte". Savinio regista dell'*Armida* agli albori della Rossini Renaissance', *Rivista italiana di musicologia* 26 (1991), 79–94

Bartlet, M. Elizabeth C. with Mauro Bucarelli, '*Guillaume Tell' di Gioachino Rossini. Fonti iconografiche* (Pesaro, 1996)

Biggi, Maria Ida and Carla Ferraro, eds., *Rossini sulla scena dell'Ottocento. Bozzetti e figurini dalle collezioni italiane* (Pesaro, 2000)

Cagli, Bruno and Franco Mariotti, eds., *Il teatro di Rossini. Le nuove edizioni e la messinscena contemporanea* (Milan, 1992)

Cohen, H. Robert and Marie-Odile Gigou, eds., *Cent ans de mise-en-scène lyrique en France (env. 1830–1930)* (Stuyvesant, NY, 1986)

Povoledo, Elena, 'Les Premières représentations des opéras de Rossini et la tradition scénographique de l'époque', *Anatomy of an Illusion: Studies in Nineteenth-Century Stage Design. Lectures of the Fourth International Congress on Theatre Research, Amsterdam 1965* (Amsterdam, 1969), 31–4

Viale Ferrero, Mercedes, '*Guglielmo Tell* a Torino (1839–40) ovvero una "procella" scenografica', *Rivista italiana di musicologia* 14 (1979), 378–94

Reception

Bini, Annalisa, '"Accidente curioso a proposito di *Un curioso accidente*". Un contestato pasticcio rossiniano (Parigi, 1859)', *Ottocento e oltre. Scritti in onore di Raoul Meloncelli*, ed. Francesco Izzo and Johannes Streicher (Rome, 1993), 339–53

Cagli, Bruno, 'Proposte rossiniane tra le due guerre', *Nuova rivista musicale italiana* 34 (2000), 311–22

Carnevale, Nadia, '". . . That's the barber!": Henry Rowley Bishop e l'adattamento del *Barbiere* rossiniano', *Ottocento e oltre. Scritti in onore di Raoul Meloncelli*, ed. Francesco Izzo and Johannes Streicher (Rome, 1993), 99–113

Everist, Mark, 'Lindoro in Lyon: Rossini's *Le Barbier de Séville*', *Acta musicologica* 64 (1992), 50–85

Music Drama at the Paris Odéon, 1824–1828 (Berkeley and Los Angeles, 2002)

Fabbri, Paolo, 'Rossini e Bellini a paragone', *Musica Franca: Essays in Honor of Frank A. D'Accone*, ed. Irene Alm, Alyson McLamore and Colleen Reardon (Stuyvesant, NY, 1996), 283–95

Girardi, Michele and Pierluigi Petrobelli, eds., *Messa per Rossini. La storia, il testo, la musica* (Parma, 1988)

Graziano, John, ed., *Italian Opera in English: 'Cinderella' (1831)* (New York, 1994)

Hensel, Christoph, 'Tell in Tirol: Zu einer antirevolutionaren Rossini-Bearbeitung', *Musik befragt, Musik vermittelt. Peter Rummenhöller zum 60. Geburtstag*, ed. Thomas Ott and Heinz von Loesch (Augsburg, 1996), 405–20

Lazzerini Belli, Adriana, 'Hegel e Rossini. Intelligenza e cuore del belcanto', *Studi musicali* 24 (1995), 283–306

Nicolodi, Fiamma, 'Rossini a Parigi e la critica musicale', *Studi e fantasie. Saggi, versi, musica e testimonianze in onore di Leonardo Pinzauti*, ed. Daniele Spini (Florence, 1996), 193–219

Pirrotta, Nino, 'Semiramis e Amneris, un anagramma o quasi', *Il melodramma italiano dell'Ottocento. Studi e ricerche per Massimo Mila*, ed. Giorgio Pestelli (Turin, 1977), 5–12

La recezione di Rossini ieri e oggi, Atti dei convegni Lincei (Rome, 1994)

Steffan, Carlida, ed., *Rossiniana. Antologia della critica nella prima metà dell'Ottocento* (Pordenone, 1992)

Internet sites

The publisher has used its best endeavours to ensure that the URLs for the following websites are correct and active at the time of going to press. However, the publisher has no responsibility for the websites.

Fondazione Rossini: http://www.fondazionerossini.org

Center for Italian Opera Studies at the University of Chicago: http://humanities.uchicago.edu/orgs/ciao

Deutsche Rossini Gesellschaft: http://www.rossinigesellschaft.de

Index